BAPTISM OF FIRE:
THE BIRTH OF THE MODERN BRITISH FANTASTIC IN WORLD WAR I

EDITED BY
JANET BRENNAN CROFT

Other Titles from the Mythopoeic Press

Chad Walsh Reviews C. S. Lewis
by Chad Walsh
preface and bibliography by Joe R. Christopher
with a memoir by Damaris Walsh McGuire

The Masques of Amen House
by Charles Williams
introduction by Bernadette Bosky
edited and annotated by David Bratman

The Pedant and the Shuffly
by John Bellairs
illustrated by Marilyn Fitschen
foreword by Brad Strickland

Sayers on Holmes: Essays and Fiction on Sherlock Holmes
by Dorothy L. Sayers
introduction by Alzina Stone Dale
bibliography by Joe R. Christopher

Tolkien on Film: Essays on Peter Jackson's The Lord of the Rings
edited by Janet Brennan Croft

The Travelling Rug
by Dorothy L. Sayers
introduction and bibliography by Joe R. Christopher
annotations by Janet Brennan Croft

Past Watchful Dragons: Fantasy and Faith in the World of C. S. Lewis
edited by Amy H. Sturgis

*Intersection of Fantasy & Native America:
From H. P. Lovecraft to Leslie Marmon Silko*
edited by Amy H. Sturgis and David D. Oberhelman

Mythlore Index Plus
edited by Edith Crowe and Janet Brennan Croft

Perilous and Fair: Women in the Works and Life of J. R. R. Tolkien
edited by Janet Brennan Croft and Leslie A. Donovan

BAPTISM OF FIRE:
THE BIRTH OF THE MODERN BRITISH FANTASTIC IN WORLD WAR I

EDITED BY
JANET BRENNAN CROFT

 Mythopoeic Press • Altadena, CA • 2015

Mythopoeic Press is an imprint of the Mythopoeic Society (www.mythsoc.org). Orders may be placed through our website at www.mythsoc.org/press. For general inquiries or requests to reprint material from our publications, contact:

Editor, Mythopoeic Press
c/o Mythopoeic Society
P.O. Box 6707
Altadena, CA 91003
USA
press@mythsoc.org

Copyright 2015 by the Mythopoeic Press
All rights reserved

Published in the United States of America

ISBN: 978-1-887726-03-0

LCCN: 2015909682

ACKNOWLEDGEMENTS

Unpublished material from the Owen Barfield Papers held by the Bodleian Library is used with the kind permission of Owen A. Barfield and the Owen Barfield Literary Estate.

The following essays originally appeared in Mythlore *and are reprinted with permission from the authors:*

> Carlson, David J. "Lord Dunsany and the Great War: *Don Rodriguez* and the Rebirth of Romance." *Mythlore* 25.1/2 (#95/96) (2006): 93–104.
> Carter, Steven Brett. "Faramir and the Heroic Ideal of the Twentieth Century: Or, How Aragorn Died at the Somme." *Mythlore* 30.3/4 (#117/118) (2012): 89–102.
> Christie, E. J. "Sméagol and Déagol: Secrecy, History, and Ethical Subjectivity in Tolkien's World." *Mythlore* 31.3/4 (#121/122) (2013): 83–101.
> Livingston, Michael. "The Shell-shocked Hobbit: The First World War and Tolkien's Trauma of the Ring." *Mythlore* 25.1/2 (#95/96) (2006): 77–92.
> Melton, Brian. "The Great War and Narnia: C. S. Lewis as Soldier and Creator." *Mythlore* 30.1/2 (#115/116) (2011): 123–42.

Cover illustration: *Battle of the Battles* by Philippe Laferrière (oil painting, 2012)
Cover design by Chloë Winegar-Garrett
Internal layout by Leslie A. Donovan; set in Palatino Linotype
Index by Janet Brennan Croft

Printed and produced by CreateSpace, a division of Amazon.com

Contents

Introduction: "The Purest Response of Fantastika to the World Storm"
Janet Brennan Croft 1

Section 1: The Inklings

The Shell-shocked Hobbit: The First World War and Tolkien's Trauma of the Ring
Michael Livingston 9

Faramir and the Heroic Ideal of the Twentieth Century; or, How Aragorn Died at the Somme
S. Brett Carter 23

Wounded By War: Men's Bodies in the Prose Tradition of *The Children of Húrin*
Margaret Sinex 38

Sméagol and Déagol: Secrecy, History, and Ethical Subjectivity in Tolkien's World
E. J. Christie 60

The Preservation of National Unity by [Dis]remembering the Past in Tolkien's *The Hobbit* and *The Lord of the Rings*
Nora Alfaiz 80

"Now Often Forgotten": Gollum, the Great War, and the Last Alliance
Peter Grybauskas 92

Beyond the Circles of this World: The Great War, Time, History, and Eternity in the Fantasy of J. R. R. Tolkien and C. S. Lewis
Shandi Stevenson 110

Silent Wounds
Andrew Krokstrom 131

The Great War and Narnia: C. S. Lewis as Soldier and Creator
Brian Melton 144

Horses, Horoscopes, and Human Consciousness: Owen Barfield on Making Meaning in His Post-WWI Writings
Tiffany Brooke Martin 165

Section 2: Outside the Inklings

The Door We Never Opened: British Alternative History Writing in the Aftermath of World War I
Nick Milne 187

"A Deplorable Misfit": The Symbolism of Desire in
G. K. Chesterton's *The Crimes of England*
    Philip Irving Mitchell 209
Lord Dunsany and the Great War: *Don Rodriguez* and the Rebirth
of Romance
    David J. Carlson 234
From *Lolly Willowes* to *Kingdoms of Elfin*: The Poetics of Socio-Political
Commentary in Sylvia Townsend Warner's Fantasy Narratives
    Meyrav Koren-Kuik 245
The Conqueror *Worm*: Eddison, Modernism, and the War to End
All Wars
    Jon Garrad... 263
E. R. Eddison and the Age of Catastrophe
    Joe Young 279
T. H. White and the Lasting Influence of World War I:
King Arthur at War
    Ashley Pfeiffer... 299

Contributors 311
Index 315

Introduction:
"The Purest Response of Fantastika to the World Storm"

JANET BRENNAN CROFT

WORLD WAR I HAS BEEN CALLED "the poets' war," as it was characterized by a massive outpouring of works of literature during and after the war. "[P]oetry figures [...] largely in public perceptions of the conflict (seemingly the last time it performed such a role)" (O'Brien 7), and during the Great War, "[i]t was possible for soldiers to be not merely literate but vigorously literary," with an appreciation of literature considered something "very near the center of normal experience" (Fussell 157–58). Much of this vast literary harvest, as Paul Fussell brilliantly demonstrated in *The Great War and Modern Memory*, hinged on an ironic response to the deadly absurdities of World War I and its contrast to the "paradoxical combination of hedonism and puritanism" characteristic of typical prewar literature (Simonson and Gilete 230), or to the modernist movement "which in its prewar form was a culture of hope, a vision of synthesis" (Eksteins 237).

Yet Fussell also acknowledges that fantasy could be a legitimate literary response to the war, when he uses Northrop Frye's theory of modes to delineate the place of fantasy on the cycle of possible literary reactions to trauma: for Frye, the ironic mode "moves steadily towards myth, and the dim outlines of sacrificial rituals and dying gods begin to reappear in it" (qtd. in Fussell 312). As I have noted elsewhere, "[t]he creation of a world in which both heroic deeds could be done and determination without hope might be rewarded" could be a way of transforming the horrible experiences of the war into something more bearable, applicable, and relevant; into "Escape" in the sense that Tolkien used the term in "On Fairy-stories" (29).

This present volume sprang from a desire to examine selected examples of the fantastic response to World War I among British authors. It is not meant to be an exhaustive collection by any means, but rather an initial exploration of the topic of fantasy as a reply to World War I in the hands of a limited group of authors. Much more remains to be done and said on the topic, particularly as we proceed through the years of the war's centenary.

The contents comprise a mix of five classic articles from the pages of *Mythlore* and twelve new essays. The first half of the book considers the Inklings, the Oxford literary group centered on Tolkien and Lewis, while the second half deals with other authors.

Section 1: The Inklings

The Inklings were a loose society of Oxford writers and friends, all male and nearly all Christian, who primarily met at The Eagle and Child pub or in C. S. Lewis's rooms to talk and read their works to each other. Of the Inklings represented in this volume, Owen Barfield served in the Royal Engineers, C. S. Lewis in the Somerset Light Infantry, and J. R. R. Tolkien in the Lancashire Fusiliers. Among the others considered members or frequent attendees, Nevill Coghill, Jim Dundas-Grant, Hugo Dyson, and Warren Lewis also served. Charles Williams was the only core member with no military record. Norman Cantor has observed that Tolkien and Lewis shared "a more positive response" to the inter-war world "than the postimperial stoicism, cultural despair, and resigned Christian pessimism that were the common response of their British contemporaries" (212).

There has been a steady growth of scholarship on Tolkien and his World War I experiences since the early 2000s, led in particular by British scholar and journalist John Garth. So pervasive has such scholarship become that nearly any article in the popular press will now allude to the facts of Tolkien's service record and take as a given that his fantasy was inspired by these experiences.

We begin this section with a classic article, first published in *Mythlore* in 2006, that provides a good overview of Tolkien's war experiences and his literary response to them. In "The Shell-shocked Hobbit," Michael Livingston describes the Battle of the Somme and Tolkien's participation in it. Pointing out the parallels between the battle-scarred landscapes of Northern Europe and Middle-earth, Livingston notes that while they are worth cataloging, it is Tolkien's nuanced and sympathetic depiction of Frodo's post-traumatic stress disorder that is the most compelling result of the author's war experiences.

After Frodo, Faramir perhaps best represents Tolkien's thinking on war and processing of his World War I experiences. In another classic *Mythlore* article, first published in 2012, S. Brett Carter investigates "Faramir and the Heroic Ideal of the Twentieth Century." Carter reveals Faramir to be a far more modern warrior than any of his compatriots, particularly in contrast to Aragorn and Boromir, who are representative of much older and rapidly obsolescing models of heroism and methods of warfare.

Introduction: "The Purest Response of Fantastika to the World Storm"

With Margaret Sinex's essay "Wounded by War," we return to the issue of shell-shock, but also consider bodily wounds as well. Tolkien's engagement with the story of Túrin Turambar over a period of decades shows an evolution in his treatment of the theme of the "grievous fragility of the human body and psyche" (40). This is especially evident in the story of Flinding/Gwindor, who in each successive retelling is increasingly damaged, as are other characters in this tale. Sinex supports her study with examples of World War I shell-shock and physical disability documented by contemporary field doctors and others.

E. J. Christie, in the third of our reprinted *Mythlore* articles (this one from 2013) uses the characters Sméagol and Déagol as jumping-off points to explore issues of secrecy, surveillance, propaganda, and censorship that were increasingly coming to the fore during World War I and the inter-war years. Although significant issues in their own right, these trends also point to a growing individual privileging of self-concealment and discretion over openness and intimacy, a process that dehumanized and eroded the social fabric. The Ring crystallizes these concerns into a single object, and Gollum's relationship to it especially creates a tangle of themes of revealing and concealing.

In "The Preservation of National Unity," Nora Alfaiz looks at related themes of silence, selective forgetting, and propaganda at a larger level, using historiographical theory to bring to light the way nations and races form their identities by controlling collective memory. Tolkien's Dwarves, Hobbits, and Men of Gondor in particular reflect early twentieth-century concerns with nationalism and race identity that were part of the motivations for the world wars.

Peter Grybauskas similarly examines issues of the representation of history, also by using Gollum as a focal character. Gollum is shown to be a surprisingly astute collector of lore and teller of tales, particularly in contrast with other characters who are more driven by motives of national or personal pride, concealment and equivocation, or even lack of interest in history. Tolkien's own interest in history, as a reader of classical and medieval literature, colored his attitudes toward the conduct of World War II in particular.

The next paper, "Beyond the Circles of this World" by Shandi Stevenson, compares the reactions of C. S. Lewis and J. R. R. Tolkien to the war. Both authors, as scholars of literature and history and as Christians, took a long view of history that set them apart from other writers of the inter-war era. Nostalgia and a sense of loss are evident in the ways they related "morality to time, meaning to history, and hope to eternity" (109). Stevenson contrasts their approaches to those of the modernists, for whom the war meant an overturning of all certainties; with these fantasists, loss was transformed to a sense of hope.

Next, we include two papers on C. S. Lewis, whose war experience has not been as closely studied as Tolkien's. In "Silent Wounds," Andrew Krokstrom considers World War I in Lewis's autobiography and letters, paying particular attention to the lacunae—the details of his war service that Lewis glossed over or suppressed. While Lewis was known for his tendency to compartmentalize his life, Krokstrom also finds a motive for concealment in contemporary dismissive and discriminatory social and official attitudes toward sufferers of post-traumatic stress disorder, or shell shock.

Brian Melton takes a different approach in "The Great War and Narnia," a classic article that first appeared in *Mythlore* in 2011. While Melton also addresses the issue of gaps in Lewis's autobiography, the main subject of his essay is the way war is depicted in the Narnia books, written as they were for children.

The third Inkling considered in this collection is the often-overlooked Owen Barfield. Like Lewis and Tolkien, Barfield also served in the war, and several of his short stories show the influence of the conflict and his philosophical reaction to it. Tiffany Brooke Martin's "Horses, Horoscopes, and Human Consciousness" discusses some of Barfield's thinking on meaning in a post-war world and his non-fiction and literary criticism, especially his review of the collected works of war poet Wilfrid Owen.

SECTION 2: OUTSIDE THE INKLINGS

In the second half of the collection, we consider works by non-Inklings fantasists published during and after the war, proceeding more or less chronologically. The first essay, "The Door We Never Opened" by Nick Milne, examines a genre rather than a specific author; in this case, the genre of alternate history or counterfactual speculation, which suddenly became a popular form of "revisionist escapism" in the years immediately following World War I. Bookended with quotations from T. S. Eliot, Milne's paper investigates the causes of the genre's sudden rise and the issues raised by its practitioners.

The vastly prolific G. K. Chesterton is the subject of the next essay. Philip Mitchell, in " 'A Deplorable Misfit,' " closely studies Chesterton's problematic 1915 pamphlet *The Crimes of England*, a propagandistic retelling of European history full of "fantastic and chivalric imagery" (203) and fairy tale tropes. Mitchell considers Chesterton's choice of fantasy symbolism in light of some of his other writings on war and politics.

Introduction: "The Purest Response of Fantastika to the World Storm"

In our final classic paper reprinted from *Mythlore* (2006), David J. Carlson considers Lord Dunsany's response to the Great War and modernized conflict in general in *Don Rodriguez*. In a pivotal section of this Quixotic romantic adventure, the character of Rodriguez is shown visions of modern war that cause him to question not just his heroic warrior ideals, but the purpose of Creation itself; his following adventures are increasingly in the ironic mode. But, as in the fantasies of the Inklings, Rodriquez is able to transcend his experiences in the end.

The only female author considered in this anthology is Sylvia Townsend Warner. Much work, obviously, remains to be done on the fantastic response to the war by women writers. Meyrav Koren-Kuik examines social-political commentary on the post-war years from Warner's non-combatant and female point of view in *Lolly Willowes* and *Kingdoms of Elfin*. In both, fantasy is used subtly, or not so subtly, to critique the stagnation of consensus reality and the patriarchal social order through the upheaval of the war.

Two papers on E. R. Eddison offer different views of this especially interesting author. Jon Garrad, in "The Conqueror Worm," interprets *The Worm Ouroboros* as not just a fantasy, but also, in many ways, as in tune with the contemporary modernist movement—though Eddison's aims were not in sympathy with the modernists, and in fact his high romanticism proposes an alternative to modernist realism and pessimism.

I place Joe Young's paper on Eddison and "The Age of Catastrophe" next as it continues to explore these ideas, offering an interpretation of Eddison's philosophy as it grew from these roots and developed in his later, World War II era, Zimiamvia trilogy. Eddison's more fully developed personal religio-philosophic complex in this work is a direct development of his earlier literary concerns.

We close with Ashley Pfeiffer's essay on T. H. White, who directly and unequivocally incorporated a critique of modern war as a major theme in his retelling of the Arthuriad, *The Once and Future King*. White's Arthur uses modern strategies and tactics to defeat the ossified traditions of his opponents; in turn he is unable to withstand Mordred's even more modern innovations, and the cycle continues without foreseeable end.

Conclusion

John Clute is speaking specifically of the literature of horror in the quotation used for the title of this essay, but it may also be said that fantasy in general is among the truest of responses "to the world storm" (27).

Much work remains to be done on the fantastic response to World War I, of course. Some authors have not been touched on at all in this collection: David Jones, Kenneth Grahame, A. A. Milne, Mervyn Peake, James Stephens, Rudyard Kipling, etc. Female authors are sadly underrepresented, and certainly much more can be said about the authors who have been included. For further study on this topic, Edward James has developed *Science Fiction and Fantasy Writers in the Great War*, an excellent web resource designed to be a comprehensive record of science fiction and fantasy writers who were involved in the war.

But the issues and themes that concern the authors included in this collection range widely and give a good sense of the outlines of the territory—the home fronts, the infirmaries, the salients, the trenches, the wounded landscapes—both interior and exterior, and hope for healing.

Works Cited

Cantor, N. F. *Inventing the Middle Ages: The Lives, Works, and Ideas of the Great Medievalists of the Twentieth Century*. New York: Morrow, 1993. Print.

Clute, John. *Pardon this Intrusion: Fantastika in the World Storm*. Harold Wood: Beccon, 2011. Print.

Croft, Janet Brennan. *War and the Works of J. R. R. Tolkien*. Westport: Praeger, 2004. Print. Contributions to the Study of Science Fiction and Fantasy 106.

Eksteins, M. *Rites of Spring: The Great War and the Birth of the Modern Age*. New York: Anchor, 1990. Print.

Fussell, Paul. *The Great War and Modern Memory*. 25th anniv. ed. New York: Oxford UP, 2000. Print.

Garth, John. *Tolkien and the Great War: The Threshold of Middle-earth*. Boston: Houghton Mifflin, 2003. Print.

James, Edward. *Science Fiction and Fantasy Writers in the Great War*. N.p., n.d. Web. 4 Feb. 2015.

O'Brien, Sean. "A Grimly Voice." *Times Literary Supplement* 7 Nov 2014: 7–9. Print.

Simonson, Martin, and Raúl Montero Gilete. "*The Chronicles of Narnia* and *The Lord of the Rings*: Two Imaginative Responses to the Great War." *Doors in the Air: C. S. Lewis and the Imaginative World*. Ed. Anna Slack. Vitoria: Portal, 2010. 229–50. Print.

SECTION I:
THE INKLINGS

The Shell-shocked Hobbit:
The First World War and Tolkien's Trauma of the Ring

Michael Livingston

In a letter to Professor L. W. Forster written on New Year's Eve, 1960, J. R. R. Tolkien reemphasized his insistence that the mythology of Middle-earth was not reliant on the events of the two World Wars that spanned much of the first half of his life: "Personally I do not think that either war (and of course the atomic bomb) had any influence upon either the plot or the manner of its unfolding. Perhaps in landscape. The Dead Marshes and the approaches to the Morannon owe something to Northern France after the Battle of the Somme" (*Letters* 303).[1] There are some critics who have fought Tolkien on this point, insisting that *The Lord of the Rings* be read as a massive allegory for one or both of the World Wars, and it is certainly tempting to do so.[2] There are, after all, a number of intriguing parallels between Tolkien's Middle-earth and twentieth-century Europe: Saruman's destruction of Fangorn, for example, has much in common with modern industrialization at the expense of nature, and his technological tampering with nature is eerily reminiscent of the arms race of the World Wars that culminated in the Manhattan Project. Even a quick glance at the geography seems strangely familiar, with the island-like Shire representing England, Gondor for France, and Mordor in the place of Germany.[3] And, even though he vociferously denied the accusation that his work was an allegory for the events of the twentieth century, Tolkien admitted: "An

---

1. For further contemporary descriptions of the Western Front and its relation to the Dead Marshes in particular, see Wayne G. Hammond and Christina Scull's *The Lord of the Rings: A Reader's Companion* (453).

2. Tolkien's fellow Inkling C. S. Lewis perhaps unintentionally provided fuel for just such a search when he commented in an early review that the War of the Ring "has the very quality of the war my generation knew. It is all here: the endless, unintelligible movement, the sinister quiet of the front when 'everything is now ready,' the flying civilians, the lively, vivid friendships, the background of something like despair and the merry foreground, and such heaven-sent windfalls as a cache of choice tobacco 'salvaged' from a ruin" (C. S. Lewis 39–40).

3. Such contemporary similarities were noticed even before the book was printed: on 12 November 1949, Warren Lewis (brother of C. S. Lewis) read a MS copy of the text and noted in his diary that "a great deal of it can be read topically—the Shire standing for England, Rohan for France, Gondor the Germany of the future, Sauron for Stalin" (W. Lewis 231).

author cannot of course remain wholly unaffected by his experience [...]. One has indeed personally to come under the shadow of war to feel fully its oppression" (*The Lord of the Rings* [*LotR*] Foreword.xvii). And as a young man Tolkien had, indeed, "come under the shadow of war," for he lost some of his best friends to the First World War, and he personally fought at the Battle of the Somme.[4] No surprise, then, that the psychological realities of the horrors that Tolkien saw at the "carnage of the Somme," as he called it (*Letters* 53), should have left indelible marks on his writings. Tolkien, as we have already seen, admits that the geography of the Somme might be reflected in his portrayal of parts of Middle-earth, but he denies further specific influence.[5] The purpose of this essay, then, is two-fold: I would like not only to recall some general influences of the Somme on Tolkien's Middle-earth, but also to delve a bit deeper into the strong influence of Tolkien's war experiences on the character of Frodo in *The Lord of the Rings* and in particular on his odd behavior following the destruction of the One Ring at Mount Doom. Frodo, as we shall see, bears all the qualities of a veteran soldier returning from combat. To put a modern term to the transformation in Frodo's character at the end of *The Return of the King*, it appears that Frodo is suffering from Post-Traumatic Stress Disorder, more commonly known as "shell-shock."[6]

That Tolkien was at the Battle of the Somme is without question, yet it is still worth recalling the nature of this five-month slaughter in order to begin to understand its effects on the young writer:

---

4. The argument that follows might be thought to imply that the Second World War had little impact on Tolkien, but this is not my intention. Indeed, one need look no further than the criticism of Tom Shippey for positive signs of Second World War influence on his work ("Post-War"). Also of note is John A. Ellison's "The Legendary War and the Real One: *The Lord of the Rings* and the Climate of Its Times."

5. The most specific study of Tolkien's war experiences is the recent work of John Garth: *Tolkien and the Great War: The Threshold of Middle-earth*. Though Garth's project is primarily biographical in nature, he provides many insights into how this period gave new impetus to Tolkien's mythology.

6. Since the completion and acceptance of this essay, a number of other studies have appeared, making similar connections between Frodo's behavior and that of traumatized war veterans. Chief among these studies are Anne C. Petty's *Tolkien and the Land of Heroes: Discovering the Human Spirit*, especially 282, and Janet Brennan Croft's *War and the Works of J. R. R. Tolkien*, especially 133–38. To Croft is owed particular notice, since after taking editorship of *Mythlore* she allowed the publication of this present study despite its being pre-empted and out-classed by her own fine and far-ranging work.

> The British began with a week-long artillery barrage that chewed the ground into a pockmarked obstacle course and obliterated the German outposts and front trenches, but left the main body of defenders untouched in their meticulously constructed dugouts, some as deep as forty feet underground. When the bombardment lifted on 1 July [1916], all possible resistance seemed to have been blown apart, and the British advanced almost nonchalantly in formations learned on the parade ground—six feet separating each man across the line, a hundred yards between each assault wave, and each soldier carrying a minimum backpack of sixty-six pounds. The Highland Regiments marched into battle behind their pipers. Meanwhile the Germans had scrambled up their steep tunnel-like shafts, pulling their machine guns with them, and were ready for action. (Kleine-Ahlbrandt 30)

Thus the battle proper began when roughly 100,000 men rose up out of the Allied trenches and marched across the crater-torn and razorwire-strewn waste of what was called No-Man's Land. The official opening day casualties for the British army alone have gone down to history as 57,470, of which 19,420 were fatal. Both numbers still stand as gruesome world records for loss of life in one day's fighting.[7] By contrast, the United States lost less than 60,000 men during the entire duration of the Vietnam War. In his memoirs, David Lloyd George writes of the course of the battle:

> It is claimed that the Battle of the Somme destroyed the old German Army by killing off its best officers and men. It killed off far more of our best and of the French best. The Battle of the Somme was fought by the volunteer armies raised in 1914 and 1915. These contained the choicest and best of our young manhood. The officers came mainly from our public schools and universities. Over 400,000 of our men fell in this bullheaded fight and the slaughter amongst our young officers was appalling. (Lloyd George 9–10)

The addition of at least another 200,000 casualties among Allied forces by the time the campaign ended in November brings the total Allied losses to nearly 600,000 men—all lost in order to press the lines 10 kilometers closer to Germany.

Tolkien was in reserves on the day of the opening battle, but one of his best friends, Rob Gilson, was killed in the first wave (though Tolkien would not learn of his death until some weeks later).[8] And even in

---

7. Arguments have been made that the Battle of Towton on 29 March 1461 in Yorkshire, the battle in which Edward IV won his crown over Lancastrian forces, saw heavier death-tolls: some estimates hover around 28,000 killed. It is also worth noting that the fall of Singapore on 15 February 1942 saw 60,000 soldiers of the British army taken captive, though that day's fatalities were far fewer.

8. A detailed account of Tolkien's war experiences is provided by Garth in *Tolkien and the Great War*.

reserves Tolkien would have witnessed "clear signs that things had not gone according to plan on the battlefront: wounded men in their hundreds, many of them hideously mutilated; troops detailed for gravedigging; and a sinister smell of decay" (Carpenter 82). Then, on 14 July, Tolkien and his company were called into action and he saw for himself the results of what he would later call "the 'animal horror' of trench warfare" (Carpenter 84). The account of another participant in the Battle of the Somme is perhaps useful here for another perspective on the events Tolkien witnessed. John Raws had to apply to the Australian Corps twice before he was accepted, and just weeks before his own death in the battle, he described what he saw in a letter to a friend:

> The glories of the Great Push are great, but the horrors are greater. With all I'd heard by word of mouth, with all I had imagined in my mind, I yet never conceived that war could be so dreadful. The carnage in our little sector was as bad, or worse, than that of Verdun, and yet I never saw a body buried in ten days. And when I came on the scene the whole place, trenches and all, was spread with dead. We had neither time nor space for burials, and the wounded could not be got away. They stayed with us and died, pitifully, with us, and then they rotted. The stench of the battlefield spread for miles around. And the sight of the limbs, the mangled bodies, and stray heads.
> We lived with all this for eleven days, ate and drank and fought amid it; but no, we did not sleep. Sometimes, we just fell down and became unconscious. You could not call it sleep.
> The men who say they believe in war should be hung. And the men who won't come out and help us, now we're in it, are not fit for words. Had we more reinforcements up there many brave men now dead, men who stuck it and stuck it and stuck it till they died, would be alive today. Do you know that I saw with my own eyes a score of men go raving mad! I met three in 'No Man's Land' one night. Of course, we had a bad patch. But it is sad to think that one has to go back to it, and back to it, and back to it, until one is hit. (Raws)

For the next months, Tolkien was in and out of these trenches, somehow managing to survive unscathed until he was felled by trench fever on 27 October; he was pulled from the lines and eventually sent back to England. He had survived the war, but he had not left it. On 3 December he learned that another of his best friends, Geoffrey Smith, had died from gas gangrene in northern France. By the end of the First World War, Tolkien later wrote, "all but one of my close friends were dead" (*LotR* Foreword.xvii).

That the "shadow of war" would leave marks in Tolkien's writing, then, is not surprising. And, in addition to Tolkien's admitted borrowing of geographical description in the Dead Marshes and the approaches to Morannon, critics have discovered a number of intriguing parallels between the Somme (and the First World War in general) and *The Lord of the Rings*.⁹ Barton Friedman, for instance, points out the similarity of the faces in the bogs of the Dead Marshes to specific descriptions of the Somme, of the No-man's Lands of northern France to the "Nomanlands" (*LotR* IV.2.617) between the Dead Marshes and Morannon, of the shrieking of the Nazgûl to incoming mortar rounds and their respective effects on men (Friedman 121). Hugh Brogan has also seen similarities: in how the description of Sauron's destruction echoes contemporary descriptions of shell-bursts, in the polarizing of consciousness between "us" and "them," in the reversal of day and night, in the road that leads from home to the front, and in even such small details as the orc who snarls "Don't you know we're at war?" (*LotR* VI.2.910)— perhaps an echo of the wartime "Don't you know there's a war on?" (Brogan 362). William H. Green has shown that the technological leanings of Tolkien's goblins owe much to the machinery of war that the author saw utilized to such horrible effect at the Somme (Green 70–71),¹⁰ and Wayne G. Hammond and Christina Scull have pointed to the similarities between the vast camps of Mordor and the "extensive army camps to which Tolkien was posted during the First World War, in particular those situated in Staffordshire on Cannock Chase," and between Sam and the "typical foot soldier" (Hammond and Scull 608, 610). In his recent study of Tolkien's war experiences, John Garth lists a number of additional reminiscences:

> the atmosphere of pre-war tension and watchfulness, Frodo Baggins's restless impatience with his parochial countrymen in the Shire, the world's dizzying plunge into peril and mass mobilizations; tenacious courage revealed in the ordinary people of town and farm, with camaraderie and love as their chief motivations; the striking absence of women from much of the action; the machine-dominated mind of Saruman. (Garth 311)

Brian Rosebury perhaps goes furthest of all in likening "the emotional ambivalence" of Tolkien's works to "the mingled relief and regret of the war-survivor," concluding that *LotR* "might indeed be seen

---

9. I have limited this discussion to *LotR*, but traces of the First World War are to be found in his other works, as well. Garth, for instance, shows how the Hammer of Wrath in "The Fall of Gondolin" is quite possibly a partial allusion to the actions of the "C" Company of Tolkien's 11th Lancashire Fusiliers (294–95). A more lengthy account of war influences on Tolkien's work can be found in Croft 16–32.

10. Tom Shippey's observation that the Rammas Echor in Gondor has certain similarities with the Maginot Line in France might also be worth including in this list (*Century* 165).

in certain respects as the last work of First World War literature, published almost forty years after the war ended" (126). These are all interesting observations, of course, but few of them contain what I would call real substance: they are mostly the cataloging of Tolkien's borrowing of details (probably inadvertent for the most part) from the memory of one terrible event in the describing of another. Frodo's behavior at the end of *LotR*, however, is no small thing. And it is my belief that his change in personality directly reflects the real changes that Tolkien witnessed in surviving veterans of the Great War.

As the historian Ben Shephard has observed, the term "shell-shock" was coined in February 1915 by Dr. C. S. Myers on the battlefields of the First World War (1).[11] But it was at the Somme that that psychiatrists and psychologists really began to take note of the condition now known clinically as Post-Traumatic Stress Disorder since

> On the Somme, shell-shock and 'nervous disorders of war', hitherto a marginal medical problem, became a major drain on manpower. According to the British official history, 'In the first few weeks [of July 1916] several thousand soldiers were rapidly passed out of the battle zone on account of nervous disorders and many of them were evacuated to England'. The inadequate official figures show that the numbers of men returned as 'shellshock battle casualties'—suffering 'shell-shock' after actually being shelled […] tripled in the last six months of 1916 […]. These are the only surviving British figures and do not cover 'Shell-shock Sick'. They probably need to be multiplied by at least three to give a real sense of scale of the problem. (Shephard 41)

The earliest doctors to study Post-Traumatic Stress Disorder found that symptoms could last anywhere from months to years, and that the cause of the condition, not surprisingly, was the experience of a disturbing trauma that led to persisting recollections of that trauma over long periods of time. In psychiatric terms, the traumatic event that is the first criteria for diagnosing Post-Traumatic Stress Disorder is termed a *stressor*, and it must meet two basic requirements: the situation must have mortal consequences, and the person's reaction to the situation must have been one of "intense fear, helplessness, or horror" ("Posttraumatic Stress Disorder" 467).[12] War, especially of the brutal, horrific

---

11. A good, albeit dated, bibliography on combat stress can be found in John Keegan's *The Face of Battle: A Study of Agincourt, Waterloo, and the Somme* (337–43).

12. I am pleased to acknowledge that the appropriateness of a direct clinical diagnosis of Frodo via the *DSM-IV* was first pointed out to me (independently) by two observant students in one of the courses I taught on Tolkien at the University of Rochester many years ago. My thanks, then, to both Jennifer Case and Lisa Richards.

kind that was trench warfare, clearly meets such criteria; but what of Frodo's experiences?

Like many of the members of the Fellowship, Frodo saw war, and he certainly was in mortal danger on many other occasions: his injuries on Weathertop and in Shelob's lair, for instance, or the flight from Moria, or his capture at Cirith Ungol. While none of these events substantially sets him apart from other members of the Fellowship, they are, taken as a whole, indicative of a clear history of trauma. And setting Frodo even further apart, of course, is the Ring. As bearer of the One Ring, the Ring of Power that is ever-leeching upon his mind and upon which the fate of Middle-earth itself rests, Frodo exists in psychological state that is unnaturally tenuous: for him, even small moments of trauma carry substantial weight and make substantial impact. In clinical terms, then, we might say that Frodo is under two stressors: the primary stressor of the weight and power of the One Ring and the secondary stressor of life-threatening physical situations at the hands of monster, demon, and man alike.

Once the existence of a stressor is established, Post-Traumatic Stress Disorder is typically diagnosed by one of three distinct symptoms: (1) the reliving of the event in the form of nightmares and, particularly, flashbacks; (2) the "[p]ersistent avoidance of stimuli associated with the trauma and numbing of general responsiveness"; and (3) the changing of personal demeanor and behavior ("Posttraumatic Stress Disorder" 468). The third of these symptoms, a generalized change in demeanor and behavior, is clear enough throughout the course of Frodo's journey to Mordor; but it is only after the destruction of the One Ring (his primary stressor) at Mount Doom that we can begin to speak of Frodo post-trauma.

The first sign of lasting change in Frodo's character occurs within hours of his rescue from Mordor, immediately after his reunion with the surviving members of the Fellowship in Ithilien. Removing his old raiment and preparing to dress for a feast in his honor, Frodo is very reluctant to wear a sword, even an ornamental one (*LotR* VI.4.933).[13] Such behavior would be familiar to Tolkien from his war experiences, as an aversion to violence is a common post-traumatic symptom of combat veterans in particular. This is not to say that Frodo was a violent, hardened warrior before his journey to Mordor—just as one cannot say the

---

13. It is worth noting that Frodo's aversion to violence is so strong that he is later unwilling to shed the blood of Saruman, who has caused so much grief to the Shire (VI.8.996). For more on Frodo's pacifism, see Croft 130–33.

same for the generation of young men who went to the trenches of northern France—but Frodo *had* previously worn (and used) blades with pride. His unwillingness to wear one in Ithilien seems to be the result of a change in his character: he is simply no longer comfortable with bearing a weapon. The lingering trauma of his experiences destroying the Ring is already beginning to prey upon his still-fragile mind.

Frodo's symptoms of Post-Traumatic Stress Disorder grow stronger as he begins to journey back toward the Shire. Indeed, it is at the Ford of Bruinen, the site of his miraculous escape from the Ringwraiths, that the form of Frodo's anxiety comes into startling clarity:

> At last the hobbits had their faces turned towards home. They were eager now to see the Shire again; but at first they rode only slowly, for Frodo had been ill at ease. When they came to the Ford of Bruinen, he had halted, and seemed loth to ride into the stream; and they noted that for a while his eyes appeared not to see them or things about him. All that day he was silent. It was the sixth of October.
>
> "Are you in pain, Frodo?" said Gandalf quietly as he rode by Frodo's side.
>
> "Well, yes I am," said Frodo. "It is my shoulder. The wound aches, and the memory of darkness is heavy on me. It was a year ago today."
>
> "Alas! there are some wounds that cannot be wholly cured," said Gandalf.
>
> "I fear it may be so with mine," said Frodo. "There is no real going back. Though I may come to the Shire, it will not seem the same; for I shall not be the same. I am wounded with knife, sting, and tooth, and a long burden. Where shall I find rest?"
>
> Gandalf did not answer. (VI.7.967)

All the major symptoms of shellshock are here. Frodo is "ill at ease," a far cry from the young and vibrant hobbit who set out from the Shire. Surely all of the members of the Fellowship have been changed by their journey, but Frodo's change in demeanor is set out in particular: they do not need to ride slowly for Sam, Merry, or Pippin, but for Frodo alone. One year had passed since Frodo's injury on Weathertop, and no doubt seeing the Ford again—where he nearly died of the Ringwraith's wound—helped to trigger the recollection of that trauma. The Ford therefore represents multiple traumas for Frodo: the fight with the Ringwraiths and its resulting wound, as well as the near-death experience that resulted from it. Frodo's unwillingness to cross the stream is symptomatic of both an avoidance of trauma-related stimuli (i.e., the stream), and a sign of Frodo's flashback to his wounding on Weathertop.

Frodo's unwillingness to wear a sword in Ithilien has, by the time the hobbits return to find the Shire in the hands of Saruman/Sharkey,

The Shell-shocked Hobbit

turned into outright pacifism. At *The Green Dragon* in Bywater, the hobbits encounter the first of the ruffians who have overrun their beloved country. When one of them insults "King's messengers," Pippin is so incensed that he draws his blade (VI.8.982). Merry and Sam do likewise, but Frodo most conspicuously does not. And after the ruffians flee, Frodo is alone in his pity for Lotho. When Pippin remarks on the irony in their fighting to rescue Lotho, Frodo makes his irenic hopes clear: "nobody is to be killed at all, if it can be helped"(VI.8.983). Merry's reaction is perceptive, and worth note:

> "But if there are many of these ruffians," said Merry, "it will certainly mean fighting. You won't rescue Lotho, or the Shire, just by being shocked and sad, my dear Frodo." (VI.8.983)

That Frodo is characterized by shock, sadness, and an unwillingness to partake in violence is, once again, evidence of shell-shock. His pacifism could stand alongside similar impulses among veterans from any number of wars, though Tolkien would, of course, know it from the Somme. Again and again, Tolkien makes it a point to emphasize Frodo's pacifism: as the folk begin to gather for what comes to be known as the Battle of Bywater, Frodo once more makes clear that he has hopes for no killing, and he demurs from helping in the planning of the fight, leaving such things to Merry (VI.8.987). Though he does play a role in the battle, Tolkien pointedly states that he did not draw his sword "and his chief part had been to prevent the hobbits, in their wrath at their losses, from slaying those of their enemies who threw down their weapons" (VI.8.993). And when they surround Saruman, it is Frodo who refuses to see him slain, even after Saruman tries to stab Frodo with a hidden blade (VI.8.996). When Wormtongue kills Saruman and tries to flee, he is felled by arrows before Frodo is able to "speak a word," an implicit testament to the fact that Frodo would surely have tried to save even that miserable wretch (VI.8.996). Like many victims of Post-Traumatic Stress Disorder, Frodo simply cannot bear to see more violence enter the world.

Even after the Battle of Bywater is finished and Frodo is home in Bag End, he is unable to escape from his experiences. On 13 March, one year after being attacked by Shelob, Frodo is found ill in bed, "clutching a white gem that hung on a chain about his neck and he seemed half in a dream." The white gem is Arwen's, given to Frodo in order to help him when he is troubled by "the memory of the fear and the darkness" (VI.6.953). Frodo's half-conscious mutterings as he grasps Arwen's pendant could just as easily be the words of a shell-shocked veteran of the Somme: " 'It is gone for ever,' he said, 'and now all is dark and empty'" (VI.9.1001). Most critics have assumed that what is gone forever here is the One Ring, but this is not explicit in the text: we are not told what exactly "it" is. Might we also here understand a loss of innocence, or of hope? Answers, since they cannot be found in the text, must lie in the eye of the beholder. But perhaps knowing precisely what Frodo believes he has lost does not matter so much as the fact that it was something entirely vital to him: without it "all is dark and empty." It is well worth remembering here that it wasn't those who died in the Great War who made up Europe's Lost Generation; it was those who survived.[14] It does not seem like a stretch of the imagination to posit that Tolkien, like other writers of his generation, was somewhat disillusioned by the slaughter of the First World War.[15] Verlyn Flieger makes a similar connection when she argues that the "The literature of the post war period in which Tolkien, like many others, began to write, spoke with the voice of the 'lost generation' trying to come to terms with incommunicable experience" (219).[16] But, unlike many of his counterparts—T. S. Eliot in *The Waste Land*, for example—Tolkien does not appear to have perceived that the slaughter, incommunicable though it might be, was senseless and indicative as a loss of meaning; quite to the contrary, even while he is at the Somme he writes in a letter to his friend Geoffrey Smith that the nature of the war was "for all the evil of our own side with large view good against evil" (*Letters* 10).[17] Not a senseless slaughter, then, but its antithesis: a slaughter of the most profound importance; a position that is not surprising from a man who would create such equally profound battles between good and evil in his fiction. Still,

---

14. The Lost Generation, technically, refers to a group of American literary figures in 1920s and 1930s Paris—figures such as F. Scott Fitzgerald, Ernest Hemingway, Sherwood Anderson, and Gertrude Stein—who might be generally categorized as being disillusioned by what they perceived as the senseless slaughter of the First World War; they were cynical and "disdainful of the Victorian notions of morality and propriety of their elders" (*The Lost Generation*).

15. Tom Shippey gets close to this perspective when he writes that Tolkien's "work expresses along with a strong belief in (a kind of) Providence, the disillusionment of the returned veteran" (*Century* 156). Going even further, Verlyn Flieger speculates that Frodo is more than just a disillusioned veteran: he also represents the loss of youth and future that comes from war (224).

16. In *The Great War and Modern Memory*, still one of the finest overviews of the literary repercussions of World War I, Paul Fussell makes much of this gap between veterans and civilians, even seeing it as a parallel development to that yawning gap between pre- and post-Great War culture.

17. For discussion on how Tolkien's notions of evil can be associated with that of other post-war writers, see Shippey ("Post-War" 92).

The Shell-shocked Hobbit

Tolkien realized that the horrors he witnessed at the Somme were a sign that something had gone terribly wrong in the world. In the same letter to Smith, he writes that his "chief impression" about the war's effect on his relationship to his friends "is that something has gone crack" (*Letters* 10). Even if, like Frodo, Tolkien could not be specific about what was wrong, he could not deny that *something* was wrong.

One would hope that time could heal the psychological scars of trauma, but, at least in Frodo's case, we see that this is not so. Sam notes that "Frodo dropped quietly out of all the doings of the Shire" (VI.9.1002), and his deeds are not celebrated by the Shire-folk. If I might be clinical once more, Frodo appears to be entering into that "vicious cycle of rejection and recrimination" that is so common with victims of Post-Traumatic Stress Disorder; he cannot escape the incommunicable fear and trembling of his past and the inexplicable guilt of living (Miller 9). And the specific pains of his past continue to recur in nightmarish flashbacks:

> One evening Sam came into the study and found his master looking very strange. He was very pale and his eyes seemed to see things far away.
> "What's the matter, Mr. Frodo?" said Sam.
> "I am wounded," he answered, "wounded; it will never really heal."(VI.9.1002)

Sam later realizes that it is 6 October, the second anniversary of Frodo's wounding at Weathertop. Time has not healed his wounds, any more than time would make the loss at the Somme of Tolkien's best friends any easier to bear.

Frodo is again ill the following March (the second anniversary of the fight with Shelob) (VI.9.1002), and in September, as the third anniversary of Weathertop approaches, Frodo and Sam meet Elrond, Galadriel, Gandalf, Bilbo, and the remaining elves for the journey west to the Grey Havens; in taking the ship west, Frodo admits that he cannot find solace even in his beloved Shire. Like veterans returning to England, Frodo finds that he is a stranger in the land that he fought so long and hard to save. He might well have been speaking for the veterans of the trenches when he says to Sam: "I tried to save the Shire, and it has been saved, but not for me. It must often be so, Sam, when things are in danger: some one has to give them up, lose them, so that others may keep them" (VI.9.1006). Tom Shippey has pointed out the similarities between Frodo's words and those inscribed on a monument in honor of those who died at Imphal-Kohima in the Second World War (*Century*

156),[18] but perhaps it is more fitting to hear an echo of Siegfried Sassoon, an English poet who wrote some of his finest work in the trenches of the First World War, including some written during the opening days of the Battle of the Somme:

> You smug-faced crowds with kindling eye
> Who cheer when soldier lads march by,
> Sneak home and pray you'll never know
> The hell where youth and laughter go. (Sassoon)

I find that Sassoon's melancholic tone—delved in the actual horrors of warfare—is quite apt of Frodo and the end of *The Lord of the Rings*: Frodo does not desire to be a martyr; he does not wish to be celebrated or even remembered. He simply wishes to be whole once more. But his trauma is too great. This world, for which he fought so hard, holds nothing but continued pain for him. He cannot be healed here (Shippey, *Century* 155). The world he has saved, sadly, is one to which he can no longer relate. As Mark Eddy Smith states the matter:

> Some injustices cannot be remedied in this Middle-earth. Fingers don't grow back. Nor do friends. The Ring, though he did not ask for it, has corrupted Frodo. [...] At the final test he chose the Ring for himself alone and refused to cast it into the fire. There is no condemnation possible for this, for the task, by anyone's standards, was too big for him. But a part of Frodo was broken during the long journey to Mordor, and no one and nothing, neither plant nor animal, can restore him to wholeness. (Smith 133)

Ultimately, and perhaps inevitably, Frodo had to leave Middle-earth: only in the Undying Lands would he be able to find succor.

Sadly, there was no such "cure" for Tolkien and his fellow veterans. Like the members of the Lost Generation, they had to continue to try to continue on with their lives, to live past what they had lived through. It is interesting in this light to recall that Tolkien once said of Sam Gamgee that he was meant to be "a reflexion of the English soldier, of the privates and batmen I knew in the 1914 war, and recognised as so far superior to myself" (Carpenter 81). What it is that Tolkien sees as "far superior" to himself in other veterans might be their ability to make that final step away from the field of battle, their ability to move on. Frodo sees precisely this in Sam, saying to him: "you will be healed. You were meant to be solid and whole, and you will be" (*LotR* VI.9.1003). Tolkien, it seems, relates himself more closely with the shell-

---

18. The inscription reads "When you go home tell them of us and say / For your tomorrow we gave our today."

shocked Frodo than he does with the resilient Sam: for him, the scars of the Somme have cut too deeply to heal fully.

Gandalf's exchange with Bilbo at the end of *The Hobbit*, a tale written before the outbreak of the Second World War, is often taken as a foreshadowing of that event. Tolkien, according to this argument, was well aware that the resonance of the First World War was still working itself out, the Great War not yet finished:

> Even as they left the valley the sky darkened in the West before them, and wind and rain came up to meet them.
> "Merry is May-time!" said Bilbo, as the rain beat into his face. "But our back is to legends and we are coming home. I suppose this is a first taste of it."
> "There is a long road yet," said Gandalf.
> "But it is the last road," said Bilbo. (*Hobbit* 311)

It is true, I think, that we can hear in this passage that the resonance of the Great War was still working itself out. But I think it equally true that we should not be looking forward to the Second World War here, but backward to the painful memory of the First World War, of the blood-mixed mud of northern France, of the trench-scarred Somme and its No-man's Land, its fields of bloating corpses, its dead faces floating in water-filled craters. Tolkien often spoke about how his "mythology (and associated languages) first began to take shape" during the First World War (*Letters* 221). Gandalf and Bilbo's exchange is doubly appropriate, then, since the journey to Middle-earth was, for Tolkien, a journey into the Undying Lands, where he might eventually find healing for the wounds of war that would not heal. The road to healing is, as Gandalf observes, a long one. And, perhaps spiritually as well as physically, it is the last road.

This article was published originally in Mythlore *25.1/2 (#95/96) (2006): 77–92. It is reprinted here with permission.*

WORKS CITED

Brogan, Hugh. "Tolkien's Great War." *Children and Their Books: A Celebration of the Work of Iona and Peter Opie.* Eds. Gillian Avery and Julia Briggs. Oxford: Clarendon, 1989. 351–67. Print.

Carpenter, Humphrey. *Tolkien: A Biography.* Boston: Houghton Mifflin, 1977. Print.

Croft, Janet Brennan. *War and the Works of J. R. R. Tolkien.* Westport: Praeger, 2004. Print. Contributions to the Study of Science Fiction and Fantasy 106.

Ellison, John. " 'The Legendary War and the Real One': *The Lord of the Rings* and the Climate of Its Times." *Mallorn* 26 (1989): 17–20. Print.

Flieger, Verlyn. *A Question of Time: J. R. R. Tolkien's Road to Faerie.* Kent: Kent State UP, 1997. Print.

Friedman, Barton. "Tolkien and David Jones: The Great War and the War of the Ring." *Clio* 11.2 (1982): 115–36. Print.

Fussell, Paul. *The Great War and Modern Memory*. 25th anniv. ed. New York: Oxford UP, 2000. Print.
Garth, John. *Tolkien and the Great War: The Threshold of Middle-earth*. Boston: Houghton Mifflin, 2003. Print.
Green, William H. *The Hobbit: A Journey into Maturity*. New York: Twayne, 1995. Print. Twayne's Masterwork Studies 149.
Hammond, Wayne G., and Christina Scull. The Lord of the Rings: *A Reader's Companion*. Boston: Houghton Mifflin, 2005. Print.
Keegan, John. *The Face of Battle*. New York: Barnes and Noble, 1993. Print.
Kleine-Ahlbrandt, William Laird. *Twentieth-Century European History*. St. Paul: West, 1993.
Lewis, C. S. "The Dethronement of Power." *A Reader's Companion to* The Hobbit *and* The Lord of the Rings. New York: Quality Paperback Book Club, 1995. 37–42. Print.
Lewis, Warren. *Brothers and Friends: The Diaries of Major Warren Hamilton Lewis*. Eds. C. S. Kilby and M. L. Mead. San Francisco: Harper and Row, 1982. Print.
Lloyd George, David. *War Memoirs of David Lloyd George, 1915–1916*. Boston: Little Brown, 1933. Print.
"The Lost Generation." 2003. *Wikipedia*. Web. 26 Oct. 2003.
Miller, Laurence. *Shocks to the System*. New York: Norton, 1998. Print.
Petty, Anne C. *Tolkien in the Land of Heroes*. Cold Spring Harbor: Cold Spring Press, 2003. Print.
"Posttraumatic Stress Disorder." *Diagnostic and Statistical Manual of Mental Disorders: DSM-IV*. 4th ed., text revision ed. Washington, DC: American Psychiatric Assn., 2000. 463–68. Print.
Raws, John. *Letter to a Friend 12 August 1916*. Web. 29 August 2006.
Rosebury, Brian. *Tolkien: A Critical Assessment*. New York: St. Martin's, 1992. Print.
Sassoon, Siegfried. "Suicide in Trenches." *Collected Poems*. New York: Viking, 1949. 78. Print.
Shephard, Ben. *A War of Nerves: Soldiers and Psychiatrists in the Twentieth Century*. Cambridge: Harvard UP, 2001. Print.
Shippey, Tom. *J. R. R. Tolkien: Author of the Century*. Boston: Houghton Mifflin, 2001. Print.
—. "Tolkien as a Post-War Writer." *Proceedings of the J. R. R. Tolkien Centenary Conference, 1992*. Eds. Patricia Reynolds and Glen H. GoodKnight. Altadena: Tolkien Society, 1992. 84–93. Print.
Smith, Mark Eddy. *Tolkien's Ordinary Virtues: Exploring the Spiritual Themes of the* Lord of the Rings. Downers Grove: InterVarsity Press, 2002. Print.
Tolkien, J. R. R. *The Hobbit, or, There and Back Again*. Boston: Houghton Mifflin, 1966. Print.
—. *The Letters of J. R. R. Tolkien: A Selection*. Eds. Humphrey Carpenter and Christopher Tolkien. Boston: Houghton Mifflin, 2000. Print.
—. *The Lord of the Rings*. Boston: Houghton Mifflin, 1994. Print.

Faramir and the Heroic Ideal of the Twentieth Century; or, How Aragorn Died at the Somme

S. Brett Carter

SCENES OF COMBAT AND THE FOREBODING PRESENCE of warfare constitute many of the most memorable moments of J. R. R. Tolkien's *The Lord of the Rings*. Coming as he did from an academic background filled with warrior heroes of ancient cultures, Tolkien's depiction of war in his Middle-earth mythos is grandiose, featuring heroes reminiscent of kings and warriors from throughout history. It is evident that much of Tolkien's work with Middle-earth is in some way affected by his involvement in World War I as particular sections of his work seem to be lifted directly from his war experience. When asked about the subject, Tolkien stated that "My 'Sam Gamgee' is indeed a reflexion of the English soldier, of the privates and batmen I knew in the 1914 war, and recognised as so far superior to myself" (Carpenter 81). However, while Sam may represent what Tolkien saw and admired in the men he met in the trenches, Faramir represents a departure from ancient forms of war and the classical hero as he embodies battle strategies, uniform considerations, and equipment advancements of the twentieth century soldier. Janet Brennan Croft writes that "Faramir has a more modern and thoughtful attitude toward war, and is perhaps a more realistic model to emulate for the twenty-first-century reader" (*War and the Works of J. R. R. Tolkien* [*WatW*] 101). Furthermore, instead of simply representing the infantrymen of World War I and a modern attitude toward war, Faramir is a much broader illustration of the heroic model itself. Faramir represents the idea that with World War I the nature of the warrior which has been depicted in literature since the *Iliad* as glory-seeking and battle-driven is fundamentally altered. Despite being perhaps one of the most socially and historically relevant characters of Tolkien's *Lord of the Rings*, Faramir is rarely considered narrowly in criticism, either featured in comparison to other characters or treated cursorily.[1] In Tolkien's saga of Middle-earth, Faramir exists

---

1. Tom Shippey compares Faramir to Boromir, Éomer, and Sam in *The Road to Middle-earth*. Christopher Tolkien provides a history of the creation of Faramir in *The War of the Ring*. Paul Edmund Thomas provides an entry on Faramir for the *J. R. R.*

as a means to establish a new definition of the heroic model for the twentieth century in contrast to the ancient heroic ideals which are dissolved in World War I.

World War I was a conflict that was both psychologically and technologically different from any war that had previously occurred in history. It was with this war that the technological capabilities of man surpassed the standard practices of warfare that had been in existence for as long as there has been organized combat. The introduction of the machine gun, mortars, and chemical weaponry created a type of warfare that demanded a new position on the nature of war and the soldier. In an article for *National Geographic* in 1944, Brigadier General W. H. Wilbur wrote that in wars throughout history "soldiers and sailors measure their contribution by four considerations. First, by the degree of their isolation and loneliness; second, by the amount of physical discomfort they endure; third, by the amount of danger they undergo; and last, by the amount of real aggressive fighting that they do" (514). Tolkien and other World War I soldiers who were confined to trenches for extended periods of time, constantly under threat of bombardment and the horrifying effects of gas attacks, and under the expectation to charge hopelessly toward guns capable of out-firing entire units by themselves, demonstrate just how World War I infantrymen are set apart from warriors of the past. This demanding form of combat created a new view of war and with it the necessity for a new heroic model.

The primary way in which war was forever changed in the early twentieth century was the transformed battle tactics that were implemented to adapt to the latest technological advancements. The battle formations and tactics of the ancient world were demonstrated to be unusable and even foolish in warfare of the twentieth century. Up to this point, war was largely waged by two opposing forces marching toward each other on an open battlefield. In *A History of Warfare*, John Keegan traces this battle plan back to the ancient Greeks in the phalanx age who "confronted their like-minded enemies face-to-face" (332). With the advent of the machine gun of the twentieth century this form of face-to-face combat significantly declined in importance, making it even less effective and, in many instances, suicidal. In World War I, men such as Tea Club and Barrovian Society member Rob Gilson, while on

---

Tolkien Encyclopedia in which he discusses his role in the story as well as the character's creation. Faramir's relationship with Éowyn is analyzed in articles from Melissa McCrory Hatcher and Melissa Smith. Faramir's treatment in Peter Jackson's films is discussed in an essay from Anthony S. Burdge and Jessica Burke.

the British front, demonstrated how this way of fighting became obsolete as he and his regiment "scrambled up ladders from the trenches and into the open, forming up in straight lines as they had been instructed, and beginning their slow tramp forward" (Carpenter 82). As Gilson approached enemy lines, the opposition fired upon the British troops with their machine guns. What was once the work of an entire army was now within the capability of an individual weapon system. Attempting to use the ancient face-to-face style of warfare made it difficult for the average soldier to even survive a battle, much less win one.

The difference in battle tactics affected the conduct of war all the way from the movement of armies to the psychology of the individual soldier. The role of the individual soldier was altered in World War I from a warrior in control of the battlefield to that of a pawn at its mercy. In "Martial Illusions: War and Disillusionment in Twentieth-Century and Renaissance Military Memoirs," Yuval Noah Harari writes that "in the twentieth century [...] soldiers have become disillusioned with war, and their own image has partly changed from that of heroes to that of victims" (43). Unlike the heroic soldiers of ancient wars, soldiers from World War I were not interested in the dreams of glory and honor that can only be achieved on the battlefield. Instead, they were concerned with mere survival. The ancient heroes became inadequate representations of the hardships faced by the modern soldier. When the war first struck Europe, society still believed in the ancient heroic ideals of long dead warrior societies. John Garth quotes Richard Jenkyns: "as the long prosperous years of the Pax Britannica succeeded one another, the truth about war was forgotten, and in 1914 young officers went into battle with the *Iliad* in their backpacks and the names of Achilles and Hector engraved upon their hearts" (qtd. in *Tolkien and the Great War* [*TatGW*] 42). Thousands of young men were heading to the front aspiring to win honor and glory in combat like the classical epic heroes.

However, the conditions these soldiers endured in the trenches of France were unlike anything Achilles or Hector had ever faced. In his letters, Gilson wrote of "utter barbarism of war" and how facing "the nightmare of those wet cold trenches" ultimately destroyed for him any notion of honor in war and "shattered the noble hopes and ideals that the war gave us at first" (qtd. in Garth, "Robert Quilter Gilson, T.C.B.S: A Brief Life in Letters" ["RQG"] 83). In this new landscape of warfare, those classical heroic models were useless. Harari writes that "the old heroic rhetoric of war has come to sound increasingly pompous and ridiculous to Western ears, and has consequently been replaced by a new and much more somber war rhetoric" (45). The change in warfare inevitably led to a change in the conception of the nature of war itself. "Nevertheless," continues Garth, "the worn word 'hero' was being reforged in galvanizing fires" and the nature of the heroic warrior was being redefined for a new era of warfare (*TatGW* 69). Faramir's role in battle and the redefinition of the heroic ideal, as Croft asserts, appears in how he questions "the chivalric ideal of war as a 'high male endeavour' " and "sees war as a means but not an end in itself, and thus finds another way to confront the 'disturbing elements' of being a warrior" (*WatW* 43). While Faramir accepts the role of the warrior, he rejects the idea of the warrior society. With this rejection, Tolkien uses Faramir as a model for the new heroic figure for modern warfare. During World War I, the classical idea of war breaks down and is replaced with both a cynicism and a heroic model that, like Faramir, is grounded more in humility and peace than in glory and combat.

Within the reality of *The Lord of the Rings*, the common outlook on war is one that is more closely aligned with ancient epic heroes than with Tolkien's own personal views. Tolkien's views on war were problematic; as Garth states, "despite his taste for romance and high diction, […] Tolkien did not find the war adventurous, dashing, or sacred. He summed up trench life as 'animal horror' " (*TatGW* 290). Although his opinion of war may have been harsh and unfavorable, this sentiment is not readily evident in *The Lord of the Rings*, which seems to glorify battle as Aragorn and the Fellowship cleave their way through countless hordes of orcs and characters such as Legolas and Gimli turn slaughter into a game, competing with one another by comparing the number of kills. While all combatants in the War of the Ring fight out of necessity and for an undeniably righteous cause, it is easy to differentiate those who follow ancient ideals of the warrior society from those less interested in glory. It is in the humility of characters such as Sam and the honest language of Faramir that Tolkien's true vision of war and the new heroic model that emerges in World War I is shared.

The character of Faramir initially appears with his group of rangers late in *The Two Towers*; his men reveal an enormous amount of detail and insight into the methods and strategy of their leader. When travelling through the woods in an attempt to find a more covert way of entering Mordor, Sam and Frodo are confronted by a group of Gondorians who come upon the hobbits suddenly and from several directions. Tolkien's initial description of the rangers includes an inventory of items that reveal exactly how the unit operates by describing their equipment and clothing.

> Four tall Men stood there. Two had spears in their hands with broad bright heads. Two had great bows, almost of their own height, and great quivers of long green-feathered arrows. All had swords at their sides, and were clad in green and brown of varied hues, as if the better to walk unseen in the glades of Ithilien. Green gauntlets covered their hands, and their faces were hooded and masked with green, except their eyes, which were very keen and bright. (Tolkien, *The Lord of the Rings [LotR]* IV.4.657)

The rangers under the command of Faramir are armed with long bows, giving them the capability to wage war over distances greater than most of their foes. This is the same type of warfare deemed cowardly and dishonorable by the chivalric knights, but is far more effective and less perilous than the face-to-face equivalent, especially when used from cover. A bowman, such as one of Faramir's unit, could "without any of the long apprenticeship to arms necessary to make a knight, and equally without the moral effort required of a pike-wielding footman, kill either of them from a distance without putting himself in danger" (Keegan 333). The traditional warrior class protested such tactics and the men who used them "on the ground that their weapon was a cowardly one and their behaviour treacherous" (333). This tactic also reveals Faramir to be a conscientious leader, minimizing the risk to his subordinates while maximizing their effectiveness in battle. Faramir was considerate of the risk he put his men to and sacrificed the idea of glorious face-to-face combat in favor of a weapon system that would be less desirable in the eyes of men such as Boromir, but also much more efficient.

The colors worn by Faramir's rangers also set them apart from other combatants in Tolkien's work as well as align them with more modern military forces. Until the twentieth century the British military dressed its men in colorful and dramatic uniforms, most notably with the famous scarlet tunics. With the coming of the twentieth century and World War I, however, the British army implemented a khaki uniform, in order to camouflage the soldiers fighting in the dirt and mud of the trenches. Faramir shows a modern sense of warfare by discarding the shining mail and other bulky garments worn by Boromir and Aragorn in favor of a streamlined uniform with colors to blend in with the environment, giving the rangers the advantage of stealth. Camouflage is also discussed during another notable occasion in *The Lord of the Rings* and is again associated with a grander ideal of heroism. When leaving Lothlórien, each member of the Fellowship received a bundle of gifts from the elves.

> For each [member of the Fellowship] they had provided a hood and cloak, made according to his size, of the light but warm silken stuff that the Galadhrim wove. It was hard to say of what colour they were: grey with the hue of twilight under the trees they seemed to be; and yet if they were moved, or set in another light, they were green as shadowed leaves, or brown as fallow fields by night, dusk-silver as water under the stars. (Tolkien, *LotR* II.8.370)

The elves, Tolkien's most revered race and the wisest group of beings in Middle-earth, gift the Fellowship with cloaks that have the ability to change colors and blend with their surroundings instead of dazzling in gold or silver. By giving the Fellowship garments of camouflage, Tolkien is affirming that the heroic model must be renewed and that the hero must adapt to the new standard of warfare. Since face-to-face warfare and posturing made up such a large part of military life until World War I, the concept of camouflage was a radical change when implemented by an entire force. Although stealth tactics existed in early wars, it was in World War I that their use became widespread and absolutely necessary. With Faramir's reliance on camouflage, Tolkien demonstrates a need for adaptability and change with regards to the modern heroic figure.

Instead of the elaborate systems of posturing and face-to-face confrontations preferred by Boromir and the chivalric armies of history, Faramir's men use stealthy tactics to sneak up on their targets and avoid making themselves known until "flight and hiding were no longer possible" (*LotR* IV.4.656). This directly opposes the position of Boromir established during *The Fellowship of the Ring* as he expresses an interest in posturing even when it is unwise. As the Fellowship first sets forth from Rivendell, Boromir "blew a blast [from his horn]. And the echoes leapt from rock to rock, and all that heard that voice in Rivendell sprang to their feet" (*LotR* II.3.279). Elrond warns Boromir against sounding his horn, to which Boromir replies "always I have let my horn cry at setting forth, and though thereafter we may walk in the shadows, I will not go forth as a thief in the night" (II.3.279). Going forth as thieves in the night is exactly how Faramir chooses to conduct war. Instead of making the enemy aware of his presence and facing them in traditional combat, Faramir sets an ambush for the Southron men, taking advantage of the element of surprise and attacking from cover in order to efficiently and systematically eliminate the enemy. As Sam sits and watches the rangers prepare for battle, "he could see [the rangers] stealing up the slopes, singly or in long files, keeping always to the shade of grove or thicket, or crawling, hardly visible in their brown and green raiment, through grass and brake. All were hooded and masked […]. Before long they had all passed and vanished" (*LotR* IV.4.660). Using camouflage and stealth, the warriors under Faramir's command set themselves apart from all other military units besides the elves in *The Lord of the Rings* and ultimately align themselves more closely with the soldiers of modern warfare than with the ancient heroes prevalent in the work of Tolkien.

The rangers of Ithilien also employ tactics that are less common in Tolkien's work as well as in ancient combat but more closely aligned with the British strategy of World War I. Croft discusses the theory behind emerging strategy in World War I in "The Hen that Laid the Eggs: Tolkien and the Officers Training Corps," in which she writes that just before World War I, the English decided to draw on the young, educated men of the country and establish them as leaders, creating an "underlying cultural model valuing preparedness" (97). Instead of creating a military of fighters, the English government was concerned with creating an army of thinkers who could lead forces of men to success by means other than simply applying force. Croft gives a number of examples of "the dangers of lapsed vigilance in Middle-earth" (102) including Sauron's reestablishment of Barad-dûr and Saruman's negligence of the ents. Faramir's ability to coordinate several covert ambushes in *The Lord of the Rings* may also lend itself as an example of good military preparedness as Faramir is able to exploit the weaknesses of Sauron's forces and the classical ideas of conventional warfare. It is when Faramir abandons his own combat strategy in favor of the classical model endorsed by his father Denethor that he loses a battle. Capitalizing on preparedness, just as the English did in World War I, Faramir's rangers dressed efficiently, wearing inconspicuous colors and equipping themselves only with what they could carry. In his article on Gilson, Garth reveals the soldier's "joy of battalion unity, of carrying all one's possessions, and of never staying in one place for more than a night" ("RQG" 89). Faramir stalked the enemy and took advantage of their lack of preparedness by employing camouflage, constant movement, and surprise tactics to aggressively attack Sauron's forces.

Faramir's relationship with his subordinates is also peculiar in comparison to other military units and relates to the new model of heroism that arose during World War I. In *The Great War and Modern Memory*, Paul Fussell writes that "a standard experience during the war was the company officer's discovery that his attitude toward his men [...] had turned into something close to devotion. [...] The men trusted their officer not just to safeguard their lives if he could but to deal with them decently when out of danger. They responded with wry admiration and affection, as to an odd twenty-year-old 'father' " (164). Although Faramir maintains a level of authority over his men suitable to his rank, he is more commonly depicted as well-respected and often loved by his fellow Gondorians. One of the primary ways in which Faramir is able to break down the class barriers between himself and his subordinates is by wearing the same uniform as his men. When fully uniformed with mask and hood, Faramir is indistinguishable from any of the men under his command. A level of affection also follows Faramir which does not seem to exist between other higher ranking men and the soldiers. The character of Beregond especially illustrates the love between the rangers and their commander. As Beregond shows Pippin around Minas Tirith, he gives the hobbit a description of Faramir's strengths as a leader, comparing him to Boromir:

> He is bold, more bold than many deem; for in these days men are slow to believe that a captain can be wise and learned in the scrolls of lore and song, as he is, and yet a man of hardihood and swift judgement in the field. But such is Faramir. Less reckless and eager than Boromir, but not less resolute. (*LotR* V.1.766)

In this passage, Beregond not only demonstrates his respect for Faramir but places him higher than Boromir, who is the more traditional hero in the story. By saying that men are slow to believe in his wisdom, Beregond implies that, though it is a desirable quality, such wisdom is not typical of higher ranking soldiers. Referring to Faramir as less reckless and eager than Boromir leaves the impression that these are actually negative traits in Boromir's character. As Croft describes Faramir, she writes that "he is as beloved and charismatic a leader as Aragorn and as effective and skilled in battle; he has the same leadership style and characteristics, but thinks (or at least speaks) more deeply about why he fights" (*WatW* 101). Faramir is just as efficient a leader as either Boromir or Aragorn, and because of his sympathetic and morally conflicted character he is perhaps even more qualified to represent the heroic model of the twentieth century.

Tolkien would be familiar with the sense of camaraderie and closeness between officers and their subordinates. Garth writes that although Tolkien's experience in the army "enshrined old social boundaries, it also chipped away at the class divide by throwing men from all walks of life into a desperate situation together" (*TatGW* 94). The desperate situation of Tolkien and the lower ranking soldiers is mirrored in Faramir's journey through Ithilien and his attempt to defend Osgiliath. Faramir travelled with his men through the wilderness on the outskirts of his realm, brushing shoulders with Mordor as they attempted to interfere with any soldiers attempting to join with Sauron's forces. When later asked to ride to Osgiliath in anticipation of the Battle of Pelennor Fields, a futile and almost suicidal mission, Faramir does not ride alone, revealing that he has formed an intense bond with his men, who are willing to follow him to their deaths. In his letters, Tolkien writes that he had "a deep sympathy and feeling for the 'tommy,' especially the plain soldier from agricultural counties" (*Letters* 54). This level of respect is exhibited only rarely within military hierarchies of Middle-earth, revealing that the new heroic figure leads with sympathy as well as with discipline.

Faramir not only sets himself apart from other leaders in Middle-earth with his use of modern military strategy, but embodies the characteristics that are necessary for military success in modern warfare. Fussell identifies the two major causes of the allied failure at the Somme as the lack of both imagination and surprise. He writes that the British staff had little confidence for the rapidly trained army and "it was felt that the troops would become confused by more subtle tactics like rushing from cover to cover, or assault-firing, or following close upon a continuous creeping barrage" (13). Faramir, however, demonstrates himself as being both confident in his subordinates and a capable tactician within *The Lord of the Rings*, setting himself apart from the imperfect leadership that created the disaster that Tolkien witnessed first-hand.

The fact that Faramir is considered wise and learned reveals another aspect of Tolkien's definition of the heroic figure. The atmosphere of society during the early twentieth century was not focused solely on battle and glory, but instead emphasized wisdom and academic success. Fussell writes that the intellectual landscape of the twentieth century military was unique as, perhaps for the first time in history, "it was possible for soldiers to be not merely literate but vigorously literary," creating a more thoughtful and introspective soldier, much like Tolkien's Faramir (157). The men in the trenches were not necessarily interested in military careers, but instead called upon to fight for their country in a time of need though their true passions lied elsewhere. Tolkien's own passions were found in his academic achievements, which were greatly respected within his community. The English school results, issued just before Tolkien's entry into the ranks of the English armed forces, revealed that he had earned First Class Honors. After the publication of his achievement, Tolkien received a letter of congratulations telling him that the honors were "one of the highest distinctions an Englishman can obtain" (qtd. in *TatGW* 83). This sense of accomplishment felt by Tolkien and his peers reveals the appreciation for academic success within Tolkien's society. Honor and glory could be accomplished through scholarly pursuits as well and were not reserved for the brave and valorous warriors such as in other, more ancient societies. Garth writes that "Faramir, of course, is an officer but also a scholar, with a reverence for the old histories and sacred values that helps him through a bitter war" (*TatGW* 310). Like Tolkien, who was more interested in studies than in war, Faramir longs for a time of peace when he can set aside his sword and instead take up a book. Tolkien and the T.C.B.S. were forced to put their studies on hold with the coming war and Tolkien "was facing the relinquishment of long-cherished hopes" (78). Faramir embodies this new wise and learned heroic model since his best qualities, as interpreted by himself and his men, do not lie in his strength as a soldier, but in his gentle wisdom and interest in glory away from the battlefield.

Another major scene featuring Faramir in *The Lord of the Rings* that reveals much of the warrior's moral code and value system is his conversation with Frodo concerning the One Ring, which mirrors many of the ideals present in the infantrymen of World War I and Tolkien himself. After taking Frodo and Sam captive, Faramir has a long discussion with the hobbits concerning the fate of his brother and the nature of Isildur's bane. Tolkien writes in a letter that it is during this scene that Faramir offers "some very sound reflections no doubt on martial glory and true glory," and it is in these first few pages of his appearance that Faramir reveals much of his character (*Letters* 79). In another letter, Tolkien writes that Faramir "had been accustomed to giving way and not giving his own opinions air, while retaining a power of command among men, such as a man may obtain who is evidently personally courageous and decisive, but also modest, fair-minded and scrupulously just, and very merciful" (323). Faramir demonstrates this honesty and mercy during his first meeting with Frodo when he announced that he "would not snare even an orc with a falsehood" (*LotR* IV.5.664) and when he states that he will "not slay man or beast needlessly, and not gladly even when it is needed" (IV.5.665). In this passage, Faramir is portrayed as a compassionate warrior who refuses to kill recklessly or without reason, even possessing the capacity to look at an orc with sympathy. This compassion strays from the heroic model established by Aragorn and Éomer, who kill indiscriminately during wartime.

It is also during this scene that Faramir encounters the temptation of the One Ring, which previously led to the downfall of his older brother, Boromir. In the Appendix to *The Lord of the Rings*, Tolkien describes Faramir as able to "read the hearts of men as shrewdly as his father, but what he read moved him sooner to pity than to scorn" (*LotR*

App.A.1056). This kingly intuition leads Faramir to the revelation that Frodo carries the One Ring, but he does not use this knowledge to try and gain power, and instead sympathizes with his burden. During this scene, Faramir describes himself as "wise enough to know that there are some perils from which a man must flee" (IV.5.681). In this moment, Faramir conveys an understanding as to how Boromir could have been tempted by the One Ring. Since Boromir represents the ancient heroic tradition of warriors that pursued glory and honor to their death, he would selfishly be drawn to the Ring. Even though he could claim to want the Ring for good intentions, knowing the evil power of the One Ring should make Boromir fearful of taking it. Instead, he is driven by his pride and longing for glory to take the Ring. "True-hearted Men," as Boromir calls himself and his people, "will not be corrupted. [...] We do not desire the power of wizard-lords, only strength to defend ourselves, strength in a just cause" (II.10.398). However, to use the Ring is fundamentally evil in itself, and it crosses a line that Faramir refuses to consider breaching. When discussing the One Ring with Frodo, Faramir says "Fear not! I do not wish to see it, or touch it, or know more of it than I know (which is enough), lest peril perchance waylay me and I fall lower in the test than Frodo son of Drogo" (IV.5.681). Unlike Boromir, whose pride and honor deceive him into believing he could take the power of the Ring for himself, in his humility Faramir knows that the Ring's power is beyond him. Boromir wishes to use the Ring to bring the fight to the enemy while Faramir would avoid warfare unless absolutely necessary.

Like the intellectual soldiers of World War I such as Gilson, who would admit in his letters to having a "late-night conversation about the ethics of war with his closest friend in the battalion," Faramir and Sam, as representatives of the twentieth century heroic figure, are also capable of such discussions ("RQG" 88). During his long conversation with Frodo and Sam, Faramir reveals his thoughts about war and his moral code. "For myself," says Faramir, "I would see the White Tree in flower again in the courts of the kings, and the Silver Crown return, and Minas Tirith in peace" (*LotR* IV.5.671). In these lines, Faramir reveals that he has no ambition for power. Although he is next in line for the stewardship of Gondor, he would prefer that the king return to rule Minas Tirith and the realm of men. Like Gilson, who thought that to survive the war would "cast a rosy glow over everything [thereafter]" ("RQG" 90) Faramir too enjoys the idea of the reestablishment of a peaceful government after the war. However, Faramir does recognize the necessity of war, stating that "War must be, while we defend our lives against a destroyer who would devour all; but I do not love the bright sword for its sharpness, nor the arrow for its swiftness, nor the warrior for his glory" (*LotR* IV.5.672). Faramir reveals in these lines that he does not have the same drive for glory that his brother and other heroes of *The Lord of the Rings* possess. The role of the warrior that defined heroes since the poetry of Homer is cast aside in favor of a heroic model that prefers peace and only fights when his way of life is threatened and there is no alternative.

As he reveals in his letters, Tolkien shares the view that war is at times necessary for a society to defend itself. In a letter to his son Christopher, who was serving in the Royal Air Force during World War II, Tolkien writes that "the utter stupid waste of war, not only material but moral and spiritual, is so staggering to those who have to endure it. And always was (despite the poets), and always will be (despite the propagandists)—not of course that it has not is and will be necessary to face it in an evil world" (*Letters* 75). In this statement, Tolkien condemns the destructive effect of war on society as well as its glorification in popular culture. However, he ends the passage by stating, like Faramir, that there are moments when force is necessary in order to combat evil. Croft writes that "Tolkien may have hated war as only a veteran could, but he also felt that sometimes it was necessary to take up arms" (*WatW* 8). This understanding of the nature of war while not idealizing it is one quality that is perfectly shared by Tolkien and Faramir.

Faramir's decision to ride to Osgiliath to land the initial blow of the Battle of Pelennor Fields, even though it essentially amounts to a suicide mission, shares some similarities with the plight of Tolkien and his friends during the first years of World War I. A characteristic of Tolkien's generation that was unlike previous generations was the obligation of all citizens to join the war effort whether or not each man was interested in the pursuit of warrior ideals. In his study on the history of warfare, John Keegan writes about some of the changes that took place during World War I:

> By 1914 an entirely unprecedented cultural mood was dominating European society, one which accepted the right of the state to demand and the duty of every fit, male individual to render military service, which perceived in the performance of military service a necessary training in civic virtue and which rejected the age-old social distinction between the warrior—as a man set apart whether by rank or no rank at all—and the rest, as an outdated prejudice. (355)

Tolkien felt an immense anxiety about finishing his undergraduate work and being forced into joining the war effort, just as many other young men were uninterested in going to war. Tolkien and his friends "felt that they were all being pitched into maturity" with the coming war (*TatGW* 87). While willing to leave in order to serve their country, Tolkien and his friends always looked forward to reuniting in the T.C.B.S. Faramir acknowledges Denethor's command and accepts his orders, just as Tolkien followed the call of King George V. Like Faramir, Tolkien and countless other British citizens fulfilled their duty to their country, but only in the capacity of a duty. They did not live for battle the way men such as Boromir and Éomer did. Garth writes that "Now they felt that, for [Tolkien and the T.C.B.S.], the war was only the preparation for the task that lay in store. It was a 'travail underground' from which they would emerge enriched" (*TatGW* 137). To Tolkien, Faramir, and the average young man swept up into World War I, war was a brief interruption in their life and a learning experience, but never the central purpose.

Near the conclusion of *Tolkien and the Great War*, Garth argues that "Middle-earth contradicts the prevalent view of literary history that the Great War finished off the epic and heroic traditions in any serious form" (287). However, though Tolkien celebrates the ancient heroic model by recalling figures such as Beowulf and Beorhtnoth in valiant characters like Aragorn, he also uses *The Lord of the Rings* to show that these heroic ideals no longer have a place in modern society and in warfare after World War I. Fussell writes that while "the war was relying on inherited myth, it was generating new myth, and that myth is part of the fiber of our own lives" (ix). Many works of literature written on war can be drawn back to this idea of the reliance on myth while simultaneously establishing new myth. Writings such as Tennyson's "Charge of the Light Brigade" attempt to celebrate classical ideas of heroic glory in battle and others, such as Remarque's *All Quiet on the Western Front*,[2] endeavor to dismiss such ideas entirely. Tolkien, however, does something much more ambitious with *The Lord of the Rings* as he replaces an antiquated and impossible mythology with a current set of ideals for the twentieth century. As Garth describes in "Tolkien, Exeter College and the Great War," Tolkien was extremely interested in the idea of "a *national* myth, the embodiment in poetic language of one cohesive culture's imagination and values" (44). Tolkien's *The Lord of the Rings*, which records the success and nobility of a more thoughtful and

---

2. In the film version of the novel, lines from Homer's *Odyssey* can even be seen on the blackboard behind the jingoist schoolteacher who encourages his students to enlist, further emphasizing the irrelevance of classical ideas of martial glory in modern society.

reluctant soldier, demonstrates the qualities necessary in the twentieth century and beyond.

Through the character of Faramir, as well as the implementation of other, more subtle elements, Tolkien shows the impossibility of the ancient heroic model in twentieth-century warfare. Faramir embodies a redefined form of the heroic model that is more representative of the modern warrior by accepting war as a necessary part of western civilization, but preferring peace. Instead of longing for combat and the possibility of gaining honor and glory like his brother and others, Faramir does his duty to his state without becoming absorbed by these ancient ideals. Though characters such as Aragorn and Boromir are not necessarily as glory-driven as their classical counterparts, Aragorn's eagerness to reclaim the throne of Gondor and Boromir's desire to take the fight to the enemy set their heroic figures apart from the distinctly more reserved Faramir. The humility and wisdom of Faramir is evident in men such as Tolkien and the T.C.B.S. who went into service with caution and awareness, not selfish dreams of decorations and promotion. In Carpenter's biography of Tolkien, he notes that Faramir was an accidental addition to *The Lord of the Rings* whom he had not previously conceived until his arrival in Ithilien. "A new character has come on the scene," reveals Tolkien. "I am sure I did not invent him, I did not even want him, though I like him" (Carpenter 198). Later Tolkien writes that "as far as any character is 'like me' it is Faramir—except that I lack what all my characters possess [...] *Courage*" (*Letters* 232). With his accidental arrival and embodiment of some of Tolkien's own viewpoints, Faramir was constructed by Tolkien as a way to correct what he saw as flawed in the classical heroic tradition, especially when applied to what he had experienced at the Somme. In *The Lord of the Rings*, Faramir is certainly set apart from other, more classically traditional heroes such as Aragorn and Boromir and is ultimately revealed to be a critical component of Tolkien's version of the national myth as a character that embodies the heroic ideal of the twentieth century.

This article was published originally in Mythlore *30.3/4 (#117/118) (2012): 89–102. It is reprinted here with permission.*

Works Cited

All Quiet on the Western Front. Dir. Lewis Milestone. Universal Pictures, 1930. Print.

Burdge, Anthony S. and Jessica Burke. "Humiliated Heroes: Peter Jackson's Interpretation of *The Lord of the Rings*." *Translating Tolkien: Text and Film*. Ed. Thomas Honegger. Zurich: Walking Tree Press, 2004. 135–64. Print.

Carpenter, Humphrey. *Tolkien: A Biography*. Boston: Houghton Mifflin, 1977. Print.

Croft, Janet Brennan. "The Hen that Laid the Eggs: Tolkien and the Officers Training Corps." *Tolkien Studies* 8 (2011): 97–106. Print.

—. *War and the Works of J. R. R. Tolkien*. Westport: Praeger, 2004. Print. Contributions to the Study of Science Fiction and Fantasy 106.

Fussell, Paul. *The Great War and Modern Memory*. London: Oxford UP, 1975. Print.

Garth, John. "Robert Quilter Gilson, T.C.B.S.: A Brief Life in Letters." *Tolkien Studies* 8 (2011): 67–96. Print.

—. "Tolkien, Exeter College and the Great War." *Tolkien's The Lord of the Rings: Sources of Inspiration*. Eds. Stratford Caldecott and Thomas Honegger. Zurich: Walking Tree Press, 2008. 12–56. Print.

—. *Tolkien and the Great War: The Threshold of Middle-earth*. Boston: Houghton Mifflin, 2003. Print.

Harari, Yuval Noah. "Martial Illusions: War and Disillusionment in Twentieth-Century and Renaissance Military Memoirs." *The Journal of Military History* 69.1 (2005): 43–72. Print.

Hatcher, Melissa McCrory. "Finding Woman's Role in *The Lord of the Rings*." *Mythlore* 25.3/4 (#97/98) (2007): 43–54. Print.

Keegan, John. *A History of Warfare*. New York: Vintage Books, 1993. Print.

Remarque, Erich Maria. *All Quiet on the Western Front*. Trans. A. W. Wheen. New York: Fawcett, 1987. Print.

Shippey, Tom. *The Road to Middle-earth*. London: George Allen and Unwin, 1982. Print.

Smith, Melissa. "At Home and Abroad: Éowyn's Two-fold Figuring as War Bride in *The Lord of the Rings*." *Mythlore* 26.1-2 (#99/100) (2007): 161–72. Print.

Tennyson, Lord Alfred. "The Charge of the Light Brigade." *The Norton Anthology of English Literature*. Ed. M. H. Abrams and Stephen Greenblatt. 7th ed. Vol. 2. New York: Norton. 1280–81. Print.

Thomas, Paul Edmund. "Faramir." *J. R. R. Tolkien Encyclopedia: Scholarship and Critical Assessment*. Ed. Michael D. C. Drout. New York: Routledge, 2007. 196–97. Print.

Tolkien, Christopher. *The War of the Ring: The History of* The Lord of the Rings, *Part Three*. Boston: Houghton Mifflin: 1990. Print.

Tolkien, J. R. R. *The Lord of the Rings*. Boston: Houghton Mifflin, 1997. Print.

—. *The Letters of J. R. R. Tolkien*. Ed. Humphrey Carpenter. Boston: Houghton Mifflin, 1981. Print.

Wilbur, W. H. "Infantrymen—The Fighters of War." *National Geographic* 86.5 (1944): 514–38. Print.

Wounded by War:
Men's Bodies in the Prose Tradition of *The Children of Húrin*

MARGARET SINEX

VERSIONS OF TÚRIN'S STORY reveal a steady engagement with the value of the male body over decades and they also reveal an intensification of the injuries the male body sustains, most especially in the case of Flinding/Gwindor. They pose the following questions. Once visibly disfigured, lacking a member (hand or foot) or possessing a shriveled leg or ruined arm, is the male body fully adult, or has it become much more like the body of a disabled child? Does the dismembered male body retain any sexual appeal? After the devastation wrought by war, does the male body have an aesthetic value?

As my title indicates, I confine my analysis of the wounded body to *The Children of Húrin*, the text edited by Christopher Tolkien and published posthumously in 2007. Tolkien first conceived this stern, dark tale about a brother and sister during the First World War. He called their story one of the three Great Tales set in the First Age of the world, and over the decades he retold it in both verse and in prose. Christopher Tolkien believes that the wartime prose version "[was] certainly in existence by 1919, if not before" and it bears the title *Turambar and the Foalókë* ('Conqueror of Fate' and the Dragon) (*Children* 9). The theme of the dragon-slayer and his foe is tightly intertwined with Tolkien's own experience of the war. It was in Tolkien's mind before he saw action in the summer of 1916 and remained with him afterward. In their *Reader's Guide* Scull and Hammond note an entry in Tolkien's *Qenya Phonology and Lexicon* for "Fentor—the great worm slain by Ingilmo or Turambar" which they date to 1915 and believe "certainly preced[es] the first written tale of Túrin. [...] This first account [they continue] written out in pencil, was erased when overwritten by a revised version, apparently in the summer of 1919" (1057).

I find that this attentiveness to the damaged body persists throughout the numerous prose versions that follow *Turambar*; it does not diminish over the decades, but rather, it intensifies. My method has been to read these prose iterations in the context of work by three contemporary medical authorities, all of whom were influential contributors to war-time debates about the definition of shell-shock, its range of symptoms, and treatment methods. Part I of this study focuses on Túrin and

Húrin, exploring symptoms that prove either transient or that permanently scar the body in minor ways, as well as the paralysis suffered by both father and son and those symptoms arising from the emotional shock sustained by Túrin following Beleg's death.

Part II demonstrates that the experiences of three maimed characters (two returned veterans and one civilian) reflect those of many disabled veterans and civilians late in the war and in the post-war period. For all three figures, their disablement determines the nature of their reception and treatment; for two of them (Flinding/Gwindor and Tamar/Brandir) it delimits their social status, their influence on military policy in particular, and their suitability for leadership.

I suggest that Tolkien should be counted among those WWI veterans—memoirists, novelists and especially the poets—who highlight the grievous fragility of the human body and psyche caught up in the battlefield slaughter of the Great War.

PART I: WOUNDS VISIBLE AND INVISIBLE
With the original *Turambar* of 1919, Tolkien establishes a scrutiny of the wounded male body, and all subsequent prose versions reveal a mounting preoccupation with it. In 1926, Tolkien completed a short version of Túrin's story, usually called the "Sketch of the Mythology" (Christopher Tolkien, *Shaping*). This *Sketch* forms the basis of the prose version of 1930 called the *Quenta Noldorinwa* or the *Quenta* that contains the tale of Túrin.[1] A much longer, more fully developed version of the tale, called *Narn I Hîn Húrin* (the *Tale of the Children of Húrin*) or *Narn*, written at the end of the 1950s, is found in the *Unfinished Tales of Númenor and Middle-earth* published by Christopher Tolkien in 1980. To compile the chapter 'Of Túrin Turambar' in the *Silmarillion* (1977), Christopher Tolkien relied on several versions of the tale: portions of the *Quenta Silmarillion* (late 1937 and discussed in footnote 1), the *Narn* (late 1950s)

---

1. Christopher Tolkien notes: "the Quenta Noldorinwa was in fact the only complete version of 'The Silmarillion' that my father ever made. Toward the end of 1937, he interrupted work on a new version, *Quenta Silmarillion*, which extended to part way through the story of Túrin Turambar, and began *The Lord of the Rings*" (*Shaping* vii). Two chapters of the Quenta Silmarillion are devoted to Túrin: "(16) 'Of the Fourth Battle: Nírnaith Arnoediad'; (17) 'Of Túrin Turamarth or Túrin the Hapless' (abandoned as Túrin leaves Menegroth after killing Orgof)" (Scull and Hammond 803). See also Christopher Tolkien's account in *Children* 275–78.

and the *Grey Annals* (c. 1951).² The text of the *Children of Húrin* published in 2007 relies chiefly on the *Narn* and the *Silmarillion*.³

I have considered each prose iteration of his story in the context of several contemporary medical authorities published during the war or directly following it: G. Elliot Smith's *Shell Shock and its Lessons* (1917), F. W. Mott's *War Neuroses and Shell Shock* (1919), and E. E. Southard's *Shell-shock and Other Neuropsychiatric Problems* (1919).⁴ It is clear that many injuries (both permanent and transient) in *Turambar* correspond very closely to those experienced and reported during the War years.

I will begin with a case found among the over 500 medical histories found in Southard's *Shell Shock and Other Neuropsychiatric Problems*. In the section "Shell-Shock: Nature and Causes" is the following case study about the accidental slaying of a fellow soldier, recorded in April 1916. Here, we find a cluster of symptoms, two of which are of interest to us: the physician notes the fixity and persistence of his patient's horrified facial expression and his unwavering focus on his memory of firing and killing his fellow soldier. The doctor observes that "[a] physical expression of horror, together with an intense sweating and a very marked stammer, persisted for months." Further, during the day, the incident crowds out all others however much the patient tries to distract himself. He quotes his patient saying: "I cannot forget it no matter how I skylark" (Southard 463). The circumstances of the shooting were as follows:

> [The patient was] placed on outpost duty. It was dark, and he was in a state of considerable tension. He heard a noise which he thought came from somewhere in front of him. Suddenly the space around him was illuminated by a flare of light, and he saw a man crawling over the bank. Without challenging, he fired and killed the man. Next morning, he found to his horror that he had killed a wounded Englishman, who had advanced beyond his comrades and was crawling back. (Southard 463)

We find these two symptoms, as well as other commonly reported ones, when we read Túrin's reaction to mistakenly slaying his comrade and advisor Beleg. In the immediate aftermath, a temporary paralysis

---

2. See Scull and Hammond's discussion on page 1061.

3. For Christopher Tolkien's account of editing the text, see his Preface to the edition (7–11) and Appendix (2) The Composition of the Text (283–92).

4. G. Elliot Smith was Professor of Anatomy at Manchester University Medical School. Col. F. W. Mott held prestigious appointments in the "Neurological Section of the 4th London General Hospital and later at the Maudsley Neurological Clearing Hospital" (Mott vii). Dr. E. E. Southard was Director of the U.S. Army Neuropsychiatric Training School in Boston from 1917–1918 and Professor of Neuropathology at the Harvard School of Medicine.

seizes him—"he stood as one stricken to stone" (*Turambar* 80).⁵ We are left to imagine Túrin's fixed facial expression indirectly by means of its effect on Flinding his companion. So ghastly was its aspect, it terrorizes the Elf into silence. Further, Túrin's frozen body is only set into motion once shaken by Flinding, not by his own volition. The Elf must direct his course because Túrin would otherwise wander "dazed." "[T]hen Túrin did as he was bid but yet as one dazed" (*Turambar* 80). He is said to be "careless" and indifferent to his own and Flinding's safety. He "wander[s]" without purpose.

Túrin manifests here (I would argue) a "non-resistant" state the medical authorities treating the war-wounded often reported. They called it an anergic stupor. It was classified as "a form of dementia in which the patient is quiet, listless, and non-resistant."⁶ The sufferer is obedient when guided but otherwise "without purpose." For the wartime medical establishment, "dazed" was a technical term defined as "benumbed in mental faculties; stupefied, bewildered" (*OED*).⁷ And like the soldier in the case study for whom "the incident crowds out all others" in the daytime, Túrin's field of vision is filled with Beleg's "white" face. Without Flinding's guidance, "soon would he have been recaptured or lost, for he thought only of the stark face of Beleg the huntsman, lying in the dark forest" (*Turambar* 81). The revelation renders him wordless and we do not "hear" Túrin speak again until he tries to rally Orodreth and his chieftains to attack their enemies openly.

These elements—the paralysis together with the simile "as one stricken to stone," the terrifying frozen stare, the strange non-resistant state, and the silence—are retained in later versions of the scene. The length of time they persist, however, is lengthened considerably and was also consistent with the duration often reported in these case studies. So, we have in *The Silmarillion*:

> Never once as they wandered together on long and grievous paths did Túrin speak, and he walked as one without wish or purpose, while the year waned and winter drew on over the northern lands. But Gwindor was ever beside him to guard him and guide him [...]. (208–09)

---

5 .The *Sketch* has: "seeing Beleg's face he is turned to stone" (32).

6. The *Oxford English Dictionary* cites a source from the immediate pre-war period, the influential *Dorland Medical Dictionary* (1913). See Mott's account of the symptoms that he regards as the result of shell-shock (81).

7. See Southard for a write-up of a dazed patient recorded in 1915 (491). See also page 502.

Further, later versions also highlight his paralysis especially. One function of the great storm that erupts that night following Beleg's slaying is to dramatize how extraordinarily unnatural Túrin's bodily stillness is. While the *Sketch* introduces the outbreak of thunder, lightning and dense rain, the *Quenta* creates the contrast between his immobility and turbulence surrounding him: "But through all the storm Túrin sat without movement" (149). After it passes Flinding struggles to stir Túrin to action; "scarcely could he be roused" even to care for the body of his friend (149). As in *Turambar*, even a desire for self-preservation does not ignite him. This element survives in the *Silmarillion* as well; there, Túrin makes no move, speaks no word and drops no tear throughout the night (208).

When he finally does stand up the next morning, the *Silmarillion* also compares the stuporous Túrin to a sleepwalker: "and [Túrin] rose as one who walked in sleep" (208). Somnambulism (also called "spontaneous hypnosis") appears in reports of wartime physicians as well. This somnambulistic state seems to share some symptoms with the non-resistant anergic stupor. One physician's report from 1915 describes a patient who remained in this condition for twenty-seven days. Southard regards this patient as an example of shell-shock also and includes his case in the section of his text "Shell-shock: Nature and Causes." Entering the hospital on August 26th, the wounded man had just fought in a battle standing beside his brother when hit with machine gun fire. Later, the physician learns that his patient had searched the corpses and, failing to find his brother, assumed he had died. From that moment the soldier had no memory:

> He lay on the bed, eyes closed as if asleep, insensible to excitation, irresponsive. Flies crawled upon him with impunity. [...]
> Next day he had to be fed like a child and looked after. Lifted from bed, once on the ground he stood up with flexed legs, as if to crouch. It seemed as if he was about to fall, but he did not.
> The next day he was in the same immobile state. Upon removal from bed he again made as if to fall, but got his balance. He kept his legs flexed, his head lowered in a fixed posture, with his eyes on the ground. He would walk quickly without falling, if taken by the hand, feet dragging, and even holding back with a certain amount of force. His walk suggested that of a somnambulist. He was left in a standing posture by his bed throughout the medical visit. [...] [On September 1] he was in the same immobile, somnolent state. [...] He would rise only when pushed and walk only when pulled, but had begun to eat a little better. (Southard 506)

The stunning suddenness of this patient's recovery recalls Túrin's equally abrupt healing at Eithel Ivrin. The soldier's grief (and possibly also his guilt for having survived) vanishes when he learns from another soldier that his brother was still alive. The doctor reports that from that very instant his patient "began to speak, opened his eyes, and began to talk" (Southard 507). In the *Quenta, Silmarillion,* and *The Children of Húrin* the virtue of the waters, their elemental purity maintained by Ulmo, Lord of Waters, heals Túrin instantly once he drinks from the spring. In keeping with the image of Túrin as somnambulist, Gwindor exhorts his suffering companion: "Awake, Túrin son of Húrin" (*Silmarillion* 209, *Children* 157). He then moves of his own volition without guidance, and sobbing openly, laments Beleg's death. The *Quenta* has no exhortation but suggests that until this moment, his "frozen tears" are stone hard like ice and need to melt (149).[8]

Once cured of his "madness" Túrin can vocalize his feelings for his friend and create art through the musical tribute he composes and sings. Twenty-first century readers will likely consider his song of praise cathartic. Interestingly, while the musical forms and the goals of the singers are not perfectly parallel, Mott notes the link between music and maintaining health in after treatment programs for recovering veterans. Mott's explicit aim was to cultivate "cheerfulness" and "that sense of well-being so essential for mental and bodily recuperation" through the singing of choral music (297). He notes: "singing classes, under the direction of proper instructors, have been a great success in France and in the camps in England" (297).[9]

We have considered a range of behaviors in Túrin following the emotional shock of realizing that he himself slew his friend Beleg. His fixed facial expression, his unnatural bodily stillness, his non-resistant passivity, and his silence together suggest symptoms that Southard, Mott and Smith regarded as indicative of shell-shock. While these symptoms prove to be transient, three versions of his story describe permanent changes to Túrin's body. *Turambar* names the catastrophe as Túrin's "third anguish" and records that it imprints his body permanently until his own death day: "nor did he lose the mark of that sorrow utterly in all his life" (81). Exactly what constitutes that "mark" remains

---

8. *Turambar* has no visit to Eithel Ivrin. Túrin weeps after hearing Flinding's report about Beleg (81).

9. Mott continues: "the Vocal Therapy Fund has been started to provide teachers of singing, and has already commenced to do useful work in hospitals and convalescent camps in England" (297).

somewhat unclear.[10] Whereas before Túrin's immobile body was likened to stone, here stone is the metaphor for his face and the verb used is one for gouging, cutting and carving: "that grief was graven on the face of Túrin and never faded" (*Silmarillion* 208, *Children* 156).

His grief and guilt also alter the color of his hair. Despite his youth, Túrin's hair begins to grey following this harrowing loss in the *Turambar*, but this detail does not survive in subsequent versions (81).[11] Yet in the *Quenta*, the hair of one profoundly shocked, anguished character (Brandir) "turned grey in that night" after he overhears Níniel's last words before she throws herself over the "Silver-bowl" (156). Physicians treating the war-wounded recorded several startling cases of uncanny (even overnight) changes in patients' hair color to white or grey.[12]

While Túrin's physical paralysis is temporary, the bodily paralysis his father endures stretches for decades, not hours. Úrin/Húrin's epithet "Thalion" means "the Steadfast" or "the Strong," and honors his defining trait and the many ways in which he exhibits it. In answering the Elves' call to battle he is unshaken in his loyalty to that race. When the fortunes of battle turn in the Nirnaeth Arnoediad, he refuses to abandon the field, and so embodies the old sense "steadfast" as "a soldier in battle: Maintaining his ground" (*OED* 1 c). He is immoveable in his defiance of Melko/Melkor/Morgoth, despite Melko's best efforts to subvert him through bribery or break him by torture. And throughout, his love for his family remains whole and vital.

The particular form of torture Melko/Melkor designs for Úrin perverts this laudable defining characteristic and reifies it in his victim's body using physical paralysis. In so doing he creates a grotesque pun on Úrin's epithet: "but upon deeds of mine that will be little to thy liking shalt thou sit here and gaze, nor be able to move foot or hand against them" (*Turambar* 71).[13] Immobilized by Melko's magic, Úrin

---

10. The *Turambar* implies that it is his face that is stamped with suffering. Subsequently while living with the Rodothlim his aspect is one of "gloom and sadness" and Túrin is said to be "weighted with the death of Beleg" (82). The text also states that later, the people of Hisilómë fear to speak to him because "his face [was] haggard and drawn as with unquenchable sorrows" (88). The marking of Túrin's face is absent from the *Sketch* and the *Quenta*.

11. One Russian physician concludes his write up of a patient treated for injury to his sciatic nerve: "Incidentally, this patient had his hair grow white in a few months of war" (Southard 755).

12. See the very precise and detailed description of just such an overnight transformation in case 211 from 1915 in Southard (291). See also page 292.

13. The *Quenta*'s wording suggests that possibly the "chains" are literal ones: "upon the highest peak of Thangorodrim he set him chained upon a chair of stone, and he cursed him with a curse of never-sleeping sight like unto the Gods, but his

embodies the meaning of "steadfast" when used of an inanimate object such as a column that can be neither shifted nor dislodged (*OED* 1 c.). He languishes stone still.

Like war veterans suffering paralysis of one or more limbs, Úrin retains his other senses (albeit distorted by his torturer). He can speak, see, and hear. Southard furnishes a number of cases in which the patient suffers from paraplegia (inability to move the lower body) but whose hearing, speech and sight remain unaffected.[14] When we consider that Melko/Melkor manipulates Húrin's perceptions (sight and hearing especially), the following case history of a soldier suffering hemiplegia (inability to move one side of the body) is suggestive. While the patient can hear the sounds of his immediate environment, they are interrupted by or blended with the cacophony of the battlefield. His physician records:

> He kept looking to one side and to a distance, as if listening, sometimes bending his head downwards. [...] Battle hallucinations, visual and auditory, sometimes occurred, the commands of superiors and the noise of guns, rifles, yelling, and groans; the man would see trenches or redoubts, or a field full of wounded soldiers or attacking columns of the enemy. (Southard 357–58)

The doctor also reports that the patient recognized these sounds and images as hallucinations; alone "upon a high place of Thangorodrim" Úrin has no such luxury.

PART II: MUTILATION AND DISMEMBERMENT

As it develops over the years, the tale of Túrin and Niënor features three maimed figures: Sador/Labadal, Flinding/Gwindor and Tamar Lamefoot/Brandir. Two are war veterans and one a civilian; we may see them as representing several subgroups of the disabled population of Britain during the war and into the 1920s. Taken together, the fates of these three suggest the range of ways a person may become disabled. One veteran, Sador/Labadal, accidently maims himself performing "civilian" work following his military service; he is injured on the job so to speak. The other, Gwindor, loses his hand as a direct consequence of

---

kin and seed he cursed [...] and bade Húrin sit there and watch the unfolding of it" (144). The *Narn* has: "[Morgoth] set him in a chair of stone upon a high place of Thangorodrim [...]. There he was bound by the power of Morgoth; and Morgoth [...] cursed him again and set his power upon him, so that he could not move from that place, nor die, until Morgoth should release him" (67–68). See also the *Silmarillion* (197) and *The Children of Húrin* (65).

14. See pages 332–38 for cases illustrating this phenomenon.

being a fighter and a prisoner of war. Brandir is a disabled civilian whose leg is deformed either congenitally or by a childhood accident.

The tragedies of these three figures reflect several possibilities experienced by Britain's disabled population (both military and civilian) during the war and in the years immediately following it. Most especially their tragedies reflect the public's treatment of disabled men: in the reception of the elf Gwindor in Nargothrond, the treatment of Sador after his military service in Dor-lómin, and the treatment of Brandir by the folk of Brethil, we witness both elf and men suffer agonizing frustration, shame, loss and dishonor. Throughout the iterations of the tale of Túrin and Niënor we find portraits of societies that, like Britain, had moved well past the sympathetic reception of dismembered soldiers during the war and in the early 1920s described by Joanna Bourke and others. Bourke traces the eroding social status of disabled civilians following the war noting that it was "partly because of the increased callousness and neglect toward the weak in general—*even* the heralded heroes back from the battlefields" (56).

The war-wounded who returned to Britain to recover joined thousands of other disabled children, women, and men whose disfigurement resulted from a range of causes. Disabled children, often living in acute poverty, became crippled as a result of diseases such as rickets and infant paralysis or through accidents in over-crowded urban areas (Bourke 35). Industrial accidents dismembered many adults: occupations such as mining and construction were particularly hazardous as were factory and dock work (37). The returning limbless veterans constituted a group that was unique. They returned with an unforeseen suddenness and in numbers inconceivable to civilians. No previous war (such as the Boer War) or colonial conflict had prepared them for this tsunami of disabled veterans (33). Because of their numbers, they were visible to the public, especially in cities and towns where they were sent to recuperate, and this visibility rendered them unusual among the general disabled population (34). They were unusual too because their bodily mutilations were far more drastic and far-reaching than those of limbless civilians (33).

Further, the war devastated a distinctive kind of body, one that was young and fit, having been molded by military training (37). Not surprisingly perhaps, there developed a "popular myth" as Bourke calls it, about the appeal of this unique male body to women: "popular myth has it that women were particularly fond of falling in love with the wounded" (56). The bodies of the young, maimed veterans were very different from those of the impoverished, chronically malnourished working men and women of the factories, mines and ports.

For these reasons and others, this novel group of dismembered men stimulated numerous questions for the British public. Their lives raised issues that challenged the British people during the war and afterward. In *The Children of Húrin*, events in the lives of these characters echo several of these challenging questions. Sador/Labadal's experiences pose the question of whether or not a dismembered veteran can ever again be considered (or consider himself) a fully adult male. If not, is a disabled man closer to being a child than a whole-bodied adult? Flinding/Gwindor and Tamar/Brandir's experiences raise the issue of masculine aesthetics. Can a damaged man be considered attractive, physically appealing? Can he remain sexually desirable? By Finduilas of Nargothrond or Níniel of Brethil? The lives of Sador and Flinding/Gwindor especially challenge the myth that a returned veteran is held in high esteem by his fellow citizens. The portraits of Flinding/Gwindor and Tamar/Brandir explore the roles deformed men may play in their respective societies that are intermittently at open war with Morgoth.

Sador's nickname Labadal, meaning 'Hopafoot,' and Tamar's epithet Lamefoot signal how central their maimed bodies are to their identities. And we will see that Gwindor ceases to use his given name altogether in later versions of the tale. Further we will see that their disfigurement determines the status of all three. Flinding/Gwindor and Tamar/Brandir's disabled bodies also determine their fitness as leading counselors, and in Brandir's case, his fitness to rule his people. This is true even though Flinding/Gwindor and Tamar/Brandir acquire their deformities very differently, the former in warfare and the latter in civilian life. The elf of Nargothrond (Gwindor) loses his hand as he escapes imprisonment by the Enemy and the man of Brethil (Brandir) is either congenitally deformed or he sustains damage to his leg in childhood.

TAMAR/BRANDIR

Tamar/Brandir's fortunes improve as his character develops in later versions of the tale; the disdain that the woodmen feel for him is most intense in *Turambar*. And this is curious for two reasons. He is the son of Bethos, ruler of the woodmen, and like his siblings, he is half-elven as their mother is an unnamed elf woman. But he is the only child who does not inherit his elven mother's "fair[ness]." Consequently his foot, which is malformed in some unspecified way, and his lack of beauty set him apart. The *Quenta* reiterates that he is not handsome and that he is also physically weak "uncomely and of less might than many" (155). This text also clarifies the nature of his disability: he is a civilian casualty—the child victim of an orc arrow.

For these reasons Tamar is "held of little account" (101) in *Turambar*. Indeed, he is passed over in favor of Túrin to succeed his own father Bethos, who dies sometime after Túrin's arrival. They value Túrin because they know he is the son of Úrin; they know of his prowess in battle, his knowledge of elves, and his "wisdom great beyond his years" (*Turambar* 102). Yet *Turambar* also establishes Tamar's traits of wisdom and kindness that might have made him a revered figure even in wartime. Subsequently, the *Quenta* also stresses that Brandir remains loving and loyal to Túrin even when he loses his beloved Níniel to the newcomer. But in the woodmen's estimation, wisdom, kindness and gentleness are less valuable in a man; "to [them] strength was safety and valour the greatest pride of men" (*Turambar* 106). In this early text, the woodmen openly express their contempt for Tamar when he takes up his sword to defend Níniel after her husband and his companions leave to confront Glorund: "many had scoffed at him for that" (*Turambar* 106). In this moment of crisis Tamar's disability renders him ridiculous in their eyes, a man without worth.

In the *Quenta*, the woodmen accept Brandir as ruler after his father Handir despite his deformity; yet they force him to relinquish his leadership when the whole bodied Túrin arrives among them. The woodmen acclaim the newcomer as their leader (*Quenta* 155). As we will see, the treatment of Flinding/Gwindor shares some similarities with the treatment of Tamar/Brandir. The elf is also blessed with wisdom and is a member of the King Orodreth's council. Yet, his absent hand and ruined arm override his other valuable qualities in the eyes of the elves.

In the *Narn*, the *Silmarillion*, and *The Children of Húrin*, Brandir's stature among the people of Brethil increases over that in the earlier texts. As in the *Quenta*, he rules after his father's death, and in these three versions the "stockade" atop Amon Obel bears his name—Ephel Brandir (*Narn* 110). The cause of his laming also shifts from an orc arrow to an unspecified childhood accident that broke his leg (*Narn* 110).[15] His gentle nature survives and other traits appear: he "lov[es] wood rather than metal, and the knowledge of things that grow in the earth rather than other lore" (*Narn* 110; *Children* 193). And in these three texts we learn that like Orodreth of Nargothrond, Brandir pursues a

---

15. This is echoed in *The Children of Húrin* (193).

policy of "silence and secrecy" to preserve his people, a policy that has served both Elves and Men well (*Narn* 112).[16]

Yet, despite his status as their ruler, Brandir "was no man of war" in the eyes of the people of Brethil (*Narn* 110). As the threat from Nargothrond slowly approaches, and Túrin and Dorlas determine that only an aggressive ambush of Glaurung will serve to preserve the people of Brethil, the last of Brandir's authority seeps away: "for now he [Túrin] ordered things as he would, and few gave heed to Brandir" (*Silmarillion* 220). The public scorn for Brandir also survives in the *Silmarillion*, this time voiced by Dorlas who ridicules him by observing that he cannot fight as a representative of his family, the House of Haleth (221). Brandir's words have no power of command or persuasion, and many of his people refuse his advice and disobey him, following Níniel to learn the fate of her husband and companions.

As his love for his people is extinguished entirely, the only love that remains to him is his hopeless love for Níniel. The *Turambar*, the *Sketch*, the *Quenta*, and the *Silmarillion* allude to his love only very briefly; only the *Narn* and *The Children of Húrin* develop the love triangle of Turambar, Brandir, and Níniel. When she begins to recover her health and learns enough of their language to speak with him, Níniel is eager for Brandir's company on walks because she is keen to learn from him more about the flora and fauna of Brethil's woods (*Narn* 123). At this point, their power dynamic is reversed. When she arrived among them, Níniel was the passive patient and Brandir the healer, but as her body strengthens, she serves as his physical support, offering him her arm to lean on as they walk (*Narn* 123). In doing so, Níniel displays the consideration and kindness that win her the love of the people, and she in turn grows to love Brandir as her brother (124).

Her sisterly love runs absolutely counter to the myth alluded to earlier that women were prone to fall in love with the dismembered veteran. Brandir's own words underscore this clearly: " '[w]ise brother?' he answered. 'Lame brother, rather, unloved and unlovely' " (*Narn* 124). He substitutes "lame" for wise" and again we see that deformity trumps wisdom. The replacement is an erasure. He is cognizant that his knowledge of healing and the woodlands are devalued or dismissed altogether because of his ruined limb. And his alliterative word play (the repetition of the "l" sound) ties all three terms together, stressing the causal link. His disability ensures that he will never arouse the passionate love of a beautiful woman, even a kind and thoughtful one. While it

---

16. *The Silmarillion* has slightly different wording (216).

is true that Brandir is a civilian and not a returned veteran, and that therefore this dynamic is not perfectly congruent with dynamic of the myth, we will see that the dismembered veteran Flinding/Gwindor fares no better when he too is locked in a love triangle that includes Túrin.

Sador/Labadal

Like Tamar/Brandir, who as we have seen is "held of little account," Sador/Labadal is also "of small account" (*Children* 41). He is a servant in the House of Hador and those objects that he makes or repairs are "things of little worth" (*Children* 41). He can perform only modest tasks for his Lord and Lady because he has cut his foot off with his wood axe, rendering his leg shrunken and malformed. The texts ascribe this to bad luck or to his own clumsiness: "by his own want of skill" as Morwen would have it (*Narn* 64). In the hierarchy of values in Dor-lómin, a maimed limb is an honorable disablement *only* if it results from battle not from "civilian" labor. He says that if he had fought in the Bragollach (Battle of Sudden Flame), he "might have got[ten] my hurt with more honour" (*Narn* 60). Húrin sympathizes with the anguish of Sador's shame, but his words nevertheless underscore the disgrace of his dismemberment: "the harm may be harder to bear than the work of a foe" (*Narn* 65).

Further, the texts suggest that as a result of his dismemberment Sador is now not a fully or entirely adult male. And I would argue that his experiences reflect the connection the British public forged between the limbless veteran and the maimed child in the post-war years. Both the *Narn* and *The Children of Húrin* refer to "the short days of his *full* manhood before his maiming" (my emphasis, *Narn* 60; *Children* 41). It is significant, I think, that readers see him only in the company of a child and not of other adults when Sador tells Túrin about himself in this early scene.

Following the war, limbless veterans had lost their novelty; "limblessness had become normalized" as Bourke demonstrates (60). The public began attribute to these men the passivity and helplessness they already associated with disabled children: "for the war-maimed, the link between themselves and disabled children eventually removed their claim to a special status. By the mid-1920s, they too had become identified with passivity—the helplessness of children who needed to be looked after for the rest of their lives" (Bourke 75). In Morwen's eyes Sador is not a useful servant: "he spends much time on trifles unbidden" (*Narn* 64). Some of these "trifles" are wooden men and animals that he makes for Túrin "[to reward] as he could the kindness of the child" (60). Small-scale crafts, such as "stitching bags," are precisely the kind of "curative work" staff at some recovery centers had dismembered veterans perform before they graduated to operating machines (Bourke 74). Bourke quotes a speech which voices shame veterans endured as a result of such infantilizing:

> In the words of Harry Smith, a character in a play entitled *The Unknown Warrior* (1923) who had been given a job making toys, 'I'm fed up with making silly toys. It's not work for a man—but we're not men now, with half our insides and half our limbs gone; it's a good enough job for us, I suppose'. (75)

Yet Sador does fight well. He volunteers and serves at Barad Eithel for some years and fights (successfully) to hold the fort against the Enemy's assault. Afterward, he gains permission to return to the woods of Dor-lómin. He has had his fill of battle. "My love of battle was sated, for I had seen spilled blood and wounds enough" (*Narn* 60). His response to battlefield carnage hardly seems disreputable to modern readers, but he ascribes his motive to cowardice saying: "for a man that flies from his fear may find that he has only taken a short cut to meet it" (*Narn* 60). His assessment is perhaps harsh, because when he grasps the elven knife Túrin gives him, he says that he has yearned to feel such a weapon again: "a blade of elven steel. Long have I missed the feel of it" (*Narn* 64, *Children* 49). We sense, I think, that if he could have marched to the Nirnaeth Arnoediad with his Lord Húrin, he would have done so. Years later, an old man reduced to begging, Sador says as much to Túrin: "a cursed axe in the woods long ago, or I would be lying in the Great Mound now" (*Narn* 105).

FLINDING/GWINDOR

While he shares dismemberment with Sador, Flinding/Gwindor's body (like that of his brother) is the one that reveals most clearly Tolkien's attentiveness to the abuse and desecration the male body sustained in war. Studying the versions of Túrin's story we see Tolkien's concern come into increasingly sharper focus; consequently, the elf's homecoming in Nargothrond is the one that receives the most detailed and nuanced treatment. The repercussions from his disablement share some similarities with those of Brandir, especially regarding social status and political influence. The two also share the humiliation of competing with Túrin for the love of a female. We find, in fact, that the love triangle is the chief site for the exploring the value of the disabled male body in these texts.

In *Turambar*, Flinding's body appears unmarked when Beleg finds him, and the text focuses on his crushed spirit, his courage. Startled from sleep "[the] Elf started up in great fear and anguish" (78). He confesses to cowardice when he relates how he saw Túrin's agony when tied to a tree by Orcs and heard him moaning and calling on his parents by name. He admits "being a craven from long captivity, I fled heedlessly" (79). And yet, Flinding's time as a prisoner of war has altered his appearance in some as yet undefined way; when he returns to his people, the Rodothlim, "few knew him again [because he was] so changed by the anguish of his slavery" (82). It is the *Quenta* that begins to define more distinctly the nature of those injuries: "Flinding Fuilin's son, who had escaped from the mines of Morgoth, [was] a bent and timid shadow of his former shape and mood" (148). This phrasing survives into the *Silmarillion* and into *The Children of Húrin*. We are left wondering about "bent"—is he deformed or twisted? He is a "shadow"; is he indistinct, insubstantial? Morally tainted? And finally at the scene's fullest development in *The Children of Húrin* we learn that Gwindor is maimed during his escape from Morgoth's mines and loses his hand (152).

His dismemberment is one of the clearest instances in which the violation of the male body escalates over the iterations of the story. But further, Gwindor's loss of his hand partially mirrors the mutilation of his brother Gelmir's body. Gelmir fills the same function as an earlier, unnamed character, an Elven herald in *Turambar*. The herald, in the service of Fenweg/Fingon, had the misfortune to be taken alive by Morgoth's forces prior to the Nirnaeth Arnoediad. At the beginning of the battle, for strategic reasons, Morgoth wishes to engage his enemies on the western front as quickly as possible and orders his Captain to provoke an assault by Fenweg/Fingon and his allies who have assembled there; so Morgoth's servants parade the herald, kill him, and abandon the body in front of the aghast allies.

The herald figure also appears in the *Quenta*, but later, in the *Silmarillion*, his role is taken by Gelmir, Gwindor's brother. This substitution in the *Silmarillion* begins a marked intensification of bodily desecration. Morgoth's servants display the captive Gelmir whom they have blinded during his imprisonment. They then hack off both Gelmir's hands and his feet and "his head last" (191) and abandon his body in full view of the allied ranks. And lastly, in *The Children of Húrin*, the mutilation of the blind Gelmir changes; instead of hands they cut off his arms, and instead of feet they slice off his legs (55). They leave his head still attached to his limbless torso and withdraw. Morgoth's plan succeeded; discipline in the allied army broke and they began their assault. It is Gwindor who breaks discipline, goaded beyond bearing by the calculated, public mutilation of his brother. Accompanied by mounted elves, he charges, slicing through Morgoth's army and reaching the Gates of Angband itself. Gwindor's company broaches the Gates and inflicts such casualties that "Morgoth trembled upon his deep throne" (56). But, as we know, Gwindor is captured alive and his companions slain. This spectacular charge establishes Gwindor's reputation for bravery and, as Christopher Tolkien notes, gives greater poignancy to his timidity and dread when Beleg later urges him to action (*Shaping* 217).

With the loss of his hand Gwindor joins the famed company of Beren and Maedhros, heroes of the First Age who suffer the same loss. And further, had he lived, Túrin himself might have joined their circle also (in a sense) because the *Turambar* reports that when the "evil blood" of the dragon Glorund fell "upon his hand [it] burnt it, and it was withered" (108).

Further, Gwindor's maiming leads to a shift in his sense of self, a shift that is mirrored in the way he identifies himself to others. In the *Turambar* no visible signs of outrage are mentioned when Beleg discovers him, and we learn that Flinding identifies himself formally; he "named himself Flinding bo-Dhuilin of an ancient house of the Gnomes" (78). In the *Quenta*, neither Beleg nor Túrin ask him to identify himself and in the *Narn* this section is missing. But in the *Silmarillion* Túrin does ask Gwindor who he is after he is healed at Eithel Ivrin. Gwindor responds: " 'A wandering Elf, a thrall escaped, whom Beleg met and comforted,' said Gwindor. 'Yet once I was Gwindor son of Guilin, a lord of Nargothrond, until I went to the Nirnaeth Arnoediad, and was enslaved in Angband' " (209). The wording in *The Children of Húrin* is virtually identical on these two points. Gwindor's answer articulates a rupture between who he was before the war and who he is now. Only his war experience now defines him.

His own people adopt this view as well. Gwindor's value to the elves hinges on the value they assign to his dismembered body. His maiming determines his power as a returned veteran and prisoner of war, expressed here through his political prestige and influence as a counselor to his king. Further, as has been mentioned, his disfigured limb determines his appeal as a male to females. Gwindor's humiliating experiences bear out Bourke's assertion: "[t]hus, the shape and texture of the male body was not simply emblematic of functional considerations: it could be suggestive of both power and attraction" (209). In the post war years, the British public was interested in the value of the male body apart from what the military required to wage war. And they concluded that the adult male body needed help: "[it] was […] widely maintained that without physical training, 'the naked body of a modern grown man [was] not beautiful" (209). Training systems proliferated to sculpt men's bodies into forms that captured an ideal masculine aesthetic.[17] "The ideal of the handsome male body expressed a reconstruction of manliness" following the war, Bourke writes and "competition [between men] became increasingly concerned with aesthetics and included a repudiation of the mutilations of wartime" (209).

Gwindor's visible disability dominates his attempts to resume his place as a lord of Nargothrond and a respected advisor to his King. In the *Silmarillion* he loses his status and influence in the council, although subsequent events prove that his advice to his King was sound. He argues against Túrin's call for vigorous offensive action against Morgoth and his forces. It is his disability, not the strength or weakness of his reasoning that leads the other lords to disregard him: "he fell into dishonor and none heeded him, for his strength was small and he was no longer forward in arms" (211). His value to his community rests entirely, it would seem, in his ardor for bold, aggressive action and his fighting prowess. He can offer them neither.

Interestingly, their public, verbal sparring includes the question of what constitutes manliness, and specifically, what masculine behaviors appeal to females (both Elves and mortals). Gwindor urges Orodreth to continue his policy of secrecy and stealth in order to preserve the women and children of both races until the day prophesized by the elves arrives; at that time "Manwë will hear and Mandos relent" (*Children* 162). "[f]or not all can fight and fall, and those we must keep from war and ruin, while we can" (162). The disabled Gwindor finds himself now a member of this segment of the community, in the company of women and children needing protection. Túrin's rebuttal characterizes Orodreth's strategy of secrecy and the elves who carry it out most unfairly:

> 'And do those that you speak of love such skulkers in the woods, hunting strays like a wolf, better than one who puts on his helm and figured shield, and drives away the foe, be they far greater than all his host? At least the women of the Edain do not. They did not hold back the men from the Nirnaeth Arnoediad.'
> 'But they suffered greater woe than if that field had not been fought,' said Gwindor. (162–63)

---

17. See Bourke's discussion of clubs devoted to the physical training of boys and men such as The League of Health and Strength and the Boy Scouts, 137–44.

By branding the elves of Nargothrond "skulkers" Túrin charges them with avoiding their duty (as he sees it); the word carries altogether negative connotations. He questions whether or not elven females could ever love such males. They are no better than animal predators who pick off their prey one by one—they are less than Men. Readers may feel that Gwindor is a rather odd choice for Túrin to be lecturing on this head since Túrin himself was a child at the time of the Nirnaeth and the elf the warrior who left his beloved behind and rode to war, who watched his brother dismembered by the Enemy and left to die, and who stormed the gates of Angband.[18]

And, despite what Túrin says here, Gwindor *had* earned the love of Finduilas and *was* betrothed to her. Readers might also expect that Gwindor's spectacular charge in the Nirnaeth, the casualties he inflicts upon the Enemy, and his endurance as prisoner might have assured him an honored place in the king's council whatever his physical condition. They do not. When he returns home, Gwindor's reception enacts the nightmare that visited many soldiers before they were shipped out—the prospect of returning grotesquely mutilated to their wives or girls and the unsupportable shame they would endure in consequence (Bourke 73-74). Gwindor judges that his ruined body bars him from marriage and he releases Finduilas from their betrothal: "[b]ut go whither love leads you; for I am become unfit to wed you; and neither my prowess nor my counsel have any honour more" (*Silmarillion* 210, *Children* 167).

But as we have seen the value assigned to male bodies (both dismembered and whole), the attraction they hold for females and choices of war strategy are all intertwined and not easily disentangled. Consequently, Túrin's claim that in Orodreth's council the two debate *only* matters of policy is somewhat disinguous: "I have opposed your counsels; but a man must speak as he sees, nor hide the truth that he believes, for any private cause" (*Children* 166-167). And as we trace the development of Túrin's years in Nargothrond, we see that in the later texts, the *Silmarillion* and *The Children of Húrin*, the focus on the contrast between the two male bodies—the one maimed and painful, the other whole and beautiful–narrows and intensifies.

The love triangle as it takes shape later in these two works is embryonic in the *Turambar*; only Failivrin falls in love (83). For his part, Túrin feels as a brother would toward her, saying that he had "found a

---

18. His choice of "wolf" adds further irony perhaps since Túrin himself had been a "wolf-man" when earlier he had joined an outlaw company of *gaurwaith*—"wolf-men."

fair sister" in her (84). His love for his "fair sister" agonizes Failivrin much as Níniel's sisterly loves does Brandir. Further, Túrin is unaware of the attraction he holds for her. In addition, *Turambar* joins pity and love together introducing the possibility of confusing the two. And perhaps Túrin does. So sharp is his pity for Failivrin when Morgoth's host annihilates the Rodothlim (including her father) and their homes that, when she pitches into his arms, he believes that he loves her deeply at that moment (85).

The *Sketch* and the *Quenta* present the love triangle fully formed.[19] In these two versions Túrin does love Finduilas but struggles against his growing attachment because he feels he must remain loyal to Flinding for rescuing him from the orcs and for his kind reception among the Rodothlim (*Sketch* 33; *Quenta* 150).[20]

Interestingly, elements from the *Turambar* reappear in the *Silmarillion* and *The Children of Húrin*. Again, Finduilas's love for Túrin remains unrecognized by him. She believes he reveres her as "a mother" and a "queen" rather than loving her as his sister as in the *Turambar* (*Children* 169). The only way into his heart she confides to Gwindor is through pity (169). But she is quite clear that she will not be the recipient of either Túrin's pity or his love (*Silmarillion* 211; *Children* 168–169). Finduilas both pities and loves Gwindor, but no longer loves him as she did before he rode to war.[21] And further, for his part, Túrin also fails to understand that Gwindor's passion for Finduilas has survived battle, enslavement and disfigurement; indeed he appears unaware that the two were betrothed before the Nirnaeth Arnoediad.[22] Túrin remains unconscious of his role as the potent third member of a triangulated relationship.

Despite Turin's incomprehension, his personality and his body are very much part of the dynamic among the three. *The Children of Húrin* explicitly juxtaposes Gwindor's dismemberment with Túrin's radiant young manhood. *The Children of Húrin* intensifies the pathos of Gwindor's suffering by adding: "the pain of his maimed left arm was often

---

19. The *Narn* does not contain this scene.
20. This is also the case in the parallel section of *The Grey Annals* (83–84).
21. *The Grey Annals* is absolutely clear that after Túrin inflicts such losses on the enemy with the newly forged *Gurthang*, Finduilas' love for Gwindor dwindles *because of* his physical ruin: "Then the heart of Finduilas was turned from Gwindor (who because of his pains in Angband was half crippled) and her love was given to Túrin" (83).
22. In *The Grey Annals*, Túrin *is* aware of the elves' love for each other and he *does* love Finduilas. But he will not pursue it because he does not wish to infect her with Morgoth's curse that lies upon him and does not wish to cause Gwindor further suffering (84).

upon him" (163). The sentence immediately following begins the long description of Túrin's appearance and carriage,[23] a description establishing him as the embodiment of the masculine ideal for *both* Elves and Men (*Silmarillion* 210; *Children* 163–64). The text continues:

> But Túrin was young, and only now reached his full manhood; and he was in truth the son of Morwen Eledhwen to look upon: tall, dark-haired and pale-skinned, with grey eyes, and his face more beautiful than any other among mortal men, in the Elder Days. His speech and bearing were those of the ancient kingdom of Doriath [...]. (163–64)

From head to toe, Túrin's form embodies all that was held to be beautiful in the male elf or mortal, as the name the Elves of Nargothrond bestow upon him—*Adanedhel* 'Elf-man'—conveys. His mother too seems to have a trace of this duality. While it was his father who lived for a time with the elves of Gondolin, Túrin seems to have inherited elvish physical traits from his mortal mother. Her epithet *Eledhwen* 'Elf-sheen' reminds readers that men found the light of her eyes elvish rather than merely human. At the very least, Túrin's countenance is the most aesthetically pleasing of any man's in the First Age. Further, his deportment and the dialect he speaks are themselves elvish. The passage continues explaining that, upon first meeting him, an elf might mistake Túrin for an elf lord of distinguished lineage.

CONCLUSION

Túrin's is the perfected male body, comprising every feature Elves and Mortals, males and females, admired in the masculine form. *The Children of Húrin* pits the ideal male body against the damaged ones of the civilian Brandir, and the war veteran Gwindor especially, creating an excruciating contrast. The reception that the people of Dor-Lómin and Brethil and the Elves of Nargothrond extend to these characters captures a particular period in postwar British culture. The unkindness Gwindor and Sador endure reflects the waning of the respect and sympathy initially felt for dismembered veterans during the war and in the years immediately following. As Bourke describes it: in these years, "[p]ublic rhetoric judged soldiers' mutilations to be 'badges of their courage, the hall-mark of their glorious service'" (56). Missing limbs "came to exert a special patriotic power" (59). These attitudes were short-lived as Bourke's work demonstrates so thoroughly.

The response of Men and Elves to these bodies mirrors the hardening attitudes toward the visibly disabled. They also mirror the point at which the "reconstruction of manliness" was underway in Britain;

---

23. The *Silmarillion* contains the same long description (210).

clubs and organizations were busy improving boys' and men's bodies, and the public schools continued to shape and extoll an ideal physical form to which the British public attached increasing value.

Túrin himself, of course, is hardly unmarked by his war experiences when he arrives in Nargothrond. But the visible, physical signs arising from his staggering emotional shock—his fixed facial expression, his prolonged silence, his non-resistant stupor and his temporary paralysis—are all just that: temporary. The shock leaves only minor outward changes, the greying hair and an undefined trace of sorrow on his face.

But returned veterans afflicted with symptoms like Túrin's (and numerous other, grievous, permanent ones) discovered that their status as adult males was destabilized as a result. As Elaine Showalter has demonstrated, some wartime medical authorities contended that shell shock was a form of male hysteria. And since hysteria had traditionally been an illness gendered as female, the shell-shocked survivor was considered unmanned and feminized by some.[24] Further, Jessica Meyer's work has described another discourse that shaped British discussion of shell-shock. It relied on the dichotomy of childishness and maturity, the difference between the boy and the man.[25]

While not wishing to press the point too far, I find a trace of this destabilization in *The Children of Húrin* as well. (162). As noted earlier, Gwindor himself states in council: "[f]or not all can fight and fall, and those we must keep from war and ruin, while we can." Gwindor's dismemberment proves feminizing, consigning him to the company of women and children requiring protection. And Sador's maiming seems to make him childlike, or at least the companion of a child, carving wooden men and animals (and eventually a chair for his lord) instead of joining the host Húrin led to the Nirnaeth with other men.

If these dichotomies are subtly at work in *The Children of Húrin*, their presence further supports the idea that Tolkien should be considered a "marginal modernist." Sarah Cole applies this term to those novelists and poets who have "a slightly equivocal status in modernism" because they did not pursue the radical experimentation in form undertaken by the High Modernists (14). Cole names Conrad, Forster, and the war poets as marginal modernists in her work on male intimacy.

---

24. See Showalter's *The Female Malady: Women, Madness, and English Culture, 1830–1980*, 167–94 especially.

25. Meyer argues: "[m]asculinity in the era of the First World War was defined as much by distinctions between the child and the adult, the boy and the man, as by those between the man and the woman" (5).

Like the works of the war poets and others, *The Children of Húrin* explores the terrible frailty of the male body and psyche "caught in youth by 1914" (*LotR* Foreword.xxiv).

WORKS CITED

Bourke, Joanna. *Dismembering the Male: Men's Bodies, Britain, and the Great War.* Chicago: University of Chicago Press, 1996. Print.

Cole, Sarah. *Modernism, Male Friendship, and the First World War.* Cambridge: Cambridge UP, 2003. Print.

Meyer, Jessica. "Separating the Men from the Boys: Masculinity and Maturity in Understandings of Shell Shock in Britain." *Twentieth Century British History* 20.1 (2009): 1–22. Print.

Mott, Frederick. *War Neuroses and Shell Shock.* London: Henry Frowde, Oxford UP, 1919. Print.

Scull, Christina, and Wayne G. Hammond. *The Reader's Guide. The J. R. R. Tolkien Companion and Guide.* Vol. 2. Boston: Houghton Mifflin Harcourt, 2006. Print.

Showalter, Elaine. *The Female Malady: Women, Madness, and English Culture, 1830–1980.* New York: Pantheon, 1985. Print.

Smith, G. Elliot, and T. H. Pear. *Shell Shock and its Lessons.* Manchester: Manchester UP, 1917. Print.

Southard, Elmer E. *Shell-Shock and Other Neuropsychiatric Problems presented in Five Hundred and Eighty-Nine Case Histories from the War Literature, 1914–1918.* 1919. New York: Arno Press, 1973. Print.

Tolkien, Christopher. "Preface." *The Lays of Beleriand.* J. R. R. Tolkien. Boston: Houghton Mifflin, 1985. 1–2. Print.

Tolkien, J. R. R. *Narn i Hîn Húrin. Unfinished Tales of Númenor and Middle-earth.* Ed. Christopher Tolkien. Boston: Houghton Mifflin, 1980. 57–162. Print.

—. *The Children of Húrin.* Ed. Christopher Tolkien. Boston: Houghton Mifflin, 2007. Print.

—. *The Earliest 'Silmarillion' (The 'Sketch of the Mythology'). The Shaping of Middle-earth.* Ed. Christopher Tolkien. New York: Ballantine, 1986. 11–91. Print.

—. *The Lord of the Rings.* 50th anniv. ed. Boston: Houghton Mifflin, 1994. Print.

—. *The Grey Annals. The War of the Jewels.* Ed. Christopher Tolkien. Boston: Houghton Mifflin, 1994. 1–170. Print.

—. *The Quenta. The Shaping of Middle-earth.* Ed. Christopher Tolkien. New York: Ballantine Books, 1986. 92–254. Print.

—. *The Silmarillion.* Ed. Christopher Tolkien. Boston: Houghton Mifflin, 1977. Print.

—. *Turambar and the Foalöke. The Book of Lost Tales, Part Two.* Ed. Christopher Tolkien. Boston: Houghton Mifflin, 1984. 69–143. Print.

Sméagol and Déagol:
Secrecy, History, and Ethical Subjectivity in Tolkien's World

E. J. Christie

In 1911, under a rising fear of war and a growing espionage hysteria caused by the movement of a German gunboat off the coast of Morocco, the British Government hurriedly passed a sweeping revision of the Official Secrets Act (see Hooper, Aitken, and Thomas). In that same year, nineteen year old John Ronald Reuel Tolkien, an Oxford-bound student at King Edward's School in Birmingham, formed a "secret society" with fellow students. The "Tea Club and Barrovian Society" (T.C.B.S.) was mostly dedicated to the covert appreciation of tea (Carpenter, *Tolkien* 45–47). By 1918, war had claimed three members of the T.C.B.S. and as Tolkien himself records, "all but one of my close friends were dead" (*The Lord of the Rings* [*LotR*] Foreword.xxiv). Although Tolkien disavowed the notion that his fantasy was an allegorical representation of the wars that defined his age, it is nevertheless accepted that the central thematic concern of *The Lord of the Rings* with power and moral responsibility reflects the devastation of those wars, both to Tolkien personally and to Britain (Garth and Croft).

While Tolkien's mythopoeic literature obviously alludes to ethical ramifications of concealment allegorized by mythical rings, the specific historical conditions of secrecy and contemporary ideas about secrecy during Tolkien's life have rarely been considered as keys to his fantasy. The "modern" world into which Tolkien was born, in which he formed his own intimate fellowships and indulged in his own "secret vice" of imaginary language creation, was a world with pressing political and moral questions about both the necessity and the abuse of secrecy. This essay examines both the modern culture of secrecy and the secrecies that pervade *The Lord of the Rings* and its mythical past. It shows how Tolkien draws on Old English semantics to channel the social and theological theme of revealing and concealing through the characters of Sméagol and Déagol.

Prior to World War I, a growing sense of the need for state secrecy had been on the rise throughout the late-nineteenth century. The Official Secrets Act, originally penned in 1889, was expanded and reinforced not only in 1911 but again in 1920 and yet again 1939. The legislation, ostensibly designed to guard against espionage, was one of the most all-encompassing laws in English history. It is, for example, one of the only laws in western jurisprudence to lay the burden of proof on the defense. It was used repeatedly in the decades that followed to prosecute, or at least threaten, citizens who passed information deemed prejudicial to state security as well as authors whose memoirs revealed knowledge gained while they held positions in the civil service. The Act thus appears to have been used more as a vehicle of state censorship, as a way to protect government ministers from embarrassment (Aitken 2; Hooper 7–10).

The Official Secrets Acts, moreover, is only one refined expression of a rising culture of secrecy. During the late-nineteenth century, an emerging consciousness of public life and family privacy "exposed the deep vein of class discrimination which informed the concept of legitimate secrecy" (Vincent 23). In 1872, the Ballot Act had also been passed amid concern from many privileged corners of the political class who believed that secrecy might place the political desires of increasingly enfranchised lower classes "beyond the supervision and influence" of their betters (93). Despite a mistrust of the "public" to cast informed votes, the intention of the act to "[protect] the individual voter from the scrutiny of his peers and betters" by ensuring a secret ballot was eventually accepted as a necessary evil (92). At the same time, however, charitable visits to working class homes with the intention of individualized moral education, increasingly involved long-term surveillance. Middle-class volunteers of the Charity Organization Society took and filed notes on the poor families they visited. "Over time," this kind of intrusive charity "raised acute and eventually insoluble difficulties about the rights to secrecy of the subjects of the visitations" (96). The late nineteenth and early twentieth centuries, then, saw an increasing formalization of relations between the secrecy intended to secure the state and the moral imperative to protect the privacy of individuals even as surveillance and documentation of citizens was increasingly institutionalized.

Next to civic debate about secrecy, academic work on the prominent role of secrecy in society also rose during Tolkien's early career. Georg Simmel's influential essay on the "Sociology of Secrecy," published in 1906, proclaims the necessity of concealment to the management of social relations. Georg Lukács described Simmel as "the most significant and interesting transitional figure in the whole of modern philosophy" (98–102). Simmel's reflections on the sociology of secrecy are often impressionistic, yet his observation of both the necessity and dangers of secrecy, as well as the association of secrecy with the sacred, remain touchstones in sociological studies of secrecy. They reach back to Plato's reflections on the intimate relationship between secrecy and subjectivity, freedom and moral choice, and are reinforced by later philosophers like Sisella Bok, Emmanuel Levinas, and Jacques Derrida. Levinas, for example, also presents secrecy as the grounds for the singularity of the self, but also therefore as the "basis for sociality with others in general" (Boothroyd 48). This individuation, both Derrida and Bok remind us, is intimated in the etymology of Latin *secretum*, which means separate or apart (Derrida 15; Bok 6).

According to Simmel, "reciprocal knowledge, which is the positive condition of social relationships [...] actually presuppose[s] also a certain nescience, a ratio, that is immeasurably variable to be sure, of reciprocal concealment" (448). The extent to which men reciprocally "know" each other is thus managed on a scale of revealing and concealing. The interior life of human beings is, in Simmel's estimation, a kind of "spiritual private property" (454). The indiscretion of "psychological observation and reflection" on this property "may be quite as violent, and morally quite as unjustifiable, as listening at keyholes and prying into the letters of strangers" (455–56).

Simmel's essay is pervaded by a rather subjective certainty that the modern world has, through its increasing complexity and "objectivity" rendered impossible the kind of complete intimacy once attained in classical society. Such a "complete intimacy of confidence," he writes, "probably becomes, with the changing differentiation of men, more and more difficult. Perhaps the modern man has too much to conceal to make a friendship in the ancient sense possible" (Simmel 458). The modern world, then, has produced a new condition of subjectivity in which the balance of self-revelation and self-concealment have shifted to privilege discretion, to place concealment at the heart of the self. Carl Jung drew similar conclusions about the pressure of mass culture and the modern state on individual will. In *Modern Man in Search of a Soul* (1933), Jung expounds at length on the link between secrets in psychotherapy and in the rituals of ancient societies and thereby on the pscyho-social effects of maintaining or sharing secrets. In his late work, *The Undiscovered Self* (1957), Jung pursued these themes with particular concern for the modern state's oppressive and dehumanizing effect on individual psychology. Nevertheless, Simmel insists, the "differentiated" relationship may still lead to the same depth of feeling and the same "capacity to sacrifice" as previous epochs and as friendships that evolve in cultures where the extent of shared outlook creates more total intimacy (459).

Tolkien's mythology represents the complex alignments of human history with the "secrecy" of interiority, and of moral choice with the pre-occupation with death. The philosopher's serene mastery of life is produced by turning beyond the material to focus on what is beyond. In this way, Plato claims, philosophy is nothing more than "practicing death." In the close reading of Jan Patočka that constitutes *The Gift of Death*, Derrida summarizes the history of contemplation that follows from this Platonic declaration: the anticipation of death awakens both self-consciousness and conscience, instigating both the interiority and responsibility that distinguishes men from beasts. This sense of responsibility likewise separates Platonic philosophy, and Christian history following it, from the orgiastic indulgence of preceding religions. As Derrida also points out, however, this "vigil" of the self against death does not eliminate, but merely incorporates, the "the orgiastic secret that it subordinates" (17). This secret is never more potent and poignant than in the experience of war, where the encounter with the enemy as a readiness both to kill and to die involves not only "identification *of* the enemy" but also "identification *with* the enemy" (19). The grieving survivor enjoys life as a "surfeit," and his affirmation of life in the wake of war constitutes also an obsessive denial of mortality (20). Derrida writes with the benefit of hindsight. In 1906, Simmel could not have foreseen the way in which the approaching war would test his assertions about the quality of friendship and the capacity for sacrifice, but the dynamic of secrecy he describes resonates in *The Lord of the Rings*, which represents a similar cogitation on interiority and society.

The moral power of secrecy was never more visible than during the great wars of the early twentieth century. War propaganda posters from throughout Europe and the United States emphatically express the theme that for non-combatants the most important duty in war was to maintain secrecy (Paret, et al.; Stanley; Rickards). Posters with pithy epigrams like "loose lips sink ships" are still familiar today, but many others reinforce the moral duty of secrecy: "He's in the silent service—are you?" asks one, depicting a grim submarine commander with a determined face and a partially raised pair of binoculars. One American poster, issued in 1942, depicts the German foe as a looming disembodied shadow whose bright white eyes peer out from beneath the silhouetted rim of the iconic German *stahlhelm* (Paret, et al. 159). This imagery was almost universal in propaganda posters of the time. Both Russian and German anti-Bolshevik posters similarly depicted their enemy as monstrous beings or dark, disembodied faces and claws looming over towns and pastoral communities and often, as in Britain, depicted the heroic response with iconic warriors of the nation's ancient or medieval past, in chainmail and on horseback (Paret, et al.)[1] While other posters imply the universal responsibility of secrecy as a duty to remain silent, to avoid talk, this one notably invokes a panoptical paranoia, reinforcing the symbolic message of those eyes with the assurance that "[he's] watching you." Though Tolkien despised propaganda, his fiction evokes the same opposition: the enemy is looming, dark, disembodied, and he's always watching, while the hero is conceived an embodiment of national character and symbolized by the warrior of the past. Tolkien, like Simmel, is skeptical about the emerging surveillance society of the twentieth-century and seems to oppose a vision of ancient fellowship to the invasion of the self by a probing, disembodied Other.

As both his letters and his imagined history indicate, Tolkien recognized the relationships between intimacy and mass society, responsibility and the contemplation of death. As a man for whom "fellowship" played such a prominent role in life as in fiction, and one nostalgic for the pre-industrial life he depicted in *The Lord of the Rings*, Tolkien had his own experience of the pressure that pits intimacy against publicity. Tolkien sought and achieved deep intimacy on many fronts—his devoted marriage to his first love, for example, and his celebrated friendship with C. S. Lewis. In his inclination toward societies like the T.C.B.S and the Inklings, he was, as Lewis writes, "a man of cronies" (Carpenter, *Tolkien* 236). As his biographer notes, Tolkien was essentially optimistic and affable, but plagued by "bouts of profound despair" (31, 129, and 236). Modern war formed one prominent source of his despair: Tolkien identified modernity's machinery and mass-culture with propaganda and the destruction of war.

For Tolkien, propaganda is the signal mode of communication of an impersonal, mass-produced world. It pits a sociolinguistic illusion aligned with horrifying violence against the more personal experiences of war related, for example, in letters to his son. In a letter to Christopher Tolkien in 1944, he writes of the "tragedy and despair of all machinery laid bare. Unlike art," he argues, which is content to imagine, "[machinery] attempts to actualize desire, and so create power in this World" (*Letters* 87). There is, in Tolkien's estimation, a direct link between the legendary fall of Daedalus and Icarus, the "Giant Bomber," and other such "Mordor-gadgets." The failure to recognize this connection is "a world-wide mental disease" (*Letters* 88; cf. 111 on Tolkien's equation of

---

1. See 107, 111, 124, and 172 for images of the disembodied threat; see 13, 51, and 161 for images of the ancient warrior.

machinery and war). In another letter later in that same year, he wonders, "when it is all over, will ordinary people have any freedom left [...] or will they have to fight for it, or will they be too tired to resist?" (*Letters* 89). In the face of "mass-produced notions and emotions," and especially of imperialist propaganda, he hopes that "at least in our beloved land of England, propaganda defeats itself" (*Letters* 89; cf. 115–16 on imperialism and patriotism). He laments in a third letter from the same year that "the future is impenetrable especially to the wise; for what is really important is always hid from contemporaries, and the seeds of what is to be are quietly germinating in the dark in some forgotten corner" (*Letters* 79). Tolkien thus shares with the thinkers of secrecy like Simmel and Jung a sense of the alienation of the "spiritual private property" of the individual in the industrial world. Mass production leads to machinery of war as inexorably as mass culture leads to propaganda. Wrestling against the unknowable future, he possesses a grim sense of history-as-secrecy and produces a fable that evokes, in his own words, a "heart-racking sense of the vanished past" (*Letters* 110).

Further indications of Tolkien's contemplation of secrecy and interiority are revealed in his non-fiction essays, where secrecy is firmly connected with imagined languages and with the sense of both community and of isolation associated with their invention. In his belated "Valedictory Address to the University of Oxford," Tolkien admits to a certain solipsism in his profession: he teaches philology because he likes it, with no special sense that it should be "thrust down the throats of the young" as if it were "necessary to salvation" (225). He explains, nonetheless, that curiosity about language is always a trait of those who achieve great success as scholars. All forms of knowledge demand sacrifice, he argues, for "their roots are in the desire for knowledge, and their life is maintained by those who pursue some love or curiosity for its own sake [...]. If this individual love and curiosity fails, their tradition becomes sclerotic" (226). As a champion of the inseparable study of language and literature, Tolkien is also a champion of curiosity. In this essay, he uses the imagery of roots and mountains positively to represent the achievement of knowledge loved for its own sake and out of personal enjoyment rather than for the good of humanity. It seems to this degree that Tolkien felt a kinship between his own nosing in language and the curiosity of the creature he created in Sméagol. Later in the same essay, Tolkien recounts how he once refused to explain how he found philology "profitable or enjoyable" when asked "as if I were some curious wizard with arcane knowledge, with a *secret recipe* that I was unwilling to divulge" (237; my emphasis).

In another essay, Tolkien describes the invention of languages as a "secret vice," though also as a "delicate pleasure" ("Secret Vice" 200). On his way to discussing the invention of entirely new languages, Tolkien considers the partial or code-languages of childhood and their function in confirming close community among friends who imagine themselves members of a "secret and persecuted society" (201). Tolkien begins the essay deflecting and deferring until finally reaching an anecdote through which to confess his own pleasure in imaginary linguistics: he describes a man he sat next to during a military training lecture who suddenly but quietly blurted out "I shall express the accusative case by a prefix!" Tolkien further characterizes this man as "a queer creature—ever afterwards a little bashful after inadvertently revealing his secret—[who] cheered and comforted himself in the tedium and squalors of 'training under canvas' by composing a language, a personal system and symphony that no else [sic] was to study or hear" (199–200). Tolkien's explanation of this soldier depicts a certain self-referential solace to inventing a language that will never be used to communicate or reinforce a community. He imagines a secrecy so great that it will never perform one crucial social function of secrecy: to reinforce membership in a society. This soldier, as a "queer creature," suggests a model for Gollum, who also occupies an interior world in which he escapes from the tedium of his surroundings by talking to himself.

Such secrecies, establishing a relationship between language, society and isolation, pervade *The Lord of the Rings*. In particular, secrecy manifests itself along racial lines according to which the histories, languages, and moral fates of the races are reflected in their reaction to the rings of power. The secrecy effected by cultural divisions is evident even in *The Hobbit*, where Thrór's Map—the map to the secret door in the side of the Lonely Mountain—is encrypted in dwarvish runes and by the cultural knowledge that a dwarvish map is drawn with East at the top. This secret door prefigures the door to the Mines of Moria, hidden and doubly encrypted by a riddle written in runes. But this secrecy becomes deeper still in historical perspective. The dwarves, as Tolkien explains, used "the languages of men" in their transactions across Middle-earth. "Yet," he writes, "in secret (a secret which unlike the Elves, they did not willingly unlock, even to their friends) they used their own strange tongue […] and they tended it and guarded it as a treasure of the past" (*LotR* App.F.1132). Despite the excessive greed caused by their possession of rings of power, these dwarves could not be brought under Sauron's control because "the thoughts of their hearts are hard to fathom"

(*Silmarillion* [*S*] 188). Tolkien thus posits intrinsic psycho-social characters for dwarves, elves, hobbits, and men. Dwarves are possessed not only of particular stubborn toughness, but also with thoughts encrypted and obscure even if one can magically penetrate their minds. Their language is a "treasure" that both expresses and conceals their identity.

Many similar examples could be proffered: The elves, as guardians of mystical knowledge and as immortals who have witnessed events now also lost to the view of men, represent an especially intensified form of secrecy: the hidden past of ancient wisdom and forgotten worlds. Again, even at their most simple, in *The Hobbit*, elves seclude themselves in forests, so much so that Hobbits are not sure they exist. The Council of Elrond meets in the "secret valley" of Rivendell (*Hobbit* 90). Aragorn as "Strider" has a dual identity as the last of an ancient line of Kings who, being almost forgotten to history, represents a concealed lineage. As the action of the story builds in *The Lord of the Rings*, the competition over using or destroying the ring becomes a central ethical question. Gandalf refuses the Ring and adjures Frodo to "keep it safe, and keep it *secret*" (*LotR* I.1.40, emphasis added). As a "servant of the Secret Fire" (*LotR* II.5.330; a cosmogonic fire that, as we learn in the *Silmarillion*, Tolkien's Creator-God Ilúvatar "sent to burn at the heart of the World" [25]) he fears the consequences of attempting to control the Ring himself.

The imagery of revealing and concealing and the connection of subjectivity with concealment is powerfully symbolized in the invisibility-visibility bestowed by the Ring, which allows its wearer to hide from literal eyes while simultaneously exposing his "subjective entirety" (Simmel 449) to the gaze of Sauron, whose oppressive image is frequently some variation of a ceaselessly watching eye. This eye does not merely seek Frodo physically, but invades his person with a "horrible growing sense of a hostile will that strove with great power to pierce all shadows of cloud, and earth, and flesh, and to see you: to pin you under its deadly gaze, naked, immovable (*LotR* IV.2.630). Sauron's most horrifying violence is psychological—the penetration of Frodo's "spiritual private property" with his own gaze and his own, far more powerful, consciousness. The Ring which makes Frodo physically invisible nevertheless reveals him to the consciousness of the Dark Lord, under whose gaze he his individual will is threatened. Over time, under the burden to remain visible rather than slip into the safe invisibility provided by the ring, and the concomitant effort to resist the will of the Dark Lord, the ring bearer "fades" and will eventually become a twilight being like the Nazgûl, who were "kings, sorcerers, and warriors of old" (*S* 289).

Such effects on "modern" ring-bearers like Frodo and Sméagol-Gollum are prefigured in the history of the Ring. Secrecy has a theological depth that brings moral force to almost every action. Tolkien's history thus weaves together mythical themes connecting secrecy with power and death. After the defeat of Morgoth, Sauron "dissembled in his mind and concealed the dark designs that he shaped in his heart" (*S* 287). In disguise as the "Lord of Gifts" he tries to sway both elves and men by offering them the knowledge and skill "which those have who are beyond the Sea" (287). While they forge rings of power under his guidance, Sauron "secretly [...] made One Ring to rule all the others [...] and while he wore the One Ring he could perceive all things that were done by means of the lesser rings, and he could see and govern the very thoughts of those that wore them" (287–88). Sauron does not foresee that this magical awareness will be reciprocal. The elves immediately become aware of his consciousness and his deception upon wearing their own rings; they remove them and successfully hide three, giving them to "the Wise, who concealed them and never again used them openly while Sauron kept the ruling Ring" (288). This foundational moment in the pre-history of *The Lord of the Rings* is essentially a story of deception and espionage. Whatever the various powers of the rings, including the One Ring, it is their transmission of consciousness, their penetration of intention and interiority that constitutes their greatest danger.

Sauron's special desire for the three elven rings is their particular power to "ward off the decays of time and postpone the weariness of the world" (288). In the Second Age, Sauron persuades the proud Númenórean King Ar-Pharazôn, who "felt the waning of his days and was besotted by the fear of Death" to attack the Valar and "wrest everlasting life from the Lords of the West" (*LotR* App.A.1037). The effect of nine rings possessed by men also evokes a paradox of eternal life, since the affected ring-bearers "had, as it seemed, unending life, yet life became unendurable to them." As they become invisible to men, they can also "see things invisible to mortal men" (*S* 289). In this the Ringwraiths suffer a similar fate to the Elves. As the *Silmarillion* recounts, the elves, though superior to men in strength, wisdom, and power, are tied to the fate of the world: "[T]he elves remain until the end of days, and their love of the Earth and all the world is more single and more poignant therefore, and as the years lengthen ever more sorrowful. For the Elves die not until the world dies, unless they are slain or waste in grief." By contrast, "Men die indeed, and leave the world; wherefore they are called the Guests, or the Strangers. Death is their fate, the gift of Ilúvatar, which as Time wears even the Powers shall envy" (42). Death is a consequence of their detachment from fate, which allows men "to shape their life [...] beyond the Music of the Ainur, which is as fate to all things else" (41). In Tolkien's imagination, the greatest sorrow is history: the sorrow of endurance suffered alike by elves whose lives are woven into the fabric of the world and who can therefore remember things long since lost others. A similar fate is suffered by those whose will is surrendered to the power of the One Ring. The freedom of men from this pattern of fate, their ability to choose, is intimately linked to Ilúvatar's "gift" of death. Against such a backdrop, in which the mythic history of Middle-earth evolves through the hidden cultures of its many races and Sauron's deceptive secrecy, the local history of less glamorous characters takes on more profound meaning. The imagery of revealing and concealing especially surrounds the character of Sméagol-Gollum.

Many critics identify Gollum as a central symbolic entity, for all his apparent insignificance as a being. Patricia Meyer Spacks, in one of the earliest essays to treat *The Lord of the Rings* with critical seriousness, writes that though "comparatively weak in evil, [Gollum] has become the symbolic representative of evil" (95). Gergely Nagy points out the central role of Gollum in figuring the constitution of subjects in language. For Nagy, Gollum's name provides an etymological equation with the Ring, linking him ineluctably with ideas of both treasure and monstrosity and thus making Gollum's name "just a variant for this central signifier" (60). Gollum's character is iconically identified by the characteristics of his speech: the repetitive hissing and solipsistic monologue in which he seems endlessly engaged is often dismissed as infantile or whining,[2] but its key feature is the use of the first person plural. Though the narrator of *The Hobbit* remarks that the name "Gollum" derives from the swallowing noise he makes, "he always called himself 'my precious' " and "always spoke to himself, through never having anyone else to speak to" (*H* 120). Later it seems that Gollum refers to the Ring as his precious, but Tolkien makes it clear here that Gollum is his own "precious." The moniker thus suggests Gollum's attempt to maintain an identity in secrecy, splitting his consciousness to form an intimacy with himself. Referring to himself as "we" and addressing himself as "my precious," Gollum represents the psychological toll of his isolation and the symbolic burden as the erstwhile possessor of the ring. On one level, Gollum is a "philologist-figure"

---

2. For example, see Flieger, *Splintered Light*, 7.

(Shippey, *Road* 274), reflecting Tolkien's own philological self-consciousness about the invention of private languages. Behind the name is another name, moreover, and the character another character. In Sméagol, Tolkien portrays the deep symbolic role of secrecy in the constitution of moral subjectivity, and his own preoccupation with historical-linguistic encryption is cast within a secrecy both more profound and more sinister. As we'd expect from Tolkien, the names Sméagol and Déagol tell this story etymologically as these names reflect the theological symbolism of concealing (**dēagan*) and revealing (*smēagan*) in Old English wisdom literature.

We first meet Gollum when Bilbo Baggins does, in "Riddles in the Dark," the fifth chapter of *The Hobbit*. This meeting is crucial for the entire story of the closing of Tolkien's Third Age, and Tolkien's revisions for the second edition suggest he intended this meeting to foreshadow the story of the Ring evolving in *The Lord of the Rings*. That this meeting should take the form of a riddle competition appears *prima facie* to provide a point of folk-cultural contact between the two characters, but it also involves them in a ritualized probing of each other's intentions that reflects profounder subjects: fear, loneliness, suspicion, the ability of two "differentiated" hobbits to trust each other, and ultimately the intrusion of the will of the Ring's creator. The ritualized concealing and revealing of the riddle game cedes to a more hostile mutual interrogation when Bilbo breaks the rules of the confrontation and simply asks Gollum to guess what is in his pocket. As Gollum begins to guess Bilbo's secret the two are a deadlocked: Bilbo asks what Gollum has lost, and Gollum insistently responds with his own question about what Bilbo has in "its pocketses" (*H* V.126). The legitimate secrecy of the ritual becomes deceit, both characters retreat into interior preparations for violence, and the scene concludes with Bilbo inadvertently escaping by means of invisibility conferred by the ring.

The association of Gollum with secrecy becomes even more plain in *The Lord of the Rings*. In *The Fellowship of the Ring*, Gandalf explains Gollum's identity, telling Frodo a newly reconstructed story of the rediscovery of the One Ring by two hobbit-like creatures called Sméagol and Déagol. The differences in their character are slight but significant. Both are "clever-handed and quiet-footed," but Sméagol is "the most inquisitive and curious-minded" of his family who, "interested in roots and beginnings," sought out the deep and dark places where he might find them (*LotR* I.2.52–53). As Tolkien himself explains, Sméagol is "meaner and greedier" (*Letters* 292). When Sméagol and Déagol take a boat trip to the Gladden Fields, Sméagol is driven to investigate the natural recesses of the pond, "nosing about the banks," while Déagol fishes serenely from a boat (*LotR* I.2.53). Throughout Gandalf's short reconstruction, Sméagol is characterized repeatedly as a furtive being whose curiosity compulsively and inevitably carries him into ethically dangerous territory. After he murdered Déagol for the ring, he hid the body "cunningly." When he discovered that the ring granted him invisibility, he "concealed it" and "used it to find out secrets, and he put his knowledge to crooked and malicious uses." Gandalf observes that the ring "had given him power according to his stature" (I.2.53), endowing him with the kind of petty maliciousness that fitted his already cleverhanded and quiet-footed curiosity. It is no coincidence that, ejected from his society as the power of the ring allows him ever more bankrupt behavior, Sméagol-Gollum sets out for the Misty Mountains, where since "[t]he roots of those mountains must be roots indeed," he imagines "there must be great secrets buried there which have not been discovered since the beginning" (I.2.54). It is only later, as Gandalf moralizes toward the end of this vignette, that Sméagol will discover "[a]ll the 'great secrets' under the mountains had turned out to be just empty night" (I.2.55).

This is a tightly organized story in which diction continually reinforces the thematic links between an obsession with origins, secrecy, and the sinister kind of solipsism that marks Gollum's final wretchedness. The relationship between Sméagol's secret murder of Déagol, his desire to conceal and to be concealed while he compulsively searches out "secrets," is concretized in the names Sméagol and Déagol and the drama of their discovery of the ring. The meaningfulness of these names has been noted before, but their centrality to the theme of secrecy in *The Lord of the Rings* is worth much deeper explication. Douglass Parker's early review of *The Lord of the Rings* includes a long footnote giving examples of how names in the trilogy reflect a philologist's imagination (605; note 4). J.S. Ryan also noticed, in 1966, the association between the names Déagol and Sméagol and the OE verbs **dēagan* and *smēagan*. Ryan's observation forms part of a catalog of examples of Tolkien's "considerable awareness of the residuum of association in words and names from the Germanic world" (45). These critics take the resonance of such names with Old English vocabulary as a curiosity associated with a philologist's outlook, one that adds to the characterization of beings like Sméagol and Déagol or that contributes linguistically to the much celebrated depth of Tolkien's imagined world. As Tom Shippey points out, however, Tolkien's words are not embellishments of his story, but part of a "philological method" of story-telling through which words encrypt entire tales (*Road* 33–39). Considering Tolkien's choice of these words as a function of a "philologists heart" risks reducing them to the idle fascinations of a sequestered scholar, and thereby missing the important connections between the secrecy of the philologists heart—a secrecy that Tolkien himself seems to have anxiously guarded—and the broad social and philosophical ramifications of secrecy in the formation of group and individual responsibility.

The names Sméagol and Déagol associate these characters with Old English verbs meaning "to peer into" or "investigate" on the one hand and "to hide" or "secrete" on the other (Ryan 53). Tolkien himself indicates that he has used modernized versions of "ancient English" words to represent the way that "Hobbit words of northern origin" were related to the language of the humans of Rohan. As Tolkien explains them, the names Sméagol and Déagol are thus equivalents whose archaic Englishness represents archaic Northern words of Middle-earth: *Trahald* meaning "burrowing, worming in" and *Nahald* "secret" (*LotR* App.F.1136). At the most obvious level Sméagol-Gollum can be taken as a figure of dangerous curiosity. Déagol fights Sméagol for the ring and his motive does not seem simply to throw it away or hide it again. He is equally self-interested in his struggle, but wishes to keep the ring for a different reason to "bury" it or hoard it for himself. The struggle between the two characters can thus be read as an allegory about the appropriate response to secrets—to dig them up, or let them lie. The depth of their meanings for Tolkien can, of course, be found in etymology, but also in Old English literature, where the revealing and concealing play a predictable role in the expression of sacred and social meaning. In religious prose, wisdom literature and heroic verse, the verbs *smēagan* and **dēagan* evoke the many sociological and sacred functions of secrecy. Both words taken together indicate the necessary proximity of wisdom and secrecy, as well as astuteness and suspicion.

Sméagol, derived from these Old English words as Tolkien confirms, is thus a reflex of the Indo-European root **meug-*. A brief list of other reflexes shows how powerfully the semantic field of this root suggests Gollum's character: in addition to Old English words *smēagan* (v. to seek, investigate), *smēag* (adj. shrewd, cunning) and *smēag ol* (adj. narrow) we may add a different Old English verb, *smūgan* (to sneak, or crawl) and the noun *smygel* (which glosses Latin *cuniculos*: a burrow, rabbit hole, excavation, or secret device). Then there are Present Day English reflexes like meek, moist, and smuggle, as well as

Latin *mucus* (slime, including of course, nose slime) (*Indo-European Documentation Center*).

Smēagan is a very common verb, used particularly in Christian discourse. *Smēagan* glosses *investigare* in a Kentish glossary (Zupitza), and as it means to meditate, consider, or deliberate, is also a verb associated with wisdom. Ælfric of Eynsham's late-tenth century Glossary, indeed, offers several direct indications of what he took this verb to mean. Ælfric posits "ic smeage" as a gloss of *scrutor* (search, probe), *meditor* (consider, meditate), and *rimor* (search, explore, rummage). The heavy duty performed by this word reflects its constant use in describing Christian contemplation.

Old English translations of the Gospel demonstrate the potential implications of this word. In the Gospel of Mark, when Christ is questioned by Scribes and Pharisees, the concepts of interrogation and meditation themselves become subjects of scrutiny. When "the Pharisees came forth and began to question with him […] tempting him" (Mark 8:11), *smēagan* is the verb for their interrogation as it is when Jesus asks "what do you question about among yourselves" (Mark 9:16 [Skeat]). At Mark 12:28, *smēagan* renders "reasoning together" (*interrogavit*). As well as between people, however, *smēagan* can represent the interior process of meditation, as it does in the Gospel according to Luke (2:19), when Mary "ponders the words" of shepherds in her heart ("geheold ealle þas word on hyre heortan smeagende" [Skeat]). In this instance, *smēagende* glosses the Latin participial *conferens*, "bringing together," "matching against each other," "comparing," or as the Douay-Rheims Bible renders it "pondering." In King Alfred's Old English version of Boethius, Wisdom similarly asks whoever hears her lessons "mid innewearde mode hi ongiton and smeagean" (Sedgefield 50). Later in Luke, *smēagan* represents interior thought again, when a Pharisee "thinking within himself" ("on him smeagan"), questions Jesus's cleanliness (11:38 [Skeat]). This question provides an opportunity to consider the hypocrisy of the Pharisees who "wash the outside of the cup, and of the platter" but whose "inside is full of rapine and iniquity" (Luke 11:39). In this biblical context, such investigation leads to a lesson about inner and outer purity. *Smēagan* thus suggests interrogation, hostile and cynical in the case of Pharisees testing Christ, whose interrogations we might compare to the riddle contest of Bilbo and Gollum, or worse, the gaze of Sauron searching out Frodo: an inquiry intended to penetrate a veil and to expose the true interior of the other. The hostility of this form of penetration is captured in the meanings of related adjectives. *Smēah* is pejorative, for example, extending the striving and investigating of *smēagan* to a crafty form of penetration or "sneaking in," while *gesmēah* means "intrigue" (Bosworth and Toller; s.v.v. "smeah;" "gesmeah").

From Sméagol to Gollum, then, we witness a degeneration from curiosity to furtive, isolated seeking. Rather than an interior dialogue like that of Mary in the Gospels, or like that encouraged by Boethius' Wisdom, Sméagol ends in a tortured conversation with himself as he literally seeks in the dark for his "precious." The concepts of concealing and revealing, furthermore, confront and define each other in these names: Déagol might have been an appropriate name for Sméagol in his later manifestation as Gollum, since it extends to include "stealthy" and "surreptitious" (*Dictionary of Old English*; I.b, I.c). If the Old English verb *smēagan* has suggested the potential harm of "investigating," **dēagan* tells us even more about the value of secrecy.

As a verb, **dēagan* is reconstructed on the basis of a single, past tense occurrence in *Beowulf* (line 850). The same root nevertheless derives many adjectival forms, including a widely attested *dīgol* or *dēogol*. This adjective means secret or hidden from sight. In *Beowulf*, early rumors of Grendel that reach the Geats describe him as a *dēagol dædhata*, an "hidden evildoer" (line 275) and his isolated home is also known as a *dygel lond* (line 1357) (Fulk, et al., 11, 47). It is used figuratively especially to refer to those things that are hidden from men, though not from God—since *dēagol* refers to sacred things, arcane knowledge, divine mystery (*Dictionary of Old English*; 3.a–d).

The importance of secrecy as a mystical concept in Anglo-Saxon literature—and as a source of imagery in *The Lord of the Rings*—can be perceived in the use of *dēagol* in Riddle 40 of the Exeter Book:

> Hyrre ic eom heofone,   hateþ mec heahcyning
> his deagol þing   dyre bihealdan;
> eac ic under eorþan   eal sceawige
> wom wraðscrafu   wraþra gæsta. (Krapp and Dobbie III.201)
>
> [I am higher than heaven, the high-king commands me carefully to watch over his secret things; I also examine everything under the earth and the blighted caverns of evil spirits]

This riddle is a "translation" of Aldhelm's one-hundredth Latin enigma, *Creatura* ("Nature"). It expresses the medieval mystical idea of creation itself as a text, as a surface encrypting divine reason, but which here also contrasts the "secret things" belonging to God with the evil spirits that are hidden in the earth. Old English literature recognizes, then, that the secrecy of deep and sacred knowledge is also fraught with dangers.

Furthermore, the words for secrecy and value overlap in meaning, so that the alliterating adjectives *dēogol* and *dyrne* often appear together.

Christ II, for example, summarizes a poem recited by Job (28:7) that describes Christ as a bird. The Old English version, found in the Exeter Book alongside the famous riddle collection, depicts the flight of that bird as hidden from enemies on earth (Wæs þæs fugles flyht feondum on eorþan / *dyrne ond degol*, þam þe deorc gewit / hæfdon on hreþre, heortan stænne) (Krapp and Dobbie III.20–21). A similar collocation occurs again in Riddle 83, whose solution may be "ore," "money," or perhaps combine both in "gold":

> Hæbbe ic wundra fela,
> middangeardes   mægen unlytel,
> ac ic miþan sceal   monna gehwylcum
> *degolfulne dom   dyran cræftes*,
> siðfæt minne. (Krapp and Dobbie III.236).
>
> [I have many wonders, not least among miracles of middle-earth, but I must conceal my journey from each man a hidden craft's mysterious law.]

The riddle emphasizes a contrast between money, a social circulation of gold, and its origin as a hidden seam, tapped only by means of special knowledge. These Anglo-Saxon images echo in Tolkien's story of the secret creation of the rings of power, as well as Gollum's coveting of his ring in darkness under the mountain.

In some examples, words of particular note as sources of Tolkien's stories and characters appear all appear together, as for example in *Maxims I*, where secrecy is a defining concept in the characterization of wisdom (*frōd*), which can dwell in the recesses of the heart, but which *should* be exchanged openly among the wise:

> Frige mec frodum wordum!   Ne læt þinne ferð onhælne,
> degol þæt þu deopost cunne!   Nelle ic þe min dyrne gesecgan,
> gif þu me þinne hygecræft hylest   ond þine heortan geþohtas.
> (Krapp and Dobbie III.156–57)
>
> [Share with me your wise words. Do not let your mind be hidden, a secret of the things you most deeply understand. I will not say my secret knowledge, if you hide your wisdom from me, and the thoughts of your heart.]

Despite its loose organization, sometimes appearing to be a list of non sequiturs, *Maxims I* is nevertheless thematically consistent. It focuses on the contrasts between men as part of society and the doleful exposure of the friendless ones to the ravages of fate and nature, symbolized by the ravenous wolf. Secrets play their role in the functioning of a harmonious society: Counsel should be spoken, but secrets written (line 13). A wife must "keep secrets" (line 86). But secrets are also associated with the disintegration of society. The poem views the ocean grimly, as "the

deep path of the dead" which "will be hidden longest" ("deop deada
wæg, dyrne bið lengest" line 78). Ultimately, secret killing is opposed
to the "fitting death" a man may earn in an age the poem recognizes as
doomed to violence:

> Mægen mon sceal mid mete fedan, morþor under eorþan befeolan
> hinder under hrusan, þe hit forhelan þenceð;
> ne biþ þæt gedefe deaþ, þonne hit gedyrned weorþeð.
> (Krapp and Dobbie III.160)
>
> [One must nourish strength with food, murder [must be] consigned
> beneath the earth deep under ground, by he who thinks to conceal
> it, that is not an honest death, when it comes to be in secret.]

By contrast, a good death is public. "A dead man's property must be
shared," the poem declares, and "[d]om is best" (yrfe gedæled / deades
monnes. Dom biþ selast," line 79b–80). *Dōm* may mean "law" this context, but also more poetically "favorable judgment after death" (*Dictionary of Old English*; s.v. *dōm*). While this view of death might be aligned
with the folk-wisdom of heroic societies, Old English Christian literature expresses an even closer allegiance of secrecy and death. Ælfric's
Homily for the Common of a Confessor, for example, allegorically portrays Death as a threatening stranger. "The hidden thief who secretly
comes," Ælfric writes, "is the Death common to mankind, who by his
secret arrival brings man's body to death" ([S]e dyrna þeof, þe diʒollice
cymð, / is se ʒemænelica deaþ, ðe þæs mannes lichaman / mid his diʒelan tocyme to deaðe ʒe-brinʒð) (Assmann 54). In this version, Death is
the ultimate secret, common to all men (*gemænlica*) and his coming in
secret suggests a sinister parallel with the unfitting death portrayed in
Maxims I. The world portrayed by *Maxims I*, in other words, is a world
that takes war and grief for granted. One in which society and the sacred are stitched together by a hidden fabric. A world like that Tolkien
described, in which the future is hidden from the wise. The poem
weighs responsibility through the structure of its gnomic imperatives
(*sceal*) stating what men "must" do, but it also measures the interiority
of wisdom and intimate promises against the social world of *dōm*. It
depicts, in other words, the situation described by Patočka and Derrida,
in which the affirmation of life is expressed as an obsessive confrontation with death.

These examples demonstrate the complex interactions of secrecy,
wisdom, and death in the words *smēagan* and **dēagan* in the Old English
word-hoard on which Tolkien drew. *Smēagan* appears frequently in
homiletic prose and other learned literature. It suggests various activities of the mind, mostly directed outward as a form of investigation or

interrogation, though as we saw above it could also characterize "pondering" as a kind of interior dialogue involving comparing or weighing two sides. This verb, however, never occurs in Anglo-Saxon poetry. *dēagan*, or rather the adjectival *dēagol*, on the other hand, occurs frequently in wisdom literature like maxims and riddles, where it characterizes the mysterious wisdom hidden in dark places of the earth. It is frequently associated with evil (as in *Beowulf*), gold (as in *Riddle 83*), and death (as in *Maxims I*). *Smēagan* and **dēagan* are not merely opposites, however, as "seeking" and "hiding" seem to be. Rather, they intersect in meaning, as "investigating" can become penetrating and sneaking and as a *smygel* is a dark hole or secret device. The *dēagol* of hidden threats and demonic caverns is also the secrecy of men's minds and of God's mystery. It is also the secrecy of the future, which as *Maxims II* declares, is "digol and dyrne" (dark and hidden).

The Lord of the Rings is celebrated for its effective evocation not of actual history, but of a sense of history. Tolkien succeeds in creating the "heart-racking sense of the vanished past" he aimed for, especially through imagining fictional languages that encrust glimpses of meaning in ancient words. Because of this pre-occupation with the past, however, the profound modernity of Tolkien's work is less often examined. Though Tolkien's use of names like *Sméagol* and *Déagol* resonates with meanings constructed in Old English verse, their purpose in his own fiction is not simply to recapture an idealized past, but rather to express the grief of modern survivors and the sense of the violation of interiority Tolkien perceived to result from mass culture and the resulting mass destruction. In the early-twentieth century, concern over the boundaries of individual privacy and the importance of secrecy in both social and political relations were newly pressing modern concerns. Like Simmel, Jung, and many other thinkers of his age, Tolkien perceives modern life, characterized by mass-production and mass culture, as the root cause of the horrors of the world wars. It is thus no coincidence that his characterization of evil in *The Lord of the Rings* revolves around the penetration of individual minds by the distant and oppressive consciousness of the "all-seeing eye" of Sauron. It is, similarly, not only Tolkien's Ring, but also the characters of Sméagol, Déagol, and Frodo (whose names connote revealing, concealing, and wisdom respectively) through which the author's theme emerges. From the meanings of such names and their resonances in Old English literature, Tolkien evokes a sense of secrecy and interiority at the root of life itself.

This article was published originally in Mythlore *31.3/4 (#121/122) (2013): 83–101. It is reprinted here with permission.*

WORKS CITED

Assmann, Bruno. *Angelsächsische Homilien und Heiligenleben*. Kassel: Georg Wigand, 1889. Print.
Aitken, Jonathan. *Officially Secret*. London: Weidenfeld and Nicolson, 1971. Print.
Bok, Sisella. *Secrets*. New York: Pantheon, 1982. Print.
Boothroyd, Dave. "Off the Record: Levinas, Derrida and the Secret of Responsibility." *Theory, Culture & Society* 28: 7–8 (2011): 41–59. Print.
Bosworth, Joseph, and T. Northcote Toller. *An Anglo-Saxon Dictionary*. Last updated 29 July 2011. Web. 2 Apr. 2013.
Carpenter, Humphrey. *Tolkien: A Biography*. Boston: Houghton Mifflin, 1977. Print.
Croft, Janet Brennan. *War and the Works of J. R. R. Tolkien*. Westport: Praeger, 2004. Contributions to the Study of Science Fiction and Fantasy 106. Print.
Derrida, Jacques. *The Gift of Death and Literature in Secret*. Trans. David Wills. 2nd ed. Chicago: U of Chicago P, 2008. Print.
The Dictionary of Old English Corpus. Toronto: DOE Project, 2009. CD-ROM.
The Dictionary of Old English: A-F. Toronto: DOE Project, 2003. CD-ROM.
Flieger, Verlyn. *Splintered Light: Logos and Language in Tolkien's World*. 2nd ed. Kent: Kent State UP, 2002. Print.
Fulk, R. D., Robert E. Bjork, and John D. Niles. *Klaeber's Beowulf*. 4th ed. Toronto: U of Toronto P, 2008. Print.
Garth, John. *Tolkien and the Great War: The Threshold of Middle-earth*. Boston: Houghton Mifflin, 2003. Print.
Hooper, David. *Official Secrets: The Use and Abuse of the Act*. London: Secker & Warburg, 1987. Print.
The Indo-European Documentation Center. U of Texas-Austin. Web. 11 Nov. 2012. Print.
Jung, Carl. *Modern Man in Search of a Soul*. San Diego: Harcourt Brace, 1933. Print.
—. *The Undiscovered Self*. Boston: Little, Brown, 1958. Print.
Krapp, George P. and E. V. K. Dobbie. *The Anglo-Saxon Poetic Records*. 6 vols. New York: Columbia UP, 1936–1942. Print.
Lukács, Georg. "Georg Simmel." *Theory, Culture and Society* 8.3 (1991): 145–50. Translated by Margaret Cerullo. Rpt. in *Georg Simmel: Critical Assessments*. Ed. David Frisby. New York: Routledge, 1994. 98–102. Print.
Nagy, Gergely. "The 'Lost' Subject of Middle-earth: The Constitution of the Subject in the Figure of Gollum in *The Lord of the Rings*." *Tolkien Studies* 3:1 (2006): 57–79. Print.
Paret, Peter, Beth Irwin Lewis, and Paul Paret. *Persuasive Images: Posters of War and Revolution from the Hoover Institution Archives*. Princeton: Princeton UP, 1992. Print.
Parker, Douglass. "Hwaet We Holbytla..." *The Hudson Review* 9:4 (1957): 598–609.
Rickards, Maurice. *Posters of the First World War*. New York: Walker, 1968. Print.
Ryan, J. S. "German Mythology Applied—The Extension of the Literary Folk Memory." *Folklore* 77.1 (1966): 45–59. Print.
Sedgefield, Walter. *King Alfred's Old English Version of Boethius*. Oxford: Clarendon, 1899. Print.
Shippey, Tom. *J. R. R. Tolkien: Author of the Century*. New York: Houghton Mifflin, 2001. Print.
—. *The Road to Middle-earth*. Rev. and expanded ed. New York: Houghton Mifflin, 2003. Print.

Simmel, Georg. "Sociology of Secrecy and of Secret Societies." *American Journal of Sociology* 11 (1906): 441–98. Print.

Skeat, W. W. *The Four Gospels in Anglo-Saxon, Northumbrian, and Old Mercian Versions*. 4 Vols. (Cambridge: Cambridge UP, 1871–87). Rpt. in one volume Darmstadt: Wissenschaftliche Buchgesellschaft, 1970. Cited from the *Dictionary of Old English Corpus*. Print.

Spacks, Patricia Meyer. "Power and Meaning in *The Lord of the Rings*." *Tolkien and the Critics: Essays on J. R. R. Tolkien's* The Lord of the Rings. Ed. Neil David Isaacs. Notre Dame: U of Notre Dame P, 1969. Print.

Stanley, Peter. *What Did You Do in the War Daddy?: A Visual History of Propaganda Posters*. New York: Oxford UP, 1983. Print.

Thomas, Rosamund. *Espionage and Secrecy: The Official Secret Acts 1911–1989 of the United Kingdom*. London: Routledge, 1991. Print.

Tolkien, J. R. R. *The Annotated Hobbit*. Ed. Douglas Anderson. 2nd ed. Boston: Houghton Mifflin, 2002. Print.

—. *The Letters of J. R. R. Tolkien*. Ed. Humphrey Carpenter. 2nd ed. Boston: Houghton Mifflin, 2000. Print.

—. *The Lord of the Rings*. Boston: Houghton Mifflin, 2004. Print.

—. "A Secret Vice." *The Monsters and the Critics and Other Essays*. 2nd ed. New York: Harper Collins, 1997. 198–223. Print.

—. *The Silmarillion*. Ed. Christopher Tolkien. 2nd ed. Boston: Houghton Mifflin, 2001 Print..

—. "Valedictory Address to the University of Oxford." *The Monsters and the Critics and Other Essays*. 2nd ed. New York: Harper Collins, 1997. 224–40. Print.

Vincent, David. *The Culture of Secrecy: Britain 1832–1998*. New York: Oxford UP, 1998. Print.

Zupitza, J. "Kentische Glossen des neunten Jahrhunderts." *Zeitschrift für deutsches Altertum* 21: 1–59. Cited from *The Dictionary of Old English Corpus*. Print.

The Preservation of National Unity by [Dis]remembering the Past in Tolkien's *The Hobbit* and *The Lord of the Rings*

Nora Alfaiz

J. R. R. Tolkien formed a complex legendarium by drawing from his experiences in war, his love of languages, and his knowledge of history and myth. His achievements have been so great that even the word "legendarium,"[1] which was not recorded in the *Oxford English Dictionary* in his time, is now the common term used to describe the tales of his world of Arda in the aggregate. While much attention has been paid to nationalist themes in the legendarium, the complex structures of the novels *The Hobbit* and *The Lord of the Rings* have been comparatively neglected. One question we might ask is how Tolkien's fiction represents nations and nationalisms in a war-ridden reality. Additionally, how does Tolkien address the project of historiography and does his work present a project of history writing? Applying Maurice Halbwachs's and Pierre Nora's theories of memory, history, and historiography to Tolkien's letters and works will demonstrate how memory can be both useful and treacherous in forming national unity. The complex nature of Tolkien's fiction is a source for answering these questions and understanding the various ways he addresses nationalist formations of memory and history.

The Hobbit and *The Lord of the Rings*, among other tales, are represented to readers as the contents of a leather-bound book named the Red Book of Westmarch. The writers of the Red Book are none other than the quiet, and mostly inconspicuous, race of the Hobbits. Tolkien uses the Red Book as an authentic frame narrative that unifies the children's story *The Hobbit* with the sophisticated events of *The Lord of the Rings*. The Red Book functions as a tangible historiographic text that traces the workings of memory in relation to national history. Among the many questions the Red Book's structure complicates are: What is memory's role in forming a unified nation? What happens to a nation once its history, whether violent or peaceful, turns into legend or myth

---

1. "[L]*egendary* itself would not quite do, as it usually denoted a physical object; nor would *mythology*, as many of his writings were too 'historical' to be described as myths" (Gilliver et al. 154).

throughout the years? The stories in the Red Book provide different examples of how history can exploit memory. In the dwarves' case in *The Hobbit*, they maintain a distant memory from their ancestors' time in order to reconstruct a sense of national unity and retrieve their land. A nation can also silence its violent past or forget it in order to maintain national unity, which is what happens to the men of Gondor when their forgotten past could have enabled the tyrannical Sauron to possess Middle-earth. Applying the theory outlined in Homi Bhabha's influential essay "DessemiNation," in which he critiques a nation's intentional forgetfulness of its national memory, helps us understand why the people of Gondor have forgotten the darkness in their past. His critique can assist in explaining the significance of having Hobbits as the writers of historiographical accounts, which incorporate the violence of a nation's past in a written form that guarantees remembrance.

Recent scholarship on Tolkien has found many ways to address the ideas of nationalism, memory, and mythology in his works. John Garth notes in a review he wrote for *Tolkien Studies* that "(like no one else on earth) [Tolkien] could capture the deeper patterns of the war in ways that were primarily unrealistic, through symbolism, nightmare, fantasy, myth" (235). Prior to this argument, Garth's review pays tribute to the realistic features of the novel, arguing that the depth of the material causes the stories' lasting impression on their readers. However, he gives more attention to the way Tolkien's ability to capture his experiences and transfer them to paper was primarily based on the methods of realism. As this paper will argue, the manner in which the characters react to their history during wartime is realistic: dwarves resort to oral songs to capture the war that ruined their kingdom, men forget the historical violence of a momentous war in their past, and hobbits write all of these events in a book so that no one forgets these dark yet significant events. All of these important events are presented realistically, lending them depth, which leads to the claim that Tolkien's technique is primarily realistic even if his world is not.

Much attention has also been paid to the biographical aspect behind the nationalist themes in Tolkien's work. Tom Shippey perfectly categorizes twentieth-century authors like J. R. R. Tolkien, C. S. Lewis, T. H. White, George Orwell, and William Golding as "traumatized authors" whose works dealt with fantasy and fable (*J. R. R. Tolkien* xxx) to describe the horror of the evil they faced in the wars they fought. He explains that the authors who spoke most powerfully about the events of the twentieth century "have for some reason found it necessary to use the metaphoric mode of fantasy, to write about words and creatures we know do not exist" (viii). Shippey explains that the horrors of wars and mass destruction that these authors witnessed were too gruesome for conventionally realistic descriptions. Tolkien's personal letters prove that he was indeed frustrated with humanity, supporting Shippey's claim. He was upset with the nationalist tendency to forget the horrors of past wars, and he wanted to challenge people to remember these events so that they would not be repeated.[2]

Tolkien's letters and works reflect his interest in history and historical accounts. He shares in a letter to his son in 1944 that "[S]o short is human memory and so evanescent are its generations that in only about 30 years there will be few or no people with that direct experience which alone goes really to the heart" (*Letters* 75–76). As a man who fought in the Battle of Somme and had direct experience of the First World War, Tolkien was one of the few survivors amongst his friends who were pulled into the same war. He extends his anxiety over forgetfulness in the Foreword that was added to the second edition of *The Lord of the Rings*. He states that

> One has indeed personally to come under the shadow of war to feel fully its oppression; but as the years go by it seems now often forgotten that to be caught in youth by 1914 was no less hideous an experience than to be involved in 1939 and the following years. By 1918 all but one of my close friends were dead. (*The Lord of the Rings* [*LotR*] Foreword.xxiv)

Tolkien uses this explanation to refute the claim by some critics that *The Lord of the Rings* is specifically about the Second World War, and many scholars follow his lead.[3] What should be noted is Tolkien's reference to his "close friends" and how the First World War robbed him of their company. The friends in question were members of the T.C.B.S. (Tea Cup and Barrovian Society), a group that formed when Tolkien was at King Edward's School in Birmingham. It was a loss that anyone would find difficult to overcome, and even though he found friends in his fellow Inklings later in life, his abhorrence for war seems to have a tinge of bitterness due to this early irredeemable loss.[4]

---

2. See letters numbered by Carpenter as 5, 43, 45, 61, 81, and 92 for more of Tolkien's views on war. He forms a mathematical equation to express his views in a letter:
> How stupid everything is!, and war multiplies the stupidity by 3 and its power by itself: so one's precious days are ruled by $(3x)2$ when x=normal human crassitude (and that's bad enough). However, I hope that in after days the experience of men and things, if painful, will prove useful. It did to me. (*Letters* 73)

3. John Garth, Verlyn Flieger, and Tom Shippey, to name but a few.

4. Letters 64 and 102, for example.

Tolkien's statement, in which he describes himself and his fellow soldiers as coming "under the shadow of war," reflects their inability to escape from the war that caused the death of a young generation. Additionally, "to be caught in youth" conveys the sense of entrapment his generation felt: the young were drafted, were expected to fight and had no say in it unless they wanted to face discrimination from their peers, after which they would be sent to the front anyway. As Tolkien wrote to his son Michael in 1941: "In those days chaps joined up, or were scorned publicly" (*Letters* 53). It could also be argued that the words "caught in youth" were deliberately picked to emphasize that his dead friends were permanently stuck in their young age. Tolkien wasn't stuck in his youth like they were because he managed to escape death's grasp, and his combat against history's forgetfulness of violence and war pushed him to portray the anguishing results of war in his work.

Tolkien's writing quest was difficult;[5] as Paul Fussell notes, soldiers labored to find ways to express the horrifying experiences they witnessed. "Whatever the cause," Fussell observes, "the presumed inadequacy of language itself to convey the facts about trench warfare is one of the motifs of all who wrote about the war" (170). Ultimately, Tolkien's investment in his experiences and loss in war metamorphosed into cautionary tales that go "really to the heart" in the form of a fantasy novel. C. S. Lewis, a friend of Tolkien and an author who also served on the Western Front, notes Tolkien's realistic themes in what Shippey describes as a world of "fantasy and fable" in his review of *The Lord of the Rings*:

> This war has the very quality of the war my generation knew. It is all here: the endless, unintelligible movement, the sinister quiet of the front when "everything is now ready," the flying civilians, the lively, vivid friendships, the background of something like despair and the merry foreground [...]. (Lewis 13)

C. S. Lewis's description emphasizes the emotional depth of Tolkien's writing. Tom Shippey recently asserted, in an article on *The Hobbit*'s 75th anniversary, that emotional depth is one of the chief reasons behind its ongoing success. He comments that just as J. K. Rowling "brought back length [in children's stories], so Tolkien boldly, or maybe unthinkingly, brought back emotional depth." To add to Shippey's claim, the strength of readers' emotive response to Tolkien's work

---

5. Other writers who experienced the Great War also found it difficult to describe the horrific event. The poet Siegfried Sassoon remarks in *Memoirs of an Infantry Officer* that it is "a weary business [...] to be remembering and writing it down [...] how difficult it is to recover the details of war experience" (67–68).

is also due to the universal symbolism of war which transcends his stories and influences readers. Moreover, Tolkien's stories have a timeless quality that reminds readers of the horrors of war, when the direct line that links one war generation to another ceases to exist.

The Hobbit addresses the long-term collective memory a broken nation has of its lost nationhood and violent past. The plot focuses on the dwarf Thorin Oakenshield and his thirteen companions as they attempt retrieve their stolen country. Bilbo Baggins is persuaded by the wizard Gandalf to join their quest to kill the dragon Smaug who seized the treasures they prize and drove the dwarves from their rightful home in the Lonely Mountain. The dwarves first share their sad history in the form of a song that tells the story of their lost kingdom. All thirteen of them chime in as they sing "Far Over the Misty Mountains Cold," a song that summarizes how the "dragon's ire more fierce than fire / Laid low their towers and houses frail" (45). The song ends as follows:

> Far over the misty mountains grim
> To dungeons deep and caverns dim
> We must away, ere break of day,
> To win our harps and gold from him! (45)

There are many bleak paths that they must pass, the song goes, and it is necessary to risk whatever it takes to retrieve stolen treasures and glory for their race. These sentiments reflect the strength of the dwarves' will to pursue their dark task. The recital of the song is uninterrupted by stumbling singers or descriptions of the chaos of the crowded room, which indicates that the song is one that the dwarves are familiar with and have recited together before.

Naturally, the function of collective memory in this scene is crucial for an understanding of how these dwarves form a sense of national unity when they were driven out of their home. The sociologist Maurice Halbwachs argues that memory is a structured activity that is characteristically a social interaction. Although Halbwachs's general argument clarifies the beneficial impact of the social setting as a place for recollecting memory, he further maintains that any who come after the community that directly experienced the event will have a historical recollection that is, at best, a shadow of the previous generation's memory. He famously observes that the act of reconstructing a past depends on an individual's reliance on other members of his or her group:

> One may say that the individual remembers by placing himself in the perspective of the group, but one may also affirm that the memory of the group realizes and manifests itself in individual memories. (40)

As such, any society's formation of its national memory depends on collaborations and interactions between individuals. By viewing the scene using Halbwachs's theory, it is clear that the dwarves are able to draw from their social interaction—the act of singing a song they have memorized—some verification of the accuracy of their individual remembrance of their history. Additionally, the song they sing also represents an oral tradition that assists them in preserving their collective memory of their history. Not only can they remember their history, but they even manage to relive it through reciting "Far Over the Misty Mountains Cold" and experience it as if it were their own memory. In this case, the dwarves' usage of the oral song is contrary to Halbwachs's theory that a memory turns to history when its owners die. The song is, as Verlyn Flieger notes in *Interrupted Music: The Making of Tolkien's Mythology,* a song that does not have an author, making it a piece that is comparable to "a bardic tradition of preserved communal history and prophecy" (64). The prophetic state of the song is triggered by the final regrouping of these dwarves in one contained space, as it is only by meeting at Bilbo's home that they can begin their journey. Additionally, the anonymity of the author does not impact the strength of the song's themes of nostalgia and revivification of community; rather, the hegemonic power of the song even influences Bilbo, an individual from another race, who suddenly feels the dwarves' love of metals and stones, "the fierce and jealous love" (45) that dwarves have for what their smiths craft and design with the substances they excavate from their mines. The spark of communal relation immediately brings out the Took side of his heritage, the side that loves to go on adventures, and it is the Took side that slowly and hesitantly, but surely, takes possession of Bilbo. The dwarves' collective recital of the song, therefore, reiterates their historical past in a way that aids their remembrance of it. Similarly, the dwarves' shared collective memory of their past, as represented in the song, benefits their community when they are able to influence individuals from other communities to empathize with their culture and help in retrieving it.

By using the song as an object that retrieves a national memory, Tolkien makes it the perfect medium to mirror the dwarves' unyielding obsession with the retrieval of a unified nationalism through regaining their stolen lands. As a result, the song's location in the first chapter, and its recurrence in the end of the same chapter when Thorin hums the song to himself (59), becomes a motivator that drives the plot of the novel. What happens in these moments early in the novel is a retrieval of a memory, not a dead history that is stuck in the past. To understand memory's role in such a scene, let us turn to Pierre Nora's definition of memory: "a perpetually actual phenomenon, a bond tying us to the eternal present" (8). The act of reciting the song, therefore, acts as a constant reminder that makes the dwarves relive the violent events of their ancestors' time and reignites their determination to retrieve the unified kingdom they once had. As such, the song takes memories from the dwarves' past and links them to their present condition, strengthening bonds between them.

Although it is true that the dwarves assert their own memory of their history, Gandalf is able to communicate them and add to their memories even though he is not part of their culture. His special innate agency as an Istari, an immortal being who resembles the race of Men but has superior mental and physical prowess,[6] makes him an outsider who can enter the dwarves' culture and support the dwarves' memory. He becomes one of the social communicators within the group and regulates their social arrangement and their identity by revealing methods to aid them in their mission. Gandalf shares a map that was drawn by Thrór, the grandfather of the dwarf leader Thorin, and reveals a hidden entrance that the dwarves are unfamiliar with; this proves to be the only passage that the dragon Smaug has no knowledge of. Thus, Gandalf enacts Halbwachs's theory that it is "in society that people normally acquire their memories. It is also in society that they recall, recognize, and localize their memories" (38). In the society of dwarves, and in the cozy home of a perplexed hobbit, Gandalf is finally able to provide Thorin with material objects that have a significant link to the memories that stir them in their present state. Though Gandalf's position has no easily identifiable counterpart in real life, his ability to enter different societies saves the creatures of Middle-earth from destruction as he takes the role of a historiographic object due to his vast and inclusive omniscience.

Moreover, Nora bolsters Halbwachs's theory about the social act of constructing a group's history by validating the role objects play in reviving a national memory. In addition to serving simply as a map and a memory trigger, the object in this scene also has a revelatory function. The illustrated document, runes and all, is significant in recovering their lands but not in maintaining their memory of their past. Such objects produce, as Nora describes, "moments of history torn away from the movement of history, then returned; no longer quite life, nor yet

---

6. Tolkien defines his unconventional usage of "wizard" in the section named "The Istari" from his *Unfinished Tales:* a "Wizard is [...] one of the members of an 'order' (as they called it), claiming to possess, and exhibiting, eminent knowledge of the history and nature of the World" (388).

death, like shells on the shore when the sea of living memory has receded" (12)—like the map and key which are objects that are provided by someone who is no longer alive. Gandalf knew Thrór and kept his map and key until his grandson was ready to retrieve their kingdom; therefore, his presence guarantees that the "moments of history" will be "returned" when the community is prepared to reclaim its nation.

In contrast to the dwarves' innate memory of their race and their recoverable past is Gondor's dis-remembrance of its monarchy's unflattering history. *The Lord of the Rings* is set sixty years after Bilbo finds a magical ring when joining the dwarves and Gandalf on their journey to the Lonely Mountain. As the events are described in the Red Book, the Ring proves to be a treacherous magical item that the dark lord Sauron devised to enable him to control the creatures of Middle-earth. The story follows the hobbit Frodo and his companions as they attempt to destroy the Ring in the only possible way: by throwing it in the flames of Mount Doom, the volcano where the Ring was forged. The chapter that unveils the story of the Ring and its relation to the land of Gondor, the greatest kingdom of Men, is "The Council of Elrond." The elf Elrond's memory is unwavering as he teaches the council about events that span thousands of years. "My memory reaches back even to the Elder Days," he informs the astonished Frodo who cannot comprehend an elf's capacious recollection (*LotR* II.2.243).

The semi-omniscient storyteller Elrond tells how Gondor's history darkened when King Isildur ignored his companions' advice to destroy the Ring. Isildur decides to claim it as an heirloom for his house, and his hubris eventually results in his murder; his history is forgotten as Gondor maintains national stability. When Elrond reaches this part of the story, he is interrupted by Boromir, the emissary from Gondor:

> "So that is what became of the Ring!" he cried. "If ever such a tale was told in the South, it has long been forgotten. I have heard of the Great Ring of him that we do not name; but we believed that it perished from the world in the ruin of his first realm. Isildur took it! That is tidings indeed." (II.2.243)

Boromir's note that the story "has long been forgotten" in indicative of the state of the memory of the people of Gondor, the greatest kingdom of the race of Men. The citizens of Gondor have forgotten such a tale if they were ever told it, or so Boromir claims. He speaks on behalf of Gondor when he uses the plural "we believed" to verify that the whole nation has one shared notion of the history that unifies it. Boromir's statements are problematic because Gondor is also the source of the history Gandalf unearths from the "hoarded scrolls and books" (II.2.252) archived in its capital: "there lies in Minas Tirith still, unread, I guess, by any save Saruman and myself since the kings failed, a scroll that Isildur made himself" (II.2.252). The long-neglected archives rest in their similarly forgotten history and are only sought by powerful figures like Saruman and Gandalf. Gandalf adds to his previous revelation:

> [A]nd *that is not remembered in Gondor, it would seem* [own emphasis]. For this scroll concerns the Ring, and thus wrote Isildur therein:
> *The Great Ring shall go now to be an heirloom of the North Kingdom; but records of it shall be left in Gondor, where also dwell the heirs of Elendil, lest a time come when the memory of these great matters shall grow dim.*
> (II.2.252)

Isildur never successfully keeps the Ring as the heirloom he wants it to be, for his pride causes him to underestimate the Ring's power and finally leads to his death. The records he writes for his heirs remain in their possession, yet these records are forgotten along with the pride that caused his demise. Isildur feared the time when "the memory of these great matters shall grow dim," yet it is the dissipation of his nation, caused by his selfish ownership of the Ring, that would have resulted. It is due to Isildur's pride that Gondor, the closest to the source of history, forgets this significant memory. Denethor, Steward of Gondor, is proud of his high position even though he cannot sit on the empty throne while Gondor hopelessly awaits its legendary king's return. Denethor's seat is located "[a]t the foot of the dais, upon the lowest step which was broad and deep" and is "a stone chair, black and unadorned" (V.1.754), yet he rules with the power of a king. The council might have noticed Denethor's pride and its danger to Gondor's stability had Isildur's hubris been widely known; but it is forgotten in the interests of maintaining a glorified image of its past.

Gandalf, repeating his role in *The Hobbit*, conveys knowledge to the distressed members of the council. As he points out, the scroll "is not remembered in Gondor, *it would seem* [own emphasis]." The last three words allow the possibility of a conscious effort in Gondor to repress the of Isildur's dark deed. The political function of such an act is to maintain the harmonious state of the kingdom though the rightful king is inconclusively absent. Gondor's state is illuminated by Homi Bhabha's "DissemiNation," which argues that "[b]eing obliged to forget becomes the basis for remembering the nation, peopling it anew, imagining the possibility of other contending and liberating forms of cultural identification" (311). The citizens' obligation to forget is indicative of "the construction of a discourse on society that *performs* [author's emphasis] the problematic totalization of the national will" (311).

Gondor's negligence and inability to read the significant scroll, as a result, is indicative of a society that has forgotten its own memory and has relied on the constructed historical accounts it has made. Gondor's denial of its past, however, becomes dangerous to its people and to other kingdoms when Saruman learns about their history and becomes more powerful as a result. Consequently, the scroll becomes a symbol of what Nora, in his differentiation between memory and history in *Representations,* describes as *lieux de mémoire.* He explains the term as a "memorial consciousness that has barely survived in a historical age that calls out for memory because it has abandoned it" (12). What the discussion at the council reveals is that the scroll barely survived. It would have been lost had Gandalf not deciphered its forgotten language. The scroll's significance as a symbol of memory is undermined and pushed aside by the society of Gondor because it associates the scroll with the past while it is struggling to live in its kingless present.

The importance of the scroll as a retriever of a forgotten memory is comparable to the Red Book; both function as a historical text. Nora claims that "it is memory that dictates while history writes; this is why both history books and historical events merit special attention" (21). Since the "special attention" Gandalf pays to the scroll reveals information regarding the Ring and its eventual destruction, special attention should also be paid to the Red Book and what it reveals. Tolkien refers to the Red Book in more than one of his works, and such references establish the validity of the book as a reliable source of information. Of a poem about Tom Bombadil which was published separately from *The Lord of the Rings*, Tolkien notes that "the Red Book contains a large number of verses. A few are included in the narrative of *The Downfall of the Lord of the Rings* or in the attached stories and chronicles" (*Bombadil* 7). His representation of the Red Book reaches its most complex form in *The Lord of the Rings,* where he claims that he is merely a compiler of the texts that are provided to the readers. Flieger aptly points to the importance of the Prologue, declaring that Tolkien's role as a compiler of the texts "maintains that a manuscript tradition of some antiquity underlay the texts of both *The Hobbit* and *The Lord of the Rings*" (68). Tolkien explains that the reason readers have the story from hobbits is due to the hobbits' awakened "interest in their own history; and many of their traditions, up to that time still mainly oral, [which] were collected and written down" after the end of the War of the Ring (*LotR* Prologue.14). He also relates that the provided "account of the end of the Third Age is drawn mainly from the Red Book of Westmarch" (Prologue.14), which originated in Bilbo's diary and was later finished by Frodo and Samwise

(VI.9.1027). The accumulation of these accounts, since Bilbo wrote *The Hobbit* and he and his fellow hobbits wrote *The Lord of the Rings*, is what reaches the readers of the text.

The three hobbits create a national memory through their written documentation of the events that happened to them as they participated in the preservation of Middle-earth's freedom. They empower their race because the memories they historicize in the act of writing put them in charge of the history of the other races they portray in the story. Fittingly, the last hobbit who controls the contents of the Red Book is none other than Samwise Gamgee, the hobbit with the least income and social status among the three writers. He represents the inversion of the master-servant role when he becomes the owner of the book; he becomes the most important character because his role as the bookkeeper includes teaching people the events in the text. The memory of the hobbits, which Sam controls because he is its last owner, then becomes both the memory of their generation and the memory that the readers will form. In *Imagined Communities*, Benedict Anderson compares the act of keeping a national record to the individual's documentation of his or her own life through the act of piecing lost memories together in an attempt to form a solid identity (204–05). Like Anderson's claim, the hobbits aim for solid unity through their documentation of their experiences. However, the reason they collect evidence is not due to the simple inability to remember their personal details. The hobbits' aim behind writing the Red Book, as Frodo Baggins explains, is similar to Tolkien's goal: to provide a "direct experience which alone goes really to the heart" (*Letters* 76). As Frodo tells Sam, "[Y]ou will read things out of the Red Book, and keep alive the memory of the age that is gone, so that people will remember the Great Danger and so love their beloved land all the more" (*LotR* VI.9.1029). Although Frodo's rationale has a stronger sense of nationalism and national unity in it, it also encompasses Tolkien's call for a solution to national forgetfulness of the horrors of the wars it has experienced and seen. As such, The Red Book becomes for the inhabitants of Middle-earth what Tolkien's stories have become for its readers: the direct experience that influences others.

The horrifying experiences Tolkien witnessed in the Great War marked him and enabled him to teach readers most about war. He becomes the "burnt hand [that] teaches most about fire" (*Letters* 76), which is a description that befits his writing. The Red Book and the stories it contains, particularly the scenes this paper has explored, make visible the complex structure of Tolkien's work in the way it represents national unity through remembrance and dis-remembrance. His legendarium presents realistic issues of memory, history, and nationality, and it challenges readers to understand the problems these issues present. The Red Book's representation of a historiographical text constitutes a frame narrative that pressures readers to consider the various methods that nations use in manipulating memory for the formation of a unified nation or a national history. These texts, in their complexity, function as cautionary tales that aim to remind readers of the dark histories that our nations are in the process of forgetting.

WORKS CITED

Anderson, Benedict. *Imagined Communities: Reflections on the Origin and Spread of Nationalism.* Rev. ed. London: Verso, 1991. Print.

Bhabha, Homi. "DissemiNation." *Nation and Narration.* Ed. Homi Bhabha. New York: Routledge, 1990. 291–322. Print.

Flieger, Verlyn. *Interrupted Music: The Making of Tolkien's Mythology.* Kent: Kent State UP, 2005. Print.

Fussell, Paul. *The Great War and Modern Memory.* 1975. 25th anniv. ed. New York: Oxford UP, 2000. Print.

Garth, John. Rev. of *War and the Works of J. R. R. Tolkien,* by Janet Brennan Croft. *Tolkien Studies* 3 (2006): 234-38. Print.

Gilliver, Peter, Jeremy Marshall, and Edmund Weiner. *The Ring of Words: Tolkien and the Oxford English Dictionary.* Oxford: Oxford UP, 2006. Print.

Halbwachs, Maurice. *On Collective Memory.* Trans. Lewis A. Coser. Chicago: U of Chicago, 1992. Print.

Lewis, C. S. "The Dethronement of Power." *Understanding* The Lord of the Rings: *The Best of Tolkien Criticism.* Ed. Rose A. Zimbardo and Neil D. Isaacs. Boston: Houghton Mifflin, 2005. 11–15. Print.

Nora, Pierre. "Between Memory and History: *Les Lieux de memoire."* Trans. Marc Roudebush. *Representations* 26. Special Issue: Memory and Counter-Memory (1989): 7–25. Print.

Sassoon, Siegfried. *Memoirs of an Infantry Officer.* London: Faber & Faber, 1930. Print.

Shippey, Tom. "*The Hobbit*: What Has Made the Book Such an Enduring Success?" *The Telegraph.* 20 Sept. 2012. Web. 29 Apr. 2014.

—. *J. R. R. Tolkien: Author of the Century.* Boston: Houghton Mifflin, 2001. Print.

Tolkien, J. R. R. *The Adventures of Tom Bombadil and Other Verses from the Red Book.* London: Allen and Unwin, 1962. Print.

—. *The Annotated Hobbit:* The Hobbit, Or, There and Back Again. Ed. Douglas A. Anderson. Boston: Houghton Mifflin, 2002. Print.

—. *The Letters of J. R. R. Tolkien.* 1981. Ed. Humphrey Carpenter and Christopher Tolkien. Boston: Houghton Mifflin, 2000. Print.

—. *The Lord of the Rings.* London: HarperCollins, 1999. Print.

—. *Unfinished Tales of Númenor and Middle-earth.* Ed. Christopher Tolkien. Boston: Houghton Mifflin, 1980. Print.

"Now Often Forgotten":
Gollum, the Great War, and the Last Alliance

Peter Grybauskas

"In other cases you can't even tell a true war story. Sometimes it's just beyond telling." – Tim O'Brien

EVEN A CURSORY SCAN of J. R. R. Tolkien's major fiction reveals a world saturated by war. Like our own, Middle-earth's history, geography and chronology are—despite all their fantasy—defined and measured by great conflicts: wars of jewels and wars of rings; of great victories, fruitless ones, and unnumbered tears; of sudden flame and torrential water; battles between five armies and sometimes just two. While the literary merits of Tolkien's treatment of war were once blithely overlooked,[1] a significant number of recent scholarly efforts have begun to explore biographical and thematic connections[2] between Tolkien's legendarium and the two World Wars which bracket the publication of *The Hobbit* and much of the composition of *The Lord of the Rings*.

One of the great advantages of such scholarship is that it repositions Tolkien's work—so long considered an aberration[3]—within the literary and historical contexts of his own time. While the label of "20th century war writer" has a certain loose-fitting appeal, the lengthy gap between Tolkien's service in World War I and the publication of *The Lord of the Rings* in 1954–1955 has tempted some scholars toward more precise taxonomy. Is he a World War I writer, as John Garth would argue in tracking Tolkien's mythopoeic foundations through the Somme trenches? Or is it more appropriate to point to the late publication dates, to consider him a World War II writer, principally concerned with the nature of evil, as Tom Shippey suggests in "Tolkien as a Post-War Writer"? In the 2nd edition Foreword to *The Lord of the Rings*, Tolkien

---

1. Not all critics of course, were blind to its relevance. A review by C. S. Lewis remarked, "this war has the very quality of the war my generation knew" (14).
2. Book length studies on the subject include John Garth's *Tolkien and the Great War*, Janet Brennan Croft's *War and the Works of J. R. R. Tolkien,* and Tom Shippey's *J. R. R. Tolkien: Author of the Century*.
3. To some it seemed a medieval throwback; to others like the stories Tolkien describes in *On Fairy-stories*, leading through "a door on Other Time" or "outside Time itself, maybe" (*OFS* 48).

himself (ironically) fuels this "controversy" somewhat, all while documenting his disdain for biographical approaches to literary study. After dismantling a reductive reading of his story as a World War II allegory, he goes on to reflect:

> One has indeed personally to come under the shadow of war to feel fully its oppression; but as the years go by it seems now often forgotten that to be caught in youth by 1914 was no less hideous an experience than to be involved in 1939 and the following years. By 1918 all but one of my close friends were dead. (*The Lord of the Rings* [*LotR*] Foreword.xxiv)

Definitive classification of Tolkien's work is not my intention; rather, I wish to draw attention to the accusation of collective amnesia here—that a mere quarter century on, the experience of the Great War "seems now often forgotten." Tolkien found this sort of forgetfulness very troubling indeed, and the implications of his reflection cut through the Foreword and deep into the heroic romance which follows it.

For in moving beyond cursory scan into careful perusal of his work, especially *The Lord of the Rings*, we might say that it is not so much a story about war as it is about war stories: telling them, reading them, remembering and reflecting on them.[4] Certainly no war story in the text exerts a more pronounced or problematic influence than the Last Alliance. This legendary war which concludes the Second Age of Middle-earth is remembered and misremembered, its tales told and untold, often with substantial effect on the narrative present. In the invitation to untangle these Alliance yarns we find not only a critical thematic parallel with Tolkien's own war experience and his efforts to come to terms with its legacy both of heroism and horror,[5] but also a gateway into the very fabric of his fantasy, the text's commentary on imagination, myth-making, and the narrative art.

In beginning to explore the Alliance tradition and its reverberations, I should like to take a curious point of departure: to consider Gollum's keen ear for story, how it solidifies his role as a knowledgeable historian, and, from a certain point of view, a hero.

---

4. As Andrew Hallam says in "Thresholds to Middle-earth," Tolkien's works "function allegorically as allegories of *reading*, for their characters perform acts of interpretation; they become figures of the modern Reader as they move through the mythic landscape of Middle-earth" (26, emphasis in original).

5. For a comparison between Tolkien and trench poet Siegfried Sassoon on a life-long preoccupation with World War I, see Aaron Isaac Jackson's "Authoring the Century: J. R. R. Tolkien, the Great War and Modernism."

GOLLUM THE GREAT

Ironically enough it is Sam who first entertains the notion of Gollum as a hero. During a respite in the Gollum-led expedition to Mordor in Book IV of *The Two Towers*, he and Frodo engage in a reflective (and perhaps reflexive) discussion on the nature of stories and their own brief cameos in what they call the "Great Tales." As if out of a grudging politeness, the hobbits' talk shifts to include the third member of their unlikely trio, with Sam quipping: " 'I wonder if he thinks he's the hero or the villain?' 'Gollum!' he called. 'Would you like to be the hero—' " (*LotR* IV.8.713) Jarred somewhat by their guide's disappearance, Sam's joke is interrupted, and this last invitation never receives formal response.

Scholars of Tolkien's work have often, and with good reason, mined the riches of this exchange before the Stairs of Cirith Ungol, finding in it the invitation to a number of readings. It is surely meta-Tolkien of some weight; the hobbits' self-referential discourse is music to the postmodernist's ear, and, as Verlyn Flieger argues in "A Post-Modern Medievalist," it seems to presage if not directly call for later stories like John Gardner's *Grendel*, re-told from the moor-stalker's perspective (260). It is another opportunity to advance the elaborate conceit of the story's transmission, from the original Red Book of Westmarch, all the way to an Amazon near you;[6] a final tragic reminder of Gollum's agency in the upcoming betrayal of his companions;[7] or perhaps just a bit of hobbit humor that Tolkien could not bring himself to excise—just a joke.

I should like to revisit this multi-faceted gem of a passage by advancing yet another reading: Like it or not, Gollum *is* the hero, his final act a tacit acceptance to Sam's invitation (he gave no other options, after all). But his accidental heroics are enabled by the old war stories; Gollum too is a reader, or a listener, interested in the storytelling art and the way his own tale interacts with others.[8] Foremost among these tales, not only in terms of Gollum's pet interest but for the fate of Middle-earth itself, is that of the Last Alliance. Gollum's last feat of arms (or rather teeth) and unwitting sacrifice bring the Quest to fruition, but the deed echoes and is modeled in the tradition of the shadowy old tales of

---

6. For more on this, see Flieger, "Tolkien and the Idea of the Book."

7. Tolkien, in a letter to his son in 1945, mentions both "Sam's disquisition on the seamless web of story" and the near repentance of Gollum which soon follows it as personal highlights (*Letters* 110).

8. Gergely Nagy's investigation of Gollum's subjectivity and speech patterns is useful here. However, the present reading focuses more on Sméagol than Gollum, and thus calls into question the notion that he is "marginal, not in a discursive position of power," unable to "partake in interpretation" ("The 'Lost' Subject of Middle-earth" 59).

the Alliance, in which Isildur cuts the Ring from Sauron's hand. If we can accept (or at least entertain) that Gollum is our hero, then Isildur is his role model, and the Alliance tradition in whatever form—be it the *Fall of Gil-galad* in its original language or the vague oral traditions of the Stoors—his inspiration. In beginning this inquiry into the overlooked debt owed the Alliance in the War of the Ring, I will first consider Gollum's aptitude for reading generally; then, his knowledge concerning Isildur and the great war of the Second Age specifically; and finally, I will revisit Gollum's ultimate act at the Cracks of Doom.

While our own ignorance of the ways of Middle-earth is often shared with the largely provincial hobbits, we have less in common with Gollum, who has been around the block (and more than once), and is characterized by an extensive knowledge of lore. In this he functions more like an Elrond, Gandalf or Aragorn; indeed at times he is a kind of ironic surrogate for the latter two, taking over where they leave off in guiding Sam and Frodo to Mordor. Although largely consumed by his desire for the Ring, he recalls still the pleasure of exchanging stories: "We used to hear tales from the South, when Sméagol was young, long ago. O yes, we used to tell lots of tales in the evening, sitting by the banks of the Great River" (*LotR* IV.3.641). Setting aside his loathing for an instant, Sam at least recognizes a shared affinity with his unlikely tour guide: "he used to like tales himself once, by his own account" (IV.8.713). This much is reaffirmed by Gandalf, whose brief biographical sketch of Sméagol characterizes him as "inquisitive and curious minded"; his research interests are "in roots and beginnings" (I.2.53). While he had no access to the libraries of Rivendell or Gondor, the matriarch of his community was "wise in old lore, such as they had." Even if written lore is beyond his means, he can learn much from the hearing and telling of oral history. His healthy appetite for stories, coupled with advanced age and furtive travel all help to account for his accumulation of lore.

Once in possession of the Ring, Gollum's inquiries turn almost exclusively toward mischievous ends, but his "sharp" ears and aptitude for "listening secretly and peering" (I.2.57) remain well suited to gaining knowledge of all sorts. He is no mere passive receiver and gatherer of knowledge, either, but an important voice of transmission—a medium through which the stories live on. His knowledge is a prized commodity on both sides of the conflict, and he is handled ungently, if not tortured, by Gandalf and Strider as well as Sauron.

That Gollum is versed in both canon and apocrypha of the Last Alliance there can be little doubt. Tellingly, the Lord of the Rings himself only discovers "where Isildur fell" through torturing Gollum; this lowly creature surpasses even the wisest in Ring-lore (I.2.59). The breadth of his grandmother's knowledge is perhaps dubious, but the proximity of their ancestral Stoor community to the Gladden Fields, the site of Isildur's disappearance, strengthens the case. It is not then implausible that her particular area of expertise would concern the folklore surrounding this greatest of local legends. He recalls fondly

> tales out of the South [...] about the tall Men with the shining eyes, and their houses like hills of stone, and the silver crown of their King and his White Tree: wonderful tales. They built very tall towers, and one they raised was silver-white, and in it there was a stone like the Moon, and round it were great white walls. O yes, there were many tales about the Tower of the Moon. (IV.3.641)

Like a good hobbit, he shows a particularly keen interest in the bloodier tales out of the past. Guiding Frodo and Sam (expertly, it has to be said) through the Dead Marshes which have swallowed up one of the key battlegrounds of the old war, he reminisces on the memorable oral traditions of his youth:

> There was a great battle long ago, yes, so they told him when Sméagol was young, when I was young before the Precious came. It was a great battle. Tall men with long swords, and terrible Elves, and Orcses shrieking. They fought on the plain for days and months at the Black Gates. (IV.2.628)

While these musings suggest beyond doubt a familiarity with stories of Isildur and accounts of the great war, they appear fairly generic and sparse in detail. However, Gollum's knowledge of more specific evidence, including the crucial detail of Isildur's stroke, is revealed in an exchange as they draw near to Minas Morgul. "Yes" he says, confirming Frodo's recollection that it was Isildur who cut the Ring from Sauron's hand, "He has only four [fingers] on the Black Hand, but they are enough" (IV.3.641). Of all the many epithets used to name (or not name) Sauron, this one is used seldom, and only by Gollum (IV.3.638). Certainly his unrelenting lust for the Ring goes a way toward explaining this semiotic choice, equating Sauron with that part of him which wields the Ring. But it might also, in some corner of his mind, bring comfort and hope. It grounds Sauron to a more tangible corporality[9]

---

9. From Gergely Nagy's discussion of Sauron: "But the way he is represented by the other fictional authors is of course also an interpretation, and it is *theirs*, not

(than the shadow, nameless fear, or the all-seeing Eye), and though it is an undoubtedly powerful and menacing Hand, its fingers can be cut, as history and legend have it.

The nebulous and generally unsatisfactory accounts of the last combat in the Alliance render direct comparison of the Second and Third Age Ring-reavings impossible; nevertheless, some compelling similarities can be teased out. Perhaps the most reliable, if not the most detailed, account of "the last combat on the slopes of Orodruin" comes from Elrond, who describes the event from memory at the Council: "Gilgalad died, and Elendil fell, and Narsil broke beneath him; but Sauron himself was overthrown, and Isildur cut the Ring from his hand with the hilt-shard of his father's sword, and took it for his own" (II.2.243). A few yards and an age of history removed, it is Sam who bears witness to the decisive conflict of his time. At the Cracks of Doom, he sees Gollum struggling with the invisible Frodo, before his "white fangs gleamed, and then snapped as they bit" (VI.3.946). Gollum's chompers pale in comparison to a legendary sword from Telchar's forge, but their gleam might be likened to the flash of a blade. Nor is this the only instance in Tolkien's work associating the two; recall Smaug's rather blunt boast: "my teeth are swords" (*The Hobbit* [H] 12.238). The potential for reading "snapped" fangs as breaking, too, suggests an uncanny similarity, for Narsil breaks under Elendil when he falls, and it is with the hilt-shard that Isildur reaps his *weregild*. The fact that this moment is described from Sam's point of view (a lover of tales in his own right) certainly supports Gergely Nagy's theory of typological readings;[10] the storytellers and redactors may have chosen to cast the scene with a nod to the older legends. But its eerie similarity also encourages us to investigate Gollum's tactic as borrowed from the annals of military history.

Fittingly it is Frodo who offers the highest praise and most moving eulogy for Gollum: "But for him, Sam, I could not have destroyed the Ring. The Quest would have been in vain, even at the bitter end" (*LotR* VI.3.947). Thus Gandalf's prediction that Gollum would yet have a part

---

Sauron's, based on the fictional traditions of representing this being, and the experience they themselves have with his power and effects" ("A Body of Myth" 126). Nagy makes no mention of this particular nickname.

10. On the allusion to Túrin in relation to Sam's battle with Shelob: "an embryonic *typological interpretation* is presented by the narrator, with Túrin as type and Sam as antitype, proving the affinity of these texts to each other" ("Great Chain of Reading" 243). Flieger similarly discusses Frodo's maiming as "cruel and even less rewarded replication of Beren's lost hand" ("Tolkien's Mythology for England" 240).

to play comes off. And, perhaps more importantly, his ambiguous assertion made in Bag End at the beginning of the story, that the Alliance is a "chapter of ancient history which it might be good to recall," proves truer than even he could have guessed (II.2.52). And so, rather than waving a dismissive "goodbye to all that,"[11] Tolkien asserts that the shadow of the past is worth remembering.

THE FOG OF WAR

Although there is, as Gollum demonstrates, much to be gained by such remembrance, it does not come easy. Inquiry into what Gollum knows and how he acts on that information draws us inevitably to consider what others know (or think they know) and what happened in the first place—questions not readily addressed. Much of this difficulty can be attributed to a deliberate authorial move, as I have argued elsewhere,[12] for the Last Alliance is perhaps the finest exemplar of the elliptical, digressive untold tales deeply characteristic of his narratives. That they find purest expression in a war story (or lack thereof) is not surprising.

There are a number of explanations for this association, although I am unsure that Tolkien would need any other beyond its essential storytelling power: a power of suggestion, of conjuring up the illusion of depth he found so moving in ancient works, in *Beowulf* and the *Aeneid*.[13] For one, the war story needs a witness, a survivor, and this may prove difficult. To tell it "true," of course, the teller struggles with the polarized inclination to romanticize or de-romanticize (dramatized in the voices of Totta and Tída in *The Homecoming of Beorhtnoth*), whether actually present (Elrond), not present (Totta and Tída again), or unconscious (Bilbo). Even eyewitnesses may find themselves tongue-tied, unwilling or unable to tell their stories.[14] There is in fact something sublime and ineffable about the war experience that makes it particularly suited to the inexpressive, the ultimate understatement of an untold tale.

Given the practical constraints on the dissemination of old war stories, Gollum's knowledge of these events becomes all the more impressive. When measured against peers, elders, and betters, it is they who

---

11. Title of Robert Graves's 1929 autobiography, emblematic of the trench poet's disillusion.

12. See "Untold Tales: Solving a Literary Dilemma."

13. Shippey says of *Beowulf*: "the poem is absolutely full (and quite apart from the monsters) of something we know Tolkien liked very much indeed, which is, 'lost tales'" ("Tolkien's Two Views of *Beowulf*").

14. Gandalf refuses to tell his companions all of what transpires in his clash with the Balrog (III.5.501). Gimli "will not speak of" his adventures on the Paths of the Dead (V.9.874).

come up wanting. Boromir, for instance, is said to care little for ordinary lore, though he does at least cultivate a taste for "the tales of old battles" (*LotR* App.A.1056). This interest notwithstanding, the heir to the Steward of Gondor is shocked enough to interrupt Elrond upon hearing of the aftermath of the last combat with Sauron. He breaks in:

> 'So that is what became of the Ring!' he cried. 'If ever such a tale was told in the South, it has long been forgotten. I have heard of the Great Ring of him that we do not name; but we believed that it perished from the world in the ruin of his first realm. Isildur took it! That is tidings indeed.' (II.2.243)

Faramir, the younger and more widely read brother, fares somewhat better: He recalls Gandalf's frequent questions "concerning the Great Battle that was fought upon Dagorlad" and his eagerness "for stories of Isildur, though of him we had less to tell; for nothing certain was ever known among us of his end" (IV.5.671). In spite of the uncertainty, his hypothesis concerning Isildur's Bane is not far from the mark: "But this much I learned, or guessed, and I have kept it ever secret in my heart since: that Isildur took somewhat from the hand of the Unnamed, ere he went away from Gondor, never to be seen among mortal men again" (671). Sam studied lore under Bilbo, and heard snatches of his translation of *The Fall of Gil-galad*, but though there is "a lot more" to it, he can only clearly recall three short stanzas (I.11.186).

Unlike many of the other moments of narrative withholding in Tolkien's texts, the Last Alliance tradition proves essential to plot and theme. It is, we might say, Tolkien's Ur-war story; a shadowy measuring stick against which the battles of the immediate narrative are sized, its various interpretations exert substantial influence over the fate of Middle-earth. And, like many good war stories, much is left to our imaginations. While we are assured of the tale's importance at every turn, no one seems particularly keen to spill the beans.

Gandalf sets a precedent for both a lack of transparency and a preoccupation with the tale's implications. Others follow his example, so that, were it not so deadly serious, it might be seen as something of a running joke. The wizard's cautious analysis precedes any actual account of the war; he deems it a "chapter of ancient history which it might be good to recall; for there was sorrow then too, and gathering dark, but great valour, and great deeds that were not wholly vain" (I.2.52). His hedging and equivocation suggests a reluctance to offer final judgment on the events. Taken together, his Virgilian excuse of it being such a "long" tale that, were he to attempt a full telling, "we should still be sitting here when Spring had passed into Winter" and his placating (but false) assurance—"One day, perhaps, I will tell you all the tale, or you shall hear it told in full by one who knows it best"—are the Middle-earth equivalent of a teacher including uncovered material on the final exam (I.2.51, 52). The few crumbs he does let slip—"for the moment [...] all that [he] will say"—grant stirring glimpses of a bygone heroic age:

> It was Gil-galad, Elven-king and Elendil of Westernesse who overthrew Sauron, though they themselves perished in the deed; and Isildur Elendil's son cut the Ring from Sauron's hand and took it for his own. Then Sauron was vanquished and his spirit fled and was hidden for long years. (52)

The value Gandalf places (or seems to place—again, his remark is not unequivocal) on the story here likely stems from its hints of possibility and inspiring heroism, rather than any special tactical revelations. While frustrating to readers, it reflects a deep understanding of his audience within the text; Frodo is no general or politician who might benefit from lessons of diplomacy or battlefield movements. Realization of his predicament and burden overwhelm Frodo, the shadow of the past towers over his once comfortable hobbit hole, and Gandalf, by his brief summation, seeks to encourage him, to remind him that, daunting as it may seem, there is historical precedent for Sauron's defeat.

We have the distinct feeling of missing a step, as the lore-masters continue to sidestep the tale itself, focusing instead on the lessons to be gleaned from it, or on secondary concerns of propriety and timeliness. While Gandalf at least regards the story as one to remember, others are more skeptical of its value, and it is in part for this reason that hope of a detailed account is repeatedly frustrated. After the wizard's introduction, Strider takes up the desultory narrative several chapters later in "A Knife in the Dark." The ranger, too, is a respectable historian, his memory a repository of old tales—he strikes the hobbits as learned in old lore and they "wondered how old he was, and where he had learned" it all (I.11.191). Like Gandalf, he is often tight-lipped, preferring laconic suggestion to elaboration: Before hiring him on to join the expedition, Frodo's first question is, "What do you know?" to which he replies, "Too much; too many dark things" (I.10.163).

Strider strikes a delicate balance in his storytelling practices while leading the hobbits toward Rivendell. When pressed to reveal more of Gil-galad and the Alliance, he balks, arguing, "I do not think that tale should be told now with the servants of the Enemy at hand" (I.11.191). He then takes Gandalf's dubious claim one step further, dangling the tale as a reward for later, should fortune and courage hold—"If we win through to the house of Elrond, you may hear it there, told in full" (191).

Sam's visceral response to parts of the Gil-galad lay—"There was a lot more [...] all about Mordor. I didn't learn that part, it gave me the shivers" (186)—suggests that Strider's taboo is wholly justified. Yet both the hobbits and their guide at least intuit a palliative (if not greater) potential in stories. Dreading the arrival of the Riders, Aragorn "began to tell them tales to keep their minds from fear," and they, in turn, "begged" for more (190). With even the name of Mordor off limits, he settles instead on another, even more ancient tale, that of Tinúviel. Though his "brief" treatment is yet more thorough than any accounts of the Alliance, it too is preceded by a sort of prefatory assessment: "It is a fair tale, though it is sad, as are all the tales of Middle-earth, and yet it may lift up your hearts," a concise description indeed applicable to much of Tolkien's work (191). Strider's role as storyteller brings us no closer to a clear picture of the Alliance, but his provocative silence further complicates the questions of value and interpretation.

Though the hobbits do ultimately win through to the Last Homely House, a thorough account is, unfortunately (but unsurprisingly), not forthcoming from Elrond. This is all the more frustrating, as it becomes plain that the Elf lord is the referent in Gandalf's "one who knows it best." He is no mere scholar—he "remember[s] well the splendour of [the Alliance] banners" (II.2.243). Elrond was *there*, the only living witness to the event, and he reminisces before a captive audience and a dumbfounded Frodo. His terse and disappointing recapitulation begins, like the others, with commentary on what to make of the Alliance. A veteran of many wars,[15] Elrond is initially dismissive, counting it one among the "many fruitless victories" he has witnessed (243). A brief overview then follows, with his own role as witness and testimony emphasized:

> I was the herald of Gil-galad and marched with his host. I was at the Battle of Dagorlad before the Black Gate of Mordor, where we had the mastery: for the Spear of Gil-galad and the Sword of Elendil, Aiglos and Narsil, none could withstand. I beheld the last combat on the slopes of Orodruin, where Gil-galad died, and Elendil fell, and Narsil broke beneath him; but Sauron himself was overthrown, and Isildur cut the Ring from his hand with the hilt-shard of his father's sword, and took it for his own. (243)

---

15. It is noteworthy that Elrond's impressive memory, stretching deep into the First Age, seems at least partly the cause of his initially negative reading; with a fitting sense of nostalgia, both the Alliance's pageantry and results seem to pale in comparison to the memory of the War of Wrath which ends the First Age (II.2.243).

These striking but brief reminiscences are immediately followed by a partially revised assessment, more in line with Gandalf's initial reading: "Fruitless did I call the victory of the Last Alliance? Not wholly so, yet it did not achieve its end" (244). Though he remains cautious in his review, the shift is nonetheless significant. But why such a sudden change of heart? It could be that, as in Gandalf's place in Bag End, he feels that those attending the Council are in need of some encouragement, a glimmer of hope. Or perhaps his heart is stirred by calling to mind once more his first-hand recollection of "the mastery" of Gil-galad and Elendil, of the "Spear" and "Sword" that "none could withstand," and of "Sauron himself [...] overthrown" (243).

Tolkien further complicates the situation by muddying the textual waters of the Alliance tradition. Interpretation of history's successes and failures—separating great deeds from fruitless vanity—is evidently a challenge even for the Wise and naturally hinges on certain textual considerations. A difference of opinion between scholars on the war's takeaways would certainly be plausible in its own right, but when we consider the possibility that our heroes might be relying on different editions, another layer of complexity is added. Gandalf of course names the story a "chapter" but does not specify author, title, or ISBN. Given his close relationship with Elrond, and the ways in which the language of their separate accounts is similar, we might assume that Gandalf's version is at least in part derived from Elrond's. On the other hand, the wizard's extensive research outside of Rivendell—the discovery of Isildur's scroll and his other visits to Gondor's libraries come to mind—suggests that Gandalf has other sources, perhaps then accounting for the variance in their views.

An additional branch of the tale's complex textual history emerges during Strider's lectures to the hobbits on the history of Weathertop. The lay that Sam begins to chant is privileged with a proper italicized title, *The Fall of Gil-galad,* suggestive of a more formal, physical manuscript history. Sam, of course, is mistaken about the poem's origins; book-learned writer of poetry though the old hobbit may be, Strider assures him that "he did not make it up. [...] Bilbo must have translated" *The Fall* from its original, in an "ancient tongue" (I.11.186). Thus we are led to consider also the vexing issue of translation and the potential excesses, errors, flourishes, and arbitrations on the part of the translator.[16] While we glimpse only three stanzas of Bilbo's effort, the

---

16. See also Nagy's discussion of retextualization and genre in the "Great Chain of Reading" (249–50).

title alone is telling; its apparent emphasis on Gil-galad's defeat over other more positive elements (the league between Men and Elves, the victory on Dagorlad, the Ring-winning, and so on) points toward a potentially epic but surely tragic poem[17] which, given the situation on Weathertop, it might in fact be better to forget than recall. Strider offers little more to go on, but surely having been fostered in Rivendell he is likely to be familiar with Elrond's version of events. As the heir of Elendil and bearer of Narsil, the great heirloom of his house, he is deeply invested in the story and its origins, and, through his service in Rohan and Gondor and legendary periods of errantry, may have provided seasoning for his own bowl of Alliance soup, to borrow from Tolkien's Cauldron of Story metaphor in "On Fairy-stories."[18]

The subject of the story's written records is again raised at the Council, when the narrator bizarrely cites these texts as rationale not to bore us with the whole story.

> Then through all the years that followed [Elrond] traced the Ring; but since that history is elsewhere recounted, even as Elrond himself set it down in his books of lore, it is not here recalled. For it is a long tale, full of deeds great and terrible, and briefly though Elrond spoke, the sun rode up the sky, and the morning was passing ere he ceased. (II.2.242)

Elrond's "clear voice" is undoubtedly a pleasure for those at the Council, but for readers it rings the death knell for our hope of hearing the tale told in full. In spite of the story's apparently meticulous documentation, it remains out of reach.

In addition to its subtle integration and narrative significance, this apparently impassable distance is another aspect of the Alliance which sets it apart from verifiable untold tales. To more fully appreciate many of the narrator's allusions and digressions, we can, thanks in large part to the work of Christopher Tolkien, refer to a number of texts. Of the tales of Túrin or Tinúviel, the 1977 *Silmarillion* gives at least a taste, while the *History of Middle-earth* offers a heartier portion; for more on Arwen and Aragorn, we have only to turn to the Appendices. Now, if posthumous publication by a literary executor is not a perfect measure of authorial intent and vision,[19] then, by the same token, the surprising dearth of resources on the Last Alliance is not a definitive

---

17. The bleakness of Tolkien's own unfinished *Fall of Arthur* provides a useful comparison.
18. See *OFS* 44–47.
19. This authorial vision is itself ever-changing, as Tolkien certainly illustrates.

statement of Tolkien's insistence on leaving the tale forever untold. Regardless of future intent, the effect within the individual text remains the same, and what little recourse we do have beyond the immediate narrative only strengthens it.

The Appendices avail us little in an attempt to more deeply engage with the Alliance tale; the timeline offered in "The Tale of Years" makes Elrond's account appear elaborate in comparison. The last three entries for the Second Age in Appendix B read as follows:

> 3434 The host of the Alliance crosses the Misty Mountains. Battle of Dagorlad and defeat of Sauron. Siege of Barad-dûr begins.
> 3440 Anárion slain.
> 3441 Sauron overthrown by Elendil and Gil-galad, who perish. Isildur takes the One Ring. Sauron passes away and the Ringwraiths go into the shadows. The Second Age ends. (1084)

The revelation that the Siege of Barad-dûr took place over seven years seems only to exacerbate frustrations about knowing so little. Questions linger: Why does the fighting shift to the slopes of Mount Doom? How does it become almost a duel between the Alliance leaders and Sauron? What was the nature of Gil-galad's wound?[20] Does Isildur strike the decisive blow or merely despoil Sauron's body in the aftermath?

For this last query we may refer to Isildur's words in the published *Silmarillion* for an indication: "This I will have as weregild for my father's death, and my brother's. Was it not I that dealt the enemy his death-blow?" (295). Yet without a straightforward account of the battle to corroborate his statement, it remains somewhat suspect; we could certainly point to examples of bent truths, equivocations, and outright lies told in service of laying claim to the Ring (both Bilbo and Gollum are notably guilty of this).

While I do not wish to stray too far from the focus on the Alliance's treatment, dissemination, and impact within the covers of *The Lord of the Ring*, "The Disaster of the Gladden Fields" material included in the posthumous *Unfinished Tales* casts further light on Tolkien's continued preoccupation with the great war of the Second Age, one which seems not to have diminished over time: Christopher Tolkien's introduction calls "Gladden Fields" a " 'late' narrative [...] it belongs in the final period of my father's writing on Middle-earth" (*UT* 10). The first thing to notice is

---

20. They are teased further, but not answered. A note on "The Disaster of the Gladden Fields" further hints at a duel with its description of the "last challenge upon Orodruin" (*UT* 280n11). Isildur's scroll makes a chilling reference to the heat of Sauron's hand and Gil-galad's demise (II.2.253).

that the war itself is once again skirted: the account begins, agonizingly, "After the fall of Sauron [...]"(*UT* 271). The final section of this chapter is titled "The sources of the legend of Isildur's death," chiefly concerned with the story's transmission: establishing "eye-witnesses," naming the "escaped" survivors, and weighing hearsay against "surmise...well-founded" (*UT* 275-6). Its conclusion bears all the hallmarks of Tolkien's preferred literary device. On discovery of the Elendilmir in the treasure hoard of Orthanc, the narrator muses:

> Why then, though an age had passed, were there no traces of his bones? Had Saruman found them, and scorned them—burned them with dishonour in one of his furnaces? If that were so, it was a shameful deed; but not his worst. (*UT* 277)

It seems fitting that the last word on Isildur would be one of ambiguity and mystery, his missing bones almost a reflection of the great lacunae which elide so much of the heroic chapter of the Alliance.

This aftermath scenario of the Gladden Fields narrative is one which Tolkien often exploited. His "Homecoming of Beorhtnoth" picks up with the sun set and the blood barely congealed from the Battle of Maldon; "The Passage of the Marshes" sees the hobbits traverse the bog which covers the hallowed Battle Plain. His camera, unlike Peter Jackson's, seems often to pull away just as the swords are joined: Bilbo passes out at the beginning of The Battle of Five Armies, likewise Pippin at the Black Gate, and with them goes our narrative presence.

Fragments Shored against Ruin

In spite of obstacles, the allure of piecing together the old stories, the desire to uncover origins, remains ever present. Ultimately, however, the hierarchy Tolkien establishes for primary world tales in "On Fairy-stories" goes for the Last Alliance as well; it is the story's use now which matters, more even than its definition or roots. The threads of the Alliance tale may ultimately be impossible to untangle—soup and bones inseparable—but its applications are unmistakable; Gollum is not the only character whose acts reflect the story's lasting relevance.

It is in a way fitting that Strider first encounters Gollum near the Dead Marshes, the haunting but fertile landscape of story which proves so important to them both. Not only does the Alliance tale assert its significance in Strider's tactical decisions and travel plans during the War of the Ring, it also exerts a more fantastic influence in his ability to summon the very specters of characters on the fringes of the tale. In his haste to reach Gondor under siege, Strider treads a path and enlists the help of a people kept alive only in the old stories. The opportunity to travel "the swiftest way" east and muster such formidable support rely on

Aragorn's application of Alliance lore. It is Elrohir who jogs his memory, bringing counsel from Elrond, "*If thou art in haste, remember the Paths of the Dead*" (V.2.775). The advice is not to take, seek, tread, or walk—but first *remember*. Théoden's skepticism—"If there be in truth such paths," he doubts—likely speaks for many, but Aragorn can take solace in his education (V.2.779). He demonstrates this deep well of knowledge in reciting the words of Malbeth the Seer and then kindly summarizing the story of the oathbreakers for his friends:

> But the oath that they broke was to fight against Sauron, and they must fight therefore, if they are to fulfil it. For at Erech there stands yet a black stone that was brought, it was said, from Númenor by Isildur; and it was set upon a hill, and upon it the King of the Mountain swore allegiance to him in the beginning of the realm of Gondor. But when Sauron returned and grew in might again, Isildur summoned the Men of the Mountains to fulfil their oath, and they would not: for they had worshipped Sauron in the Dark Years.
>
> Then Isildur said to their king: 'Thou shalt be the last king. And if the West prove mightier than thy Black Master, this curse I lay upon thee and thy folk: to rest never until your oath is fulfilled. For this war will last through years uncounted, and you shall be summoned once again ere the end.' (V.2.782)

The summoning of the Dead emphatically asserts the relevance, the redemptive potential—even the real presence—of the past.

Elendil's sword, Narsil, or what is left of it, serves as another link to the past—a tangible reminder passed down with the same care as the stories themselves. If the songs have withered somewhat, as Totta would say, still the sword has been revered ("Homecoming" 85). We learn through Elrond at the Council that Isildur's squire, Ohtar, escaped the orc ambush that killed Isildur and delivered the shards to safety. This escape at all costs is recounted in "The Disaster of the Gladden Fields" as Isildur's last command to Ohtar, suggestive of the significance he placed on the heirloom, in spite of its disrepair. Aragorn honors this commitment even to the point of encumbrance, evidently carrying the broken sword with him on his many perilous journeys: "Not much use, is it Sam?" he asks, brandishing it before the hobbits in Bree (I.10.171). Such reverence seems only just, not out of respect for its original wielder alone, but in recognition of the blade's impact in the wars against Sauron. The fact that it merits mention in Elrond's account of the Alliance victory, where words are at a premium, is telling. Unlike most swords, its value is not wholly diminished when broken, as the hilt-shard alone is enough to strike the legendary blow. Like the stories themselves, the broken sword represents a latent possibility.

The sword's eventual re-forging as Andúril brings this latent potential to fruition. If Elrond's negative assessment of the Alliance legacy is based in part on its unfinished business—the dark tower broken but its foundations remained—the opposite is also true. The broken sword can be salvaged, repaired, made whole and perhaps even stronger than before. Hard lessons of history, inspiring lessons, these can be preserved, shared, learned from, and put to use. Aragorn demonstrates the same reverence for the restored heirloom, declaring it against his will to "put aside [his] sword" even among allies in Edoras (III.6.510). The blade's long and secret safekeeping begins to pay dividends in its effect on both friends and foes. At the battle of Helm's Deep, sight of the weapon serves as a morale boost and rallying cries proclaim its pedigree: "Andúril goes to war. The Blade that was Broken shines again!" (III.7.534). Aragorn's swordsmanship aside, mere sight of it appears to have the opposite effect on his enemies—"the terror of the sword for a while held back the enemy" (537). Orcs and Uruks, it would appear, are not wholly ignorant of heroic legend either.

Exploitation of the sword's legend indeed proves every bit as critical as manipulation of the sword itself. Aragorn says as much when he judges his contest with Sauron via the *palantír* "a struggle somewhat grimmer […] than the battle of the Hornburg" (V.2.780). Somewhat like the War of the Last Alliance, this episode too is narrated only afterward, vaguely, and in brief, as Aragorn reflects on the experience to Gimli and Legolas:

> It was a bitter struggle, and the weariness is slow to pass. I spoke no word to him, and in the end I wrenched the Stone to my own will. That alone he will find hard to endure. And he beheld me. Yes, Master Gimli, he saw me, but in other guise than you see me here. If that will aid him, then I have done ill. But I do not think so. To know that I lived and walked the earth was a blow to his heart, I deem; for he knew it not till now. The eyes in Orthanc did not see through the armor of Théoden; but Sauron has not forgotten Isildur and the sword of Elendil. Now in the very hour of his great designs the heir of Isildur and the Sword are revealed; for I showed the blade re-forged to him. He is not so mighty yet that he is above fear; nay, doubt ever gnaws him. (780)

Aragorn relies on the suggestive power of the Isildur legend, knowing that the Enemy with whom he communicates would be intimidated by the sight of Elendil's heir and the "Sword that robbed him of his treasure re-made" (V.9.879). It is a tactical feint, made to provoke a panicked response, because, as Aragorn reasons, "the hasty stroke goes oft astray" (V.2.780). While it is no guarantee of ultimate success, this gamble is largely dependent on the mystique of the Alliance story.

In 1944, during the composition of *The Lord of the Rings* but long before there could be any hope of a second edition Foreword in which to vent frustrations about short-term historical memory, Tolkien wrote to his son Christopher expressing his dismay over what "seems almost a world wide mental disease." Christopher was training in the Royal Air Force at the time, and the frustration was perhaps brought into focus by his son's involvement in this most recent installment of the "War of the Machines," as he called it. "Even if people have ever heard the legends (which is getting rarer)," he wrote, "they have no inkling of their portent. How could a maker of motorbikes name his product Ixion cycles! Ixion, who was bound for ever in hell on a perpetually revolving wheel!" (*Letters* 88).

This sensitivity to the legends and language of the past—in private correspondence as well as in fiction—has been one of the major impediments to Tolkien's acceptance in literary discussions. "I was always embarrassed by the words sacred, glorious and sacrifice and the expression in vain," confessed Lieutenant Frederic Henry in Ernest Hemingway's 1929 novel *A Farewell to Arms* (184), neatly summing up the aura of disillusionment now taken for granted in the literature of the First World War. Hugh Brogan saw manifest in this remark the incredible linguistic gulf between Tolkien and his contemporaries. Yet, if we return again to Gandalf's words about the need to remember, that "there was sorrow then too, and gathering dark, but great valour, and great deeds that were not wholly vain," we find in Gandalf's hedging a strange half-echo of Henry's words and an opportunity for further discussion. The whole truth of the Last Alliance remains untold, cannot be captured, known or recorded by any one tale or any one teller. Nevertheless, as Gollum, Strider, and others demonstrate, much depends on our attempts to remember, understand, and interpret the shadows of the past.

Works Cited

Brogan, Hugh. "Tolkien's Great War." *Children and Their Books: A Celebration of the Work of Iona and Peter Opie*. Eds. Gillian Avery and Julia Briggs. Oxford: Clarendon, 1989. 351–67. Print.

Croft, Janet Brennan. *War and the Works of J. R. R. Tolkien*. Westport: Praeger, 2004. Print. Contributions to the Study of Science Fiction and Fantasy 106.

Flieger, Verlyn. "A Cautionary Tale: Tolkien's Mythology for England." *Green Suns and Faerie: Essays on J. R. R. Tolkien*. Kent: Kent State UP, 2012. 237–41. Print.

—. "A Post-Modern Medievalist." *Green Suns and Faerie: Essays on J. R. R. Tolkien*. Kent: Kent State UP, 2012. 251–61. Print.

—. "Tolkien and the Idea of the Book." *Green Suns and Faerie: Essays on J. R. R. Tolkien*. Kent: Kent State UP, 2012. 41–53. Print.

Hallam, Andrew. "Thresholds to Middle-earth: Allegories of Reading, Allegories for Knowledge and Transformation." *Mythlore* 30.1/2 (#115/116) (2011): 23–42. Print.

Hemingway, Ernest. *A Farewell to Arms*. 1929. New York: Scribner's, 1957. Print.

Jackson, Aaron Isaac. "Authoring the Century: J. R. R. Tolkien, the Great War and Modernism." *English* 59 (#224) (2010): 44–69. Print.

Lewis, C. S. "The Dethronement of Power." *Tolkien and the Critics*. Ed. Neil D. Isaacs and Rose A. Zimbardo. Notre Dame: U of Notre Dame Press, 1968. 12–16. Print.

Nagy, Gergely. "The Great Chain of Reading: (Inter-)Textual Relations and the Technique of Mythopoesis in the Túrin Story." *Tolkien the Medievalist*. Ed. Jane Chance. New York: Routledge, 2003. 239–58. Print.

—. "The 'Lost' Subject of Middle-earth: The Constitution of the Subject in the Figure of Gollum in *The Lord of the Rings*." *Tolkien Studies* 3 (2006): 57–79. Print.

—. "A Body of Myth." *The Body in Tolkien's Legendarium*. Ed. Christopher Vaccaro. Jefferson: McFarland, 2013. 119–32. Print.

O'Brien, Tim. "How to Tell a True War Story." *The Things They Carried*. Broadway Books. New York, 1990. 67–85. Print.

Shippey, Tom. *J. R. R. Tolkien: Author of the Century*. Boston: Houghton Mifflin, 2001.

—. "Tolkien as a Post-war Writer." *Proceedings of the J. R. R. Tolkien Centenary Conference, 1992*. Eds. Reynolds, Patricia and Glen H. GoodKnight. Altadena: Milton Keynes Tolkien Society, 1992. 84–93. Print.

—. "Tolkien's Two Views of Beowulf." *Lord of the Rings Fanatics Plaza*. 25 July 2010. Web. 9 June 2014.

Tolkien, J. R. R. *The Hobbit*. Boston: Houghton Mifflin, 1966. Print.

—. "The Homecoming of Beorhtnoth Beorhthelm's Son." *Poems and Stories*. Houghton Mifflin, 1994. 77–109. Print.

—. *The Letters of J. R. R. Tolkien*. Ed. Humphrey Carpenter. 2nd ed. Boston: Houghton Mifflin, 2000. Print.

—. *The Lord of the Rings*. 50th anniv. ed. Boston: Houghton Mifflin, 2004. Print.

—. *The Silmarillion*. Ed. Christopher Tolkien. 2nd ed. Boston: Houghton Mifflin, 2001. Print.

—. *Tolkien On Fairy-stories*. Ed. Verlyn Flieger and Douglas Anderson. London: Harper Collins, 2008. Print.

—. *Unfinished Tales*. Ed. Christopher Tolkien. Boston: Houghton Mifflin, 1980. Print.

Beyond the Circles of this World:
The Great War, Time, History, and Eternity in the Fantasy of J. R. R. Tolkien and C. S. Lewis

SHANDI STEVENSON

THE EMERGENCE OF MODERN FANTASY from the cauldron of World War I has recently begun to attract the scholarly attention it undoubtedly merits. While the obvious influence of the war on the great works of mainstream modernism has often been explored, its influence on the development of modern fantasy has only in recent decades begun to receive serious analysis. Too often dismissed simply as an escapist or nostalgic response to the upheaval of the war years and the dreamlike horrors of the Western Front, the fantasy of the first half of the twentieth century is in fact a complex, multifaceted response both to the war itself and to the cultural landscape of the postwar world. As such, these influential works deserve and repay examination not only as psychological and artistic artifacts, but also as serious and sophisticated articulations of an alternative response to the issues of their time.

Of the pillars of western culture shaken by the Great War, perhaps the most irreparably damaged was the predominantly optimistic vision of history that had emerged during the modern period as a hybrid of Judeo-Christian and Enlightenment thought. As John Gray points out, not only "political religions" such as Jacobinism, anarchism, and communism, but also the belief of the western liberal tradition in "progress as a slow incremental struggle," functioned not simply as political theories but also as myths to meet the human need for meaning (2). Thus, the political philosophies that dominated the two centuries leading up to the war shared the basic assumption that human history was progressing, however gradually, along a timeline that led from chaos to order, from barbarism to civilization, from poverty and war to plenty and peace. The scale, the destructiveness, and the far-reaching effects of the Great War cast doubt on this narrative. Henry James called the war a plunge into darkness that "gives away the whole long age during which we have supposed the world to be [...] gradually bettering," and wrote of "the treacherous years" which had created hopes now revealed as meaningless (qtd. in Fussell 8).

In the aftermath of the war, several responses to the destruction of this narrative emerged. These ranged from attempts to shore up the liberal paradigm of peaceful human progress, to political projects that sought to create new historical frameworks in its place, to the rejection of any overarching meaning in history. The last was rare in political theory, but dominated the important literature of the postwar period. In the flowering of literary genius that blossomed in the 1920s, such writers as Joyce, Lawrence, Woolf, Kafka, Elliot, Hemingway, and Fitzgerald explored what they considered the characteristic twentieth-century experience of disillusionment, disorientation, and ambiguity. The undermining and obfuscation of moral values, the erosion of direction and meaning in history, and the loss of confidence in human progress characterize the great literature of the period. The distortion of the experience of time itself and the pervasive rootlessness and ambiguity caused by losing the sense of participation in a larger narrative are both highlighted by stream of consciousness, the unreliable narrator, and other experimental techniques developed by the great writers of this period.

In contrast, the emerging genre of fantasy was characterized by its defense—or more accurately its assumption—of a teleological historical narrative and a concomitant sense of moral clarity and transcendent hope. Yet this vision was emphatically not the same one embodied in the confident prewar liberal optimism. In particular, the Christian fantasy of J. R. R. Tolkien and C. S. Lewis responded to the postwar disorientation by seeking to recreate a cohesive vision of history, but one without the horizontal, linear orientation and the confident clarity that had characterized Enlightenment political theory and its descendants. Instead, their view of history was clouded with uncertainty and tinged with loss and sorrow, even while sustained by a sense of hope and ultimate meaning that had largely withdrawn from mainstream literature. This vision was anchored in an ultimately hopeful Christian view of history, but it was also permeated by the elegiac quality of loss and fragility characteristic of the early European culture both Tolkien and Lewis loved and studied—a sense of nostalgia and vulnerability which, for them, the Great War reawakened rather than created.

Both Tolkien and Lewis served in World War I. Tolkien, who later wrote that he began to create his mythology "in grimy canteens […] or by candle light in bell-tents, even some down in dugouts under shell fire" (*Letters* 78), attributed to his wartime experiences the early development of his mythology, and the "quicken[ing] to full life" of his love for fairy stories (qtd. in *Music 16)*. "You couldn't write," he explained years later, "You'd be crouching down among flies and filth" (qtd. in Garth 186), but undoubtedly the "anxieties of war," in Garth's words, "stoked [his] creative fires" (187), and at a mental and emotional level

Tolkien must have laid the foundations for much of his future life and work during this period of loss, disruption, and danger—of "the collapse of all my world," as he would later describe the outbreak of war (*Letters* 393).

C. S. Lewis's writing seems less directly influenced by his wartime experiences. They must be presumed to have illuminated several brief references in Lewis's work (*HHB* 197–99; *LB* 148–49; *THS* 384–85), but do not seem to have played the catalytic role in the development of his imagined worlds that Tolkien's did in his. Perhaps this was in part because the philosophical foundations of Lewis's fantasy would rest in the Christian worldview he would not adopt for many years after the war. Also, Lewis's emotional response to the war seems to have been very different from and far less fully articulated than Tolkien's. John Bremer, in his insightful *C. S. Lewis, Poetry, and the Great War*, points out that there is an emotionally detached quality to much of the young Lewis's writing from the wartime and postwar period (210–11). Certainly the difference in the emotional resonance of Lewis's diary from the postwar years and of his later work is striking. If Tolkien in some sense explored and processed his wartime experiences through his fiction, as many have argued, Lewis's very different temperament may have simply found memories of the war best left as far behind as possible. "My memories of the last war haunted my dreams for years," Lewis wrote on the threshold of the Second World War. "The flesh is weak and selfish, and I think death would be much better than to live through another war" (qtd. in Arnott 74).

But to focus too much on the degree to which specific experiences of war did or did not influence specific aspects of Tolkien's and Lewis's fantasy is to miss the greater significance of cultural and generational disruption and loss. War as a defining experience in the life of an individual author is one thing; the Great War as a defining experience in the life of a generation—shaping and permeating the ideology, culture, language and imagery of a generation of British writers—is another. While the first is interesting to consider in the cases of Tolkien and Lewis, the second is more significant to our understanding of two writers self-consciously engaged in creating a fictional world that intersects with and responds to the real one.

This paper will examine how Tolkien's and Lewis's fantasies relate morality to time, meaning to history, and hope to eternity through a historical paradigm rooted both in the Christian tradition and in the older traditions of Northern Europe. To construct this paradigm, both

Tolkien and Lewis reach back in the western tradition beyond the narrative of progress established by the Enlightenment, and incorporate both classical and pre-Christian European influences into their ultimately Christian understanding of history and time. By doing so, they reject the radical novelty many of their contemporaries saw in the war and its aftermath, positioning the upheavals of their own time in a much larger historical and metaphysical context.

It is important to acknowledge, before proceeding, that the fantasies of Tolkien and Lewis are very different, with many important contrasts of emphasis and approach. Much could be and has been written on the differences between their works. However, for the purposes of this discussion the similarities between their works are more important. The focus of this analysis is on the vision of history, time, and eternity Tolkien and Lewis shared; for this reason, the parallels between their fantasy worlds, rather than the contrasts, will be emphasized.

THE DOOM OF CHOICE: MORALITY AND TIME

In much postwar literature, the corruption or at least the evolution of morals is a major theme. The erosion of old values is portrayed not merely as coincidental with the war, but as the result of the war's betrayal and destruction of timeworn ideals. It was as if the Great War was a test which such ideals as courage, honor, chivalry, loyalty, and sacrifice had failed to pass—as if they were empty shells that had crumbled at the fiery touch of war, revealing hollow centers. A trusting obedience to unbending moral imperatives, in the face of their obvious corruption or futility, was seen by many as a cause not only of the outbreak of the war, but of its horrifying length and destructiveness. Thus, all the great words had been "cancelled" for the war generation, as D. H. Lawrence writes: "[A]ll these great, dynamic words were half dead now, and dying from day to day" (63). The contrast with the prewar generation, to whom, in Fussell's words, "terms like *heroism* and *decency* and *nobility* conveyed meanings that were entirely secure" (136), is striking. Now that the "old men's lies" (Pound 190) for which so many died had been exposed and undermined by the harsh realities of the war, the prewar ideals were seen, not merely as outgrown values that were nostalgically regretted, but as treacherous and tainted instruments of deception. They could be spoken of only with "irony and pity," in Hemingway's wry phrase (113–14). Most important literature of the twenties and thirties proceeds on this assumption, either exploring the bankruptcy of the old moral codes or embracing the opportunity to discover new values to illuminate new realities. In contrast, much of both the popular appeal and the critical disdain that greeted the emergence of fantasy literature stemmed from its distinctive insistence on a degree of moral certainty, which had come to seem both arrogant and naïve to mainstream literature. As we shall see, however, Tolkien's and Lewis's moral vision is far from a black and white caricature. Instead, it is the organic outgrowth of a serious and nuanced view of time, history, and the nature of the universe.

When Éomer of Rohan meets Aragorn, Legolas, and Gimli early in *The Two Towers*, his words might well speak for the postwar generation's moral disorientation. "The world is all grown strange," Éomer says. "How shall a man judge what to do in such times?" Aragorn, who says he brings Éomer "the doom of choice," captures Tolkien's alternative vision in his reply: "As he ever has judged. [...] Good and ill have not changed since yesteryear; nor are they one thing among Elves and Dwarves and another among Men" (*Lord of the Rings* [*LotR*] III.2.434, 438).

Tolkien's fiction thus reverses the epistemological order characteristic of modernist literature. While the modernists paint a world in which individuals struggle to find a moral and psychological foothold amid shifting and conflicting values, seeking to understand their own selfhood in order to work outward to an understanding of the world, Tolkien portrays a world in which moral absolutes can—and must—be known and trusted before the psychological data beloved of modernist writers can be understood. In Tolkien's world, characters such as Éomer, Aragorn, or Faramir may be uncertain or conflicted about which duties and loyalties should govern specific decisions, but they never doubt that moral certainties exist and are both accessible and relevant to them. Indeed, a recurring theme in Tolkien's fiction is that moral imperatives are often the only things that can be certainly known. The practicability, the dangers, and the probable outcome of many choices his characters face are impossible to predict. The one certainty that can be trusted is that what is right must be attempted, however impossible it may seem, or however great the sacrifices it will cost. "We must walk open-eyed into that trap, with courage, but small hope for ourselves," says Gandalf to the captains of Gondor. "For [...] it may well prove that we ourselves shall perish utterly in a black battle far from the living lands; so that even if Barad-dûr be thrown down, we shall not live to see a new age. But this, I deem, is our duty" (V.9.880).

So far, Tolkien's moral outlook may seem a Victorian one, surviving precariously into a world it no longer fit. But it is important to note that Tolkien's vision is not, in fact, the simplistic one sometimes associated with the centuries between the Enlightenment and the First World

War—one in which good is rewarded and evil punished with reassuring promptness. The Enlightenment, and especially its more radical embodiment in the French Revolution, had stressed the idea that moral values could be recognized—and should be embraced—because they were beneficial to society. Values that were seen as tainted with theological or superstitious associations were increasingly suspect, and those of obvious utility in combatting poverty, ignorance, and war and advancing wealth, education, and tolerance were seen as the "real" moral absolutes. The value of virtues and ideals might be ascertained by assessing their tendency to advance human progress and happiness. Thus the staggering impact of the war on the old moral codes and the sense of betrayal that followed in its wake. How could the values of honor and sacrifice still be trusted after the appalling destruction of human lives and societies that had been perpetrated in their name? And what could the old virtues still offer the world, transformed as it was almost beyond recognition?

Tolkien's response to this view rests on his belief that the foundation of and justification for moral absolutes is to be sought outside, rather than inside, human history. Not time but eternity would ultimately determine the "right" and the "wrong," he believed. It was not so much the old ideals of honor and virtue, then, as their hypocritical subordination to the utilitarian advantages of human society that had been unmasked by the horrors of the war. In Tolkien's world, its utility or success does not demonstrate the rightness or value of an idea. Conversely, the likelihood—even the seeming certainty—of failure is no excuse for refusal to uphold the moral code his characters embrace. This code comprises not only the more obvious martial virtues of heroism, honor, loyalty, and sacrifice, but also such "bourgeois" ideals as courtesy, compassion, kindness, and humility—as when Faramir defends gentleness to his stern father (*LotR* V.4.812–13). For Tolkien, the fact that the old values had been coopted by the machine of war and tainted by its mud and blood did not mean they were either outdated or corrupted. Rather, it proved that honor and sacrifice viewed as means to utilitarian ends were not really honor and sacrifice at all. Such ideals, for Tolkien, transcended social, economic, and political goals, rather than simply being the quasi-Marxist machinery used to achieve those goals.

C. S. Lewis's fiction reflects a similar view that the experience of moral ambiguity is peripheral or accidental in human life, rather than central or essential, and that it often stems from lack of courage, from distraction, or from self-deception. In *The Silver Chair,* Lewis portrays the descent from the ethereal realm of Aslan's country into that of everyday life as one in which moral absolutes do not disappear, or cease to exist, but become harder to recognize—even as, Lewis might have argued, they had become harder to recognize in postwar culture. Aslan, having given Jill Pole the "signs" that will guide her on her quest, warns her:

> Here on the mountain I have spoken to you clearly: I will not often do so down in Narnia. Here on the mountain the air is clear and your mind is clear; as you drop down into Narnia, the air will thicken. Take great care that it does not confuse your mind. [...] [T]he signs which you have learned here will not look at all as you expect them to look, when you meet them there. That is why it is so important to know them by heart and pay no attention to appearances. (25–26)

In *That Hideous Strength* [*THS*], Lewis further elucidates his view that modern life can conceal and distort moral realities. The ambitious Mark Studdock, gradually being drawn into the web of evil concealed behind the scientific and benevolent façade of the sinister National Institute for Coordinated Experiments, agrees to write a fraudulent article for use as propaganda. "This was the first thing Mark had been asked to do which he himself, before he did it, clearly knew to be criminal," writes Lewis.

> But the moment of his consent almost escaped his notice; certainly, there was no struggle, no sense of turning a corner. There may have been a time in the world's history when such moments fully revealed their gravity, with witches prophesying on a blasted heath or visible Rubicons to be crossed. But, for him, it all slipped past in a chatter of laughter, of that intimate laughter between fellow professionals, which of all earthly powers is strongest to make men do very bad things before they are, individually, very bad men. (145)

Again and again, Mark's refusal to recognize the significance or even the existence of the moments at which he is making moral choices proves his undoing. "The moment of Mark's decision had passed by him without his noticing it," writes Lewis of another unacknowledged crisis in Mark's moral deterioration (*THS* 242). In contrast, the first step in Mark's eventual redemption is the enforced recognition of the moments of decision he has refused to acknowledge: "He was aware, without even having to think of it, that it was he himself—nothing else in the whole universe—that had chosen the dust and broken bottles" (*THS* 288). Only the possibility of death, like that faced by the soldiers of Lewis's generation, reveals to Mark the moral choices he is making.

Lewis's work often explores the idea that such moments of moral clarity interrupt the normal experience of time and divide life into "before" and "after" periods. Interestingly, Fussell notes that a similar idea—the sharp division that interrupts and distorts the flow of time and bifurcates experience and memory—is characteristic of the discourse of the Western Front (80–81). It is as if Lewis recreates through fiction, in a moral sense, what the war created in a psychological sense through its violence and strangeness. "This moment contains all moments," says an angel in *The Great Divorce* to a soul whose eternal destiny is being decided (176). The bifurcation and refraction of time experienced by many under the stress of war is thus echoed in Lewis's fantasy, and becomes a metaphor for the moral choices human beings make without noticing them in the misleading ordinariness of everyday life. As Screwtape explains to his demonic apprentice, the disruption and danger of war can illuminate aspects of reality which ordinary life allows human beings to refuse to recognize (28). Like Tolkien, then, Lewis rejects a moral vision that is merely nostalgic longing for the undisturbed routines of prewar life. For both, fantasy fiction can resemble war in clarifying the real issues of human life, and in forcing human beings to consider things from the perspective of eternity rather than time.

ERE THAT PURPOSE IS MADE KNOWN: THE TELEOLOGY OF HISTORY

History can imbue a culture with a sense of purpose and outline the trajectory along which it believes itself to be travelling. John Gray writes, "The dominant western myths have been historical narratives." After discussing the competing narratives that dominated the twentieth century, Gray notes, "In all these accounts history is told as a coherent narrative, and nothing is more threatening than the idea that it is a meandering flux without purpose or direction." What Gray calls "the belief that history has an underlying plot" has been predominant in western culture (204).

With the shift toward secularization characteristic of the Enlightenment and perhaps best typified in the French Revolution, the telos of history had become resolutely earthly and horizontal, as opposed to transcendent and vertical, in orientation. While the Judeo-Christian view had been that human history is continually influenced, periodically interrupted, and ultimately ended by divine intervention, the eighteenth- and nineteenth-century secular version of an unfolding historical narrative was that history itself, whether through the heroic actions of Carlislian great men or through the mindless processes of Darwinian or Marxist determinism, tended ineluctably toward a largely positive conclusion. At some time in the future, this narrative ran, problems such as poverty, war, injustice, disease, ignorance, superstition, and crime would be eliminated, or confined to the fringes of human society.

It was this sense of nearness to a (largely desirable) "end" of history that was wounded to the death in the Great War. "The break with the past that took place with the onset of the Great War birthed a new conception of time and a new distrust in linear progress" (Simonson and Gilete 230). The western vision of historical progress was one of the great casualties of the "war to end war," and no small part of the disorientation typical of much postwar art and literature arises from this sense of having lost touch with the overarching narrative that had so long given context and meaning to events. Much late Victorian and Edwardian literature, such as Hardy's, Swinburne's, and Housman's, partakes of and anticipates this anxiety and uncertainty; the dividing line between prewar and postwar literature is a very blurred one. But the war greatly intensified the feeling of having lost the plot of history. Much literature characteristic of the postwar period is notable for its novel approach to time and history. Such important writers as Joyce, Woolf, and Kafka explore not only a world in which history, in the sense of a coherent organizing narrative, but also time, in the sense of an individual's personal experience of the flow of minutes, hours, and days, had become elusive, misleading and contingent. This literature looks to the future with a sense of disorientation and to the past with a deep sense of disillusionment and betrayal. Thus, the collective trauma of the war recast the whole western literary experience of history. As Fussell notes, "the Great War was perhaps the last to be conceived as taking place within a seamless, purposeful 'history' involving a coherent stream of time running from past through present to future" (21). After the war, a feeling that history had no discernible plot was strongly present in literature and in culture.

This cultural disillusionment and disorientation were, to some extent, rooted in the individual wartime experience of being caught up in a vast, mechanized, unintelligible process that denied any sense of purposive action to its participants. Eric Leed points out that the experience of the Great War was one of a breakdown in teleology. "The rationality, purposes, and intentions of the war were increasingly mysterious to combatants" (131). And later: "[F]amiliarity with combat distanced the individual from the purpose and the significance of the project in which he was engaged" (132).

Much postwar literature thus embodies a double disorientation—that induced by the loss of prewar confidence and clarity, and that induced by the experience of war itself. Many authors suggested that the experience of participating in a chaotic, incomprehensible series of events beyond one's control—the experience that defined the war for so many of its participants—revealed a truth about the nature of life and time which prewar society had concealed. Many of the great modernist masterpieces explore the same fragmented, impressionistic experience of life that the war had introduced to many of its participants. These works suggest that the chaotic and directionless universe revealed by the war was the reality, and the apparent order and purpose of peacetime life was the illusion.

Both Tolkien and Lewis, in contrast, reject the postwar assumption that the experience of chaos and meaninglessness in daily life reveals chaos and meaninglessness at the heart of reality. But they also reject the bold optimism of the prewar era, with its confidence about the progress and improvement of human society—a confidence that tended to see the worst in the past, the best in the future, and each major event as fitting easily into its place in the spectrum. Lewis and Tolkien instead portray worlds in which the ultimate, metaphysical teleology is magnificently certain, but in which individuals, generations, and nations often find themselves struggling through the dark, uncertain of the part they are playing. The ultimate guarantee of victory, in the transcendent Christian sense, is there, but so is the likelihood of danger, uncertainty, loss, and tragedy between us and that distant goal. As Tolkien points out in the famous conversation between Sam and Frodo on the nature of stories, it's impossible for the characters in a story to know what kind of story it is: "[T]hat's the way of a real tale. [...] You may know, or guess, what kind of a tale it is, happy-ending or sad-ending, but the people in it don't know. And you don't want them to" (*LotR* IV.8.712).

Thus, in *The Lord of the Rings*, the characters frequently grapple with doubt about their individual destinies, but they seldom doubt their participation in a larger story. Indeed, the only characters who do lose faith in that larger story are those who fall into despair and evil—e.g. Saruman and Denethor. The others cling to and act upon their conviction that it is enough to see the next step, and that the ultimate righting of wrongs and unravelling of riddles lies beyond their ken. "[I]t is not our part to master all the tides of the world," says Gandalf to the Captains of the West, "but to do what is in us for the succor of those years wherein we are set, uprooting the evil in the fields that we know, so that those who live after may have clean earth to till. What weather they shall have is not ours to rule" (*LotR* V.9.879). Gandalf also tells Frodo that many wish they had lived in different days, "[b]ut that is not for them to decide. All we have to decide is what to do with the time that is given us" (*LotR* I.2.51).

Similarly, in *The Silmarillion*, even the Valar, the godlike or angelic figures in Tolkien's mythology, do not know how the universe will unfold, "[F]or to none but himself has Ilúvatar [God] revealed all that he has in store" (18). In Tolkien's beautiful metaphor, the universe is the embodiment of the music the Valar sing before Ilúvatar; each contributes his or her own theme, but none knows how they will all be combined in the great music. The Valar always encourage elves and men to trust, as they do, in the purposes of Ilúvatar, and to act on the understanding they have of their own destinies and duties. They are always portrayed as knowing enough to act upon, and as aware that they are playing a small part in a story much larger then themselves.

Tolkien thus adopts a precisely opposite approach to that characteristic of the major modernist writers. They generally emphasize the need for an individual to discover—or create—an intelligible teleology for his or her own life, while suggesting that a more ultimate and universal direction and purpose is irrecoverable. Tolkien, in contrast, suggests that certainty and clarity about the events of one's own life, or about one's own destiny, may often need to be sacrificed entirely, but that a larger purpose and significance in the universe can still be trusted.

Lewis's fantasy echoes a similar view. In *The Horse and His Boy* [*HHB*], Shasta has a transformative encounter with Aslan on his journey into Narnia. Aslan explains to Shasta how all the events he has perceived as misfortunes have had their place in a larger story, but when Shasta asks a question about his friend's life, Aslan replies "I tell no one any story but his own" (176). Similarly, in *Prince Caspian,* Aslan tells Lucy that no one is ever told what *would* have happened, but that her part is find out what *will* happen if she carries out his instructions (149). In the interplanetary trilogy, even Lewis's angelic Eldils, like Tolkien's Valar, are ignorant of many aspects not only of the future, but also of the present and the past (*THS* 233–34).

Thus, the Christian teleology inherent in the history of Tolkien's and Lewis's fantasy worlds is not the overtly linear sociopolitical narrative so obviously overturned by the Great War. Instead, it is a narrative only the beginning and end points of which can be clearly seen or certainly known, and during the unfolding of which darkness and loss will often intrude. This is important because the willingness to face uncertainty, change, loss and sacrifice is central to the message of Christian fantasy, and especially to Tolkien's work. One of Tolkien's greatest achievements is that he so powerfully captures longing and regret for a world swept irretrievably away by the tides of time and loss—what

Verlyn Flieger terms "a deep nostalgia for what has passed and is passing" (*Time* 111)—yet at the same time he explores the responsibility to accept change and loss. Most of his major characters must face a choice between letting go of a great good, and clinging to it at all costs even when its sacrifice has become a clear duty. The impulse to possess and control, however innocent its beginnings, must always ultimately be surrendered in Tolkien's world. The Elves of Rivendell and Lothlórien must sacrifice the beauty they have created over the centuries in order to destroy the One Ring and to preserve the freedom of a Middle-earth they will not inhabit. Frodo must give up the Shire to save it for others. In *The Silmarillion,* Eärendil sacrifices his own home in Middle-Earth to gain the aid of the Valar for those who still live there, and Lúthien gives up her immortal life to marry the mortal man Beren and aid him in his war against Morgoth.

As Flieger's insightful analysis demonstrates, Tolkien's genius lies in his ability to make real for his readers the hard choices and painful losses his characters face. His evocation of the intense nostalgia of the Elves and of the beauties of their fading world is all too powerful, drawing the reader, too, into a desire to hold tight, instead of let go—arguably the central temptation in Tolkien's world. In a sense, Flieger points out, the longing to preserve Lothlórien unchanged becomes the temptation of the reader, as it is of the Elves. Like the Ring of Power itself, the demand for power over time, for power to refuse to let something go, is ultimately wrong and destructive. "[T]he Elvish weakness," writes Tolkien in a letter, was "naturally to regret the past, and to become unwilling to face change [...]. Hence they fell in a measure to Sauron's deceits: they desired some 'power' over things as they are [...] to make their particular will to preservation effective: to arrest change, and keep things always fresh and fair" (*Letters* 236). In another letter Tolkien writes, "The chief power (of all the rings alike) was the prevention or slowing of *decay* (i.e. change viewed as a regrettable thing), the preservation of what is desired or loved, or its semblance [...] also they enhanced the natural powers of a possessor—thus approaching 'magic', a motive easily corruptible into evil, a lust for domination" (152). The ultimate contrast to this is the commitment of the Elves of both Rivendell and Lothlórien to sacrificing all that is good and beautiful in their own lands to remove a great evil from the world. They, like Frodo, make the ultimate sacrifice so that good they cannot enjoy may endure—as Frodo says, "It must often be so [...] when things are in danger: some one has to give them up, lose them, so that others may keep them" (*LotR* VI.9.1029). Perhaps Tolkien was thinking of his own close friends and the millions of others who died to protect their homes during the Great War; almost certainly he was also exploring the theme of the sacrifice of Christ which runs through so much of his work.

"And so there is a concealed sting in Lórien's beauty," writes Flieger:

> Its timelessness is not the unspoiled perfection it seems. Rather, that very perfection is its flaw. It is a cautionary picture, closer in kind to the Ring than we'd like to think, shown to us in all its beauty to test if we can let it go.
> *The Lord of the Rings* is, among many other things, a story about the ability to let go. (*Time* 112)

"Now I have taken my worst wound in this parting," says Gimli as the Fellowship leaves Lothlórien. Legolas replies, "[S]uch is the way of it: to find and lose, as it seems to those whose boat is on the running stream. But I count you blessed, Gimli son of Glóin: for your loss you suffer of your own free will, and you might have chosen otherwise" (*LotR* II.8.378). Like the Elves of Lórien he has learned to love, Gimli has made the choice to ride the river of time toward his destiny, leaving behind what he longs to possess forever. Loyalty and duty, not confidence about the end of history, must direct Tolkien's characters in their choices.

Lewis makes a strikingly similar point in *Perelandra*, even employing the same water imagery. In the unfallen paradise of Perelandra, the one thing forbidden to its inhabitants is to pass the night on the Fixed Land, rather than on one of the planet's floating islands. They do not know the reason for this prohibition, but after Ransom, the man from Earth, defeats the enemy who tempts the Queen to disobey the injunction, she tells him she has come to understand the law. "[W]hy should I desire the Fixed except to make sure—to be able on one day to command where I should be the next and what should happen to me? It was to reject the wave—to draw my hands out of Maledil's, to say to Him, 'Not thus, but thus'—to put in our own power what times should roll toward us…" (179).

In Lewis's most complex treatment of the same theme, Orual in *Till We Have Faces* poisons her love for her sister Psyche by clinging desperately to their shared past, and refusing to relinquish Psyche to the future and the changes it brings. It is only when her life has been embittered by loss, disappointment, and rage against the cruelty of the gods that Orual realizes her resentful longing for something that was hers to enjoy for a while, not to keep forever, has become a kind of possessiveness or desire for control that is destructive and entirely inappropriate to a mortal being. Orual's agony at the loss of her sister echoes Denethor's fierce lament in *The Return of the King:*

> I would have things as they were in all the days of my life [...] and in the days of my longfathers before me [...] But if doom denies this to me, then I will have *naught*—neither life diminished, nor love halved, nor honor abated. (V.7.854)

Thus, while a palpable nostalgia and a permeating elegiac quality are one of the most characteristic and most compelling aspects of Tolkien's and Lewis's fantasy, both in fact reject a purely escapist refusal to confront the realities of the postwar world. Tolkien wrote to his son in later life that those born between the Golden and Diamond Jubilees of Queen Victoria had experienced the loss of one certainty after another: "Both sense or imaginations of security have been progressively stripped away from us. Now we find ourselves nakedly confronting the will of God, as concerns ourselves and our position in Time" (*Letters* 393). In their own way, both Tolkien and Lewis bring at least as much open-eyed courage to the confrontation of a changed world and a new century as the most innovative modernist writers. Much that was good and precious in human life has indeed been lost, and will yet be lost, and the certainty the prewar west had once felt entitled to will never be regained. The redeeming purpose that can justify the injustices and suffering of human history can come only from outside history itself. And as the Valar tell the men of doomed Númenor in *The Silmarillion*, "[M]any ages of men unborn may pass ere that purpose is made known" (265).

HE DOES NOT PLANT TO NO PURPOSE: THE NATURE OF HOPE

In her classic account of the beginnings of World War I, *The Guns of August*, Barbara Tuchman writes:

> Men could not sustain a war of such magnitude and pain without hope [...]. [T]he mirage of a better world glimmered beyond the shell-pitted wastes and leafless stumps that had once been green fields and waving poplars. Nothing less could give dignity or sense [...] when every spring there was still no end in sight, only the hope that out of it all some good would accrue to mankind kept men [...] fighting. (489)

When this promise failed to materialize, the loss of the hope that had guided so many generations was staggering. While many politicians continued to pursue the hope of a better world, the literary voices of the postwar period mourned the loss not only of some specific hope, but of hope itself. Vera Brittain writes in her compelling memoir that "the early ideals of the War were all shattered, trampled into the mud which covered the bodies of those with whom I had shared them. What was the use of hypocritically seeking out exalted consolations for death, when I knew [...] there were none?" And later: "I knew now that death was the end and that I was quite alone. There was no hereafter, no Easter morning, no meeting again; I walked in a darkness, a dumbness, a silence, which no beloved voice would penetrate, no fond hope illumine" (446).

The distinctive achievement of Tolkien's and Lewis's fantasy is that it neither echoes prewar hopes for political and cultural progress, nor does it embrace the underlying despair which characterizes so much postwar literature. For Tolkien and Lewis, it is from outside of time that hope must ultimately come. As long as we are confined by time and by "the circles of the world," in Tolkien's phrase (*LotR* App.A.1063), victory must be fragile and loss inescapable—"within Time the monsters would win," as Tolkien writes ("*Beowulf*" 22). Indeed, W.A. Senior notes in a discussion of Tolkien's work, "The issue of loss [...] may in fact be deemed central to modern fantasy" (180), even as it is, in a very different form, to mainstream modernist fiction. As Tolkien writes in *The Silmarillion*, "If [the story] has passed from the high and the beautiful to darkness and ruin, that was of old the fate of Arda [Earth] Marred" (255). Just as Beowulf triumphs over two monsters but finally falls before the dragon, just so, Tolkien believed, all human achievements must be doomed within time, and redeemed from futility only by eternity. In the words of the dying Aragorn, "In sorrow we must go, but not in despair. Behold! We are not bound forever to the circles of the world, and beyond them is more than memory" (*LotR* App.A.1063).

Lewis, too, came to believe that "progress" in the robust Enlightenment sense was illusory. He held this belief, however, not with the embittered cynicism of many writers of his generation, but with the Christian belief that hope would ultimately triumph over despair—and that, therefore, the choices and achievements of earthly life had significance. Lewis wrote to Tolkien: "All my philosophy of history hangs upon a sentence of your own, 'Deeds were done which were not *wholly* in vain'" (qtd. in Duriez 167). The quotation is from Gandalf's words to Frodo in the *Fellowship of the Ring*. Later, Galadriel tells Frodo in a similar vein that she and Celeborn have "fought the long defeat" for countless centuries, cherishing and defending Lothlórien as long as they can although they know they must lose it in the end (*LotR* II.7.357). "Not wholly vain" and "fighting the long defeat"—these phrases fittingly sum up the vision of history Tolkien's and Lewis's mythologies capture. It rejected both opposing extremes which emerged in the wake of the war to end wars—both the optimistic commitment to a future utopia, and the despairing repudiation of any hope for a better world. In doing so, it returned to a much older literary strain, echoing the melancholy flavor of early European literature—a literature in which the courage to hang on when all hope seems lost can be rewarded by what Tolkien famously termed "eucatastrophe"— the breaking in of hope from outside. Gollum may step in to ensure the destruction of the Ring when Frodo has done all he could; the Rohirrim may arrive to forestall the collapse of Gondor's defense just when all seems lost; the Valar may return to deliver the people of Middle-Earth from an enemy too great for them to face. For Tolkien and Lewis, the incarnation, death, and resurrection of Christ are the ultimate realization of this image of help arriving from outside when all hope is lost—of "Joy, Joy beyond the walls of the world, poignant as grief" ("OFS"153).

Thus, while noted for their nostalgic identification with a vanishing western tradition, both Tolkien and Lewis rejected the view that the twentieth century was a uniquely terrible period, or that things were worse than ever before. Instead, both took a longer view. "The times we live in are, as you say, grave: whether 'graver than all others in history' I do not know," writes Lewis in a letter. "But the evil that is closest always seems to be the most serious: for as with the eye so with the heart, it is a matter of one's own perspective" (*Latin* 73). Tolkien remembered that, as a young man mourning the outbreak of war, he was assured by his Roman Catholic professor that the war was not an anomaly; rather, the prolonged peace had been an anomaly. The destruction and chaos of the war were a return to the norm of a fallen world (*Letters* 393). "A small knowledge of history depresses one with the sense of the everlasting mass and weight of human iniquity," writes Tolkien to his son. "Old, old, dreary, endless repetitive unchanging incurable wickedness […]. And at the same time one knows that there is always good" (*Letters* 80).

Perhaps their familiarity with and love for the twilit atmosphere of the medieval European north made this view of history easier for Tolkien and Lewis to embrace. Tolkien was self-consciously engaged in rediscovering the neglected literary tradition of the European north and transmitting its influence. Lewis, too, deeply loved this literature, which he describes in his autobiography as awakening his early aesthetic and spiritual impulses: "[I]nstantly I was uplifted into huge regions of northern sky, I desired with almost sickening intensity something never to be described (except that it is cold, spacious, severe, pale, and remote)"

(*Surprised* 17). He later writes of "Pure 'Northernness'," which he describes as "a vision of huge, clear spaces hanging above the Atlantic in the endless twilight of Northern summer, remoteness, severity" (73).

It might be argued that the mental and emotional world opened by the First World War—a world in which defeat is often ultimate but victory is always temporary, a world against which the west had striven to brace the door for nearly a millennium—was less disorienting to the imaginations of Tolkien and Lewis because they nourished an affection for the dim, chill world of the medieval European north, in which the nightfall of earthly joys was inevitable. They had inhabited in imagination the world of the epic poem "The Battle of Maldon," in which a doomed hero declares "Mind must be the firmer, heart the more fierce, /courage the greater, as our strength diminishes" (309–10).

The Christian doctrine of the fall of man is fundamental to this vision of history. Something has been lost that can never be recovered without divine intervention, and a taint has affected even the best achievements of mankind. As Tolkien writes in a poignant letter to his son:

> Genesis is separated by we do not know how many sad exiled generations from the Fall, but certainly there was an Eden on this very unhappy earth. We all long for it, and we are constantly glimpsing it: our whole nature at its best and least corrupted, its gentlest and most humane, is still soaked with the sense of 'exile'. (*Letters* 109–10)

Thus, the Christian view of history that shaped the fantasy of Tolkien and Lewis embraced the sense of exile, loss, and rootlessness explored by so many postwar writers—that feeling, so characteristic of a whole literary generation, of having been cut off by a terrible fissure from an irrecoverable past. But in embracing it, the Christian view transformed it. In a distinctive twist that echoes the earliest Anglo-Saxon literature, hope is allied to despair, transforming it into a reservoir of endurance and resolve. From this resolve, and from a trust in the ultimate intrusion of divine purpose, comes the hope that flavors the fantasy worlds of Tolkien and Lewis.

As Michael Drout points out, Tolkien explores the differences between two sharply contrasting types of "despair." One type is the mortal sin of Catholic theology. This is a self-centered despair that springs from a frustrated desire for control or possession—the ultimate outcome of a refusal to accept the loss or change of something, however originally good, when its sacrifice is demanded by time and duty. It is the impulse to reject any hope for the world that does not include one's own safety or one's own chief desire. It is, for Tolkien, ultimately a form of idolatry—the placing of some originally good joy or desire above all else, until it is corrupted into a mockery of itself. The fatal despair of Denethor is typical: "If doom denies me this," he cries after describing his longing for Gondor to survive unchanged, "Then I will have *naught!*" (*LotR* V.7.854) When his own self-centered hope fails him, Denethor refuses any other.

In contrast, Tolkien's work also depicts a type of "despair" that is creative because it is unselfish and sacrificial. It enables characters to endure till the bitter end because they have given up hope for their personal safety or happiness—they are freed to commit themselves completely to the task they face. The despair of Galadriel over the inevitable doom of Lothlórien enables her to desire nothing but the defeat of Sauron. The despair of Éomer and the Rohirrim after the death of their king enables them to rescue Minas Tirith. The despair of Sam and Frodo carries them to Mount Doom with no hope of coming back alive.

C. S. Lewis's work explores a similar idea. Screwtape urges his apprentice, at the height of the Second World War, to get his "patient's" mind "off the simple rule ('I've got to stay here and do so-and-so')," until "what was intended to be a total commitment to duty becomes honeycombed all through with little unconscious reservations. By building up a series of imagery expedients [...] you may produce, at that level of his will which he is not aware of, a determination that the worst *shall not* come to the worst" (101). Later, after an air raid, Screwtape urges his point again: "[T]he thing to avoid is the total commitment. Whatever he *says*, let his inner resolution be not to bear whatever comes to him, but to bear it 'for a reasonable period'—and let the reasonable period be shorter than the trial is likely to last" (103). For Lewis as for Tolkien, the "total commitment" that can spring from despair of one's own safety is the source of real hope—the hope that comes from outside time, the hope that gives a redeeming significance to heroism and sacrifice.

Thus, while many postwar writers are suspicious and resentful of the ethic of personal sacrifice that had consumed so many lives, both Tolkien and Lewis reaffirm a commitment to the ideal of sacrifice, and base much of the element of hope in their fantasy upon it. On the imperiled planet of Perelandra, Ransom realizes that he alone is appointed to face the horrific task of fighting the devil-possessed "Un-Man" Weston in order to save the innocent, unfallen people of Perelandra. "Perhaps he would fight and win, perhaps not even be badly mauled," Ransom thinks, searching for some hope for himself. "But no faintest hint of a guarantee in that direction came to him from the darkness. The future was black as the night itself" (125). Despair of his own safety gives Ransom the courage and endurance to face the ultimate sacrifice and to save a world he can never inhabit.

In *The Return of the King*, Sam, too, finds hope at the end of despair when, looking up into the night sky over Mordor, he sees "a white star twinkle for a while" through the clouds:

> The beauty of it smote his heart, as he looked up out of the forsaken land, and hope returned to him. [...] [T]he thought pierced him that in the end the Shadow was only a small and passing thing: there was light and high beauty for ever beyond its reach. [...] Now, for a moment, his own fate [...] ceased to trouble him. (VI.2.922)

Stars are a compelling image of hope in Tolkien's work, and provide us with a unique insight into his understanding of hope. Paul Fussell writes in his compelling account of trench life during the Great War that "[i]t was the sight of the sky, almost alone, that had the power to persuade a man that he was not already lost in a common grave" (51). From the bottom of a trench stars could be seen with special clarity, Fussell notes; as in Tolkien's world, the stars alone remain bright, beautiful, and unstained, far above the ruin and decay of the earth.

Stars as an image of hope suggest a remote and impersonal quality, a kind of hope that offers no suggestion of personal safety. A similar image appears when Frodo and Sam find the mutilated statue of the king at the Crossroads as they journey into Mordor. The broken head of the statue is entwined with flowers "like small white stars," prompting Frodo to say "They cannot conquer for ever" (*LotR* IV.7.702). Again, the two hobbits do not derive any hope of safety for themselves, but they do find hope that one day justice will be upheld, and goodness will survive.

In *The Lion, the Witch and the Wardrobe*, Aslan explains to Susan and Lucy that the ultimate hope of Narnia, his own return to life after his execution by the White Witch, is located not within time, but in the "magic deeper still" from "the darkness before Time began" (178–79). In *The Silmarillion*, the Valar urge the men of Númenor: "Hope rather that in the end even the least of your desires shall have fruit. The love of Arda was set in your hearts by Ilúvatar, and he does not plant to no purpose" (265). Thus, the distinctive response of Tolkien's and Lewis's fantasy to the blighted hopes of the postwar world is to reject both the hopes of Woodrow Wilson and other optimists that a radiant new world could arise from the wreckage of the old, but also the almost nihilistic despair that flavors the work of many important modernists. Like the stars high above the trenches, the hope Tolkien and Lewis capture in their imagined worlds is remote, and offers no guarantee against loss and tragedy. Yet, like the stars, it is indestructible, and rendered more precious by the horrors of the war.

WORKS CITED

"Battle of Maldon." *The Anglo-Saxon World: An Anthology.* Ed. and trans. Kevin Crossley-Holland. Oxford: Oxford UP, 1984. 11–18. Print.

Arnott, Anne. *The Secret Country of C. S. Lewis.* Grand Rapids: Eerdmans, 1975. Print.

Bremer, John. *C. S. Lewis, Poetry, and the Great War 1914–1918.* Plymouth: Lexington Books, 2012. Print.

Brittain, Vera. *Testament of Youth.* 1933. New York: Seaview Books, 1970. Print.

Drout, Michael. "Tolkien and the West: Reclaiming Europe's Lost Literary Tradition." Prince Frederick: Recorded Books, 2012. CD.

Duriez, Colin. *Tolkien and C. S. Lewis: The Gift of Friendship.* Mahwah: HiddenSpring, 2003. Print.

Flieger, Verlyn. *Interrupted Music: The Making of Tolkien's Mythology.* Kent: Kent State UP, 2005. Print.

—. *A Question of Time: J. R. R. Tolkien's Road to Faerie.* Kent: Kent State U, 1997. Print.

Fussell, Paul. *The Great War and Modern Memory.* Oxford: Oxford UP, 1975. Print.

Garth, John. *Tolkien and the Great War: The Threshold of Middle Earth.* Boston: Houghton Mifflin, 2003. Print.

Gray, John. *Black Mass: Apocalyptic Religion and the Death of Utopia.* New York: Farrar, 2007. Print.

Hemingway, Ernest. *The Sun Also Rises.* New York: Scribner's, 1926. Print.

Lawrence, D. H. *Lady Chatterley's Lover.* New York: New American Library, 1959. Print.

Leed, Eric. *No Man's Land: Combat and Identity in World War I.* Cambridge: Cambridge UP, 1979.

Lewis, C. S. *The Great Divorce. The Best of C. S. Lewis: 5 Books in 1.* New York: The Iverson-Normal Associates, 1969. 110–95. Print.

—. *The Horse and His Boy.* New York: HarperTrophy, 1954. Print.

—. *Last Battle.* New York: HarperTrophy, 1956. Print.

—. *The Lion, the Witch and the Wardrobe.* New York: HarperTrophy, 1950. Print.

—. *Perelandra.* New York: Scribner, 1944. Print.

—. *Prince Caspian.* 1951. New York: HarperTrophy, 1954. Print.

—. *The Screwtape Letters. The Best of C. S. Lewis: 5 Books in 1.* New York: The Iverson-Normal Associates, 1969. 1–107. Print.

—. *The Silver Chair.* New York: HarperTrophy, 1953. Print.

—. *Surprised by Joy.* New York: Harcourt, 1955. Print.

—. *That Hideous Strength.* New York: Macmillan, 1946. Print.

—. *Till We Have Faces.* New York: Harcourt, 1956. Print.

Lewis, C. S., and Don Giovanni Calabria. *The Latin Letters of C. S. Lewis.* Ed. and trans. Martin Moynihan. South Bend: St. Augustine's Press, 1998. Print.

Pound, Ezra. "Hugh Selwyn Mauberly." *Personæ: The Collected Poems of Ezra Pound.* New York: New Directions Books: 1926. 185–91. Print.

Senior, W. A. "Loss Eternal in J. R. R. Tolkien's Middle-earth." *J. R. R. Tolkien and His Literary Resonances.* Ed. George Clark and Daniel Timmons. Westport: Greenwood Press, 2000. 173–82. Print.

Simonson, Martin and Raúl Montero Gilete. "*The Chronicles of Narnia* and *The Lord of the Rings*: Two Imaginative Responses to the Great War." *Doors in the Air: C. S. Lewis and the Imaginative World.* Ed. Anna Slack. Vitoria: Portal Editions, 2010. 229–50. Print.

Tolkien, J. R. R. "Beowulf: The Monsters and the Critics." *The Monsters and the Critics and Other Essays*. Ed. Christopher Tolkien. Boston: Houghton Mifflin, 1984. 5–48. Print.
—. *Letters of J. R. R. Tolkien*. Ed. Humphrey Carpenter and Christopher Tolkien. Boston: Houghton Mifflin, 2000. Print.
—. "On Fairy-stories." *The Monsters and the Critics and Other Essays*. Ed. Christopher Tolkien. Boston: Houghton Mifflin, 1984. 109–61. Print.
—. *The Lord of the Rings*. Boston. Houghton Mifflin, 1987. Print.
—. *The Silmarillion*. 2nd ed. Boston. Houghton Mifflin, 2001. Print.
Tuchman, Barbara. *The Guns of August*. New York: Dell, 1962. Print.

Silent Wounds

Andrew Krokstrom

WORLD WAR I left an indelible mark on all involved in its execution. None of the individuals or nations who experienced its terror could ever claim that they were the same again. Geopolitical power shifted greatly and set the stage for the war's sequel to occur two decades later. Those lucky enough to escape from the war's death grip were likely to be scarred both physically and emotionally, although those emotional effects were not appreciated in the manner that they should have been. Physical effects were seen as badges of courage. They indicated certain closeness to the enemy and participation in combat that was lionized by popular culture. Unfortunately, emotional damage that the war inflicted upon a soldier was not seen in the same way, despite the fact that it came about due to the exact same circumstances. Psychological damage was seen as a defect, brought about through either personal weakness or a lack of proper training and leadership. These factors led many men to discount the effect that the war had on them emotionally and to diminish any feelings or experiences they had that indicated the contrary. C. S. Lewis was one of those men who refused to acknowledge that the war had any effect on him later in life. Lewis spent his time in the war as an infantry officer, commanding troops in the trenches near Arras, France. His unit was on the receiving end of nearly constant shelling, resulting in a terror that made men feel helpless. Lewis, decades later, told a story of encountering a trembling field mouse in the midst of one of those terrible shellings. He recalled how neither of them made any attempt to avoid the other, as the cacophony of noise around them had debased them to the point of equals. "[A]nd a poor shivering mouse it was, as I was a poor shivering man" (*Surprised by Joy* [*SJ*] 189). But despite having countless experiences like this, and some more horrible still, Lewis refused to acknowledge that the war had any effect on him. Many similar descriptions of the primal nature of war exist in the writings of other Great War veterans. Erich Maria Remarque writes in *All Quiet on the Western Front* how "At the sound of the first droning of the shells we rush back, in one part of our being, a thousand years. By the animal instinct that is awakened in us we are led and protected. It is not conscious; it is far quicker, much more sure, less fallible, than consciousness" (176). Despite their similarities, each author took a different approach to the effect the Great War had on them after its completion. This question of the effect the war had on

Lewis is important because it can help us gain an insight into the mind of one of the twentieth century's greatest scholars and apologists. In its answer lie the roots of many a *Narnia* battle scene, and perhaps the basis for the spiritual growth of a Christian who looms quite large in many a theological debate. Additionally the question will provide further insight into the mind of a man whose voice consoled a warring nation years after his own service, and was a towering figure on which Britain relied upon for strength in the face of unrelenting attack.

In this paper, I will seek to prove that the war affected Lewis in several ways. I will first look into his thoughts before the war for insights into his attitudes and preconceived notions about the Great War and military service in general. Secondly, I will examine his war record in detail, in order to better understand the experiences that he had while in the Army, then I will delve into his reactions to the war and its effect on him, both in times proximal to and distant from his exit from the service. The inconsistencies in these reactions will also be discussed to help us decipher his true feelings on the war's impact on him, despite his constant diminishment of that trauma. Finally, the societal forces that impacted veterans in the decades following the war will be scrutinized. This will help us to discover Lewis's motives in hiding the lasting effects that the war had on him emotionally. My goal is to prove that the war affected Lewis mentally and emotionally years after its completion, how the war haunted his dreams and affected his career path later in life, and how his reaction to this supposedly non-traumatic event echoed two tragedies he endured early in his life—his time at Malvern, and the death of his mother—which he repeatedly acknowledged as being formative in his development. The Great War affected Lewis long after its completion; whether he was aware of this is up to debate, but what is not debatable is that the war did have an impact on him for decades to come.

A Looming War

Lewis never desired to fight in the Great War; as a bookish teen he did not feel a particular duty to fight, and he knew a military lifestyle did not exactly fit his personality. Lewis was uniquely suited for an intellectual life, and any involvement in the war would only delay what he had been preparing for his entire life. This inclination toward an intellectual vocation was recognized early on by Lewis's Professor William Kirkpatrick who remarked in a letter to Lewis's father that "Jack was born with the literary temperament and we have to face that fact with all that it implies" (Jacobs 59). As his biographer Alan Jacobs points out, this was more than a compliment to Lewis's intellectual abilities; it was a realization that he lacked the ability to successfully do virtually anything else (59). From this distant position the War would seem to only get in the way of Lewis's future success; this was realized by Lewis and all those around him.[1]

Lewis frequently wrote about avoiding conscription into the war, either looking for excuses to avoid that fate, or creating rosy interpretations of news from the front that would give him hope. Four times between May 1915 and June 1916 Lewis writes about his desire to avoid conscription into the war, revisiting the topic that must have been at the forefront of his mind. In a letter to his father in May of 1915 Lewis discusses his hope that "Either [...] the war may be over before I am eighteen, or that conscription may not come into force before I have volunteered" (*Letters* 1.125). One must not read his willingness to volunteer as an indication of a desire to fight. Lewis merely viewed volunteering as a better option than conscription. He feared the reactions of his future peers in the Army when they discovered he was forced to join a cause for which they had chosen to fight on their own accord. He consistently searched for an excuse to be exempt from the fighting, writing to his father in February of 1916 when the first set of conscriptions was taking place: "Are you [sure] that it applies to those who are under age, and who are also Irish?" (*Letters* 1.163).

Lewis takes no proactive steps to join the military and even sidesteps some overtures that possibly could have eased his wartime experience. Writing to his father in July of 1917, Lewis mentions a letter he received from an old Malvern friend inquiring about Lewis's intentions regarding the war. Lewis remarks that he will write the friend when his plans are settled but more importantly he states how he "should like to have a friend with [him] in the Army, but it his hardly worth while making any special provisions for [the matter]" (*Letters* 1.209). This passage provides an interesting perspective; Lewis is not merely rebuffing a friend because it's not worth the trouble, as he claims. Although serving together for a long period of time was unlikely, due to their social status the two might at least have been able arrange to go through the

---

1. This feeling did not prove to be totally accurate, as the war directly enabled Lewis's entry into Maudlin College. He had previously failed the entrance exam prior to the war due to his deficiencies in arithmetic, but as a returning solider was exempt from retaking the test. Lewis's life would have been quite different had the War not helped him gain entry into the College from which he would launch his prolific career.

Officer Training Course together.[2] Lewis was probably afraid that any inquiry about serving with a friend would result in his early entry into the war. At this time he was still reluctant to join, as he indicated many times in his personal correspondence.

But his entrance into the war eventually became inevitable. To make the best of his experience, he decided to avoid conscription, and on April 1916 he enrolled in Oxford's Officer Training Course in preparation for a commission into the British Army (Jacobs 66).

WAR RECORD

After enrolling, it was more than a month before his formal military training would commence (Jacobs 66), and during this period Lewis lived a duty-free life, spending the majority of his time reading and socializing with his new peers. Lewis came to marvel at the wealth of information he now had at his fingertips at the libraries of Oxford; "Among thousands of interesting books it is impossible to settle down to one" (*Letters* 1.308). This time of leisure was short-lived, though, and he started his actual service in the battalion of cadets in June of that year (Jacobs 66).

Entry into the Corps of Cadets drastically changed the daily routine that Lewis so eagerly enjoyed in that lazy month prior to his service. Gone were the days of swimming in the river and reading late into the night. His day was strictly regimented, starting with a 7 A.M. parade that lasted until breakfast at 8:45.[3] He then read and worked until a 1 P.M. lunch and another parade from 2 P.M. to 4 P.M. (*Letters* 1.310). This signaled the end of his military obligations for the day, and he spent the rest of the day reading and studying. Lewis did not like this life as well as the one he enjoyed previously, but in his letters he does not describe it as an awful affair. To his father he says that "It is on the whole a very pleasant life"; but Lewis had a tendency to whitewash much of the information he gave to his father, especially when it came to his military obligations (*Letters* 1.310).[4] This routine did not last for particularly long, as he was commissioned a 2nd Lieutenant in September of

---

2. Lewis's father pulled governmental strings on multiple occasions to attempt to ease Lewis's time in service, and there is reason to think he could have done the same in this instance.

3. Parade refers to a Formation of Cadets. Typically this involved activities such as calisthenics, marches, field craft training, and becoming more familiar with weapons systems.

4. This will become most apparent during their conflict on which unit Lewis is to serve in (his father secretly worked to get him into an artillery unit that he felt was safer than the infantry) and after Lewis's injury later on in the War.

1917 and was sent to the front on November 28th, hours before his 19th birthday (Gilchrist, "2nd Lieutenant Lewis" ["2nd Lt."] 47).[5]

Lewis's unit was sent to the front line trenches just outside of Arras, France ("2nd Lt." 64). He was billeted in the town itself, not the "Wilderness Camp" that lay just outside of the town limits (Gilchrist, "Continuing Research on 2nd Lieutenant Lewis" ["Continuing"] 48). This meant that he was in comparably comfortable living quarters during this initial period. He describes the area to his father as "a certain rather battered town" and later proclaims that Arras was "the jaws of a sacked village, stark and grim" (qtd. in "2nd Lt." 64). This desolation was due to the area's strategic import and foreshadows the future violence that Lewis experienced while in the area. Lewis's unit spent a good amount of time in this area and saw light action during their stay. They soon were forced to move, though as they had to counter a bloody German offensive at Mount Bernenchon ("2nd Lt." 65). The particular trench the unit stayed in was known as Pudding Trench, an area that was particularly strategic because of its vast views of the surrounding area ("Continuing" 49). From this vantage point, Lewis's unit could witness the carnage unfold as the Germans slowly advanced to their position. Lewis's unit was heavily attacked while they stayed in this position, losing eighty-three men in the short time that they were there ("Continuing" 49). This unit's location should be especially emphasized because it drastically changed Lewis's experience of the war. From this position he could see the cavalcade of death as the Germans advanced. The constant nature of the combat he experienced was particularly draining; Remarque makes note of this in *All Quiet on the Western Front*: "We lie under the network of arching shells and live in a suspense of uncertainty. [...] If a shot comes, we can duck, that is all; we neither know nor can determine where it will fall" (101). The toll this constant uncertainty about one's ability to survive had on a soldier must have been great. Lewis experienced this violence on a very personal level as many in his unit died as a result of the heavy shelling they received. It is important to remember this when one later examines Lewis's dismissive statements about the war.

The violence of the war soon personally affected Lewis, shaking him out of his innocence about the war. During a British counterattack near Mount Bernenchon Lewis was injured by a British shell that fell

---

5. Interestingly enough, Lewis's memory differs from the official regimental diary; Lewis recorded that he arrived to the trenches on his birthday, not the evening before.

short of its German target and struck his unit. The same shell killed Sergeant Ayers, the man Lewis most relied on to help lead his unit. Lewis was hit in three places by shrapnel from the shell; "in the back of the left hand, on the left leg from behind and just above the knee, and in the left side under the arm pit" (*Letters* 1.364). The wound under the armpit broke several of his ribs and left him unable to sleep on his side for several weeks, an inconvenience that irritated him endlessly. This injury effectively ended Lewis's active service in the army; he spent the remainder of the war in the hospital.

RESPONDING TO HORROR

Lewis personally witnessed and experienced vast amounts of trauma during his short time at the front. He saw the deaths of thousands from afar, and witnessed the deaths of friends up close. It is hard to imagine this kind of carnage would not affect a person later in life, but Lewis constantly diminished these experiences and insisted they did not affect his development as an intellectual or as an author, as it did with other Great War veterans. While the truth of his claims is dubious and has many incongruities, we will here focus on Lewis's statements regarding the war, and state for the record how Lewis described the war and its effects on him.

This determination to not be affected by the war manifested itself several years before he was ever to see its horrors. He writes that in the period of fighting prior to his commission "I put the war on one side to a degree which some will think shameful and some incredible" (qtd. in Jacobs 61). Lewis totally occupied himself with his studies and did not indulge in any news from the front. Not only was he determined not to let the looming war affect him prior to his entrance, but he was even set on living a post-war life free from any of burden that the war might place on him. He wrote how he "will die in your wars if need be, but till then I shall live my own life" (qtd. in Jacobs 61). His fixation on living a life free from the burdens of war seems a bit odd, but it does give insights into the origins of his desire to not be affected by the Great War.

During the war Lewis rarely made mention of its dreadfulness, or its effect on him. His correspondence tended to gloss over the revolting nature of the front, although he was slightly more willing to acknowledge some of the psychological damage that the war inflicted upon him. In his letters to his father, Lewis tended to be more reserved in his descriptions of the war, while in his letters to his friend Arthur Greeves he was a bit more liberal in what he revealed about his own feelings. Many tend to be more intimate with their friends than their families, but Lewis took this concept to the extreme. In a letter to Arthur, Lewis insists, "When I see you face to face I will tell you any war impressions quite freely *at your request*—and not otherwise" (*Letters* 1.361). Lewis chose to hide behind the notion that others would not want to hear of a subject that most "have always disliked," and used that as an excuse to not divulge any lingering feelings that he may or may not have had. This was in part due to societal stigmas associated with mental trauma, which will be examined later. He wrote repeatedly during the war about how fortunate he was to be injured, both when he had pyrexia and after he was hit by a rogue shell. Lewis did all he could to prolong his hospital stays and never once wished he was back in the trenches. While most would not wish to go back to the front, if it was not a traumatic experience, why would Lewis do all he could to avoid it? At one point he started to hope for the "forgetfulness of the authorities for [his] continued stay in the hospital" (*Letters* 1.396). This wish was eventually granted as he ended up overstaying his leave in the hospital by a couple of weeks. Despite the grave nature of his injury, Lewis states that "Never a day passes but I thankfully realize my great good fortune in getting wounded" (*Letters* 1.400). This is particularly interesting when one remembers the rather severe nature of his injuries. His hospital stay lasted from April through October, an indication of the severity of his injury. Despite all of this he found the hospital and the injury to be a blessing because it relieved him of the horror of the front. Lewis did not particularly like the experience of war; he described the ordeal as being "a slave to the state" and having the "menace of France" hanging over his head (*Letters* 1.394). While this is not a particularly revealing statement by itself, it seems more significant when compared to his later dismissal of the war's effect on his development.

    Lewis's diminishment of his war experiences seemed to grow with time, and any habit of revealing mental strain did not carry over through the postwar years. In his autobiography *Surprised by Joy*, written decades after the war's final shot was fired, Lewis is extremely dismissive about the war's effect on his development as a person. He writes that "it is too cut off from the rest of my experience and often seems to have happened to someone else" (*SJ* 190). This statement fits in perfectly with his pattern of either self-delusion or lying, when it comes to the war's effect on him. In a letter to his father only a year after he is injured, he shows the beginnings this habit: "Indeed my life is rapidly becoming divided into two periods, one including all the time before we got into the battle of Arras, the other ever since. Already last year seems a long, long way off" (qtd. in Jacobs 84). Just a year after his injury, and a few short months after his discharge from the hospital, Lewis began the process of dismissing the war and moving forward mentally and emotionally: "all this shows rarely and faintly in memory," he claimed, a dismissive attitude that was either something less than honest or something less than fully self-knowing (qtd. in Jacobs 75).

Meaningful Contradictions

World War I was, in its time, the bloodiest conflict in human history, and obviously left marks on the people and societies who were chosen to fight in its battles. Each person and culture dealt with the years of violence differently; some chose to expound on its effect and others chose to quietly move on without acknowledging its impact. Lewis's reaction to the war tended to fall toward the latter of those two reactions. He primarily dealt with the effects of the war silently, refusing to give those memories any credit for his development as a man or as a Christian.

When one begins to examine Lewis's response to the trauma he saw during the Great War, many inconsistencies surface. These inconsistencies in his thoughts and actions invariably lead one to doubt the veracity of his claims of indifference about the war and its effect on him. This section will serve to point out the words, letters, and actions that reveal a greater psychological impact he was willing to acknowledge.

Throughout his life, Lewis referred to two events as seminal in his development as a man. He was keenly aware of how the death of his mother effected his emotional and social development and his views on death, and he felt his experiences at his boarding school Malvern were some of the worst in his life and haunted his memory. He refused to acknowledge the Great War, on its own, as having a large effect on him, but he repeatedly, and most likely subconsciously, compared his war experiences with those two earlier horrific periods in his life. In a letter to Arthur Greeves in May of 1918, Lewis describes his time in the army up to that point as "quite like the Malvern days again" (*Letters* 1.372). This statement may not seem that revealing until one goes back and examines his thoughts on his time at Malvern. In his autobiography he states "As I grew more and more tired, both in body and mind, I came to hate [Malvern]. I did not notice the real harm it was doing to me" (*SJ* 95). In equating the two experiences but not equating their effects, Lewis is creating an inconsistency that is irreconcilable with his statements. If the Army smacks of Malvern, and Malvern was a hateful experience that did real harm to him, how can the Army not have had an effect on him at all? It would be understandable to say that one had a greater effect than the other, or that due to his young age Malvern had a greater effect on his development. But to equate the two and yet not acknowledge any sort of similarity indicates a lack of self-awareness or simply a miscarriage of truth. In a similar manner, Lewis throughout his life stated that the death of his mother was a formative event in his life. "With my mother's death all settled happiness, all that was tranquil and reliable, disappeared from my life. [...] It was sea and islands now; the great continent had sunk like Atlantis" (*SJ* 19). This passage from *Surprised by Joy* indicates that even decades later, Lewis recalled the trauma of his mother's death and how it uprooted the stable life that he had enjoyed as a child. No one can deny that the death of a mother is a scarring experience, and in *Joy* Lewis describes the horror of seeing his mother's corpse: "Grief was overwhelmed in terror. To this day I do not know what they mean when they call dead bodies beautiful. The ugliest man alive is an angel of beauty compared with the loveliest of the dead" (*SJ* 17). Lewis does not use his age as an excuse for why the death of his mother was formative; instead he blames thoughts of her body and his loss of security. Lewis again draws some parallels between his mother's death and his experiences at war: "Familiarity both with the very old and the very recent dead confirmed the view of corpses which had been formed the moment I saw my dead mother" (*SJ* 189). In the light of what was outlined above, it seems incredibly unlikely that an experience that immediately reminded him of one of the most formative periods in his life would have no effect on him. Lewis, however, remained adamant that the War was not a formative experience despite how he compares it to the death of his mother.

Another incongruity that surfaces in Lewis's diminishment of the war are a couple of rare comments where he hints at the lasting effect that the war had on him. These moments were ephemeral in nature, occurring only when he was most comfortable. Writing to Dom Bede Griffiths about the possibility of involvement in the Second World War, Lewis says, "I am too old. It would be hypocrisy to say that I regret this. My memories of the last war haunted my dreams for years" (*Letters* 2.258).[6] This statement is direct contrast with the diminishment of the war that Lewis all too commonly made, and strikes more true than his numerous dismissals of the war because it falls perfectly in line with his descriptions of nightmares that he had immediately after being injured. In a letter to his father in November 1918, a month after he was discharged from the hospital, he describes "nightmares—or rather the

---

6. See also Jacobs 75.

same nightmare over and over again. Nearly everyone has it, and though very unpleasant, it is passing and will do no harm" (*Letters* 1.417).[7] But the nightmares that Lewis described continued to haunt him for decades after the war's end. His descriptions of his nightmares match perfectly the experiences of many other intellectuals who also fought in the Great War. Ernest Hemingway describes similar experiences in *The Sun Also Rises*; "It is awfully easy to be hard-boiled about everything in the daytime, but at night it is another thing" (42). This quote also indicates how many war veterans (Lewis included) consciously chose to be "hard-boiled," but in the loneliness of the night, they were unable to escape their past. There were many reasons for them to choose this path, and those societal forces will be examined in the next section of the paper.

CAUSE FOR DISMISSAL
What was the motivation behind Lewis's dismissal of the war's impact on him? There were immense societal pressures facing those affected by war, and those pressures were magnified when one publically acknowledged the mental damage the Great War could cause. Even now, in the wake of the Iraq and Afghanistan Wars, we are only beginning to understand the damage that war can wreak on a mind. In Lewis's time views on mental trauma were even less developed, and significant social stigma was attached to any sort of lasting mental damage, which was seen as a personal defect. An examination of views on PTSD in Britain around the time of Lewis's war experiences will show how those views may have affected Lewis and his desire to repress any damage that the war may have done to him. The intent is not to show that Lewis's himself suffered PTSD. The broad sweeping definition of Post Traumatic Stress Disorder and the relatively little information we have about Lewis's reaction makes that a quixotic quest. Instead this section will show the societal forces that existed around Lewis at the time, and thus give us an insight into why he chose not mention the effect that the war clearly had on him.

Both sides of the war had regrettable views about PTSD and war-induced mental trauma. Neither the Central nor the Allied powers acknowledged the damage that war could cause to even the most proficient soldier. The prevailing German viewpoint at the time "was that the war-traumatized veteran was weak and selfish—one of the reasons

---

7. Again credit must go to Jacobs for his insight into this passage (75).

why Germany lost the war, and likely to bankrupt the state unless unchecked" (Wessely 270–71). The Germans ascribed selfish motives to those who had the misfortune of being damaged by war, and felt that there was some component of personal weakness to those affected mentally by war. It is as if they equated mental anguish with not finishing an exercise or being an inaccurate shot, and could not conceive that PTSD was involuntary, and no mental exercise or attitude could be adopted to prevent its onset. More damningly, it is clear that financial concerns contributed to German mistreatment of veterans. Acknowledging mental anguish as legitimate would have forced the Germans to give those with PTSD disability pay, the same as they gave those who lost limbs or suffered other physical injury. Fearing that this would be too costly a burden, the Germans instead chose to ignore and belittle their suffering brethren in an effort to save money. They "checked" the effect of mental trauma by associating a significant social stigma with that those who suffered from it.

Unfortunately for Lewis and his countrymen, the British viewpoint at this time did not differ greatly from the German perspective. The British position generally reflected the "traditional Edwardian values of courage and moral fibre. Breakdown was not inevitable, some men made better soldiers than others and some were more resilient than others" (Wessely 271). Like the Germans, the British felt that any lasting mental effect the war may have caused was due to personal weakness, a notion that surely does not match our current understanding of PTSD. They felt that "the best way to prevent breakdown was to ensure that troops were properly trained, properly equipped and properly led," as if a soldier could somehow train himself to resist emotional trauma (Wessely 272). This viewpoint continued in Britain for decades, and manifested itself in a similar manner during the Second World War. In the early years of World War II psychiatric casualties were diagnosed with "war neurosis," a condition pre-existing in the individual because of inherent weakness or defective parenting and aggravated by armed conflict (Boone 20). This perspective arose directly out of the views that the British held about Great War veterans affected with PTSD, and deeply affected the reluctance of any sufferer to reveal symptoms of mental anguish.

Lewis's decision to hide any effect that the war had on him becomes much more understandable after one examines the societal forces at play. Any public acknowledgment that the war left lasting damage on him would not have been received well, and in fact would have diminished his stature as a public intellectual and as a man. All of the societal incentives were on the side of dismissing any effect the war had as inconsequential or normal. There was no advantage to be had in telling of the private suffering that one may have been feeling; that would only compound the anguish. It is unfortunate that Britain and other countries forced their war veterans to hide their trauma in this way. These condescending viewpoints, held out of either selfishness or ignorance, caused many war traumatized veterans to live in the shadows for decades, deprived of proper treatment and vilified by the same society they gave so much to during the course of the Great War.

In addition to the societal forces which led Lewis to deny portions of his life, Lewis's personality certainly contributed to these gaps in his autobiography. The contradictions between his memories of the war and his initial description of his experiences do not stand out as aberrations to Lewis's character; instead they fall perfectly in line with Lewis's habit of segregating the different aspects of his life. For example, Lewis never mentions his complicated relationship with his adoptive mother Mrs. Maureen Moore in *Surprised by Joy*, despite the fact that she was the most important personal figure in his life for decades, and later he hid his marriage to Joy Gresham from most of his colleagues and friends for over a year (Ward 7). Lewis consistently chose to compartmentalize parts of his life; he kept professional and personal friends separate, he completely segregated his romantic affairs from the rest of his existence, and he often concealed his authorship of his works behind a pseudonym. This is not to say that Lewis was a liar or a sneak; instead, it indicates that he was a private man who did not feel the need to let the different aspects of his life blend together. He found it much more preferable to deal with each part independently. This lifelong habit of compartmentalization can help explain the various lacunae in his correspondence and autobiography.[8]

Conclusion

Lewis was not alone in his post war experiences; an entire generation was lost in the wilderness of their own minds, forced by their own countries to silently deal with the lasting damage that the war inflicted upon them. Many veterans were able to deal with their war experiences and were able to convert that trauma into the fuel for a successful life. But that did not mean that those successful men (and Lewis was surely one of them) did not realize the effect their damage could cause to themselves or society. Many who endured experiences similar to

---

8. For expansion on this theme of secrecy in Lewis's life, see Ward, specifically the first chapter of *Planet Narnia* (1–34).

Lewis's felt that the lasting trauma war caused was more impactful and damaging than the war itself. As T. S. Eliot wrote in *The Hollow Men*, "*This is the way the world ends / Not with a bang but a whimper*" (59). Eliot and others of the lost generation understood how the war's greatest effect would be in its aftermath; its wake would cause much more damage than its execution.

C. S. Lewis was greatly affected by World War I. It scarred him physically, leaving him in a hospital for over six months. It traumatized him emotionally, haunting his dreams for years. Despite this lasting impact, Lewis rarely acknowledged, privately or publically, that the war's effects were anything but ephemeral, due in part to the major European powers' official denial of the effects of PTSD. There were no positives for a veteran declaring mental trauma; it would only lead to ridicule and personal attacks. With that societal backdrop, it is easy to see why Lewis chose to hide the impact the Great War had on him. What is not so easy to believe is Lewis's claim that the war did not have an effect on him. When one delves deeply into his personal correspondence, it becomes clear that he was affected by the war, despite his claims to the contrary.

WORKS CITED

Boone, Katherine. "The Paradox of PTSD." *The Wilson Quarterly* 35.4 (2011): 18–22. Print.

Eliot, T. S. "The Hollow Men." *The Complete Poems and Plays 1909-1950*. New York: Harcourt Brace & World, 1962. 56–59. Print.

Gilchrist, K. J. "2nd Lieutenant Lewis." *SEVEN: An Anglo-American Literary Review* 17 (2000): 61–77. Print.

—. "Continuing Research on 2nd Lieutenant Lewis." *SEVEN: An Anglo-American Literary Review* 18 (2001): 47–50. Print.

Hemingway, Ernest. *The Sun Also Rises*. 1926. New York: Scribner, 2006. Print.

Jacobs, Alan. *The Narnian*. San Francisco: HarperCollins, 2006. Print.

Lewis, C. S. *The Collected Letters of C. S. Lewis*. Vol. 1. San Fransisco: HarperCollins, 2004. Print.

—. *The Collected Letters of C. S. Lewis*. Vol. 2. San Francisco: HarperCollins, 2004. Print.

—. *Surprised by Joy*. Orlando: Houghton Mifflin Harcourt, 1995. Print.

Remarque, Erich Maria. *All Quiet on the Western Front*. 1929. New York: Ballantine, 1996. Print.

Ward, Michael. *Planet Narnia: The Seven Heavens in the Imagination of C. S. Lewis*. Oxford: Oxford UP, 2008. Print.

Wessely, Simon. "Twentieth-Century Theories on Combat Motivation and Breakdown." *Journal of Contemporary History* 41 (2006): 269–86. Print.

The Great War and Narnia:
C. S. Lewis as Soldier and Creator[1]

BRIAN MELTON

WHEN IT COMES to his personal experiences in war, C. S. Lewis can be a difficult man to understand. It is not, of course, that Lewis is not clear on the subject when he speaks of it. On the contrary, when he does it is generally with the same incisive clarity that he applies to all other subjects. The trouble is that Lewis simply does not say much about it at all. While other famous veterans of the First World War speak at great length and in horrible detail of what they saw and did, Lewis says what little he must and no more. Some newer authors, such as K. J. Gilchrist in his book *A Morning After War: C. S. Lewis and WWI*, argue that in Lewis's general attitude lurks the monster of some undiscovered trauma that caused him to willfully "obscure facts" about his wartime past (Gilchrist 1). Others, such as Humphrey Carpenter, talk about Lewis's "silence" on his wartime service but believe that it is because the war did not affect him as much as it could have (qtd. in Gilchrist 8).

When viewed from the perspective of the present author, an historian who has already published a work on a soldier who left relatively few records behind (*Sherman's Forgotten General: Henry W. Slocum*), Lewis does not seem to be abnormally reticent. After all, he was not a significant figure in the war and did not define himself by his time in it, as other writers did. If he appears to be suspiciously quiet, it may be due to the fact that he speaks so prolifically on other subjects that his discussions on war seem slim by comparison. In reality, he addresses it often enough and to a depth that is appropriate for the context in which the various discussions occur. Lewis may not have expended much of his energy looking at his time in the trenches, but he gives everyone enough to get on with. His devotees—the present included—may wish he had said more, but, then again, they generally wish he had said more about every subject he addressed and *something* about quite a few he did not.

In the land of Narnia, war is as much a real facet of personal and political life as it was in Lewis's own world. Are there any possible ways in which his wartime experiences affected his Narnian creations? While

---

1. A shorter version of this paper was published in *The Lamp-Post*, the Journal of the Southern California C. S. Lewis Society in Winter 2010. Those portions are reprinted here with permission.

the tracks are somewhat elusive, they are not impossible to trace in every case, and scholars need not indulge in any shady "reading between the lines" to discover parallels. While Lewis does not exhibit every stereotypical World War I influence, and in fact at times he specifically avoided allowing his war experience to affect his writing, what he faced in World War I affected Narnia in a number of distinctive ways. There are other instances where it is likely Lewis was influenced, but scholars cannot know for certain in the absence of specific explanatory evidence straight from Lewis's own pen. In those cases, it is possible to point to distinct historical parallels between worlds—the real and the imaginary—where Lewis's experience *may* have played a role. Finally, there are a number of themes that are common to many post war writers that Lewis seems to ignore altogether. These are notable by their absence.

Before proceeding, it is important to set a few boundaries and clarify a few definitions. First, this is not an attempt to deal with the general themes of violence or conflict in Narnia. "War" in this context refers to the engagement of significant numbers of the armed retainers of two or more Narnian political factions and the individual's experience of it. This generally excludes personal combat (i.e. Peter versus Fenris in *The Lion, the Witch and the Wardrobe* [*LWW*] or his fight with Miraz in *Prince Caspian* [*PC*]) as well as small unit actions (i.e. Caspian's fights in *Voyage of the "Dawn Treader"* and Tirian versus the Calormene squad in *The Last Battle* [*LB*]). Second, this article makes use of Lewis's time in World War I exclusively. World War II or his thoughts on war in general are worthy topics to be explored elsewhere. Finally, no attempt has been made to prioritize this particular influence in the complex watershed of thought that flowed together to form Lewis's imaginary world. The author makes no claims to demonstrate that any particular example or parallel is *the* primary influence in any given instance. Given the paucity of sources from Lewis about his time in the war, such a ranking is no longer possible on the practical level. Most probably, Lewis's vast experience in literature played the dominant part in his thinking—that theme has been explored elsewhere—and his military experiences served in a supporting role. In short, there are a number of other essential tributaries that eventually merged into the whole. This is just one of them.

World War I, or the "Great War" as it was called prior to World War II, began in 1914 when a tangled web of diplomatic intrigue magnified the assassination of a relatively minor royal figure into an explosion that annihilated the peace of Europe. Soon a regional conflict between the small Balkan state of Serbia and the second-rate power Austria-Hungary became an enormous struggle that dragged in most of the world's major nations, including Russia, Germany, France, and Britain herself. What everyone expected to be a short war of movement degenerated into a murderous stalemate on the western front when the Allies checked Germany's rapid advance through Belgium and France. Both sides tried to move around the end of each other's position, extending their own lines farther and farther out. Soon, there was no longer any room left to flank and a more or less continuous line of defensive works existed from the English Channel all the way to the Swiss Alps. Having planted themselves firmly onto French soil, the Germans began a colossal entrenching program, and then dared the French and British to do something about it.

The Allies tried: again, and again, and again. Unfortunately, no one, least of all British commander Douglas Haig, really understood the situation that recent advances in technology had created on the battlefield. A combination of non-line-of-sight artillery, practical and efficient machine guns, and barbed wire made it possible for both sides to kill so many men so quickly from their defensive positions that older tactics, involving massed formations of men sent plowing across the field after a preliminary bombardment, were virtually guaranteed to fail. The German practice of building defenses in depth (one line of defenders behind the other) insured that any local successes would be quickly contained and then repulsed. For Haig, every attack he made appeared to come within an iota of success, and so he threw more and more men into the fray, which only resulted in thousands of broken and bloodied British soldiers slowly sinking into the fetid mud of no man's land—the unoccupied ground between the armies (DeGroot 1–47).

An atheistic, priggish (by his own account) Lewis spent the early years of WWI studying with William Kirkpatrick, better known as the "Great Knock," in Kirkpatrick's home in Great Bookham, Surrey (Green 41). While living there Lewis felt isolated from the war, though he noted that even in this insulated haven of study he could, if the wind was right, "hear the mutter and grumble of the far distant guns in France" (Gresham 33). Though he could have avoided service entirely, after a period of indecision Lewis chose to join up. Having crossed that important threshold, he then proceeded to segregate his mind from thinking about the war to such an extent that he later remarked that some people would likely think it "shameful." In his words, war and country "may have my body, but not my mind. I will take part in battles, but not read about them" (Lewis, *Surprised by Joy* [*SJ*] 158).

Lewis later left the presence of the Great Knock and traveled to Oxford to begin study to become a scholar. He had been there less than a term when his enlistment papers came through and he officially entered the army. He did not leave Oxford, but joined a cadet battalion stationed at Keble College. There he made the acquaintance of a number of aspiring scholar-warriors, including Paddy Moore, whose mother later played such a long and important role in Lewis's life. It is notable that of the five friends who left Keble for war, Lewis alone survived (Sayer 139). After a brief period of training, Lewis was promoted to second lieutenant and attached to the Somerset Light Infantry.

Lewis arrived on the front lines in France on his nineteenth birthday in November 1917. While he would remember portions of the next five months fondly at times, overall they proved to be one of the worst periods of his life as well. He later remarked that though he understood that war was sometimes a necessity, he would rather die than live through another (*The Collected Letters of C. S. Lewis* 2.258). Here too, he continued to demonstrate the remarkable ability to split off his intellect and imagination from the horrors surrounding him. If his letters to Arthur Greeves are any indication, while facing carnage and death on an almost daily basis, Lewis seemed to dwell more on what he was reading and on the various poems that would later be published as *Spirits in Bondage*. Walter Hooper remarked on this tendency when he observed that for his entire life, Lewis "had the extraordinary ability of being able to write almost anywhere" (Hooper 11).

In stark contrast to his still blossoming literary pursuits, Lewis experienced the awful reality that was World War I. He afterward described "the frights, the cold, the smell of H. E. [high explosive], the horribly smashed men still moving like half-crushed beetles, the sitting or standing corpses, the landscape of sheer earth without a blade of grass, the boots worn day and night till they seemed to grow to your feet" (*SJ* 196). He seems, though, to have dealt with this by withdrawing further into the shell provided by his active imagination and the literature he still managed to feed it. He observed that the reality of the war "shows rarely and faintly in memory. It is too cut off from the rest of my experience and often seems to have happened to someone else. It is even in a way unimportant. One imaginative moment [that of hearing his first bullet] seems now to matter more than the realities that followed" (*SJ* 196).

During his time at the front, he acquitted himself well. The company he commanded won awards for guard mounting and company drill and he aided in the capture of around sixty German prisoners of war (Gilchrist 99; *SJ* 197). During the winter Lewis spent a month in hospital recovering from a bout with trench fever, but he returned to his unit in time to face the massive German offensive in France in the spring of 1918. Having forced the Russians to make peace, the Germans transferred reinforcements west and unleashed a massive series of strokes designed to knock either Britain or France out of the war before the new American Expeditionary Force could make its presence felt. During the Battle of Arras, on April 14, German shells fell amongst his troops, obliterating a respected sergeant named Harry Ayres and seriously wounding Lewis. Lewis managed to drag himself back toward friendly lines where a stretcher crew picked him up. He was eventually transported to a series of hospitals in the rear. The war ended before he had recovered sufficiently to take the field again, and he returned to Oxford to continue his studies.

Even in the horrific instant of Lewis's wounding, he reported the same disconnect from his physical circumstances and retreat into his mind that he carried with him to war. As he observed in *Surprised by Joy*,

> the moment, just after I had been hit [...] I found (or thought I found) that I was not breathing and concluded that this was death. I felt no fear and certainly no courage. It did not seem to be an occasion for either. The proposition "Here is a man dying" stood before my mind as dry, as factual, as unemotional as something in a textbook. It was not even interesting. The fruit of this experience was that when, some years later, I met Kant's distinction between the Noumenal and the Phenomenal self, it was more to me than an abstraction. (197)

While Lewis claims not have been clearly aware of this distinction before then, it is obvious that for quite some time he had the practical ability to withdraw into himself and distinguish between the creative reality of his mind on the one hand and his physical circumstances on the other. For him, this amounted to a willful decision to enjoy the interior world of the mind and spirit instead of what confronted him outside. Perhaps Puddleglum described it best in his argument with the Green Witch in *The Silver Chair* when he stated,

> Suppose we *have* only dreamed, or made up, all those things—trees and grass and sun and moon and stars and Aslan himself. Suppose we have. Then all I can say is that, in that case, the made up things seem a good deal more important than the real ones. [...] That's why I'm going to stand by the play world. I'm on Aslan's side even if there isn't any Aslan to lead it. I'm going to live as like a Narnian as I can even if there isn't any Narnia. (159)

Whether or not the Marsh-wiggle is vicariously speaking for Lewis, it is a tendency he seems to share with his creator.[2]

---

2. One reviewer of this article has objected that in this selection Puddleglum is not actually advocating a retreat into an inner world at all; rather, he is taking a

This segregation of mind was well developed prior to Lewis's actual entry into the war. He had already integrated it into his larger worldview with ease, perhaps even eagerly. Thinking back on it later, he himself remarked that "even if the attitude was right, the quality in me which made it so easy to adopt is somewhat repellent" (*SJ* 159). Precisely where his ability came from is a question that will probably never be answered authoritatively. He may have been born with it, developed it as a child after his mother's death, it may stem from years of daydreaming and vicarious living through the literature he loved so much, or perhaps it grew up as a survival mechanism as a result of the torture he and Warren Lewis had endured at the hand of Robert Capron, the insane headmaster of his first boarding school. Whatever the case, it enabled him to endure the horrors of war but keep what he considered to be essentially himself separate and, to a certain extent, unaffected.

In practical terms Lewis's ability has led some Lewis scholars to misinterpret the war's apparent effect on him and therefore on his later work. Authors observe the obvious fact that Lewis does indeed willfully shut himself off from portions of his wartime experience and presume that some massive trauma must have preceded it. Gilchrist goes so far as to accuse Lewis of repeated "posing," "posturing," and "masking" when discussing the war (Gilchrist 67, 73, 108). In fact, Lewis's pre-existing intellectual defenses may have made it possible for him to emerge from the gauntlet carrying less emotional baggage than most. Lewis's silence on the details of his war service may then be exactly what it purports to be: silence and nothing more. Barring the new introduction of unreviewed evidence, to pursue this line of thought further, scholars must begin in advance of all evidence with the assumed premise that Lewis could not actually have meant what he said and then work downhill into varying degrees of absurdity from there.

The propensity to inject massive emotional trauma where it may not exist is exacerbated by the fact that many modern authors see war and its effect on people through the considerable mythology surrounding soldiers since American involvement in Vietnam. War is supposed

---

stand in favor of accepting the real world over the witch's poor imitation. That is a just criticism, when viewed from the more objective perspective of the reader, who knows very well what the witch is doing. However, at the time, inside the story, Puddleglum and his friends are no longer sure of that—in fact he admits that it seems to him like the witch is probably right and that Narnia really is nothing but moonshine. If that is the case, he is in fact saying that he preferred living in their "play" world to her "real" one. Therefore, the analogy holds, though, like all analogies, it must be taken with care.

to be so traumatic that part of what makes the experience of it valid to the larger academic culture is that it first desecrates and then dominates the individual who survives it. The deeper a person's emotional scars, the more credence their testimony seems to be given. People who can face war and then somehow emerge to live normal and productive lives are often treated as if their experiences are somehow less legitimate than those of people who can never adapt to the regular world (B. G. Burkett and Glena Whitley discuss this tendency in their book, *Stolen Valor*). This leads to either the belittling of genuine veterans or, at times, the search for some hidden trauma that the scholar assumes *a priori* must exist.

On the contrary, for all the tortured souls that war leaves in its wake, there are others who are able to adapt to their experiences and move on, and Lewis may well be one of them. In "Learning in Wartime" Lewis remarked on the notion that war must by definition consume an individual, and he thought it nonsense: "Neither conversion nor enlistment in the army is going to obliterate our human life. Christians and soldiers are still men; the infidel's idea of a religious life, and the civilian's idea of active service, are fantastic" (51–52). While it is impossible to prove a negative, there is no obvious reason to believe that Lewis must, by default, be hiding some conscious or subconscious trauma and that this must be expected to necessarily bleed through into Narnia.

Of course, this is not to say that those five violent months did not affect Lewis in significant and lasting ways. Though he understood that war could be unavoidable, he never forgot its darkness, and often took the opportunity to reprove young Douglas Gresham when the boy spoke about war or warriors with "words of admiration," emphasizing that "no matter what people or newspapers or politicians try to tell you, there is no glory in war" (Gresham 44–45). He flatly stated that war literally "threatens *every* temporal evil" ("Why I Am Not a Pacifist" 89). Lewis also noted that for years after the war he suffered from terrible nightmares about being back in the trenches (Gresham 51). Even here, though, it seems that the war mostly affected an existing problem; it did not create a new one. Lewis elsewhere references the regular "nightfears" he faced while growing up and remarked that "I would not wish to heat the fires of that private hell for any child" ("On Three Ways of Writing for Children" [OTW] 30). So the war did not so much cause his fear as provide fodder for a pre-existing condition.

In the end, Lewis emerged from the war scarred and undoubtedly carrying some sort of emotional baggage—as any sane, feeling human would—but he did not continue to be dominated by it. Much of what has been blamed on what he faced in the trenches he could just as easily have carried to war with him. Retreating into his mind, he insulated himself from what he saw and did and emerged on the other side having been influenced by his experiences, but not necessarily more so than he would be by other important eras of his life.

The Great War was, in fact, simply one of a number of incidents that Lewis likely drew from when constructing his stories. Lewis's first-hand experience must be also balanced by the important literary considerations involved in his depiction of war in Narnia. The content of his thinking shows the effects of his exposure to various genres, particularly classical literature. Lewis noted in "Learning in Wartime" that he found his own war experience mirrored in Tolstoy and the *Iliad* (51–52). The massive amount of mythology he imported into Narnia is so self-evident that it is unnecessary to do more than mention it in passing. His decision to draw from the vast wealth of information he had stored in his internal library would necessarily limit his opportunity to include his wartime experiences. There was, after all, only so much that he could fit into so few pages. Of course, these influences on Narnia have been covered exhaustively elsewhere by other authors far better qualified to discuss them than the present.

There is another practical literary concern that would check Lewis's reliance on personal experience: his goals in writing for children. Lewis did not intend to produce a hard-bitten pseudo-documentary about the Great War, nor did he wish to drag his audience through the muck and stink of the British trenches as an anti-war object lesson. Though he primarily wanted to tell a good story about a picture in his head, Lewis knew that books like his also teach. He insisted that "the only moral that is of any value is that which arises inevitably from the whole cast of the author's mind" and that we "must write for children from those elements in our own imagination which we share with children" (OTW 33). In Narnia, Lewis depicted war as he felt he would have needed to see it as a child. He wanted his audience to see real evil and real good, and he wanted them to see that by decisive, brave action, good could triumph. In one of his more famous passages on the subject, Lewis wrote,

> Since it is so likely that they will meet cruel enemies, let them at least have heard of brave knights and heroic courage. Otherwise you are making their destiny not brighter but darker. […] As far as that goes, I side impenitently with the human race against the modern reformer. Let there be wicked kings and beheadings, battles and dungeons, giants and dragons, and let villains be soundly killed at the end of the book. (OTW 31)

Lewis's purposes, then, would act much as a filter might, straining out inappropriate facts and ideas gleaned during the war from expression in a Narnian context.

Still, it is possible to point to a number of strong correlations between war in Narnia and war as Lewis knew it. The first involves a notable *exclusive influence,* meaning that Lewis's experiences probably led him to keep a theme *out* of his creative world. The second category is *inclusive,* and it is possible that Lewis inserted these ideas into Narnia due to something he saw personally in France or in the army in general. The final group contains those ideas that might be called *missing in action* (MIA), since they are themes that are prominent in the writings of other veterans—including his fellow don and Inkling J. R. R. Tolkien—but are absent from Lewis. These ideas are distinguished from those in the *exclusive* section by the fact that there is nothing to suggest one way or the other why Lewis did not address them. Their absence may be intentional or it may just be incidental; there is simply no way to tell from this distance in time.

One final disclaimer before proceeding, in the hopes of avoiding a trap Lewis himself spoke out against: the following attempts to lay out a series of parallels between Lewis's historical experience and what later appeared in Narnia, and then offer some reasonable speculations on how they *could* be connected, based on existing evidence. It does not try to psychoanalyze Lewis in the traditional sense or to produce absolute results regarding his motivations. Lewis legitimately disliked the trend amongst Freudian peers who claimed to know more about their subjects than their subjects knew about themselves. The current approach is therefore more historical than it is literary or psychoanalytic. The parallels are there, but what they mean and why they are there—whether by chance or intention—is open for debate in the absence of clear guidance from Lewis himself.

An Exclusive Effect

The primary example of Lewis excluding something from Narnia due to his wartime experience involves his attitude toward the dead. More particularly, it is evident in the complete absence of mangled bodies from the battlefields of Narnia (Aslan on the Stone Table notwithstanding). Lewis developed a visceral abhorrence for corpses at an early age, when he saw his mother's body laid out on a bed. As was custom, he had been forced to go into the room and pay his respects. This left a mark on him, which his later experiences only worsened. The dead were the World War I soldier's constant companion. At the front and in no man's land, they could be encountered anywhere, in every imaginable position and state of decay. As mentioned before, Lewis saw them lying prone, sitting where they died, and standing up, caught in mud or propped against a tree. Recalling Lewis's description of war, Gresham observed that "He learned to eat whatever food was put before him, often within both the sight and smell of dead men, both friend and foe. He learned how to tell the nationality of a dead soldier by the smell of the body as it began to rot" (43). Lewis noted that "both [...] the very old and the very recent dead confirmed that view of corpses which had been formed the moment I saw my dead mother" (*SJ* 195–96).

Despite the fact that the battles in Narnia are at times quite large, Lewis never mentions any corpses after a battle whatsoever. It is not that Lewis chose to explain the corpses away through some omnipotent literary device, like Lucy's cordial. They simply never make an appearance, anywhere. Once someone falls dead he or she simply vanishes. The closest he comes to acknowledging the presence of the dead is in *The Horse and His Boy*, when Corin observes the vultures above Anvard, and that is not a direct reference in itself (176). Lewis never mentions the harsh reality of burying the dead, friend or foe, and he never shows the aforementioned carrion in action. At some points, he seems to imply that the nasty business of cleaning up is actually being taken care of "off screen," so to speak, but in general he forgot about or avoided the issue altogether. For example, at the end of the Battle of Anvard, in *The Horse and His Boy*, somewhere between twenty-four and thirty six hours after the fight they hold a party "on the lawn before the castle, with dozens of lanterns to help the moonlight" (213). This is presumably the very same lawn that had been strewn with carcasses the day before, including men, horses, and at least one giant (who would have been quite difficult to dispose of by default). A more prominent situation presents itself earlier in Narnian history when, after having defeated and slaughtered Jadis and her dark retainers, Peter's army sits "where they were" and enjoys a "fine high tea" on the grass. They then sleep on the battlefield itself, something not likely to happen if the area really were strewn with contorted, maimed bodies (*LWW* 178). In *Prince Caspian*, the celebration actually begins before the battle itself ends, and no practical time is allowed for any burial parties, though perhaps it might be argued that Bacchus took care of this oversight with his handy ivy (204–07).

In "On Three Ways of Writing for Children," Lewis remarked that in his stories "I put in what I would have liked to read when I was a child and what I still like reading now that I am in my fifties" (22). It is clear that Lewis did not enjoy reading about mortal remains at any age.

INCLUSIVE EFFECTS

This category of influences involves ideas and depictions in Narnia that are, to at least some extent, traceable to something Lewis saw or experienced in the Great War. While not all of the lines of evidence are as obvious as would be preferred, they are clear enough to make at least a strong circumstantial case for a connection.

First, a sense of dark realism pervades Narnian war. War and its accoutrements in Narnia are no more glorious or frivolous than in real life. There is no sense of fun or grandeur in any of the various Narnian scenes. For instance, when Aslan prepared Peter for battle in *The Lion, the Witch and the Wardrobe*, his advice was purely straightforward and down-to-earth. There was no hint of war as a game, beyond a very brief scene where Peter showed off his sword to Mr. Beaver—something that is more likely a comment on young boys than on war (*LWW* 105, 143–44). Later, in the battle itself, there were praiseworthy heroics, but they were of the sort inspired by hard necessity rather than a desire for laurels and victory was purchased dearly. Edmund's fight with the Witch was the stuff of song and legend, but ended with him shattered, broken, and bloody (*LWW* 175–76). Caspian's war against his uncle was anything but glorious, with the rebels shortly pinned up in Aslan's How to be ground slowly down by Miraz's superior forces. The aftermath of the failed attack before Caspian blew Susan's horn speaks for itself: "The best of the bears had been hurt, a centaur terribly wounded, and there were few in Caspian's party that had not lost blood. It was a gloomy party that huddled under the dripping trees to eat their scanty supper" (*PC* 88). Shasta also observed the same sort of dull frankness as he watched the Narnians prepare to relieve the siege of Anvard in *The Horse and His Boy*. The archers testing their strings, the giants donning their spiked boots, the big cats prowling, soldiers checking their equipment, all took place in general silence. There was no mindless boasting, no singing, or jesting. Even the usually boisterous Corin became solemn, pointing out the vultures circling overhead, as mentioned previously. "They know we're preparing a feed for them," he said (176). Later, when Aravis remarked that it "must have been wonderful" to be in the battle, Shasta simply replied that it "Wasn't at all like what I thought," implying that he had been disabused of some of his more boyish notions (197).

The actual fighting itself is also surprisingly harsh for what modern readers would expect from a "children's book," though Lewis is careful not to carry it to excess. While Lewis described the large battle at the end of *The Lion, the Witch and the Wardrobe* in mostly general terms, in *The Horse and His Boy* he was more frank. The Hermit of the Southern March, while keeping Aravis and the horses apprised of the fighting notes that he saw one of the giants fall, "shot through the eye, I suppose." Later he stated that "King Edmund is dealing marvelous strokes. He's just slashed Corradin's head off." When judging Rabadash, King Lune plainly remarked that to "have cut his throat in the battle would have eased my heart mightily." Edmund agreed, hoping that if Rabadash broke his word again, that it would be in a place where he could "swap off his head in clean battle" (182, 184, 206).

It does not take much imagination to see in this the harsh realism of Lewis's own experience in the army. Rather than using literature to obscure reality, here he uses reality to keep literature in check. World War I taught Lewis that wars are not to be encouraged, but treated with cold practicality by those who must face them. Lewis believed that the "child as reader is neither to be patronized nor idolized: we talk to him as man to man" (OTW 34). In the Chronicles, Lewis did so.

Next, as was the case with Lewis himself, war in Narnia never seems to wholly consume those who take part in it. They emerge on the other side still essentially themselves. Probably the two best examples of this are Peter and Edmund in *The Lion, the Witch and the Wardrobe*. The war against Jadis is easily one of the largest and most costly discussed in the Chronicles, second in size perhaps only to Caspian's fight against the Telmarines. Even though Aslan and Lucy saved many injured, the implication is that there are a significant number of dead. Peter watched his soldiers die in front of him as he fought a desperate battle. Edmund had been brutally wounded by Jadis. Even Lucy's cordial would be unlikely to heal such emotional scars (*LWW* 142–86).

The transformation that the boys undergo is notable, but not complete. They are not the same, but neither are they so changed as to no longer be recognizably themselves. When Lucy arrives on the field with Aslan, she finds it odd "to see Peter looking as he looked now—his face was so pale and stern and he seemed so much older" (*LWW* 175). Rather than being left scarred and dysfunctional, Peter became "a tall and deep chested man and a great warrior, and he was called King Peter the Magnificent" (*LWW* 181). Edmund's case is less obvious, since he also benefitted from Lucy's ministrations and it is impossible to distinguish what cause resulted in which effect. Still, after the battle Edmund becomes "his real old self again and could look you in the face" (177). He later "was a quieter and graver man than Peter and great in council and judgment. He was called King Edmund the Just" (*LWW* 181). The older Edmund presented in *The Horse and His Boy* only deepens and illustrates this.

When Lewis came out of the hospital in 1918, he had earned no magnificent surname and was not likely any deeper-chested than before, but, as noted above, he was still essentially Jack Lewis. Older, graver perhaps, but not so radically changed that he did not know himself. The essential point is clear. All three youths carried a certain character into the war, and all three emerged with that same basic character intact. War marked both Lewis and the Pevensies indelibly, leaving them changed in sometimes critical ways, but the experience did not ruin them as individuals and could in fact have helped them mature. They faced it out of necessity and afterward they did not dwell on its horrors without reason. War became one more stream of experience in a much longer tale; part of them, but not the whole.

Next, Lewis's pictures—the few times they occur—of the wounded also exhibit a strong edge of realism, most likely born of his time on the front. For all the fighting and killing that takes place in Narnia and despite the fact that Lewis generally adopts a straightforward approach to war, readers see very few close descriptions of those on whom the course battle has not been kind. This, of course, is probably due to Lewis's expressed desire not to inflict "any haunting dread in the minds of children" (OTW 31). He includes these descriptions only when necessary, and pushes them only to the extent he must.

Still, when the wounded do appear, their injuries are frighteningly real. The most obvious of these is Edmund, after his battle with Jadis. Lucy found him "in the charge of Mrs. Beaver a little way back from the fighting line. He was covered with blood, his mouth was open, and his face a nasty green colour" (*LWW* 176). In *Prince Caspian*, Reepicheep is, if anything, even more gravely wounded than Edmund. He was borne to Aslan on a small litter after the battle, "little better than a damp heap of fur; all that was left of Reepicheep. He was still breathing, but more dead than alive, gashed with innumerable wounds, one paw crushed, and, where his tail had been, a bandaged stump." Even after Lucy tended him with her miracle cure, there was "a long and anxious silence" before it became clear that the chief mouse would survive (201).

While Lewis does not regale his readers with many disturbing firsthand accounts of what he saw at the front, what little he does say makes plain that he had probably seen his share of horribly wounded men. His brief but disgustingly brilliant description of them quoted above ("half-crushed beetles") could hardly be more real. He would not have had to venture too deeply into his memory to dredge up a very genuine picture upon which to base his description of Edmund and, with a few necessary modifications, Reepicheep. If anything, his self-imposed literary limitations would have to moderate his memory and prevent him from including too many details. This does not mean that he is "posing" at all; he has made no claims to writing a "real" war history.

Lucy's cordial itself may be an example of wishful thinking regarding the wounded. That small crystal vial is nothing more or less than a soldier's ideal. Lewis, jolting his way painfully from the front in an ambulance or lying frustrated in some hospital bed, may well have wished for something like it. While he no doubt wanted to avoid returning to the trenches, in hindsight, with the end of the war so near, it would make sense for him to wish vaguely for some *deus ex machina* to rescue him from the frustration of hospital life, which he later described as disagreeable. He almost certainly would have wished for something that could have saved all of his wounded friends.

Another, more personal correlation between the wounded in Europe and war in Narnia comes from Shasta, though it may not be very significant. It is interesting that Shasta had only one wound to show for his trouble when he met Aravis after the fight at Anvard. When he arrived, announced by his true name of Cor, Aravis noticed that his "left hand [...] was bandaged" (*HHB* 196). While this cannot be pressed too far, it is notable that of Lewis's own wounds, the one on his left hand gave him the most trouble throughout the rest of his life (Sayer 132). Shasta, like Lewis, found the injury to be merely annoying and not serious, though he did not receive it in nearly so dramatic a fashion as Lewis. Shasta scraped his knuckles, while Lewis survived an explosion.

An emotional parallel between Lewis's life and Narnia appears in his own description of his first experience of combat and what happens to his characters. There is a clear sense of nerves and fear, but also a feeling of the surreal. The environment around the observer seems to change somewhat from actual reality. In the case of Shasta at the Battle of Anvard, everything around him slowed down and became focused to an absolute pinpoint. Terror and necessity mingled in one moment and he saw far more than the scant few seconds would seem to allow:

> And now a gallop. The ground between the two armies grew less every moment. Faster, faster. All swords out now, all shields up to the nose, all prayers said, all teeth clenched. Shasta was dreadfully frightened. But it suddenly came into his head "If you funk this, you'll funk every battle all your life. Now or never." (*HHB* 179)

Then, suddenly, the world turns into chaos, and Shasta can no longer follow what is going on.

Here the author must retreat somewhat from the strict delineations offered earlier and allow some evidence from Peter's battle with Fenris. This is appropriate, given that in a very real way, all combat is personal; the only question is how many persons are taking part at any given moment. Peter's reaction to his first taste of combat—which Lewis himself called Peter's "First Battle" in the chapter title—was very similar to Shasta's. In the moment he charged the wolf, "Peter did not feel very brave; indeed, he felt he was going to be sick. But that made no difference to what he had to do" (*LWW* 127). There is also a hint of the same confusion and distortion of time, when there are more things going on in a "moment" than would normally be possible.

This compares favorably with Lewis's own description of the first moment he personally experienced enemy fire. For Lewis too, it seemed unreal and fantastic. His own word for it was "imaginative." He went on to state that it was "the first bullet I heard—so far from me that it 'whined' like a journalist's or a peacetime poet's bullet. At that moment there was something not exactly like fear, much less like indifference: a little quavering signal that said, 'This is War. This is what Homer wrote about'" (*SJ* 196). While Lewis did not mention a subsequent charge in his description, the same sense of a suspension of reality and some sort of tempered fear response are both present. Lewis most likely had this moment or one like it in mind when he penned Shasta and Peter's descent into war.

A more physical comparison presents itself when turning to the question of fortifications in Narnia. While most often thought of as residences for the various personalities of the world, they are also intended to serve a more militant purpose. Cair Paravel, Jadis's Castle, Anvard, and the small towers in *The Last Battle* are all designed to be comfortable and yet are also strong points from which Narnians can defend their lands. Viewed from the general context of the Great War, it is interesting that Narnians exhibit a peculiarly British attitude toward fortifications and their use. Unfortunately, in all but one example, they have reason to regret this.

During World War I, the Germans tended to build more complex trenches and then wait for their opponents to come to them. As noted previously, they could afford this luxury since, as they occupied French territory, they could expect their enemies to attack in an attempt to drive them out. The Allies, on the other hand, took less care in trench construction for the simple reason that they never planned to stay in them long. British General Haig remained fixated on restoring movement to his army, believing that each new attack would be the one to break the German line. As such, British positions were often less complicated and less well equipped. While the Germans hauled in tons of concrete and steel and wired their trenches for electricity, the British (and to a lesser extent, the French) tended to make do with the bare necessities and constantly came out of their trenches to attack their enemies (DeGroot 33).

There could hardly be a better general description of Narnia's construction and use of her strongholds. A number of them are rather simple in design and exhibit none of the post-Crusades refinements of the high Middle Ages. While readers are not given much information on the specific defenses of Cair Paravel, both Anvard and the Witch's Castle lack even a moat (In Jadis's defense, a frozen moat would do little good, but a dry moat would be practical). These oversights cost the Witch in her war with Aslan and Cair Paravel in its last defense. Anvard was able to survive only by the timely arrival of reinforcements. Had Edmund's army been delayed, the lack of a more in-depth defense would have allowed Rabadash and his force to batter down the gate with little more than a tree trunk (*HHB* 178–79).

This lack of strong fortifications seems to have been due to the fact that, like the British, the Narnians preferred the offensive when provoked. Narnians—good and evil—very rarely actually *fight* from behind their prepared works. They are constantly coming *out* of them and fighting in the open, where their defenses do not benefit them in the least. While Aslan thought that Jadis might withdraw to her castle to face a siege in *The Lion, the Witch and the Wardrobe*, she actually attacked Peter's army directly. As a result, she lost when reinforcements were freed from her undefended home and overwhelmed her in a sudden rush (164–76). In *Prince Caspian*, while Dr. Cornelius talked at length about the defensive advantages offered by Aslan's How, once Caspian's army occupied it he repeatedly launched sorties to attack Miraz's forces on open ground, where the Telmarines obviously had the advantage. The battles usually ended in stinging defeats for Caspian, who eventually relied on Aslan and an army of reawakened trees for victory (85–93). Only at Anvard in *The Horse and His Boy* did the defenders actually put their advantages to good use, and even there they emerged from the castle to go on the attack at the first opportunity (175–85).

Lewis himself never explained his reasoning on the issue, and so it is now impossible to push this claim to an absolute conclusion. Yet, there is a strong correlation between the way Lewis's own people utilized their trenches in the war in which he participated and how the

Narnians themselves used their closest equivalents. In this, the Narnians seem to be distinctively British.

MISSING IN ACTION

Janet Brennan Croft, in her book *War and the Works of J. R. R. Tolkien*, identified a number of clear and logical ways in which World War I affected "Tollers" and his epic *Lord of the Rings* trilogy. These themes are often present in a much broader sampling of post-war authors. Lewis in all likelihood heard them in Tolkien's writing as he sat listening to him in the evenings with the other Inklings, and Tolkien had an opportunity to remind Lewis of them—if he so desired—as he in turn listened to and critiqued Narnia. It is therefore interesting to note that a number of these "traditional" Great War themes do not seem to have affected Lewis as might be expected.

According to Croft, much war in Middle-earth seems to reflect war in Northern Europe, though obviously it was translated culturally and technologically. The general and complete waste of the land as a result of conflict and the large, highly organized armies Sauron marched into combat are cases in point. The treatment of the orcs bears some similarity to the British view of Germans in the first half of the twentieth century. To anyone with an even cursory knowledge of life during the Great War, these ideas make perfect sense and are, in fact, almost predictable. It would be logical for an author who experienced them firsthand to include them, but with Lewis, a significant number of Croft's themes simply do not appear in Narnia or, if they do, they are decidedly muted.

Of course, as noted above, Lewis possessed a separate, interior life where he spent much of his time and which he fed with copious amounts of imaginative material. Lewis's emphasis on his own imagination and his ability to withdraw into it meant that in a very real sense he "experienced" whatever he read first hand. The simple fact that something took place in the "real" world as opposed to his imagination did not give it any particular primacy in his scheme of Narnian influences. His experience of war in person and vicariously were therefore simply two significant strands in the much larger tapestry, and it is probable that the following are instances where the literary overshadowed the historical.

First among these missing points is presence of huge, well-organized armies. In World War I, Allied and German forces literally reached into the millions of men, and they had very well defined structures of command from a supreme commander down to the lowliest private.

There is no sense of this at all in Lewis. The armies that the Narnians fielded are generally small, numbering not more than a few thousand (perhaps hundred) soldiers at a time, though Lewis obviously never gave a detailed order of battle. There are a few references to individual leaders (Fenris Ulf, is one instance), but no detailed division of command into coherent units. In this sense, Narnian war-making was much more feudal than modern. The troops were not professional soldiers who made up an officially trained army so much as they were individuals with other lives and pursuits who make war part-time at the request of the king or queen. Even Calormen, while demonstrably more war-like, operated in a similar way.

Of course, Lewis himself was a civilian who took up arms in the war, but this analogy can only be carried so far in a broader understanding of modern warfare. In most of Twentieth Century Europe, nations maintained huge standing armies of professional soldiers, which were then expanded greatly at need by the addition of draftees from the larger populace. The draftees (or volunteers, in Lewis's case) essentially became professionals for the time they were in and were treated as such. This is, of course, a very different approach compared to the feudal or militia system evident in Narnia and Calormen.

Next, Narnian wars tend to be quickly fought conflicts of movement, rather than a longer, grinding stalemate like the Western Front. With the exception of Caspian's war against the Telmarines, most Narnian campaigns are fought in days or weeks as opposed to months and years. Even Tolkien had a complete history of diplomatic intrigue and military maneuvering worked out that took place over the course of decades in Middle-earth to explain the specific events that were accomplished in one year in his trilogy. There is no sense of this at all in Lewis.

Another significant missing theme that might be expected to appear is the general destruction left in the wake of war. Unlike France in World War I, Narnia was never laid waste as a result of war itself. Blight and destruction were present in the Chronicles, but they were a result of a pre-existing evil, not war itself. In *The Lion, the Witch and the Wardrobe*, Narnia suffered under the crushing weight of a perpetual winter, but this was a result of Jadis herself, not the war against her. In *Prince Caspian* the land of Narnia was mostly green and fertile, even if its native denizens were being hunted and Cair Paravel left to fall to ruins. In both cases, war actually freed the land to improve further; it did not desecrate or destroy it. The only hint of destruction as a result of war comes in *The Last Battle* when the Calormene soldiers began their deforestation project. Even here, though, it can easily be argued that the brief war itself did not lead to destruction—Shift's greed did.

Further, there is none of the dirt, stink, and grit that Lewis manifestly experienced in the trenches, and in fact the Narnians do not seem to be interested in trenches at all, however useful they might be as defensive positions. Spatially, Narnians tended to think upward instead of downward in terms of war. The fortifications of Narnia—castles and towers—are built on top of the ground rather than excavated into it. Even the defense of Aslan's How, the closest Lewis ever comes to anything remotely like trench warfare in Narnia, demonstrates this tendency. While the British trenches Lewis served in were obviously dug *down* into the ground, the How was heaped up *above* the stone table to make an artificial hill. Inside, there was none of the sense of cramped, disgusting filth that Lewis saw in France. Instead, it was spacious, roomy, and clean (*PC* 89).

A final obviously-absent theme is the demonization of human enemies in Narnia. In her discussion of Tolkien's orcs, Croft notes that the common attitudes evident in World War I stressed the differences between "us" and "them" *ad absurdum* (47–48). The Germans were essentially dehumanized to the point where they lost individual identities and were more a force of nature, and a very evil one at that. There is no real sense of this with Lewis's human enemies in Narnia. The two largest opponent groups—the Telmarines from *Prince Caspian* and the various appearances of the citizens of Calormen—were very much living, human races. They had unique names and personalities, like Glozelle, Sopespian, Corradin, and Emeth. Some of them were evil, but in a very human sense, meaning that their own backgrounds and experiences interacted with their free will to harden them into making consistently evil choices, such as the haughty and childish Prince Rabadash. In these cases, there was no sense that these people *must* act this way because they *were* evil beyond redemption. Other enemies simply followed evil orders in good faith, such as the "burly, decent-looking fellow" who stepped up to take advantage of Aslan's offer to return to Earth at the end of *Prince Caspian* or Emeth, the faithful Calormen soldier in *The Last Battle* who entered the Stable in search of his god and instead found Aslan (*PC* 212; *LB* 159–66). Salvation was clearly possible for all of these anti-Narnians. Aslan offered it repeatedly to Rabadash at the end of *The Horse and His Boy* while Emeth received it, as did apparently thousands of younger Telmarines in *Prince Caspian* (*HHB* 203–13; *LB* 159–66; *PC* 207–08).

That said, Lewis does demonize some enemies, but those he does are, appropriately, somewhat demonic already. Lewis only treats traditionally evil, non-human entities as beyond redemption. In these cases, he clearly gives a sense of "us" and "them," stating plainly that there is real, permanent evil that needs to be destroyed, not coddled, tolerated, or even negotiated with. The witches (white and green) were foremost among these, but Jadis herself also gave a nice list of beings when she called her retainers to do battle with Aslan's army:

> Summon all *our people* to meet me here as speedily as they can. Call out the giants and the werewolves and the spirits of those trees who are on our side. Call the Ghouls, and the Boggles, the Ogres and the Minotaurs. Call the Cruels, the Hags, the Spectres, and the people of the Toadstools. We will fight. (*LWW* 132, emphasis added)

While apparently some mythological creatures can choose which master to serve (i.e. naiads, dryads, dwarfs, giants, and Earthmen), others seem simply set in their evil ways and Aslan made no attempt to rehabilitate them. Instead, they were hunted and destroyed and "in the end all that foul brood was stamped out" (*LWW* 180).[3] This would fit the definition of "demonization" but, since the creatures involved were never human to begin with, it would require several odd anthropomorphic leaps in logic to establish any necessary connection to Germans in World War I, especially given that Lewis depicts human enemies in a very different way.

In conclusion, Lewis's time in the army affected him in definite ways, though not as much as it might be supposed. While it did not annihilate his essential self or inflict such trauma that he was unable to function afterward (as it did for some others), the war did exert a significant influence on his already extant personality. It became an important part of the much larger and complex tapestry that was Lewis, and was one of several springs which flowed into the creative pool of his considerable imagination. Lewis drew on his experience in distinguishable ways, and in a real sense the trenches of France affected how the Narnians pursued war.

This article was published originally in Mythlore *30.1/2 (#115/116) (2011): 123–42. It is reprinted here with permission.*

---

3. This is obviously at odds with the recent movie versions of the book, where there are good and bad mythological creatures on both sides—particularly minotaurs. It would seem the writers and directors missed Lewis's point about having to face real evil.

WORKS CITED

Burkett, B. G. and Glena Whitley. *Stolen Valor: How the Vietnam Generation was Robbed of Its Heroes and Its History*. Dallas: Verity Press, 1998. Print.

Croft, Janet Brennan. *War and the Works of J. R. R. Tolkien*. Westport: Praeger, 2004. Print. Contributions to the Study of Science Fiction and Fantasy 106.

De Groot, Gerard J. *The First World War*. New York: Palgrave, 2001. Print.

Gilcrist, K. J. *A Morning After War: C. S. Lewis and WWI*. New York: Peter Lang, 2005. Print.

Green, Roger Lancelyn and Walter Hooper. *C. S. Lewis: A Biography*. New York: Harcourt Brace, 1974. Print.

Gresham, Douglas. *Jack's Life: The Life Story of C. S. Lewis*. Nashville: Broadman and Holman, 2005. Print.

Hooper, Walter, ed. *C. S. Lewis: A Complete Guide to His Life and Works*. New York: HarperCollins, 1996. Print.

Lewis, C. S. *The Collected Letters of C. S. Lewis*, Vol. 2. Walter Hooper, ed. San Francisco: HarperSanfrancisco, 2004. Print.

—. *The Horse and His Boy*. New York: Collier, 1970. Print.

—. *The Last Battle*. New York: Collier, 1970. Print.

—. "Learning in Wartime." *The Weight of Glory and Other Addresses*. New York: HarperOne, 2001. 47–63. Print.

—. *The Lion, the Witch and the Wardrobe*. New York: Scholastic, 1987. Print.

—. "On Three Ways of Writing for Children." *Of Other Worlds: Essays and Stories*. San Diego: Harvest, 1994. 22–34. Print.

—. *Prince Caspian*. New York: Collier, 1972. Print.

—. *The Silver Chair*. New York: Collier, 1970. Print.

—. *Surprised by Joy: The Shape of My Early Life*. Orlando: Harvest Books, 1955. Print.

—. "Why I Am Not a Pacifist." *The Weight of Glory and Other Addresses*. New York: HarperOne, 2001. 64–90. Print.

Sayer, George. *Jack: A Life of C. S. Lewis*. Wheaton: Crossway Books, 1988. Print.

Horses, Horoscopes, and Human Consciousness:
Owen Barfield on Making Meaning in His Post-WWI Writings

TIFFANY BROOKE MARTIN

OWEN BARFIELD (1898-1997) IS USUALLY ASSOCIATED with the Inklings, and his philosophical and literary ideas factor into the profound impact that writers such as C. S. Lewis and J. R. R. Tolkien have had on literary studies, fantasy literature in particular, and the culture at large in both the English-speaking world and globally. Barfield, however, deserves a closer critical look based on his own merit as an intellectual and prolific writer of both non-fiction and fiction. Disagreeing with the materialism and dualistic thinking of the modernist era, Barfield drew on romanticism to develop his views, and he contended that how humans think and process language and meaning has changed, demonstrable in an evolution of human consciousness. Language, once unified, is now split into multiple meanings; whereas a word once represented something concrete, over time, linguistic meaning has grown increasingly abstract (*Poetic* 87–88). Barfield's vision was unity; he believed that imagination can reunite language and meaning, thereby reversing social decline into meaninglessness. In his cultural critique, Barfield advocated social reform and invited his readers to think and act on his ideas, often through the vehicle of fantasy to illustrate his redemptive, hopeful impetus and belief in harmonizing the material and spiritual through language's power and the imagination.

Barfield's theories are central to his work, but social, cultural, and biographical factors also shape his writing. Prior to World War I, Barfield and his older brother, Harry, were keenly interested in radio communications. When the war began, Harry enlisted and became a wireless officer; once Barfield was of age, he followed his brother's lead though his service was short-lived due to the armistice. This early interest and training in electricity and its theory was central to Barfield's developing ideas and life's work. The impact of WWI is also seen in how Barfield treats the subject specifically—for instance in his short story "The Devastated Area" and his review of Wilfrid Owen's poetry—as well as general themes that he developed early on and consistently returned to in his writing.[1] Recognizing the powerful possibilities fantasy presents to the reader, Barfield incorporated such elements in several fantasy stories, plays, and poems. For example, Barfield's frequent use of horses and stars as symbolic and notable appear to have their origins in his early years. They are some of the many signs he uses in his overarching message about human consciousness and how to make meaning after the devastation of WWI. Considering some of his early texts—"The Superman," "Dope," "The Devastated Area," and *The Silver Trumpet*—gives insight into not only Barfield's own ideas (and how they were shaped) but also the corresponding influence he has had on contemporary writers and thinkers.

As a British citizen and soldier, Barfield incorporates some of the cultural and social effects of WWI in his writing. Concerning WWI literature, Paul Fussell writes that "the movement was towards myth, towards a revival of the cultic, the mystical, the sacrificial, the prophetic, the sacramental, and the universally significant. In short, towards fiction" (131). This was "a world of reinvigorated myth," which "seem[s] to imply a throwback way across the nineteenth and eighteenth centuries to Renaissance and medieval modes of thought and feeling" (115). This movement toward fiction, myth, and older modes of thinking is evident in Barfield's literary choices. Fussell relates that "[t]he well-known triads of traditional myth and ritual donate, as it were, some of their meanings and implications to the military threes" (127), such as "three separate lines of trenches: front, support, reserve" (125) and the soldiers' practice of "[c]ounting off by threes" (127); consequently, "military action becomes elevated to the level of myth and imbued with much of its portent" (127). The threefold and its mythic associations in both ancient and modern thought, as well as its association with war and human action, influenced Barfield's thinking—seen in his concept of humans as threefold beings who feel, will, and think—and occurs throughout his fiction.

Fussell also writes regarding the authors of the Great War: "The roster of the major innovative talents who were not involved with the war [...] includes Yeats, Woolf, Pound, Eliot, Lawrence, and Joyce—that is, the masters of the modern movement. It was left to lesser talents—always more traditional and technically prudent—to recall in literary

---

1. Besides the impact of WWI, another often cited "great war" shaped Barfield's and Lewis's ideas and approach to writing through a series of letters ranging from approximately the mid-1920s to the early 1930s (Adey).

form a war they had actually experienced" (313–14). Barfield experienced the war in some ways more directly than those canonically heralded as literary greats, but he is not considered a major talent though some of his poetry and fiction received due notice and acclaim at the time. For example, his poem "Day" was included in *The Best Poems of 1923* (Hunter and Kranidas 6), and a few short stories appeared in modernist periodicals that published famous writers. Barfield turned, nevertheless, from this "entry into the world of fashionable letters" by "proclaim[ing] himself a maverick both stylistically and in terms of subject matter" (Hunter and Kranidas 6). As his ideas about language and meaning solidified, and as he committed himself to generally unpopular anthroposophical[2] and romantic views, Barfield's writing style and interests increasingly became what could be deemed neo-romantic.

Following his overarching principle that imagination needs actualization in daily life, Barfield blends ideas about myth and meaning from modernist and romantic interpretations in his own neo-romantic conception that reformulates the old (such as myth, tradition, and history) to inspire fresh vision. Michael Tratner writes in *Modernism and Mass Politics* that "two different senses of 'myth'—as the history of the future and as elements taken from ancient tales that will revive ancient values lost in capitalist society—appear in modernist works extensively" (37). Romanticism's view that "myth represents the recurrence of universal experience" (Von Hendy 137) shapes Barfield's neo-romantic use of myth since he intends a wide application of his principles. Verlyn Flieger explains Barfield's perspective regarding myth and meaning as "inseparable":

> Words are expressed myth, the embodiment of mythic concepts and a mythic world view. The word *myth*, in this context, must be taken to mean that which describes man's perception of his relationship to the natural and supernatural world. Barfield's theory postulates that language, in its beginnings, made no distinction between the literal and metaphoric meaning of a word, as it does today. [...] We now perceive the cosmos as particularized, fragmented, and wholly separate from ourselves. (39)

Barfield defines "myth [as] the true child of Meaning, begotten on imagination" (*Poetic* 201). Reclaiming myth with modern storytelling helps

---

2. Anthroposophy, briefly defined, is a philosophy created by Rudolf Steiner that blends spirituality, science, and Western and Eastern thought. Diener estimates that Barfield began seriously researching anthroposophy in early to mid-1923 and officially joined the Anthroposophical Society in Great Britain in 1924 (92–93).

create meaning to counteract a degenerating culture by building on ancient truths.

An avowed anti-materialist, Barfield distanced himself from what he viewed as unimportant and sought to communicate truth through the imagination, staying true to mental processes, and he also explored the importance of dreams and writing in bringing about wholeness and healing for his fictional characters. Astrid Diener writes, "The themes explored in his fiction of the 1920s are all concerned with the consequences of an outlook which separates individual thought (and experience) from reality" (114–15). This reveals Barfield's belief that "[s]eparation, dissociation, isolation [...] have finally come to dominate modern consciousness" (48). Barfield's writing often incorporates both modernist and neo-romantic techniques and themes. Well-known examples of modernist style related to time include the stream-of-consciousness technique and fragmentation in the narrative's structure (apparent in Barfield's "The Devastated Area"). Focus on the internal thoughts and conflicted emotions of characters recurs in modernist texts since the human consciousness portrays larger forces at work; "the ache of unrest in the 1920s arose not simply from a vain, nostalgic wish somehow to re-enter earlier, happier times, but from an uneasiness with the sense of time itself" (Stevenson 140). As examples of this point, although James Joyce's *Ulysses* (1922) and Virginia Woolf's *Mrs. Dalloway* (1925) both take place on a single day in June, the texts indicate the fluidity and difficult nature of time, demonstrated through the use of flashbacks and internal anxieties about the future, all happening within the (dis)order of the present.

Political unrest and WWI's devastating effects generate growing social distrust in language and its power to communicate and make stable meaning, a problem that Barfield addresses in his work. Randall Stevenson points out that "the multiplying lies of governments and official institutions—as well as advertisers—have steadily added to language's potential for distortion rather than representation; to its capacity for rhetorical manipulation almost independently of meaning or truth" (185). In addition to the abuse of language through propaganda, "[t]he war punctures time, upsetting the dynamic relationship between past, present and future which constitutes modernity: locking its protagonists in the present; rendering the past a mythic 'before'; and displacing the hopes invested in the future" (Armstrong 16). In Woolf's and Joyce's fiction, for example, death is another recurrent theme, an omnipresent shadow of the revolutionary upheavals of the past and present and a foreshadow of anticipated apocalypses. Revolutionary themes also feature in romantic writing and subsequently in neo-romantic texts with apocalyptic themes depicting spiritual ideas as well as the influence of war and the call for transformation in society and thinking, all of which occur in Barfield's literary endeavors.

Noting the problems humanity faces in the modern age, Barfield writes:

> Living in the consciousness soul[,] man experiences isolation, loneliness, materialism, loss of faith in a spiritual world, above all—uncertainty. The soul has to make up its mind and to act in a positive way on its own unsupported initiative. And it finds great difficulty in doing so. For it is too much in the dark to be able to see any clear reason why it should, and it no longer feels the old (instinctive) promptings of the spirit within. (*Romanticism* 109)

Aware of the devastating effects of such problems, Barfield addresses how humanity can face and work through these issues. The idea of the soul being "too much in the dark" appears in specific metaphors regarding light, sleep, and awakening that occur in his fiction, notably his later works. Acknowledging the importance and development of language over time, its effect on one's thought processes, and how that needs to be unified in mind and spirit can lead an individual to more richly perceive life and meaning; thereby engendering greater personal integration and certainty to improve one's overall harmony with others and nature.

Perhaps to demonstrate the need for individual and communal unity, Barfield's protagonists are often isolated and/or misunderstood. This motif presents itself in Barfield's presumably first story "The Superman," currently unpublished and written c. 1919 at Wadham College, Oxford, during the beginning of Barfield's undergraduate education.[3] The text blends modernist and neo-romantic themes, a fitting start to illustrate Barfield's early reflections and interests that he was to expand on throughout his writing career. According to Blaxland-de Lange, the story "is a thinly veiled autobiographical reflection about the mystery of individual human existence, poised between the melee of everyday human affairs and the starry cosmos. As a piece of writing, it is considerably more interesting—and, indeed, a truer reflection of Barfield's youthful spirit—than the story which he *did* succeed in publishing shortly afterwards, 'Dope' " (259). The

---

[3] Blaxland-de Lange believes that the story "probably dates from 1920" (331n230). The text at the Bodleian has "1919 or 1920" written in pen at the top of the first page.

claims that "The Superman" is more interesting and more true to Barfield than "Dope" are rather subjective and arguable, and to be kept in mind in reviewing both stories. Blaxland-de Lange also contends that "Barfield's deeper interests [did not] manifest themselves in the three other short stories published during the 1920s, although a penetrating human perception is evident in all of them" (259). First, in response to this assertion, Barfield published more than "three other short stories" during this time. Second, perhaps Barfield's ideas about the evolution of human consciousness are not as representative in these stories, if this is what Blaxland-de Lange intends by "Barfield's deeper interests"; however, that lack does not mean that these stories are less important or worth dismissing without further investigation concerning what Barfield tried to communicate through them.

To begin with this first story, the nameless protagonist, the "superman" as the title implies, is a visionary struck by "moods" and "mental trances" that come to him involuntarily and cause "the present, past, and future" to intermix and "give life to the picture in his mind, turning it from a tableau into a drama" (1). Regarding the importance of names and etymology to Barfield, while the protagonist remains anonymous, the story's title is a likely reference to the Nietzschean concept of the *Übermensch*.[4] A superman has superior qualities compared to other humans, possessing a power that separates him from others. His visionary power distinguishes Barfield's protagonist, isolating him from others yet uniting him to the greater cosmos, drawing him out of himself and urging him to reflect on deeper issues and life forces.

At a piano recital, a visionary experience comes upon him more intensely than ever, removing him from "self-consciousness" into a dream-like state that makes him aware of the humanity around him as "a stream of pitiful figures." They appear to be "stiff fantastic Things" with facial expressions that are "mechanical and without meaning," adding to the "atmosphere of anxiety and hurry" (2). Such descriptions are in keeping with modernism with its portrayal of society and people as mechanistic, meaningless, and fast-paced; yet it is also a neo-romantic scene in that it becomes a surreal moment of insight for the protagonist.

Wondering if others have had similar experiences or if he is mentally afflicted, he tries to explain these moods and visions to a friend

---

4. The modern reader might also initially associate this story's title with the Superman character of the American comic strip; though there are similarities in that they both have extrasensory powers, Barfield's character predates the comic strip, is not invincible or necessarily heroic, and cannot fly except in a more figurative sense, based on the text's language.

who replies that he has also felt that way, concluding in a modernist tone "How futile life is!" (3). The protagonist, unconvinced that his friend understands, tries to discuss his experiences with other people but feels increasingly isolated and socially withdraws. Turning to poetry, he reads a line by William Wordsworth that summarizes the visionary feelings that "all troubled me";[5] in this moment, he experiences a Barfieldian "felt change of consciousness" because he mentally and emotionally responds to the transformative quality of reading this poetry (4).[6] The line "all troubled me" returns to him during a walk home while contemplating the night sky.[7] Though he has an amateur knowledge of astronomy, the stars and their constellations are "new to him" with "some meaning" in their shapes. Wholly absorbed with the sky, "his mind left the earth and stood in the black emptiness of space," rendering him oblivious to a car speeding toward him (5). The reader, however, is aware of this impending danger, and a break in the text and the character's ruminations indicate that something has happened to the protagonist because after "fe[eling] a shock, […] it seemed that he was coming to himself" (5–6). As "pain" causes him "to remember that he was on the way home and ought soon to be there," another break occurs in the text, introducing the final paragraph that leaves the story rather inconclusive (6).

The protagonist finds himself "among the drifting stars […] that moved about each other in time to some great rhythm, of which the whole stream's motion was only a part"; he observes the stars' "interplay" and is uncertain "whether centuries or only a few moments had passed" (6). This scene seems to allude to the divine dance of the cosmos, a medieval concept that the Inklings often incorporated in their fiction as symbolic of the harmonious connection of the spheres, linking the supernatural and natural worlds, spirit and matter that are central to Barfield's concerns. Space is alive and not a void.

It is also in this outer space scene where the story abruptly stops. The reader is left to question whether the protagonist is dead or having an out-of-body experience due to his likely injury. Complicating the lack of closure is the fact that the character himself does not seem to know

---

5. See Wordsworth's poem "Resolution and Independence."
6. This concept comes from *Poetic Diction* (48–57), indicating an emotional and cognitive change that contributes to self-development and detailed appreciation of language.
7. Barfield "was […] a great lover of the stars" (Harwood 32), and this scene is the first of many in his fiction that emphasizes humanity's relationship with the cosmos.

because the concluding line "when he realised what had happened" has been marked through, apparently by Barfield since he signs off at the end of the text. This lack of finality leaves the character himself without completion, floating as it were with the cosmic powers, unsure about time and his mortality. With his first story, Barfield begins a recurrent pattern in his fiction, that of the ambiguous ending, which is a common modern/postmodern literary device. The reader does not know but can assume that the protagonist is killed, or at the least severely injured, by the speeding car. The purpose in such a fatal or potentially fatal end is open to interpretation, something Barfield is fond of inviting his readers to do, to speculate on the how and why of the story.

Barfield's insight into and representation of human consciousness is consistent with modernist writing, as well as exemplary of Barfield's concerns with mental processes, evident in two more short stories, "Dope" and "The Devastated Area," written not long after WWI. In reviewing these two tales, David Bratman writes that they "are appropriately hazy character portraits illustrating Barfield's thesis that the 'reality' we see around us is more a mental construct than anything truly existing. The characters in these stories experience the dissociation from that consensus reality that Barfield himself must glimpse" (57). If one accepts Kathryn Hume's definition that *"Fantasy is any departure from consensus reality*, an impulse native to literature and manifested in innumerable variations" (21), Bratman's observation about consensus reality alludes to the fantastic thread weaving through much of Barfield's work. Diener describes "Dope" (1923) as "perhaps the most impressive illustration of an alienating outlook which reduces the individual to a passive spectator of an external reality, whose processes are increasingly felt to be slipping out of control" (115). Ultimately, she believes that "Dope"

> embodies twentieth century fears about the predicament of modern man in an increasingly mechanized world: fears, for example, about the loss of meaning in a world where individuals feel they are doomed to coexist without relating to each other or the world around them. It also embodies fears about the loss of freedom as man increasingly feels dominated and enslaved by the machine. (116)[8]

This short story illustrates "in some ways, the dawning of the age of totalitarianism and fascism" (116). Diener also writes that the story "in spirit strikingly resembles [Eliot's] *Waste Land*" (49) and "is characterized not by meaningful interrelation, but by fragmentation and

---

8. Diener suggests that Lewis's later, incomplete story "The Dark Tower" shares similarities with the possibility of Barfieldian influence (116).

disintegration" as well as "specific fears about the alienating and dehumanizing effects of technical progress" (122). In Barfield's words, the story is "an expression of the sort of passivity with which undeveloped 20th century minds (as far as I can see) watch a mechanical world clicking past their limited field of vision" (qtd. in Diener 127).

As these descriptions attest, "Dope" is an excellent example of Barfield's employment of such modernist tropes as time schedules, mechanistic work and lifestyles, a barrage of advertising and meaningless language, and aimless trips into the countryside. The word choice increases the modernist tone: "Henry Williams, unskilled labourer [...] plodded on alone toward his Underground station with nothing particular in his thoughts except a row of the little bright screws he had been sorting all day" (71), impressing on the reader the monotony, isolation, and dullness of such a life. Throughout the story, the word "on" repeats, sometimes several times in a row like the ticking of a clock or the repetitive motion of a train. Related to these modernist problems that deaden the senses and that divorce language and meaning is the fact that humanity is a spectator and not a participant with nature, expressed through the shallow observations of city dwellers when they travel through the countryside. Hinting at this problem shows Barfield's neoromantic inclination and the themes he emphasized more over time about participating with nature and other humans meaningfully.

"Dope" ends in a cry of despair, as an unidentified man exclaims, "hide me from the bloody world!" (76). The man might represent a traumatized war veteran or a modern man sick of the monotony of common labor. His namelessness, as well as the woman he is with, corresponds with the generic nature of these people. They could be anyone, standing there "on the side of the road" (76) without any apparent purpose, underscoring their pointless, peculiar position. The title of the story itself can also apply here. A "dope" is a stupid, foolish person and as a noun can represent a character's name in a sense, thereby referring to the people caught up in the mechanized, modernized world without actively thinking about the detrimental effects it has on their lives and how they should attempt to counteract social and cultural problems. "Dope" in its slang form to denote mind-altering drugs could also imply the damaged modern consciousness that needs healing and restoration of reality and meaning in daily life. Near the story's conclusion, the word "bloody," if read as both profanity and adjective, highlights that the world is cursed perhaps in part because of the recent bloodbath of WWI. According to Lewis's diary entry of 4 Feb. 1923 (the year "Dope" was published), Nevill Coghill told Lewis "(just like Barfield) that he felt it his duty to be a 'conchy' [conscientious objector] if there was another war" (*All My Road* 191). This sidenote about Barfield, along with the information about Coghill, shows the impact that the war had on young men, as well as Barfield's views at the time on fighting.

Other contemporary short stories that responded to the war and modernism's concerns with the city and industrialization include those of Anglo-Irish writer Lord Dunsany. In the preface to *The Book of Wonder* (1912), Dunsany invites readers "who are in any wise weary of London: come with me: and those that tire at all of the world we know: for we have new worlds here" (n.p.). In the story "The Wonderful Window," a magical window lets a businessman observe a kingdom he terms Golden Dragon City, offering him respite and a utopia of sorts. Eventually he destroys the window because he thinks the kingdom is doomed, and business proves paralyzing to his spirit and imagination as wonder is lost in the daily routine and the suppressive city and work environment, similar to the drudgery illustrated in "Dope."

Another story by Dunsany with neo-romantic themes is "The City on Mallington Moor," published in *Tales of Wonder* (1916). The collection's preface marks its response to WWI because "[t]hese tales are tales of peace," offering readers a way to "turn their eyes […] from a world of mud and blood and khaki, and to read for a while of cities too good to be true" (n.p.). The story presents—unlike the gloomy, xenophobic reality of London and other world cities—an unearthly city in the countryside as one "of beauty and song" (77) that offers "strangers rest" (78). The tale's narrator sleeps but then awakens to discover that the city has vanished. Such a dream cannot last. Visions of utopia cannot be realized in the modern life except through fiction or so it would seem in Dunsany's pessimistic representation, just as "Dope" concludes with its unhappy view about the world's condition.

Continuing his cultural critique of meaninglessness in "The Devastated Area" and the motif of monotony in modernism via repetition, Barfield returns to his narration of war's effects specifically in its societal and personal consequences for veterans. First published in *The New Age: A Weekly Review of Politics, Literature and Art* (3 July 1924), "The Devastated Area" includes both biographical details and "the dark imaginings of an ex-soldier and his inability to communicate the horrors of war" (Hunter and Kranidas 13).[9] Such modernist allusions signify

---

9. Barfield attempted publishing this story with *The Criterion* before the story was published by *The New Age*. On 20 Sept. 1923, Eliot writes Barfield that
> I have indeed received your second sketch ['The Devastated Area'] and have kept it in the hope of being able to see you or write

the cultural currents of the period with the disintegration of the British Empire and the trauma of war. A well-known literary example of war-related communication problems and the effects of shell shock is the character of Septimus Smith in Woolf's *Mrs. Dalloway*.[10] Due to fighting in the war and thereby losing part of himself—stressed through the repeated phrase "he could not feel" (e.g., 131, 133)—Septimus has difficulty communicating and ends his life in despair. Though Barfield's shell shock victim Stephen does not commit suicide, he entertains the idea in response to the chaos of his mind: "I must get out of this. Plenty of people do, you know ... found with his head in a gas oven" (83). Stylistically, the story is modernist with its stream-of-consciousness representation of the character's thoughts. Extending the mechanical theme in "Dope," clockwork rhythms and engines reappear here but more closely connected with human consciousness: Stephen "felt his brain starting slowly to revolve like the engine of a great liner; it seemed to gather speed and noise, till it chugged round and round in his head as though it could never stop," contributing to his insomnia and disordered consciousness (77).

Textual breaks in the story rhetorically reflect the shattered state of the soldier's mind and emotions. He wants to forget but memory intrudes. One of the strongest impressions left on him from the war is his memory of seeing the blown-out remains of another soldier's head because "he could still draw a map with his eyes shut of the inside of that head" (78). Akin to the marital problems Septimus Smith and his wife have after his return from the war, Stephen experiences distance and miscommunication in his marriage. Stephen's wife Muriel "still believed in the British Empire" and "that on the whole the war was a righteous war" (79); however, Stephen cannot accept the war propaganda anymore due to fighting and living in the trenches and shell-holes. Contrastingly, Muriel "hadn't been bowled right over and turned inside out, and stamped into the mud; [...] her soul hadn't been disembowelled [...]

---

to you at some length about it. I must tell you frankly that I do not like it nearly as much as the one which we published ['Dope']. The latter impressed me as having a distinct individual rythym [sic] which made it remarkable; the former seems to me to have the defects of the method without this rythym [sic]. The story which we published, however, interests me so much that I shall follow with the greatest interest anything you write and hope that you be as good as to let me see other things which you have written. (*Letters Vol. 2* 217)

10. Barfield's story was published before Woolf's novel, so it would be interesting to know if she had read it or if their works merely parallel each other due to mutual social concerns.

she had somehow managed to keep her head" (79)—all of which alludes to the separation and misunderstanding that often occurred between war veterans and those who did not know war on the Front Line.

Joining the fight was not without its motivations and effects: "war experience and its recall take the form of the deepest, most universal kind of allegory. Movement up the line, battle, and recovery become emblems of quest, death, and rebirth" (Fussell 131). Moreover, "[t]he experiences of a man going up the line to his destiny cannot help seeming to him like those of a hero of medieval romance if his imagination has been steeped in actual literary romances or their equivalent" (135). Entering the war to participate in a seemingly noble and courageous effort, the returning solder's experience was usually quite the opposite, struggling to reenter a changed society as a profoundly affected and traumatized individual. In a 1921 review of poems by Wilfrid Owen, Barfield writes the following passage that notes themes he clearly registers in his own story:

> To this poet war seems to have meant above all things loneliness; he must have been haunted continually by a horrible sense of spiritual isolation, which kept whispering to him that his friends—above all, that the women—at home, loving, sympathetic, imaginative as they might be, had never once been on the edge of the threshold of *sharing* his experiences. He felt with anguish that he was gradually slipping further away from them, *isolated by his own suffering*. (454, emphasis in original)

In addition to the tragedy of the isolated feelings war veterans experienced upon returning to Britain after WWI, "the really shocking thing is not the *horror* of war alone, it is the actual *reaction* to that horror of those who stayed at home" (Diener 117). This reaction occurs in the lack of understanding on Muriel's part, leading to the couple's eventual estrangement.

Similar to the protagonist in "The Superman," this tale's protagonist feels alone "from the rest of the world" (77) but for different reasons. In "The Devastated Area," "[t]he depths of human isolation and alienation are further explored" and "[like 'Dope'] has as its theme the impotence of thought and feeling over against a hollow, this time not literally mechanical, but spiritually empty world" (Diener 116). Time is in flux for him; though Stephen wants "to let his thoughts run on into the future" now that the war is over, he finds that "memory" persistently "take[s] him backwards through time" (Barfield, "Devastated" 77). Such a mental state illustrates that "the temporality of the post-war world is a product of the war, and this 'therapeutic' view—which suggests memory must be worked over and over, and that trauma must be unlocked—is itself a product of the world the war made" (Armstrong 22). To combat his trauma and ineffective verbal communication, Stephen considers writing as an outlet but then dismisses it: "What's the good of writing? The only people who'll read it are the people who feel it already. The nice gentle people you want to get at, who go on deceiving themselves all their lives, they'll just read the first page and put it away" (83). These lines chastise individuals "who go on deceiving themselves" by not critically thinking and feeling; Stephen's thoughts also resonate with what Barfield later called his "Law of literary endeavour" meaning that "when a book appears with anything upsetting in it, the few who read it don't need it, and the many who need it don't read it" (*Night Operation* 61). Later Barfield characters find writing a much-needed personal outlet, which is especially the case for the protagonists in *This Ever Diverse Pair* and *Eager Spring*.

Though Barfield did not fight on the Front, he incorporates some of his military experience in this story with the chapel service scene (81–82), repeating the rhetoric he heard preached from the pulpit to convince soldiers about the rightness of the war (cf. Blaxland-de Lange 15–16). Furthermore, the moral, even spiritual, implications regarding Britain's view of the Great War resonate with the choice of the name Stephen, somewhat ironic yet appropriate for the story since Stephen means "crowned one." To be crowned is to wear a sign of honor and rule on one's head. With the disintegration of the British Empire, the power and respectability of the crown diminishes. In a more literal sense, "The Devastated Area" often mentions heads, brains, and thoughts, and what troubles Stephen is the memory of the dead soldier's head, his own disordered thoughts, and the pain in his head. The name Stephen can also refer to the biblical martyr, symbolizing the personal suffering that Barfield's Stephen has experienced, dying in one sense for a sacred cause as some believed the war to be.

Barfield's sympathy for war veterans is apparent in a seemingly small gesture. Among his personal papers, Barfield saved a copy of a horoscope that a veteran (John M. Thorburn [?]) made for him, dated 21 July 1931. Forty years later in August 1971, Barfield added a handwritten note at the top of the manuscript: "I got into conversation with the author of this horoscope in a restaurant. He had been badly knocked by World War I, and said he found the drawing of horoscopes psychologically remedial to him. I think I paid him £3.30 for it." This action underscores the fact that veterans need understanding and an outlet to cope with their suffering. Acquiring and keeping this horoscope also emphasizes Barfield's belief in humanity's connection with the cosmos. This point does not make any claim or suggestions about astrological beliefs but rather that Barfield understood the importance of humanity needing to be in harmony with nature and the supernatural, and thereby live imaginatively and create meaning.

Although Barfield engaged with modernist tropes and themes, his early stories also reveal his interest and incorporation of fantastic elements, even if the stories do not qualify wholly as mythopoeic fiction. Flickers of the fantastic appear and support his predisposition toward the power of fantasy to communicate important messages to readers. Horses usually with mythic qualities feature in Barfield's later fantasy works, such as *The Rose on the Ash-Heap* and numerous poems. This attention to the archetypal nature of horses appears to have come at least in part from the experience of riding as a soldier. In a letter (4 Nov. 1984) to Barfield, Dr. Lyle Dorsett asked where Barfield went riding while "stationed in Belgium, waiting to be discharged" during World War I. Barfield replied on 18 Nov. 1984: "Anywhere in the neighbourhood of Mons, where my unit was stationed, but what I especially remember is gallops [...] through pinewoods in the Spring when the pines were scenting the warm air." This memory is one of the few recorded ones in which Barfield directly refers to his war-time experience. Highlighting an activity that provided an outlet during the war also underscores Barfield's emphasis on nature's vital role in human consciousness and health.

Not long after these short stories, Barfield turned more strongly to fantasy with his first book publication, the fairy tale *The Silver Trumpet* in 1925 pre-dating Lewis's and Tolkien's published fantasy.[11] Barfield's biographer deems it as "[t]he only piece of imaginative prose from this early period which encompasses the full breadth of Barfield's mind, combining spiritual vision with incisiveness and humour [...]. This [story] had been completed by 20 October 1923, since C. S. Lewis had read it in manuscript by then and recorded his reflections in his diary" (Blaxland-de Lange 259). Walter Hooper describes it as "a fairy tale of the Hans Andersen kind" (*Lewis, Letters* III.1598), and the story was a favorite of Tolkien's children. Lewis wrote Barfield in June 1936:

---

11. This is not to say that the other Inklings had not written fantasy by this time. For example, Tolkien wrote *Roverandom* for his children in the late 1920s, but it was not published until 1998. Tolkien also wrote a series of illustrated Father Christmas letters for his children from 1920 to 1943, but these were not published until 1976.

> I lent *The Silver Trumpet* to Tolkien and hear that it is the greatest success among his children that they have ever known. His own fairy-tales, which are excellent, have now no market:[12] and its first reading—children are so practical!—led to a universal wail "You're not going to give it back to Mr. Lewis, are you?"
>
> All the things which the wiseacres on child psychology in our circle said when you wrote it turn out to be nonsense. [...] In fine, you have scored a direct hit. (*Lewis, Letters* II.198)

To turn to the story itself, it opens with the birth of the two princesses, Gambetta and Violetta, and in fairy tale fashion, a witch is on the scene. Although Miss Thomson is "a nobody" and "a witchery sort of woman in her old age," she is a kind witch (6). At the Christening Breakfast, her gift to the princesses is for them to be alike; then she adds, "As long as you both live, you shall love each other more than all else in the world. As long as one of you is living, both shall *be*" though this does not mean that the girls will necessarily be happy (9).

The characterizations of the two princesses through their names and name changes relates to Barfield's thematic focus. Gambetta and Violetta are Italian, feminine names that are then changed to English, more masculine names, Gamboy and Violet, though Violet still retains feminine connotations.[13] In his wisdom about the magical power of names, the Lord Tullywich changes their names so that the girls can be distinguished from each other. In terms of gender criticism, Violet is good because she is feminine and weds Prince Courtesy who comes on a horse with a silver trumpet seeking a queen, whereas Gamboy is bad because she is masculine and practices dark magic.[14] Gamboy strongly opposes Violet's desire to marry Prince Courtesy, but Violet's love for him overrules all else, thus breaking the spell Miss Thomson placed on the princesses (35–36). Violet and Courtesy wed, rule Mountainy Castle, and have a daughter, Princess Lily. Indicative of flowery loveliness, innocence, and purity, Violet and her daughter Lily are named after plants,

---

12. According to the editors' introduction, *Roverandom* was a fantasy that Tolkien wrote for his children likely in 1926 after a summer holiday in 1925; the text was rejected for publication in early 1937 and not published until 1998. Tolkien attempted publishing the text not long after his children clamored often for Barfield's story, which makes one wonder if his children's enjoyment of Barfield's fantasy prompted him to revisit his story and try to publish it.

13. Etymologically, "violet" has both feminine and masculine forms, with the more modern forms being masculine.

14. The Amalgamated Princesses are represented unfavorably by association with Gamboy as their leader, since as a unit lacking individuality, they are weak and easily ruled. Later on, Gamboy lies to them that they shall all be queens, when in reality, she plans to rule as much of the world as possible (137).

a connection with nature and the environment around them, indicating their participating more fully with life in contrast to Gamboy. According to the *OED*, the oldest form of the word "gam," refers to the mouth and "prominent or ugly teeth" (*n.¹*). A later form of "gam" is slang for "[a] leg" (*n.³*), which relates to the etymology for "gambit" from the Italian *gambetto* "tripping up the heels (in wrestling)"—using the legs not as a dancer but as an aggressor. Gambetta/Gamboy is reduced to body parts and therefore is incomplete. The fact that Gamboy relies on a magic book *Excerpta* demonstrates the problems of being incomplete, not whole, since the book's title refers to parts not wholes. An excerpt is a piece, an abstract, a way to pick and choose selections that meet Gamboy's immediate purposes, rather than a lasting, unified force. Her name refers specifically to the leg and mouth, which, in her misusing these parts (i.e., evil missions and abuse of language), negatively portrays what should be applied beautifully in such ways as dance and music to both engender joy and unity and reflect the harmonious spirits of dancers (e.g., Violet) and musicians (e.g., Prince Courtesy).

As a primary framework for Barfield's text, the traditional princess and the frog fairy tale appears in altered form. A dwarf known as the Little Fat Podger is Curator of the Royal Dump and makes the king laugh with his wit and dancing. The Little Fat Podger builds a mechanical toad and hopes to amuse Queen Violet with it. Instead, the toad frightens the queen to death and causes the infant princess to be scared of toads, creating misunderstanding and interfering with an adequate appreciation of the natural world.[15] The king condemns the dwarf; however, wise Lord Tullywich exiles the dwarf yet declares him dead. Aunt Gamboy takes advantage of her niece's fear, dominates Lily and the king, and brings ruin to the region.

Signifying the cultural work of the text, through Gamboy's abuse of rhetoric/language and magic, the treasury is emptied, and the townspeople are poor and restless under mismanagement. In a social critique, Diener analyzes the fairy tale as follows:

> the narrative reflects Barfield's awareness not only of his own personal weakness or that of his predecessor Coleridge, it also reflects his awareness of more general feelings (inherent, for example, in the philosophy of the early twentieth century)—feelings of resignation over the powerlessness of ideals […] [such as with] fascism […]. *The Silver*

---

15. "Robots have their origins in the mechanical toys or automata of the Middle Ages" (Ashley 96), and the dwarf's mechanical toad might be a criticism of technology since Barfield represents robots in other negative contexts in *The Rose on the Ash-Heap* and *Night Operation*.

> *Trumpet*, with its illustration of the mechanism of a brutal authoritarian regime of terror and repression, is an uncanny anticipation of what was to occur in European history. In this respect, the story is a powerful plea for the absolute and acute urgency to counteract these developments—a plea for doing so by bringing the world of ideals back to life. This ultimately meant for Barfield […] a fundamental change in the contemporary social and economic system. (154–55)

Expanding on traditional elements of the fairy tale form, Barfield neo-romantically addresses the modernist problems of language corruption, economic instability, and political division. Though the text might seem aimed at a child audience, there are layers of meaning that can appeal to a wide readership.

Change comes to Mountainy Castle several years later, when Prince Peerio arrives looking for Lily, whom he loves after seeing a painting of her. Of course, Gamboy turns the prince into a toad to obstruct his plans. Meanwhile, a stableboy goes up to a loft to sleep but finds the trumpet that Gamboy hid there long ago, and he blows it. The stable*boy* rights the evil that Gam*boy* committed. A commoner exerts change that affects the kingdom: "As the last note [of the silver trumpet] died slowly away, everybody in the Castle stirred slowly, like a man waking from sleep" (122). The music arouses memories and prompts action: the King confiscates the trumpet, the townspeople realize how Gamboy has abused her position all these years causing great harm to them and the royal family, and Lily determines that she must not live locked away in a tower. During this course of events, Prince Peerio, still a toad, encounters Miss Thomson. She cannot undo Gamboy's spell and tells Peerio someone must love him as a toad for him to be human again.

True to fairy tale form, Princess Lily manages to overcome her fear by the greatest, most unifying power, love. She kisses the toad, transforming Peerio into a prince and leading to their marriage. Peerio's name can refer to peerage indicating that he is noble, but the root form "peer" also implies that he is an equal noble and not exalted over Lily. They must mutually rescue each other from what constrains them. Marriage brings healing and hope, symbolic of unity's power to renew and restore meaning in society.

Because Barfield believed the imagination was "a way of life" (Diener 145) and expression of truth, he encouraged greater self-awareness and individual development with the implications of social reform and collective change not only in his non-fiction but also in his fiction, as a journey through these early, post-WWI works confirms. Malcolm Guite, in his 2011 talk at Cambridge, affirms that Barfield is a prophet of the imagination's power and wrote "for the future." In looking ahead, Barfield was a visionary as is often the case for writers drawn to fantasy, a key element in much of his works in dealing with the supernatural and the unknown.

Fantasy can offer hope to its readers and propose alternative courses of thought and action. Mythopoeic fantasy in particular, as Marek Oziewicz observes, contains "the regenerative powers of myth and mythmaking" and is "a literary indication of a holistic worldview and an imaginative, or 'poetic,' conceptualization of human experience within it" (66). Often characterized by addressing the need for social justice and a harmonious relationship between humans and their environment, along with affirming life's value and humanity's spiritual nature, mythopoeic writing is visionary and describes to some extent much of the fiction Barfield produced. Fantasy's attributes connects with imagination's significance because "[u]nless we use the imagination we are not fully human. Without it, we lack empathy and understanding, all of which are essential to our survival on this planet. […] Barfield thinks of imagination come of age, i.e. a trained imagination that is informed by will (political, ethical will) and by thought" (Schenkel 35), correlating with Barfield's emphasis on the threefold concept of unity in thinking, feeling, and willing. To realize individual, and by extension cultural, change, developing and balancing one's inner and outer self is paramount as a physical and spiritual being, for the physical body enacts one's imaginative ideas.

Positively using our imagination is fundamental to Barfield's concept of final participation in which we are part of a larger whole. The power of participation is to think, synthesize, redeem, wonder, create, interact, and love—all as fully and actively as possible in our creative response to life. This is what Barfield invites readers to do. Unless people take action in changing the way they think, people become passive and lose control over their worlds. Active thinking and reflection through imaginative engagement can lead to unity of mind and spirit, thereby contributing to greater self-development and potential improvement in society and culture, reversing its descent into meaninglessness, despair, and fragmentation.

Although he draws on old ideas, Barfield reimagines them with farsighted intent. Barfield wants readers to stop and think, and think about *how* we think because the mind affects our choices, actions, and interactions with self, others, God, and the environment. In response to this way of thinking, we are to keep telling stories that matter with our lives and other creative expressions. Because he was a writer and thinker of integrity and genuine goodwill, readers need not dismiss

Barfield as esoteric or as less important to the field of literature than more well-known authors. According to Gareth Knight, "Owen Barfield [...] provides much of the ground base for the work of the others [Lewis, Tolkien, and Williams] with his philosophical and literary ideas" (4), which have not been explored in great detail here. Although he had an immeasurable influence on the Inklings and many other writers, intellectuals, and readers—and subsequently extended an indirect influence on modern fantasy and fiction in general—Barfield is not an appendage or mere support or inspiration to other writers. It is through the medium of fiction that Barfield asks us how we will choose to make meaning consciously and culturally.

ACKNOWLEDGEMENT

Material from the Owen Barfield Papers held at the Bodleian Library, Oxford, is quoted with the kind permission of Owen A. Barfield.

WORKS CITED

Adey, Lionel. *C. S. Lewis's "Great War" with Owen Barfield*. Victoria: U of Victoria, 1978. ELS Monograph Ser. 14. Print.

Armstrong, Tim. *Modernism: A Cultural History*. Cambridge: Polity, 2005. Print.

Ashley, Mike. *Out of this World: Science Fiction: but not as you know it*. London: British Lib., 2011. Print.

Barfield, [Arthur] Owen. "The Devastated Area." *A Barfield Sampler: Poetry and Fiction by Owen Barfield*. Ed. Jeanne Clayton Hunter and Thomas Kranidas. Albany: State U of New York P, 1993. 77–84. Print.

—. "Dope." *A Barfield Sampler: Poetry and Fiction by Owen Barfield*. Ed. Jeanne Clayton Hunter and Thomas Kranidas. Albany: State U of New York P, 1993. 71–76. Print.

—. Letter to Dr. Lyle W. Dorsett. 18 Nov. 1984. MS. Owen Barfield Papers, Dep. c. 1060. Bodleian Lib., Oxford.

—. *Night Operation*. [UK]: Barfield P UK, 2009. Print.

—. *Poetic Diction: A Study in Meaning*. 1928. Hanover: Wesleyan UP, 1984. Print.

—. *Romanticism Comes of Age*. 1944. Letchworth: Rudolf Steiner, 1966. Print.

—. *The Silver Trumpet*. 1925. 2nd ed. Grand Rapids: Eerdmans, 1968. Print.

—. "The Superman." C. 1919. TS. Owen Barfield Papers, Dep. c. 1083. Bodleian Lib., Oxford.

—. [Unsigned]. "Wilfrid Owen." Rev. of *Poems*, by Wilfrid Owen. *The New Statesman* 16 (15 Jan. 1921): 454. Print.

Blaxland-de Lange, Simon. *Owen Barfield: Romanticism Come of Age; A Biography*. Forest Row: Temple Lodge, 2006. Print.

Bratman, David. "Landmark Barfield." Rev. of *A Barfield Sampler: Poetry and Fiction by Owen Barfield*, by Owen Barfield. *Mythlore* 21.1 (#79) (1995): 57. Print.

Catalogue of papers of (Arthur) Owen Barfield. Dept. of Special Collections and Western Manuscripts. Bodleian Lib., U of Oxford. Web. 25 Feb. 2013.

Diener, Astrid. *The Role of Imagination in Culture and Society: Owen Barfield's Early Work*. Glienicke: Galda & Wilch, 2002. Print. Leipzig Explorations in Literature and Culture 6.

Dorsett, Lyle W. Letter to Owen Barfield. 4 Nov. 1984. TS. Owen Barfield Papers, Dep. c. 1060. Bodleian Lib., Oxford.

Dunsany, Lord. *Wonder Tales: The Book of Wonder and Tales of Wonder*. 1912, 1916. Mineola: Dover, 2003. Print.

Eliot, T. S. *The Letters of T. S. Eliot Volume 2: 1923–25*. Ed. Valerie Eliot and Hugh Haughton. New Haven: Yale UP, 2011. *Amazon.com Book Search*. Web. 25 Feb. 2013.

Flieger, Verlyn. *Splintered Light: Logos and Language in Tolkien's World*. Grand Rapids: Eerdmans, 1983. Print.

Fussell, Paul. *The Great War and Modern Memory*. New York: Oxford UP, 1975. Print.

Guite, Malcolm. "Inklings 3 Barfield; Poetry and Participation." 20 Oct. 2011. PodOmatic, 2011. MP3 file.

Harwood, [Alfred] Cecil. "Owen Barfield." *Evolution of Consciousness: Studies in Polarity*. Ed. Shirley Sugerman. Middletown: Wesleyan UP, 1976. 31–33. Print.

Hume, Kathryn. *Fantasy and Mimesis: Responses to Reality in Western Literature*. New York: Methuen, 1984. Print.

Hunter, Jeanne Clayton, and Thomas Kranidas. "Introduction." *A Barfield Sampler: Poetry and Fiction by Owen Barfield*. Ed. Jeanne Clayton Hunter and Thomas Kranidas. Albany: State U of New York P, 1993. 1–17. Print.

Knight, Gareth. *The Magical World of the Inklings*. Longmead: Element, 1990. Print.

Lewis, C. S. *All My Road before Me: The Diary of C. S. Lewis 1922–1927*. 1991. Ed. Walter Hooper. San Diego: Harvest-Harcourt, 1992. Print.

—. *The Collected Letters of C. S. Lewis, Vol. 2: Books, Broadcasts, and the War 1931–1949*. Ed. Walter Hooper. New York: Harper, 2004. Print.

—. *The Collected Letters of C. S. Lewis, Vol. 3: Narnia, Cambridge, and Joy 1950–1963*. Ed. Walter Hooper. New York: Harper, 2007. Print.

Oziewicz, Marek. *One Earth, One People: The Mythopoeic Fantasy Series of Ursula K. Le Guin, Lloyd Alexander, Madeleine L'Engle and Orson Scott Card*. Jefferson: McFarland, 2008. Critical Explorations in Science Fiction and Fantasy 6. Print.

Schenkel, Elmar. "Worlds Apart: The Dialogical Imagination of Owen Barfield." *Inklings-Jahrbuch* 24 (2006): 21–39. Print.

Stevenson, Randall. *Modernist Fiction: An Introduction*. Lexington: UP of Kentucky, 1992. Print.

Thorburn [?], John M. Horoscope for Owen Barfield. 21 July 1931. MS. Owen Barfield Papers, Dep. c. 1054. Bodleian Lib., Oxford.

Tolkien, J. R. R. *Letters from Father Christmas*. Ed. Baillie Tolkien. New York: Houghton, 2004. Print.

—. *Roverandom*. Ed. Christina Scull and Wayne G. Hammond. Boston: Houghton, 1998. Print.

Tratner, Michael. *Modernism and Mass Politics: Joyce, Woolf, Eliot, Yeats*. Stanford: Stanford UP, 1995. Print.

Von Hendy, Andrew. *The Modern Construction of Myth*. Bloomington: Indiana UP, 2002. Print.

Woolf, Virginia. *Mrs. Dalloway*. New York: Harcourt, 1925. Print.

Wordsworth, William. "Resolution and Independence." *Poems: In Two Volumes*. London: Longman, Hurst, Rees, and Orme, 1807. 89–97. Google eBook. *Google Books Search*. Web. 3 Jan. 2013.

SECTION II: OUTSIDE THE INKLINGS

The Door We Never Opened:
British Alternate History Writing in the Aftermath of World War I

Nick Milne

T. S. Eliot, in "Burnt Norton,"[1] gestures poignantly toward a subject that has long been a complex focus of human imagination and memory:

> What might have been is an abstraction
> Remaining a perpetual possibility
> Only in a world of speculation.
> What might have been and what has been
> Point to one end, which is always present.
> Footfalls echo in the memory
> Down the passage which we did not take
> Towards the door we never opened
> Into the rose-garden. (171)

This fascination with "the door we never opened" is frequently given voice in works of alternate history. Alternate history—also variously referred to as retro-speculation, alternative history,[2] counterfactual speculation, or allohistory—is a genre of writing that traces historical events back to an arguably definitive turning-point, introduces a twist in some fashion, and then crafts a narrative based upon the consequences of things playing out differently. Historical events provide a ready-made framework for new and intriguing narratives, replete with established characters, personalities, politics, geographies—all waiting to be made new by the alteration of key details. What if Hitler had been accepted to a Viennese art school? What if the American Civil War had resulted in a Confederate victory? What if Napoleon had been triumphant at Waterloo? All of these possibilities and more provide rich grist for the mill of speculative fiction.

In the years following World War I, those who experienced it were faced with a host of questions of their own. What had the war meant?

---

1. The first of the *Four Quartets* (1935–42).
2. Karen Hellekson, in *The Alternate History: Refiguring Historical Time* (2001), favors this term above others for its greater grammatical correctness and for its dual emphasis upon the altered nature of the history being presented and upon the use of alternative means of understanding history (3). Nevertheless, she chooses, as I have, to continue using "alternate history" instead—it is the phrasing most favored by authors and editors in the field and has no chance of being misunderstood.

What did it mean for so many to have sacrificed so much, and with consequences so complicated and (often) disappointing? Who had been responsible? The process of working through these and other questions birthed a multi-faceted body of literature that was focused upon coming to grips with the war through the writing of creative fiction. Whether through novels, poems or plays, numerous authors attempted to better understand the war through the lens of recreated fictionalized episodes from within it. Thus Siegfried Sassoon (for example) maintains a certain distance from even his own memoirs by making them focus on the fictionalized "George Sherston" rather than upon himself; Robert Graves, in writing *Goodbye to All That*, "deliberately mixed and spiced up all the incidents he could think of to produce a bestseller because he desperately needed the money" (Bond 31). Whatever their motivation, the war authors' engagements with the history of the war were marked dually by the subjective and the creative. The war was an inescapable setting and a totalizing reality, but the stories remained theirs to shape.

A much smaller strain of literary production maintained this emphasis on understanding the war through artificial narratives, but in a somewhat different direction. Rather than simply relying upon the war as a real and monumental backdrop to whatever fictional or embellished narratives the authors wished to create, in these comparatively rare narratives the war itself is fictionalized—that is, the approach to it is no longer historical but counter-historical. The British alternate history writing that began to flourish in the war's aftermath is evocative of wider cultural and artistic concerns about the nature of history and the place of the war within it. In a fashion that corresponds in many ways with that of the speculative "invasion literature" of the pre-war period,[3] certain post-war works retroactively imagine a new version of the war in a bid to better illuminate the real one, and to imaginatively "improve" upon the results that had, in the real world, proven so complex and unsatisfying. These works take a transformative and creative approach to history, creating a new version of our world's past through the alteration of historical circumstance.

---

3. See George Tomkyns Chesney's *The Battle of Dorking* (1871), William Le Queux's *The Great War in England in 1897* (1894) and *The Invasion of 1910* (1906), Erskine Childers' *The Riddle of the Sands* (1903), Saki's *When William Came* (1913) or Arthur Conan Doyle's "Danger!" I. F. Clarke's *Voices Prophesying War 1763–1984* (1966) remains the classic overview of this style of speculative literature; Cecil D. Eby's *The Road to Armageddon: The Martial Spirit in English Popular Literature 1870–1914* (1987) places these works firmly in the context of developing British anxieties about the shifting international scene.

This revisionist escapism is a further example of the impulse already so powerfully apparent in the success of the poets and memoirists, and the chapter that follows will situate these alternate-historical writings within the wider context of both the post-war literary boom and the development of this strain of fantasy writing[4] generally. Through an examination of Stephen Leacock's "The Hohenzollerns in America" (1919), Arthur Conan Doyle's "The Death Voyage" (1929), Bernard Newman's *The Cavalry Went Through!* (1930), and J. C. Squire's *If It Had Happened Otherwise* (1931), we will see that the roots of modern alternate historical writing may be found in the post-war generation's determination to creatively engage with a war that was as much a point of historical rupture as it was an historical event. In an analysis of the very few purposefully counter-historical works of fiction about the war written in its immediate aftermath, we shall see a further manifestation of the broader cultural retreat from the pervasive anti-German sentiments of the pre- and intra-war years, and of a rising sense of dissatisfaction with how the war had been both conducted and concluded. The period's alternate history writing, then, represents an attempt to go through "the door we never opened" in hopes of finding a rose-garden rather than a graveyard.

The history of allohistorical speculation is paradoxically both long and short, and this tendency toward speculating upon happier outcomes has been present since the beginning. The genre's history is long in that the earliest examples of it to be found in print date back very far indeed — to Livy's *Ab Urbe Condita* (c. 35 CE), in fact, in Book IX: 17–19 of which the Roman historian meditates upon the likely outcome of an invasion of the Italian peninsula by Alexander the Great after the conclusion of his Persian campaigns c. 325 BCE. If the roots of such speculation run deep, however, it still took a considerable while to bloom; consequently, long-form allohistorical speculation of a sort we would readily recognize does not really begin to appear until the middle of the nineteenth century. These early manifestations took the form of novels like Benjamin Disraeli's *The Wondrous Tale of Alroy* (1833) or Louis-Napoléon Geoffroy-Chateau's *Napoléon et la conquête du monde, 1812–1823:*

---

4. Alternate history has long been a staple of a certain sort of fantastic or speculative writing, from early science fiction works like L. Sprague de Camp's *Lest Darkness Fall* (1939), Philip K. Dick's *The Man in the High Castle* (1962), or Fred Hoyle's *October the First is Too Late* (1966), through the innumerable alternate-history novels of fantasy/SF authors like S. M. Stirling and Harry Turtledove, to the current spate of overtly magical alternate-history fantasy works like Susanna Clarke's *Jonathan Strange & Mr. Norrell* (2004) or Naomi Novik's ongoing *His Majesty's Dragon* series.

histoire de la monarchie universelle (1836); the former purports to be a secret history of events in 12th c. Baghdad, while the latter is a work of faux-scholarly history looking backward upon the world Napoleon made after his triumphant (and counterfactual) victory in the Russian campaign. These early examples were followed up by several more in a similar spirit, but the great degree of popular interest the genre now enjoys[5] did not develop until relatively recently.

One check on the genre's popularity was the fact that the speculative processes demanded by such historical questions is not uncontroversial among historians. This idea of what Isaac D'Israeli described[6] as "enlarg[ing] our conception of the nature of human events," through speculation of this kind has sometimes met with criticism. Historians like E. H. Carr, Benedetto Croce and Michael Oakeshott have been less than kind about the subject, denouncing such speculation as anything from "a parlour game" and "a red herring"[7] to, in E. P. Thompson's vivid phrasing, "*Geschichtenscheissenschlopff*"—that is, "unhistorical shit" (145). Nevertheless, while historiography is one thing, creative fiction is quite another. As Geoffrey Winthrop-Young points out, "for the emergence of Alternate History proper [as a literary genre] [...] borrowings from historiography were indispensable, but the exchange between the two was so successful precisely because of their obvious distance from each other" (114).

There was little in this spirit produced in Britain in the years leading up to World War I—an essay by G. M. Trevelyan is probably the most famous such piece.[8] It is only after the war that the genre really began to take off, and this counter-historical spirit in the inter-war years is perhaps best exemplified not by a work of fiction but rather by a collection of essays—*If it Had Happened Otherwise* (1931), edited by John Collings

---

5. Recent collections of counterfactual essays on varied subjects include Niall Ferguson's *Virtual History: Alternatives and Counterfactuals* (1997); Robert Cowley's popular *What If?* series (1999; 2001); Andrew Roberts' *What Might Have Been* (2004); a trio of politically oriented volumes edited by Duncan Brack and Iain Dale (2003, 2006, 2012); Philip E. Tetlock, Richard Ned Lebow and Geoffrey Parker's *Unmaking the West: "What If?" Scenarios that Rewrite World History* (2006), and Richard Ned Lebow's *Forbidden Fruit: Counterfactuals and International Relations* (2010). Recent collections of such essays or stories on specific subjects are too numerous to list.

6. In "Of a History of Events Which Have Not Happened," from the second series of *Curiosities of Literature* (1824)—an early and influential essay.

7. For an overview of these and other criticisms, see Niall Ferguson's introductory essay in *Virtual History: Alternatives and Counterfactuals* (1997).

8. "If Napoleon had Won the Battle of Waterloo" (1907), first published in the *Westminster Gazette* and then regularly in various historical anthologies thereafter.

Squire. Squire's was a popular volume at the time, and remains influential even now;[9] the original volume included retro-speculative submissions from the likes of André Maurois, Hilaire Belloc, G. K. Chesterton, Emil Ludwig, and Sir Winston S. Churchill. The volume exemplifies a broader willingness at its time of writing to look to history as a mutable and uncertain thing rather than one that was inevitable and always trending toward progress. The war had formed what Samuel Hynes has abstractly called a "gap in history":

> [M]en and women after the war looked back at their own pasts as one might look across a great chasm to a remote, peaceable place on the other side.
> This sense of radical discontinuity of present from past is an essential element in what eventually took form as the Myth of the War. I use that phrase […] to mean not a falsification of reality, but an imaginative version of it […]. (ix)

It is in this spirit—this "imaginative version of reality" as seen through the "radical discontinuity of present from past"—that informs the allohistorical work produced in the post-war period, and it is in this spirit that the mainstream popular historical community in England, whose contributions comprised Squire's collection, willingly turned numerous settled verities on their heads in a bid to better understand them. Napoleon escaped to America after Waterloo. Lincoln survived the evening of April 15, 1865. Lord Byron became the king of Greece.

Rather significantly for our purposes, however, although it was published squarely in the middle of the War Books Boom of 1927–1933[10]

---

9. Andrew Roberts, in his own edited volume of speculative essays, refers to Squire's collection as "the greatest of all counterfactual essay collections" (ix); Stephen Badsey calls Squire's volume "the first counterfactual best-seller" (360); Niall Ferguson takes no happy view of the volume, but avows its importance in having possibly served to "discredit the notion of counterfactual history for a generation" (10). An expanded edition of the volume including several extra essays was reprinted in 1972, and is still widely available; one added piece, excerpted from A. J. P. Taylor's *The First World War* (1963), examines the contingent effect of two factors (the railway timetables of the various European powers and the love of the Archduke Franz Ferdinand for his wife) on the events of 1914.

10. This rich period of literary history saw the publication of many works now considered canonical where World War I is concerned, including Ernest Hemingway's *A Farewell to Arms* (1929), Erich Maria Remarque's *All Quiet on the Western Front* (1929), Siegfried Sassoon's *Memoirs of an Infantry Officer* (1930), Robert Graves' *Goodbye to All That* (1929), Richard Aldington's *Death of a Hero* (1929), Frederic Manning's *The Middle Parts of Fortune* (1929), Vera Brittain's *Testament of Youth* (1933) and R. C. Sherriff's sensationally popular drama, *Journey's End* (1928). For an overview of the war's canonical British writing, see Bernard Bergonzi's *Heroes' Twilight* (1965),

and is authored largely by authors who had written much elsewhere on the subject, *If It Had Happened Otherwise* contains no essays specifically and primarily dedicated to the subject of World War I at all. Thirteen years had passed since the war's conclusion, but still the only references to be found to it in this volume are oblique and in passing. Squire's own introduction unhesitatingly notes that each question is likely to be contingent upon national sympathies; in one of the volume's few specific references to the war, he declares that "the question 'If Napoleon had won the Battle of Waterloo' [...] will not arouse the same emotions in the breasts of an Englishman and a Frenchman, and we could hardly expect from a German the response evoked in us by the speculation 'If Kluck had not turned away from Paris' " (vii-viii). Significantly, Squire leaves it open as to whether the response evoked in "us" or in "the German" would be the more powerful. The ambiguities this engenders in terms of the war's conclusion are hugely intertwined with how it began: with a seemingly unstoppable German assault on France that quite unexpectedly failed.

Nevertheless, as Niall Ferguson suggests in his introduction to *Virtual History*, in spite of the war's general absence from the pages of *If...*, many of its essays are written without "conscious indifference to what is known about later events." The volume's speculations about events leading to increased French security, different stripes of Anglo-American alliance, and even a unification of interests between Great Britain and Germany consequently show that each author "takes as his starting point the burning contemporary question: How could the calamity of the First World War have been avoided?" (11).

It is a question that has often been asked. "Few events," writes the military historian Robert Cowley, "lend themselves so poignantly to counterfactual scenarios as the First World War" (*What If? 2* 195). To examine the contours of the war is to see at once why he might say such a thing; so much of it hinges upon accidents, reversals, and fateful decisions that it offers very fertile ground indeed for inquiry into alternate possibilities. What if the Archduke Franz Ferdinand had not been assassinated in Sarajevo on June 28th, 1914, or Jean Jaurès in Paris a month later? What if the Serbs had acceded to all of the terms of the Austro-Hungarian ultimatum, or that ultimatum had not been so severe? What if the assault on Gallipoli had succeeded? What if the assault on Vimy

---

Paul Fussell's *The Great War and Modern Memory* (1975), Samuel Hynes' *A War Imagined* (1991), Hugh Cecil's *The Flower of Battle* (1995), or Randall Stevenson's *Literature & the Great War, 1914–1918* (2013).

Ridge had not? What if Lord Northcliffe had been a pacifist? Anyway, some questions are more reasonable than others.

Regardless of its merits as a historiographic exercise, it is certainly the case that a great deal of allohistorical fiction concerning World War I exists—though perhaps not as much as Cowley's declaration might suggest. Stephen Badsey, in his wide-ranging survey[11] of counterfactual engagements with the events and personalities of the war, notes that, "when compared to the Napoleonic Wars, the Second World War or the American Civil War, the First World War is not a particularly popular subject for counterfactuals" (352). Badsey goes on to list a number of reasons why this might be the case, but the most important for our purposes is this:

> In many counterfactual books about wars the focus is chiefly on individual battles and how their outcomes might have differed. But in dealing with the First World War authors have almost completely neglected this issue, and instead preferred to write about how the war might have been prevented, how Great Britain might have avoided direct involvement, whether an earlier American involvement would have brought an earlier peace, whether a German victory would have made any difference, and whether the Russian October Revolution could have been stopped. In this respect, counterfactual history shares the view of the First World War of popular culture: a uniquely terrible event in which to consider victory or defeat in a battle is meaningless, and that almost any outcome would have been better, or at least no worse, than the historical one. (353)

A survey of the existing works in this field tends to support Badsey's claims; with remarkably few exceptions,[12] one will not find essays or stories dedicated to answering questions like "What if the breakthrough at Cambrai had been better exploited?" or "What if the Somme offensive had been abandoned after the first day?" They tend to focus instead on political or personal factors rather than military ones, with the elimination of Lenin or the preservation of Franz Ferdinand being particular favorites.[13] The fictional works that serve as the focus of this

---

11. This excellent essay is currently the only extant overview of alternate history writing dedicated to the war, surveying the field with a particular emphasis upon the war's oft-claimed status as an unequalled and unprecedented event.

12. One such rare exception is Guido Morselli's *Contro-passato prossimo: Un'ipotesi retrospettiva* (1975), which proposes a scenario in which the Austro-Hungarian army uses anachronistic blitzkrieg tactics against the Italians in May of 1916, thereby eventually securing a victory for the Central Powers by the following year—a situation remarkably similar (though with the factional affiliations reversed) to that of Newman's *The Cavalry Went Through*.

13. See, for example, George Feifer's "No Finland Station" (*What If? 2*, 2001), Helen Szamuely's "What if Lenin's 'sealed' train had not reached Petrograd in 1917?"

chapter provide such exceptions in some ways while remaining typical in others; while two are specifically focused on stark military differences with consequences that are very meaningful indeed, all are united in affirming that the vision they present is at least no worse and in some cases considerably better than the real history that confronts us.

The late-nineteenth and early twentieth centuries saw a boom in what came to be known as "invasion literature." The authors operating in this genre of literature were primarily concerned with envisioning future wars, whether to sound a note of warning or simply to tell an enticing story. In the main, however, the overriding feature of the "invasion fiction" genre is the degree to which it reflects—especially in Britain, where it was particularly widely-read—a broad cultural anxiety about the prospect of rising German power and the dangers the German Empire would pose in the event of a modern war.

Erskine Childers, in his speculative espionage thriller *The Riddle of the Sands* (1903), dramatically sets forth the ambivalent perspective of the British upon the German empire in the years leading up to the war:

> I described her marvellous awakening in the last generation, under the strength and wisdom of her rulers; her intense patriotic ardour; her seething industrial activity, and, most potent of all, the forces that are moulding modern Europe, her dream of a colonial empire, entailing her transformation from a land-power to a sea-power. Impregnably based on vast territorial resources which we cannot molest, the dim instincts of her people, not merely directed but anticipated by the genius of her ruling house, our great trade rivals of the present, our great naval rival of the future, she grows, and strengthens, and waits, an ever more formidable factor in the future of our delicate network of empire [...].
>
> "And we aren't ready for her," Davies would say. (90)

This sense of Germany as a modern success story—but also an imminent threat—was prevalent in the pre-war era's speculative fiction. The total Prussian triumph and the subsequent creation of the unified German empire in the wake of the Franco-Prussian War of 1870–1871 left many in England worried about the prospect of eventual war with this new power; George Tomkyns Chesney quickly wrote a novella on this subject, *The Battle of Dorking* (1871), in which a narrator fifty years in the

---

(*Prime Minister Portillo*, 2003), and Andrew Roberts's "Lenin is Assassinated at the Finland Station" (*What Might Have Been*, 2004), or Norman Stone's "Archduke Franz Ferdinand Survives Sarajevo" (*What Might Have Been*, 2004), York Membery's "What if Franz Ferdinand's assassin had missed in 1914?" (*President Gore*, 2006), Richard Ned Lebow's "Franz Ferdinand Found Alive: World War I Unnecessary" (*Forbidden Fruit*, 2010), and the whole of the same author's *Archduke Franz Ferdinand Lives! A World Without World War I* (2014).

future looks back with regret upon the successful German invasion of England and the price that was paid for a lack of English preparedness. The British Empire is dissolved; the British Isles themselves are now a German province, Canada has been ceded to the United States, and both India and Australia have been granted independence—a nightmarish vision, to be sure.

This theme of the dangers of English unpreparedness was taken up more forcefully by Field Marshal Lord Roberts, one of the Empire's most highly decorated soldiers, who made frequent use of his position to lecture Britons both young and old on the absolute necessity of an expanded program of military training and investment. The novelist William Le Queux, inspired by Lord Roberts' pleas, produced two novels on this theme—*The Great War in England in 1897* (1894) and *The Invasion of 1910* (1906). The first of the two offers an intriguing glimpse into the period's delicate diplomatic realities: the "great war" that transpires in the work sees England assailed by France and Russia, with the German Empire coming in as a staunch English ally. *The Invasion of 1910* offers a more familiar warning, however; it began appearing in serial in the *Daily Mail* in March of 1906, and took as its pretext the successful German invasion of England and the necessity of a mass popular uprising in response. The *Mail*, the flagship of the notoriously anti-German Lord Northcliffe's press empire, would prove to be a leader in prosecuting the British war effort from 1914 onward, and in Le Queux's work we see a prefiguring of many of the sensational stories of occupied Belgium and France that would appear in those pages as the war unfolded.

At the back of this German achievement and at the forefront of the German threat is the figure of Kaiser Wilhelm II, who was taken by many, for good or ill, as the embodiment of his empire's potential. In British popular opinion the Kaiser was frequently admired for his greatness, even as he was castigated for his rhetorical flourishes and ominous deeds; in Lothar Reinermann's words, "Wilhelm became a 'representative individual', whose personal characteristics were generalized to the entire German population" (469). These flames of suspicion and alienation were only fanned by the 1908 "*Telegraph* controversy," which saw the Kaiser sit for an unprecedentedly candid interview for publication in that paper. What began as an attempt to cement the bonds of Anglo-German friendship quickly degenerated into a sensational tirade, faithfully transcribed for the paper, in which the Kaiser denounced the English as being "mad, mad, mad as march hares," and warned that Germany would not long continue to be patient in having her friendly intentions doubted (Clark 240). It was a watershed moment in the development of his popular image, and one that—in Britain, at least—he would never live down.

The complexities of his status manifest themselves in the speculative fiction leading up to the war as well. Even as the heroes of Childers' *Riddle of the Sands* race to thwart the Kaiser's secret plans to invade England, they cannot help but call him "a splendid fellow" and "a man [...] who doesn't wait to be kicked, but works [...] for his country, and sees ahead" (89). In Le Queux's *Invasion* the Kaiser is a distant figure, sending out bulletins and proclamations from various far-removed locations and relying upon his underlings for their execution. Even during the war, in works like John Buchan's widely popular adventure novel *Greenmantle* (1916), the Kaiser (as encountered by the accomplished hero Richard Hannay) is an enigmatic and conflicted figure; he wears "the face of one who slept little and whose thoughts rode him like a nightmare" (90). "This man," the narrating Hannay concludes, "the chief of a nation [...] paid the price in war for the gifts that had made him successful in peace. He had imagination and nerves, and the one was white hot and the others were quivering. I would not have been in his shoes for the throne of the Universe" (91).

The cessation of hostilities on the Western Front on November 11, 1918 brought with it a powerful mixture of relief and disappointment. That the war was finally over was a cause for great celebration, but it had concluded without those features that many of its most furious proponents had long insisted upon in their attempts to justify it as an enterprise: there had been no great breakthrough, no race to Berlin, no dictation of terms to the Kaiser's face at Potsdam, no trial to which to subject him and his associates. Wilhelm, unlike the Emperor Napoleon a century before, would never spend two weeks aboard a ship in Plymouth Harbor awaiting his victorious enemies' verdict.

What did happen instead was that the rising tide of German war-weariness gave way to open revolt against Wilhelm and all for which he stood. German socialists, initially supportive of the war effort but having grown increasingly opposed to it as the years dragged by, seized many opportunities to fan the public flames of resentment against the royals, staff officers and politicians who seemed so determined to continue the war in the face of its apparent impossibility. In late October of 1918, Admiral Franz von Hipper decided to take the High Seas Fleet out of Wilhelmshaven, break the Royal Navy's blockade, and send his men and his ships to a romantic death in one last act of defiance (Herwig 442). This move rather understandably triggered a mutiny which soon spread to Kiel, and within weeks the sailors had been joined by thousands of other disaffected soldiers, workers and civilians in what would become the German Revolution. By November 9th Wilhelm had abdicated, and by the 10th he had crossed into neutral Holland. The rule of the Hohenzollerns in Germany was ended.

This denial of the opportunity for direct and immediate confrontation with the Kaiser was a disappointment to many, and attempts to procure it continued into the process of drafting the Treaty of Versailles. The concluded Treaty even carried, in Article 227, provision for his capture, arrest and prosecution, citing "a supreme offence against international morality and the sanctity of treaties" (Ashton 75n23). With even his cousin George V of England having grown convinced that Wilhelm was "the greatest criminal in history," and George's Prime Minister, David Lloyd George, echoing the popular "Hang the Kaiser" rhetoric of the penny presses, the main thing that managed to save him was the refusal of the Dutch government, at Queen Wilhelmina's urging, to permit Wilhelm's extradition. So there he stayed, a private citizen, writing his memoirs (published in English by Harper as *The Kaiser's Memoirs*, 1922), corresponding with old acquaintances, and generally keeping to himself. His relationship with the ascendant Nazis was deeply conflicted and is not exactly germane to the subject at hand, but one final note about his later life is worth mentioning: with the German conquest of the Netherlands in 1940, Wilhelm was surprised to receive a message from the British Prime Minister Winston Churchill offering him asylum in England (Gilbert 523). Wilhelm refused, and a year later he was dead.

This focus upon the figure of Kaiser Wilhelm II may seem inordinate, but he lies at the heart of two of the fascinating post-war engagements with the war's conclusion and legacy under consideration here—Leacock's "The Hohenzollerns in America" (1919) and Doyle's "The Death Voyage" (1929). Each treatment strips the abdicated Kaiser of one of the familiar elements of his popular image, but with very different motives and results; where Leacock's treatment removes Wilhelm and his family from the context of wealth and privilege that Leacock implies helped corrupt them in the first place, Doyle's instead takes from Wilhelm's shoulders the burden of being thought a bully, a coward, and a hypocrite. Both works imagine a very different fate for Wilhelm than that which actually befell him, and we may see in these complex but often sympathetic accounts a further engagement with the broader cultural shift away from the anxious anti-German sentiments of the war years.

Depending on where they lived, those reading the papers in 1919 might have encountered the first of the two remarkable allohistorical treatments of the Kaiser's great crisis that we will be examining here—Stephen Leacock's "The Hohenzollerns in America." which first began appearing in serial in *Vanity Fair* in December of 1918. The English-born Leacock made his name in Canada jointly as an economist and a humorist, and "Hohenzollerns" is a late-blooming but natural extension of his wartime propaganda writing in aid of the Commission for Relief in Belgium.

The Kaiser—or, more accurately, the Uncle William—of Leacock's "Hohenzollerns" is a figure far-removed from the pomp and splendor of yesteryear. Leacock notes in the story's brief preface that he intends to present an image of the deposed monarch and his family possessed of "none of the prestige of fallen grandeur," but rather to show "the Hohenzollerns as an immigrant family departing for America, their trunks and boxes on their backs, their bundles in their hands" (3-4). His primary hope is that "the world would have a better idea of the thin stuff out of which autocratic kingship is fashioned" (4) and thereby repudiate it.

To the modern eye there may seem in this to be a slight narrowness of vision; Leacock was a full-throated supporter of worldwide British imperialism, at that time—an imperial project then under the nominal headship of Wilhelm's cousin, George V, who was no stranger to pomp and finery himself. Leacock had embarked on a world lecture tour in 1907 at the behest of the Cecil Rhodes Trust with the mandate of promoting imperial unity, and his support for that Empire only became more pronounced in the years leading up to the war. German achievements did not impress him much. His 1910 essay "The Devil and the Deep Sea: A Discussion of Modern Morality"[14] is predicated in part upon the deleterious moral influence of German philosophy upon the mind; the citizens of Mariposa in *Sunshine Sketches of a Little Town* listen eagerly to the discourses of the local barber "explain[ing] in full the relations of Keesar to the German Rich Dog" (*Sunshine* 24). The author's comically fictional "visit" to Germany ("Germany From Within Out") in the 1916 collection *Further Foolishness* satirizes numerous German stereotypes, from the nation's exquisite orderliness to her people's amoral ruthlessness to the likelihood that every German waiter in the English-speaking world is secretly a spy.

---

14. In *Essays and Literary Studies* (1916).

Nevertheless, it seems that Leacock undertook the project not out of any personal vindictiveness toward Wilhelm, whatever he may have thought of the Kaiser's office or the empire over which he reigned, and in a letter to B. W. Willett of the Bodley Head dated March 27, 1919, declares his intention to scupper the whole volume should the tide of events render it indelicate:

> What you say is quite true; the Kaiser might be shot at any minute But in that case ~~the~~ it is not the <u>title</u> that is queered it is the book itself. Jones & I have agreed that it shall not be published if anything of that sort happens while it is in the press. But as about 75 or 80 pages deal with the Hohenzollerns in America we think that the book had better stand or fall in that. *Letters* 122)

And stand it did—over 46,000 copies sold by the end of 1920 (Spadoni 182–84).

While Peter Webb has argued that "Hohenzollerns" sees Leacock adopt "a conventional and clichéd brand of Kaiser-baiting" filled with "moments meant to elicit a gleeful spirit of revenge against the Teutonic cultural type" (44–45), the deposed monarch receives an occasionally sympathetic portrayal as the story unfolds. Much of this is a function of the narrative lens Leacock employs: the serial "diary" of Wilhelm's fictional niece, Princess Frederica, who has been sent into exile with the rest of the family. Good-natured and unsuspecting, Frederica looks upon her extended family as being at their best even when they are very obviously otherwise, but there is a sheltered naïveté in her outlook powerful enough to excuse almost anything; arriving at Ellis Island in New York, for example, she can only declare that they "have just passed a huge statue that rises out of the water, the name of which they mentioned but I can't remember, as it was not anything I ever heard of before" (19).

The former Kaiser bears the brunt of Leacock's satiric gaze, but this is a necessary consequence of him also being the most complicatedly and expansively wrought of all the Hohenzollerns in the story. Where the Crown Prince is reduced to an increasingly vicious thief and lecher, Wilhelm is presented as a man with grand illusions that are slowly—and even beneficially—stripped away. It is a mark of Leacock's skill and even (perhaps) of his cautious empathy that the reader can go from laughing aloud at the former Kaiser's presumption that he will be offered the presidency of Harvard or the governorship of an American state (18-19) to being only somewhat disappointed that he hasn't been. He instead ends up as a modestly successful and even somewhat happy street merchant (67–68), albeit one still wracked by nightmares involving the sea and the chanting of doomed, angry voices. It is this lingering sense of guilt that eventually leads to Wilhelm's death. While out walking one afternoon, he happens upon the unveiling of a new monument commemorating the sinking of the *Lusitania*. Stricken with a sudden horror he rears back, stumbles into the street, and is accidentally ridden down by a passing column of cavalry (62–63).

Leacock's decision to tie Wilhelm's death to the historical memory of the sinking of the *Lusitania* situates the story within the real world in a way that its somewhat farcical earlier chapters do not always allow. It also reflects the strong contemporary opinion in the English-speaking world that the ocean liner's sinking was a crime for which the Kaiser should feel especially guilty, stemming in part from the (long since discredited) accusation that the German government had minted a series of commemorative medals to celebrate the sinking. This integration of alternate-historical speculation into the facts of established history can take many forms, however, as Arthur Conan Doyle's subsequent meditation upon the Kaiser's character will show. In addition to rewriting the Kaiser's fate, Doyle salvages the very real and never enacted 1918 plan of Admiral Franz von Hipper to take the High Seas Fleet out into the Channel for one last desperate action, reassigns it to the Kaiser himself, and offers up an account of its devastating consequences.

"The Death Voyage," like many works of alternate history, hinges upon a "Great Man" understanding of history. Sometimes such works hinge upon it rather too heavily; as Andy Duncan has protested, "that peace is as fateful as war, that the everyday lives of you and me are as crucial to history as the lives of Napoleon and Hitler, is too often overlooked by the writer of alternate history" (216). Nevertheless, in the case of "The Death Voyage," Doyle is overtly reaching back to Thomas Carlyle's early argument in the lectures that comprise *On Heroes, Hero-Worship and the Heroic in History* (1841) that "the history of the world is but the biography of great men" (28). The tide of events, from this perspective, is contingent upon the action (or lack of action) taken by influential individuals at certain key points. In writing his alternate version of the Kaiser's fate, Doyle takes the opportunity to enact this concept explicitly:

> Musing over the great crises of history, I could see that the chief actor in each had always come to a dividing of the ways where it was within his choice to take the one path or the other. He took the one, and the annals tell us what came of it. But suppose that he had taken the other. Is it possible for the human imagination to follow up the course of events which would have resulted from that? (391)

Doyle's answer to his own question is very much in the affirmative, and "The Death Voyage" is the result. In it, the Kaiser—though forced officially to abdicate and urged to flee to the Netherlands as he did in reality—decides to travel in disguise to the port at Kiel, convinces the navy's mutineers to stand with him, and takes the whole of the German fleet out to meet the combined Anglo-American squadron in a last battle to the death. " 'No ignoble suicide will end your Emperor's career,' " he assures his astonished men; " 'there are nobler ways of dying, and it is for me to find them' " (397).

The story first appeared in the *Saturday Evening Post* of September 28, 1929, before being reprinted the following month in Doyle's favored periodical, *The Strand*. It has ended up becoming a marginal work in every sense—as a piece of World War I literature, as a short story by Doyle, as a piece of alternate historical fiction—in spite of its unique character, and last saw print in an anthology released in 1982 with no greater purpose than to collect those short works of Doyle's that no one had yet bothered to anthologize.[15] Nevertheless, this neglect masks a number of interesting features. In spite of Doyle's aggressive positioning of "The Death Voyage" at its outset as a "Great Man" narrative, as the story unfolds greater and greater challenges to this notion begin to appear. The Kaiser reflects, during the final battle, on the ways in which the war had been caused not only by his own actions or those of a chosen elite, but also by those of diplomats, statesmen, soldiers, and whole peoples in a variety of different countries. No one man is the pivot on which the wheel of history turns—and even if he were, it would be possible to turn in the wrong direction: "It was useless to go back upon the past," he ruefully concludes, condemning both his own introspection and, abstractly, the story itself; "far off, many years ago, some wrong path was taken and this was whither it had led" (410). It is a condemnation that Doyle himself echoes in its final lines: "So ran my vision of an alternative. And yet it may be that Fate was wiser, and that the path upon the level was better than that upon the hilltops" (412).

If the cavalry made an accidental end of the Kaiser in Leacock's alternate history writing, they make a purposeful end of the whole German army in Bernard Newman's *The Cavalry Went Through!*. In addition to being the only novel of its sort about the war in English at the time, it remains the only such work from the period to take the military dimensions of the war on the Western Front as its primary focus. Where Doyle provides a dramatic re-envisioning of the war's naval side during its

---

15. *Uncollected Stories: The Unknown Conan Doyle*, edited by John Michael Gibson and Richard Lancelyn Green. The same editors would continue the *Unknown Conan Doyle* series in 1986 with *Letters to the Press*, a fascinating collection of Doyle's letters to the editors of various newspapers and magazines.

closing chapter, Newman offers a no less dramatic alteration of the circumstances that had led, in reality, to four long years of stalemate in France and Flanders. Through the brilliantly unorthodox maneuvers of a fictional British general, Newman instead brings the war to a triumphantly victorious conclusion for the Allies in the Summer of 1917.

The Cavalry Went Through was Newman's first novel; the publisher Victor Gollancz brought it out in February of 1930 at a price of 7s. 6d. Certain that it would be a success, but still wishing to grease the wheels of its reception, Gollancz took the step of contacting several high-profile authors of military and adventure fiction in a bid to canvas advance opinions to be used in the advertisement campaign. Newman records in his autobiography that he was doubtful about this enterprise given his status as an unknown, but then the letters started to arrive. One, in particular, demands our attention:

> I opened a letter and read its contents with eyes protruding in excitement. "It is really a glorious yarn, and a most welcome change from the present fashionable cloacal type of war novel. I think the thing is extraordinarily well done, with such understanding of war that it deserves to be made a handbook at a Staff College! In addition it is a most thrilling story, admirably proportioned and written with the proper speed of style. I hope—indeed, I am sure—it will be a great success." (*Speaking from Memory* 61–62)

"The signature," Newman concludes, "was as thrilling as the letter—John Buchan" (62).[16] This passing of the torch, so to speak, from one writer of speculative World War I fiction to another would find a further iteration in the attention *Cavalry* won from the hugely influential British military historian Basil Liddell Hart. Liddell Hart found in *Cavalry* almost a manual of the future—an original and insightful meditation on military possibilities in spite of being predicated upon a fictionalized past: "His detailed ideas were so good," he wrote in Newman's obituary for the *Times*, "as well as vividly conveyed, and had such a clear bearing on the future, that I mentioned this book of his in several of my own, and have ever since put it on successive lists of recommended reading for military students" (10). It is in this dramatic re-envisioning of the war's conduct that *Cavalry* makes its strongest claim to originality.

---

16. Newman records later the surprise he felt at the reception accorded his book in Germany; "they studied the book seriously, and some of their new tactics emerged direct from [the fictional General] Duncan's ideas. I was distressed at this—but after all, we had the first chance. […] In Germany my book *was* used for Staff College training, as John Buchan had suggested: but not in England" (63).

Perspectives on the British military conduct of the war have typically been scathing even when tinged with pathos. This jointly held respect for the fighting men and contempt for their leaders—this love of the "lions led by donkeys"—has been an all-pervading feature of the cultural memory of the war since almost the moment the armistice was signed. It is intimately tied to the broader narrative of mud, blood and futility that came to dominate the story of the trenches during the War Books Boom, helped along in the latter half of the century by popular filmed works like *Oh! What a Lovely War* (1969), *The Monocled Mutineer* (1986) and *Blackadder Goes Forth* (1989), or by widely consumed novels like Pat Barker's *Regeneration* trilogy (1991–1995) or Sebastian Faulks's *Birdsong* (1993). This perspective has even made its way into modern alternate history writing about the war, as Stephen Badsey laments:

> [It] is being written based on formulae established in the 1930s, on views of the war in popular culture rather than on the most recent historical understanding, on the desire of some historians to indulge their fantasies and have some fun with the reading public, and not least on the basis of commercial needs to appeal to an American readership in particular. (366)

Badsey's reference to "recent historical understanding" is an important one, as the shape of the war's historiography has changed considerably in recent decades[17] even as cultural memory of the war remains much the same. At the heart of this cultural memory—which is after all a perspective laced with tragedy—is the insistence that those in charge of running the war could and should have done better or at least different things while running it. Newman was similarly convinced, but did not stop at simply making the claim; *The Cavalry Went Through* is a fictionalized, book-length case for how the war *ought*, in his opinion, to have been fought.

Unlike Doyle and Leacock, Newman had the distinction of having actually served in the Great War himself. He lied about his age

---

17. The last thirty years have seen a new wave of British historical and critical work offer serious challenges to the standard narrative attached to many aspects of the war, such as the efficacy of propaganda, the competence of the military administration, or the war's oft-purported futility. Heather Jones offers a comprehensive survey of the current state of the field in a recent article ("As the Centenary Approaches: The Regeneration of First World War Historiography"; *The Historical Journal* 56.3); for full-volume treatments of the military question, see *The First World War and British Military History* (1991; ed. Brian Bond), Paddy Griffith's *Battle Tactics on the Western Front, 1916–18* (1994), Gary Sheffield's *Forgotten Victory: The First World War, Myths and Realities* (2001), Daniel Todman's *The Great War: Myth and Memory* (2005), or Brian Bond's *Survivors of a Kind: Memoirs of the Western Front* (2008).

and joined up while only seventeen, eventually coming to serve with the Royal Army Service Corps. His service saw him mentioned in dispatches "for gallant and distinguished services in the field," and his various aptitudes eventually landed him a position in intelligence. His experience of the war and his thinking on the subject afterward inform the substantially different approaches he ascribes to his fictional general in *Cavalry*. Henry Berrington Duncan is almost unrealistically competent and efficient—as an administrator he is like a second Napoleon; as a tactician a sort of anglicized Jan Christiaan Smuts. Even more useful would be a comparison to the German General Paul von Lettow-Vorbeck (1870–1964), the quite real commander of the German army in its East African campaign during World War I. Many of the things attributed to Duncan—his shocking success in Africa, his unorthodox approach to discipline, his heavy reliance on black colonial troops—were true of Lettow-Vorbeck as well, and truly could it be said of the German commander that by the war's end he had never once been defeated in the field.[18]

All of this far-reaching competence sees Duncan bring about the war's satisfactory conclusion through a variety of unorthodox tactics. His men—many of them colonial troops from Africa—have sacrificed the expected military discipline of marching, saluting and uniformity in favor of spending time on developing the skills necessary to win the war. They stage commando raids deep into enemy territory. They develop new strategies using a type of table-top board game simulating trench tactics. They learn a basic level of German to assist in interrogating any prisoners they happen to take. They are audacious where the real army was cautious, dynamically adaptive where the real army was sluggish, and seemingly amoral in their determination to win at any price. Duncan himself is almost a tyrant, expecting and receiving his men's complete obedience. This pseudo-tyranny extends to his interactions with British statesmen, as well—a matter of considerable controversy both during and after the war. When *Cavalry* was published, the fourth volume of Winston S. Churchill's war memoirs, *The World Crisis*, had already been out for a year and had attracted considerable attention. This work, much like David Lloyd George's soon-to-be-published *War Memoirs*, did much to cement in the public mind the impression that the war had been mismanaged by generals who had refused to listen to the

---

18. For an overview of Lettow-Vorbeck's campaign, and of the African theater of World War I generally, see Edward Paice's *Tip and Run: The Untold Tragedy of the Great War in Africa* (2007) or Anne Samson's *World War I in Africa: The Forgotten Conflict Among the European Powers* (2013).

wiser council of statesmen—including that of Churchill himself. Duncan's perspective on these charges is precisely the opposite; far from seeking the advice of politicians, he would "have a virtual dictatorship. [...] Were I the Cabinet, I would choose the man fitted for the job. Having chosen him, I would not support him—I would *obey* him" (127).

For all of that, it must be said that Churchill, in particular, comes out very well in *Cavalry*'s revised view of history. Churchill—or Worton Spender, as he is called[19]—ends up serving on the Western Front as one of Duncan's right-hand men after his (very real) fall from political grace in the wake of the failure at Gallipoli, of which plan he was a significant architect. Spender is given a second chance, however, in Newman's most dramatic revision of the historical record, apart from having the war conclude in the summer of 1917: his decision to return to the Dardanelles. Duncan and his lieutenants understand well the necessity of finding a means of knocking the Turks out of the war, and so they devise a second assault in the Dardanelles—*at Gallipoli*. Reasoning that the Turks would never expect an attack on precisely the same point that had dealt such a blow to British morale, Duncan and Spender launch a fresh and amazingly successful strike in the middle of the night. In a seeming bid to dull the audacity of this idea even as a literary invention, Newman resorts to a somewhat macabre prosopopoeia[20] whereby the thousands of British dead in the Dardanelles signal their approval: "My God, I'll bet those 50,000 dead of ours are happy now. I wish they could come to life again: if they could see this sight they would not begrudge their death. We are going to victory over their bones" (148).

That victory is eventually won, at Gallipoli and elsewhere, but *Cavalry* is less concerned with the consequences of this than it is with showing how they might have been brought about. The novel concludes with an armistice being signed, and Duncan coming to visit the narrator as he recovers in a field hospital. "Our part is over, boy" he says; "the politicians have taken their cure. The war is over. And now the fun begins" (288). The "fun" in reality, as we have seen, was anything but, and it is not surprising that a book otherwise so focused on the matter of war should not bother to go into details about a new approach to peace.

---

19. Newman includes many real historical figures in the novel, but always under names that have been disguised with varying degrees of opacity. Churchill is Spender; Field Marshals Sir Douglas Haig and Sir John French have seemingly been combined into one Sir John Douglas; Lord Kitchener is Lord Khartner, etc.

20. Which is not without precedent in this particular case; see "Our Graves in Gallipoli," E. M. Forster's scathing 1922 dialogue between two skeletons.

While the writing of alternate history in the period following World War I was minor when compared to the wider literary scene, it laid the foundation for a host of later engagements with the subject from the 1930s down to the present day. Works like Guido Morselli's *Contropassato prossimo: un'ipotesi retrospettiva* (1975), Michael Frayn's play *Balmoral* (1988), Brian Stableford's *The Carnival of Destruction* (1994), and Ian R. MacLeod's *The Summer Isles* (2005) offer new and sometimes fantastical perspectives on how the war might have been. Alternate-historical engagements with the war have even carried over into film, whether in the key of supernatural horror—as in the 2002 British film *Deathwatch*, which tells the tale of an ancient evil that dwells in the heart of No Man's Land—or of science fiction—as in the 2013 faux-documentary *The Great Martian War, 1913–1917*, a History Channel production that weaves the events of the war into a narrative inspired by H. G. Wells's *The War of the Worlds*. Even at the present hour they are joined by written works like Robert Conroy's *1920: America's Great War* (2013), Richard Ned Lebow's *Archduke Franz Ferdinand Lives! A World Without World War I* (2014), and a volume of counterfactual World War I essays currently in preparation by Spencer Jones and Peter G. Tsouras. Whatever the attention the war may have received from alternate history writers in the past, it seems to be commanding a considerable amount today.

The joint preoccupation in alternate history writing with the vicissitudes of the past and the consequences for the future (both real and imagined) suggests something about the human experience of time, and the degree to which a constant stream of re-imagining what was helps us to cope with the loss of what might have been. It is perhaps fitting to close where we began—with Eliot:

> human kind
> Cannot bear very much reality.
> Time past and time future
> What might have been and what has been
> Point to one end, which is always present. (172)

WORKS CITED

Ashton, Nigel J. and Duco Hellema. "Hanging the Kaiser: Anglo-Dutch relations and the fate of Wilhelm II, 1918–20." *Diplomacy and Statecraft* 11.2 (July 2000): 53–78. Print.

Badsey, Stephen. " 'If It Had Happened Otherwise'—First World War Exceptionalism in Counterfactual History." *British Popular Culture and the First World War*. Ed. Jessica Meyer. Leiden: Brill, 2008. 351–68. Print.

Bond, Brian. *The Unquiet Western Front: Britain's Role in Literature and History*. Cambridge: Cambridge UP, 2002. Print.

Brack, Duncan, ed. *President Gore …. and Other Things that Never Happened*. London: Politico's, 2006. Print.

Brack, Duncan and Iain Dale, eds. *Prime Minister Portillo ... and Other Things that Never Happened*. London: Politico's, 2006. Print.

—. *Prime Minister Boris ... and Other Things that Never Happened*. London: Biteback, 2012 Print..

Buchan, John. *Greenmantle*. 1916. London: Penguin, 2008. Print.

Carlyle, Thomas. *On Heroes, Hero-Worship, and the Heroic in History*. 1841. Ed. Henry David Green. New York: Longmans, 1906. Print.

Childers, Erskine. *The Riddle of the Sands*. 1903. Ed. David Trotter. Oxford: Oxford UP, 1998. Print.

Clark, Christopher. *Kaiser Wilhelm II: A Life in Power*. 2000. London: Penguin, 2009. Print.

Clarke, I. F. *Voices Prophesying War 1763-1984*. London: Oxford UP, 1966. Print.

Cowley, Robert, ed. *What If?: Eminent Historians Imagine What Might Have Been*. 1999. New York: Berkley, 2000. Print.

—. *What If? 2: Eminent Historians Imagine What Might Have Been*. New York: Berkley, 2001. Print.

D'Israeli, Isaac. "Of a History of Events which have Not Happened." *Curiosities of Literature*. 2nd series. Vol. 1. London: John Murray, 1824. 99–119.

Doyle, Arthur Conan. "The Death Voyage." *Uncollected Stories: The Unknown Conan Doyle*. Ed. John Michael Gibson and Richard Lancelyn Green. Garden City: Doubleday, 1982. 391–412. Print.

Duncan, Andy. "Alternate History." *The Cambridge Companion to Science Fiction*. Eds. Farah Mendlesohn and Edward James. Cambridge: Cambridge UP, 2003. 209–18. Print.

Eby, Cecil D. *The Road to Armageddon: The Martial Spirit in English Popular Literature, 1870–1914*. Durham: Duke UP, 1987. Print.

Eliot, T. S. "Burnt Norton." *The Complete Poems and Plays*. 1969. London: Faber, 2004. 171–76. Print.

Ferguson, Niall. "Introduction." *Virtual History: Alternatives and Counterfactuals*. 1997. Ed. Niall Ferguson. London: Pan, 2003. 1–90. Print.

Gilbert, Martin. *The First World War: A Complete History*. New York: Holt, 1994. Print.

Hellekson, Karen. *The Alternate History: Refiguring Historical Time*. Kent: Kent State UP, 2001. Print.

Herwig, Holger H. *The First World War: Germany and Austria-Hungary, 1914–1918*. London: Arnold, 1997. Print.

Hynes, Samuel. *A War Imagined: The First World War and English Culture*. New York: Macmillan, 1990. Print.

Jones, Heather. "As the Centenary Approaches: The Regeneration of First World War Historiography." *The Historical Journal* 56.3 (Sept. 2013): 857–78. Print.

Leacock, Stephen. "The Hohenzollerns in America." *The Hohenzollerns in America, with the Bolsheviks in Berlin, and Other Impossibilities*. New York: John Lane, 1919. 9–72. Print.

—. *The Letters of Stephen Leacock*. Ed. David Staines. Oxford: Oxford UP, 2006. Print.

—. *Sunshine Sketches of a Little Town*. Ed. Gerald Lynch. 1912. Ottawa: Tecumseh, 1996. Print.

Lebow, Richard Ned. *Archduke Franz Ferdinand Lives! A World Without World War I*. New York: Palgrave Macmillan, 2014. Print.

—. *Forbidden Fruit: Counterfactuals and International Relations*. Princeton: Princeton UP, 2010. Print.

Liddell Hart, Basil. "Mr. Bernard Newman, Writer on Strategy." *The Times* 27 Feb 1968: 10. Print.

Moorcock, Michael, ed. *Before Armageddon*. London: W. H. Allen, 1975. Print.

Newman, Bernard. *The Cavalry Went Through*. London: Gollancz, 1930. Print.

—. *Speaking From Memory*. London: H. Jenkins, 1960. Print.

Ponsonby, Arthur. *Falsehood in Wartime*. 1928. Ed. Blanche Wiesen Cook. New York: Garland, 1971. Print.

Reinermann, Lothar. "Fleet Street and the Kaiser: British Public Opinion and Wilhelm II." *German History* 26.4 (October 2008): 469–85. Print.

Roberts, Andrew, ed. *What Might Have Been: Imaginary History from Twelve Leading Historians*. London: Phoenix, 2004. Print.

Schmunk, Robert B. *Uchronia*. n.d. Web. 15 December 2013.

Spadoni, Carl. *A Bibliography of Stephen Leacock*. Toronto: ECW, 1998. Print.

Squire, John Collings. "Editorial Notes." Editorial. *The London Mercury* Feb. 1920: 385–90. Print.

Squire, John Collings, ed. *If It Had Happened Otherwise*. 1931. London: Sidgwick and Jackson, 1972. Print.

Tetlock, Philip E., Richard Ned Lebow and Geoffrey Parker, eds. *Unmaking the West: "What-If?" Scenarios That Rewrite World History*. Ann Arbor: U Michigan P, 2006. Print.

Thompson, E. P. *The Poverty of Theory: or, an Orrery of Errors*. 1978. London: Merlin, 1995. Print.

Webb, Peter. " 'A righteous cause': war propaganda and Canadian fiction, 1915–1921." *British Journal of Canadian Studies* 24.1 (2011): 31–48. Print.

Winthrop-Young, Geoffrey. "Fallacies and Thresholds: Notes on the Early Evolution of Alternate History." *Historical Social Research* 34.2 (2009): 99–117. Print.

"A Deplorable Misfit":
The Symbolism of Desire in
G. K. Chesterton's *The Crimes of England*

Philip Irving Mitchell

> It is too late to expect Mr G. K. Chesterton to change his style, or, rather, to adapt it to his subject; so it must be said, *tout simplement*, that the style of *The Crimes of England* is a deplorable misfit. [...] As an exhibition of Mr Chesterton's miraculous cleverness, Mr Chesterton's almost fanatical earnestness, Mr Chesterton's knowledge and insight, *The Crimes of England* is, I venture to say, one of his two best works; but as an *exposé* of the crimes of England or, for the matter of that, of Germany either, it is unconvincing. The *truth* of what Mr Chesterton says is the last thing the reader thinks about. So dazzled are we by the verbal sparklings of Mr Chesterton's wit that it is as if we were trying to read by the light of fireworks; we can read nothing for the explosions and the coloured spectacles.—A. R. Orage (qtd. in Pearce 228–29)

The Crimes of England is the kind of work by G. K. Chesterton that troubles even his supporters. Published in November 1915, it is one of two pamphlets written for the War Propaganda Bureau, and along with Chesterton's columns in *The Illustrated London News*, his chief contribution to the war effort. If mentioned at all by critics, *Crimes* is typically either dismissed for its weak understanding of international affairs or bewailed for its simplistic view of warfare. For example, Margaret Canovan charges that Chesterton's imagery of medieval swords and honor ignores or justifies "that nightmare of guns, gas, barbed wire, and trenches" (108), while Joseph Pearce discounts *Crimes* as "not so much a work of intelligent rhetoric as a piece of anti-Prussian propaganda" (228). Julia Stapleton's study of Chesterton's politics admits that Chesterton's analysis hardly holds up and that his fear of wide-spread Teutonism in England was distorted (154–55). Even the venerable Maisie Ward admits that Chesterton was "oddly selective" in his targets and that the work is "an undue simplification" of matters (336).[1] Without denying these claims, I will argue that *The Crimes of England*, however, is not simple war propaganda because it

---

1. Ian Ker mentions *The Crimes of England* mostly as the first sign of Chesterton's heroic idealization of William Cobbett (366–67).

makes the epistemic risks in Chesterton's historiography immediate and questionable.[2]

Chesterton's contemporary A. R. Orage complained that *Crimes* was one of Chesterton's best works, yet also a serious failure, "a deplorable misfit" between its style and subject. I think Orage's charge has stumbled on to something important. His division between the coloristic manner of Chesterton's prose and the miscarriage of its political analysis is not just a division between its rhetoric and its logic. Rather, Orage touches on a potential fissure at the heart of Chesterton's method. His epigrammatic, paradoxical, buoyant comedy is his matter, as well as his manner. What, then, does a lover of Chesterton do with texts as wrongheaded as his WWI pamphlets? Can one justifiably use, as Chesterton does, the fantastic elements of fairy tale, chivalric romance, the mythic undead, and religious apocalypse to describe history? Can one trust popular memory and idealism to tell the tales of history accurately? Can one invoke the language of dreams and nightmares to picture historical and contemporary desires, especially if these are violent and macabre? *The Crimes of England* does not answer these questions, but it does bring them into stark clarity. Assisted by a number of insights from Paul Ricoeur's semantics of desire and his hermeneutics of suspicion and belief, I will argue that *Crimes* manifests a three-fold pattern of trust in truism, of suspicion in symbolism, and of hopeful, second naïveté. While increasing the dramatic power and developmental impact of the historical narrative, Chesterton's symbolic language runs the risk of suppressing the ambiguity and complexity of *realpolitik*. However, such symbols in turn open up the teleological dreams and desires that structure his narrative, though without negating the abuse to which such symbolism is often put. In short, the presence of the one does not annihilate the presence of the other, and both are worth our investment as readers.

Chesterton's Naïveté & Promise

For some it might seem anachronistic to bring a mid-to-late twentieth-century phenomenologist, such as Ricoeur, into conversation with an Edwardian journalist; however, Chesterton's historiography shares with Ricoeur a tri-fold pattern of investigation and desire, as well as a recognition that symbols are more rationally basic than theoretical

---

2. Chesterton's *Crimes* is also a transitional work of popular history between his *The Victorian Age in Literature* (1913) and his *A Short History of England* (1917) and shares with both texts a number of approaches and concerns.

elaboration.[3] Ricoeur's treatment of symbolism in *The Symbolism of Evil, Freud and Philosophy*, and *The Conflict of Interpretation* offers a number of ways to reexamine what Chesterton is doing in *The Crimes of England*. In particular, Ricoeur's dialectical move from an initial naïveté to a hermeneutic of suspicion to a second naïveté—a pattern of problematic trust, desacralizing analytic, and hopeful dialectic—helps us understand why a reader might be repulsed by the historical realities to which Chesterton failed to do justice and yet still be drawn to his poetic idealism. In *The Symbolism of Evil*, Ricoeur explores how the mythic conceptual language that the Western, Jewish, and Christian tradition(s) employ about misery and failure is emblematic of the way symbols work. Ricoeur narrates the symbolism of defilement, sin, and guilt and shows how these are exploratory and interpretive rather than purely explanatory; that is how they move from locating evil in exterior stain to interior action to sustained personal responsibility.

The Crimes of England is divided into ten chapters, and after the first, which is a satiric rejoinder to the distortions of German war propaganda, the chapters unfold in a chronological manner, beginning with Frederick II of Prussia (1712–1786) and William Pitt's support of his regime and ending with the First Battle of Marne in which British and French forces halted the German advance in September of 1914. Along the way, Chesterton recounts the historical crimes of England, yet in every case finds some insidious Prussian hand. The English opposition to the French revolution and to Napoleon, the occupation of Ireland, the alliance with Germany against Napoleon III, and general fascination with the Teutonic theory are all given as evidence of England's faults as well as of Teutonic corruption. Perhaps it should not surprise us, then, that in such a wide-sweeping pamphlet, Chesterton would employ his gift for generalization and broad characterization. He musters a full complement of fantastic and chivalric imagery, casting heroes and villains in a landscape of gallant and supernatural consequence. Likewise, he evokes the language of dreams, nightmares, and apocalypse to suggest that the fight at hand, rather than being simply political, is also metaphysical and epic.

Ricoeur's approach shows that while Chesterton's use of fairy tale and apocalyptic imagery in *Crimes* serves interests both personal and political, they cannot be reduced univocally to these interests alone. We are faced with the fundamental question of where evil is to be found: is

---

3. They also stand as virtual bookends to a period of extensive interaction with and critique of European theories, theologies, and philosophies of history, historiography, and historicism, though this insight is too sweeping to prove here.

it primarily an exterior contagion; is it an interior set of decisions; or is it an interdependent mixture of exterior ideology and interior corruption? As I will seek to show below, Chesterton's *Crimes* invokes all three strategies. Our initial trust in our consciousness and its intentions are challenged by those that Ricoeur has labeled the "masters of suspicion," namely Marx, Nietzsche, and Freud. All three thinkers point out our capacity for self-deception. While Marx would urge us to question if our ideologies are a form of false consciousness, working to oppress others for our own profit, Nietzsche locates within the will false forms of resentment and self-hatred. Freud goes even further, claiming to locate suppressed infantile desires that drive our images and rationales for our behavior. With Ricoeur's approach, one need not agree that these theories are correct in their analysis to accept the broad shape of their interrogation of the self. What Ricoeur argues is that our initial faith in our myths, beliefs, and perceptions should be tested by these forms of interrogation, but in doing so, our beliefs may yet arise in a new form that discovers the hope of future fulfillment in new poetic offerings.

At one level, Chesterton's whole life and career could be said to be a manifestation of Ricoeur's pattern. The young Victorian raised in a broadly Unitarian home undergoes a period of soul-testing pessimism and nihilism (while at the Slade School) only to turn to cosmic optimism and loyalty to the world. Setting himself against modern pessimism, relativism, and moral plasticity, Chesterton becomes the public defender of the tradition of not only Christianity, but also of folkways and adventure stories. And as is well-known, Chesterton re-invests the sacred center—the world, marriage, the moral life, local polity, and Christian orthodoxy—with the arresting imaginative power of fairy tales, adventure stories, and accounts of chivalry.

Chesterton would articulate this approach for historiography at various points in his career. In "Three Ways of Writing History" Chesterton argued that there are three broad approaches to writing history and all involve a stance toward the picturesque and suggest stages in maturation. The old-style Victorian history lessons, at their best, inspired students with a sense of the noble and heroic, yet they also contained much misinformation. Edwardian attempts to correct the often untrue picturesque narratives with the new "scientific" historical methods were also problematic to Chesterton's mind. Monographic history, despite its claims to objectivity and to disinterested study, distorted the

"A Deplorable Misfit"

basic humanity of the past, reducing its peoples to social phenomena[4]: "A far different class of things that makes every modern book of history as false as the father of lies; ingenuity, self-consciousness, hypocritical impartiality" (*Varied Types* 22). In short, the pose of being impartial rendered one unable to truly see *all* the evidence.

Yet a third way of writing history remained. In a manner similar to R. G. Collingwood,[5] Chesterton urged that, rather than striving for a hypothetical objectivity with its undisclosed assumptions of superiority, historians should seek to enter sympathetically into the moral, religious, and emotional context of past cultures and their folkways. Like the monographic historians, one can be engaged in widening the available evidence from history while keeping one's commitments and loyalties. Writers also should practice a "history of the historians," that is an awareness of their own prejudices and motivations ("Need for" 607–10).[6] The call for humility makes wonder possible, including respect and charity toward the past ("Paganism" 127–28). Chesterton did not hold that every culture or person possessed or even recognized it.[7] He, likewise, argued that historians should practice humility when comparing the past to their own time. Historians should own that the limitations of their own contexts, rather than giving them objectivity on the past, make it more difficult for them to truly enter sympathetically into the past's psychological milieu ("Need for" 608–10). Each age was accustomed to a certain manner of life, so readers or writers of history must decide their misery based on their standards, not ours ("Comparing" 181–83). The historian should be about uncovering what the people thought and were concerned

---

4. The *Cambridge Modern History*, under John Lord Acton, may not have set out to end in this manner, but Roland Hill concludes that the series ended up piecemeal and atomistic, something of a chore for a generation of British students (396–401).

5. See, for example, Collingwood's discussion of the outer and inner elements of an historical event, and how a historian must seek to enter the inner elements through the hard work of imaginative re-enactment (214–17).

6. The nature of the historian's "ideal" subjectivity: Historical distance and the historian's investigation bracketed from his or her pathos (*Crimes* 327).

7. According to him, Thomas Carlyle's problem as a historian came from his inability to truly sense the emotional and subjective commitment of other people to other worlds. Chesterton suggests that the truly "impartial" historian is one who can express some sympathy for the human viewpoint (mind and emotions) of other periods and cultures. Carlyle was never able to truly understand the Catholic and Jacobean worldviews because he lacked humility ("Thomas Carlyle" 29ff.). By contrast, Chesterton could praise Wilfrid Ward's biography of John Henry Newman for being able "to be strongly co-operative with another's mind," modeling an intense meekness that acts as would a benevolent friend (Ker 278).

with and should avoid treating a whole period as good or bad ("Age of Reason"185–87). Too often, certain historical failures are brought up with no attempt to contextualize that which we disapprove; for example Galileo's imprisonment by the Church or the harsh English penalty for stealing sheep ("Abuses" 379–82). Such is a failure to imagine a context in which such things might have made sense or been at least more understandable.

Chesterton's historiographical position, then, was not unlike Ricoeur's first and second naiveté. The naïve childhood response to the romance of history is replaced by political and moral complications, even forms of desacralizing challenge, that come with academic study. But, school histories that leave the picture of history overly complicated have done great disservice to students, for what remains is a third stage of adult engagement with the past that is pragmatic in its imaginative interactions, as well as in its factual understanding ("Romance" 114). Mythic language does not disappear in a true and faithful history, according to Chesterton; instead, it expands to take a stance that is general enough to be argued with and yet specific enough that it has sought to be fair to the available information.[8] What holds all three stages together is imagination and wonder, a quest for sympathy, an approach that revives the sacred character of past people and their worlds. Chesterton never lost his basic trust in the power of symbols and paradoxical generalizations to open up the truth of being human and to enlarge readerly experience.[9] In this Chesterton assumed that the picturesque narrative would continue to be the form that good historiography must take, for that form arises out of human symbolic needs.

---

8. In his essay "The Teaching of History," Chesterton sought to set out this third stage as a larger theory of historiography: He insisted that while global history is important, any single theory of history is reductive. There is a need for "intellectual independence" (317), but it comes in seeing the varied cases for various historical positions. Too many progressive historians do not see that there might even be another interpretative location from which to examine the past. "The whole object of history is to enlarge experience by imagination," Chesterton enthuses (318). Therefore, the past can be admirable, profitable, enviable, etc.

9. According to Chesterton, the experience of reading primary texts in cheap translations helps us to encounter our cultural others in a way that a teacher of our same culture and class does not ("Books" 35). When we read such sources, Chesterton holds, we open ourselves again to the humanity of past people, and this openness justifies one's personal and human responses to the picturesque, a suitable frame for the wide freedom of individuals and their cultures.

"A Deplorable Misfit"

HISTORY AND TRUISMS

By common consent, Chesterton does not achieve his ideals for historiography with *The Crimes of England*. At first glance, however, this appears an unjust judgment. The pamphlet is written as a popular text, not as one of the monographic tomes that he so distrusted. It does employ generic plots and popular memories, even exaggerations, as a better kind of history, but then Chesterton holds that these touch people emotionally and volitionally. He invokes the defiling undead—goblins, bogeys, skeletons, ghosts—as well as apocalyptic battle imagery. He also re-invests his subjects with romantic imagery from the Crusades, martyrdom, the Body of Christ, the Holy Roman Empire, and medieval romance in general. The work, by its very structure, seeks to own up to interior English faults, for Chesterton's loyalty is always one that includes critique. The patriot tells his or her people where they should repent. Yet what *Crimes* lacks is Chesterton's call for humility and little, if any, sympathy for the Prussian or German past. Likewise, while not the first time that Chesterton had been charged with getting his facts wrong or with offering a one-sided picture of his enemies, *Crimes* is a particularly clear case by virtue of being war propaganda. Part of the issue, too, may be a question of genre. Even if we give Chesterton the benefit of the doubt (that is, that he never intentionally distorted the historical record), he clearly has an axe to grind. And even if we grant that histories can never be truly objective in the sense that Chesterton critiques, he still offers a history that purports to offer evidence to which all can lay claim. His use of heavy symbolism and extensive generic emplotment embodies the initial strength of his basic trust in their truth-telling abilities, and thus, they are subject to further testing.

Chesterton had a career-long trust in generic plots to tell the truth about history and morality because they give voice to how people actually think and feel about human existence and ethical action, including about evils one must encounter and sins one has committed. This trust follows from an equal faith in common people and in received worldviews. Alan Blackstock traces how for Chesterton, as early as 1901, a truism, like folk literature, has a permanency about it, for it dwells in the *sensus communis*, so much so that it becomes aphoristic as long as it remains unquestioned. For Chesterton, this is how things were meant to be. Lived human experience is not a nest of continual qualifications. "The true modern cowardice is that no one has the courage to pronounce truisms" ("On Books," qtd. in Blackstock 5). Chesterton often made this claim. "Making generalizations is what makes him a man," he tells us in *Heretics* ("Shaw" 67). In *Orthodoxy* he observes that

"Man can be defined as an animal that makes dogmas" ("Concluding" 196). Truisms, generalizations, and dogmas are different ways of describing universal statements. Their declarative structure creates forms of mythic certainty. He insisted that a confession of faith always involves a distillation of truth that "gains something and gives up something. So long as he does both, he can create; for he is making an outline and a shape" (*Victorian* 439). Chesterton assumed that his practice of generalization and characterization was incomplete; human reason and story cannot be comprehensive since they are dramatic forms.[10]

Not surprisingly then, Chesterton believed that the motivations of Edwardian realism and skeptical history are related. If there are authors "who really hate the heroic," there are also historians who hardly admit the romantic, even when it actually happened ("Historical Skepticism" 491–92). Chesterton puts his trust in folk histories because they simplify—one is tempted to say, purify—their versions of what happened in order to emphasize its moral center. He fears "that introduction of ingenious and over-elaborate detail [...] is the whole art of telling lies" (494). Qualifications, for Chesterton, rather than attempting to offer a balanced picture of the past, are too often subtle commitments to an anthropology that will not admit the morally admirable act can occur. In *Crimes*, for example, Chesterton places front and center his trust in epic imagery and popular memory in his valorization of the French Revolution. He praises the classicism of the movement because of its universal quality, parabolic voice, and tragic memory. It came forth as "a sudden antiquity" and is invested with "the hammering of spears and the awful cap of Phrygia." Its prologue and epilogue, the storming of the Bastille and the end of Napoleon, are "primary symbols" of "visionary character" in that they reflect the justice of the community's memory. Of course, Chesterton admits that the true end at Waterloo happened after Napoleon's defeat, but the common picture that Napoleon should be there at the very end is correct, for "the mob is an artist, though not a man of science." Waterloo in popular memory had Napoleon present as a ghost, "a spectral resurrection and a second death." The actual ending

---

10. Chesterton praises William Cobbett's fiery history even if it often exaggerated for similar reasons: "And as his seemingly mad language is very literary, so his seemingly mad meaning is very historical. Modern people do not understand him because they do not understand the difference between exaggerating a truth and exaggerating a lie. He did exaggerate, but what he knew, not what he did not know. He only appears paradoxical because he upheld tradition against fashion. A paradox is a fantastic thing that is said once: a fashion is a more fantastic thing that is said a sufficient number of times. [...] Now this is extravagant. It takes the breath away; and it was meant to" (*Crimes* 333).

with its alliance of British and Prussian forces was dull and ignoble, with Gebhard von Blücher stealing "the sword of Joan of Arc" from Paris (*Crimes* 317–18). Taken together, Chesterton values the popular and the narratival because they sustain human action, and the epic language of antiquity affirms the actions of the Revolution as universal and, therefore, universally admirable and understandable.

Another example of Chesterton's approach in *Crimes* is his treatment of Bismarck's war with Denmark. Chesterton sees the plan for German unification as nothing but an aggressionist campaign by Prussia that overrode the genuine sovereignty of other German principalities, and England's refusal to help protect Denmark's territories manifested the feeble underside to English Teutonism. Yet Chesterton's analysis does not stop there, for he must unpack "the symbolical intensity of the incident." To do this, he examines the political failure as several layers of fairy-tale failures. Denmark, he holds as exemplary of "quiet freedom, quiet prosperity, a simple love of fields and of the sea," things normally associated with the not yet unified Germanys. These are what England, having prized, should have protected, but instead, the theory of Teutonism left them the obscene task of seeking to make Bismarck poetic and pious. Chesterton charges the Germans with having lost their basic pedagogical and moral resources—that is, the love of the truth found in fairy tales. And to bring this home, rather than call up the Grimms, he offers Hans Christian Andersen as the one to whom English children owe a sense that "domesticity is not dull but rather fantastic; that sense of the fairyland of furniture, and the travel and adventure of farmland." In particular, Chesterton centers down on the tale "The Tin Soldier" for it teaches that "the dignity of the fighter is not in his largeness but rather in his smallness, in his stiff loyalty and heroic helplessness in the hands of larger and lower things." Chesterton laments, "These things, alas, were an allegory," or perhaps better said, another fairy tale. The English Teutons, such as Carlyle, looked on "while the innocent toy kingdom was broken like a toy," and the toy army of Denmark like the Toy Soldier was "swept away down the great gutter, down that colossal *cloaca* that leads to the vast cesspool of Berlin." In turn, he charges the Teutonism of historians like E. A. Freeman and J. R. Green with a failure of fantasy: "King Arthur might not be historical, but at least he was legendary. Hengist and Horsa were not even legendary, for they left no legend" (*Crimes* 341–44).

Chesterton's trust in the power of fairytales and popular memory is, therefore, emblematic of the first phase of Ricoeur's hermeneutical analysis. For Ricoeur, myths are developed, narratively structured symbols. The symbols themselves, which work as primitive analogies, have primary meanings that open up other potential significance(s), and they require of us interpretation. In particular, symbols are manifested in the cosmic universe of discourse, in the oneiric world of dreams, and in the poetic structure of multiple meanings. We are born into world-pictures and rituals that confirm these narratives, and they provide stable social and personal meaning (*Freud* 8–18). In Chesterton's case, they provide the energy of conviction necessary for deep engagement from his readers. These are tales, at least in shape, which he suspects that all trusted as children. This trust, because it is extended to symbols, has to cooperate in an imaginative way with their movement. As Ricoeur notices, symbolic fecundity opens up a number of potentially limitless echoes, and in Chesterton's case this leads to "the explosions and the coloured spectacles" of which Orage complained.

In chapter two of *Crimes*, Chesterton sets out his Act I history: the lead player is Frederick II of Prussia, and his stunted maturation is narrated as a plethora of gothic tropes:

> Everything was young once, even Frederick the Great. It was an appropriate preface to the terrible epic of Prussia that it began with an unnatural tragedy of the loss of youth. That blind and narrow savage who was the boy's father had just sufficient difficulty in stamping out every trace of decency in him, to show that some such traces must have been there. If the younger and greater Frederick ever had a heart, it was a broken heart; broken by the same blow that broke his flute. When his only friend was executed before his eyes, there were two corpses to be borne away; and one to be borne on a high war-horse through victory after victory: but with a small bottle of poison in the pocket. It is not irrelevant thus to pause upon the high and dark house of his childhood. For the peculiar quality which marks out Prussian arms and ambitions from all others of the kind consists in this wrinkled and premature antiquity. (*Crimes* 303)

The execution of Hans Hermann von Katte for desertion is painted as a macabre moment in Frederick's psyche, but rather than resort to language of analysis, Chesterton summons images of corpses, poison, dark houses, and insufferable cruelty. Even if one already agrees that such a childhood event was formative in Frederick's later psyche, the narrative of tragedy and horror asks an imaginative commitment. Chesterton would say it is fitting. Indeed, not to find some equivalent narration, Chesterton would judge it as false, as burying the moral meaning of the past in a too objective psycho-social series of qualifications. This is not to say that Chesterton was avoiding these kinds of explanations; indeed, he was attempting them, but in a symbolical mode that was cosmic, oneiric, and poetic at once:

> But the spirit of the great Hohenzollern smelt from the first of the charnel. He came out to his first victory like one broken by defeats; his strength was stripped to the bone and fearful as a fleshless resurrection; for the worst of what could come had already befallen him. The very construction of his kingship was built upon the destruction of his manhood. He had known the final shame; his soul had surrendered to force. He could not redress that wrong; he could only repeat it and repay it. He could make the souls of his soldiers surrender to his gibbet and his whipping-post; he could make the souls of the nations surrender to his soldiers. He could only break men in as he had been broken; while he could break in, he could never break out. He could not slay in anger, nor even sin with simplicity. Thus he stands alone among the conquerors of their kind; his madness was not due to a mere misdirection of courage. Before the whisper of war had come to him the foundations of his audacity had been laid in fear. (*Crimes* 304)

According to Chesterton, Frederick II is a damaged man. Chesterton summons all the language of evil to identify this fault: brokenness, shame, torture, madness, fear. Frederick has become one of the undead, a skeletal figure "fearful as a fleshless resurrection," no longer operating according to even normal patterns of sin, but by a cold heartless "loathsome affection" in which he tears apart the bodies of nations, impoverishes them, and tortures them without malice, without any motivation recognizably human at all (304–05). Chesterton offers a metaphysical and spiritual judgment of the despot. Frederick's interior brokenness lends itself to the defilement of others. He becomes an instrument of force that operates without human-sized loyalties. Under such terms, Chesterton can judge Frederick's later actions as "satanic," and can insist that this word is "not a term of abuse, but of theology" (310). Such a distinction gestures toward Chesterton's belief in actual angelic and demonic beings. His symbolism carries with it some measure of commitment to their metaphysical veracity. Frederick's division of Poland, for Chesterton, is a kind of Black Mass, and Frederick's hatred of Maria Theresa of Austria is a cosmic one, for she was "firm in the ancient faith" and "brave as a young lioness," and his animosity added "something almost superhuman to the mysterious vileness of his character" (309).[11]

---

11. The friendship of Voltaire and Frederick the Great is another good example of Chesterton's continued interest in Frederick II as a spiritual and ideological signifier. Late in his career, he could picture the friendship of Frederick and Voltaire as a diabolical historical disaster: "The spiritual zero of Christendom was at that freezing instant when these two dry, thin, hatchet-faced men looked in each other's

This cosmic character of Chesterton's rhetoric in *Crimes* is often reducible to apocalyptical binaries. Its duality carries with it not only a supernatural division, but also invokes a sense of cosmic expectation, of the finality of things. The English involvement in Ireland is emblematic of the larger political and spiritual disaster, a war of two worlds, and clearly brings into focus the mythic stakes:

> Having chosen our part and made war upon the new world, we were soon made to understand what such spiritual infanticide involved; and were committed to a kind of Massacre of the Innocents. [...] Fate for once seemed to pick out a situation in plain black and white like an allegory; a tragedy of appalling platitudes. The heroes were really heroes; and the villains were nothing but villains. The common tangle of life, in which good men do evil by mistake and bad men do good by accident, seemed suspended for us as for a judgment. We had to do things that not only were vile, but felt vile. We had to destroy men who not only were noble, but looked noble. [...]
>
> The march of Pitt's policy went on; and the chasm between light and darkness deepened. Order was restored; and wherever order spread, there spread an anarchy more awful than the sun has ever looked on. Torture came out of the crypts of the Inquisition and walked in the sunlight of the streets and fields. A village vicar was slain with inconceivable stripes, and his corpse set on fire with frightful jests about a roasted priest. Rape became a mode of government. The violation of virgins became a standing order of police. Stamped still with the same terrible symbolism, the work of the English Government and the English settlers seemed to resolve itself into animal atrocities against the wives and daughters of a race distinguished for a rare and detached purity, and of a religion which makes of innocence the Mother of God. In its bodily aspects it became like a war of devils upon angels; as if England could produce nothing but torturers, and Ireland nothing but martyrs. (*Crimes* 321–22, 324–25)

What is evident in passages like these is Chesterton's desire for, even need for, larger, dramatic absolutes. Infanticide and a campaign of rape are images that he need not fear his audience will judge without harsh reproof. There is no muddling of heroism and villainy, nor is there any doubt as to oppressor and oppressed. The historic events can be safely labeled as tragic, as horrific, as atrocities. The apocalyptic symbolism is all together necessary for this. It is a matter of cosmic light and darkness, a battle between angelic and the demonic, between purity and defilement, between humane and animalistic. The fairy tale signifier "as if" becomes for Chesterton more than a rhetorical tool; it becomes the division between torturer and martyr. Yet Chesterton also invokes his

---

hollow eyes and saw the sneer that was as eternal as the smile of a skull. Between them, they have nearly killed the thing by which we live" ("Frederick" 380).

own identity as an Englishman. He shares in the guilt of deeds vile and terrible, though perhaps he declaims too much. Chesterton warms to the myth because it imparts narrative stability and ethical confidence. However, it is clear that Chesterton was only too aware that "the common tangle of life" is rather sloppy for this kind of thing; indeed, it may even be so for the case in question.

SUSPECTING SYMBOLS

According to Ricoeur, we stand between myths that make the pretense of being universal and timeless (even if they have a history which can be traced) and particular historical identifications, which are contingent and not at all of necessity axiomatic (*Symbolism* 164–65). Ricoeur's distinctions between myth and history, as well as myth and *gnosis*, raise fundamental questions about truth and history. Ricoeur held a vision of myth not unlike that of Owen Barfield in which the primeval "supernatural, the natural, and the psychological are not yet torn apart" and in which the postlapsarian myth now gestures toward that original wholeness (*Symbolism* 167). For Ricoeur, the mythic cannot be the historic because the former seeks the universal, yet still must be narratival because it looks back to what has been lost and seeks resolution in what is still to come (168–70). Because of this, a myth should never be reduced to a stationary, gnostic understanding. "A symbol starts to be destroyed when it stops playing on several registers" (*Conflict* 308–09).

Chesterton's understanding of fairyland in *Crimes* runs parallel with Ricoeur's. Chesterton warns that the horrible in fairy tales exists so that the child may learn not to fear the evil figure, but to regard it, at one level, as unreal and, therefore, unthreatening. The danger is to come to worship that which is malevolent. Demystifying evil protects the child (*Crimes* 336). Chesterton held this position from early on in his career. In "The Nightmare" (*The Daily News* 16 October 1909), Chesterton proves that he can easily construct a tale of supernatural horror, but he does it to guffaw, "Only, you see, this mood is all bosh. I do not believe it in the least" (*Alarms* 25). For Chesterton, this dismissal is a literary, ethical principle. "This luxury of fear" is acceptable as long as it does not rule one's psyche and one's ideology is "Christian and simple […] the old plain things of poetry and piety"; which is to say that Chesterton while not denying the metaphysical reality of demons or ghosts or other supernatural horrors, holds that the amusing thrill of fairy-tale evil has the benefit of strengthening the imagination (26–27). He insists in *Crimes* that going to fairyland requires coming back; that is, engaging the fantastic should not end in being held captive (*Crimes* 337).[12]

Moreover, according to Chesterton one must not "break the mirror" of fantasy with theories of "psycho-pathological abnormality" (*Crimes* 338). Chesterton charges the Prussians with having lost the child-like nature of their best fairy tales and substituting for it a philosophy of force, which rests at the heart of their worst fantasies. Chesterton says that this dilemma is an "unconscious symbolism" of "playing with terrorism" and that England's choice is either "elfland" with its "Teutonic fantasy" or Prussia with its "Teutonic fear" (338). Yet may one not ask the same questions of Chesterton's own propaganda? Ricoeur has argued that symbols must remain analogous and indirect, not univocal and reductive, if they are to retain their productive artistic powers, and Chesterton would agree. Chesterton certainly understood the oneiric qualities of symbols. The divided English attitude toward Waterloo he called "the dual personality in a dream" (318), and English trust in Pan-Germanism he pictures as "riding on a nightmare" evokes the image of an out-of-control steed to describe the chaotic near fatal fall "from a dream to a nightmare" (352). Given his caution against breaking the mirror, Chesterton offered his fairy-tale symbolism in much the same way as his defense of truisms and generalizations. They are meant to be argued with, yet to work their magic they also require a common-sense acceptance. How seriously, then, are we to take a passage such as the following?

> The crowning of the first modern Kaiser in the very palace of the old French kings was an allegory; like an allegory on those Versailles walls. For it was at once the lifting of the old despotic diadem and its descent on the low brow of a barbarian. Louis XI. had returned, and not Louis IX.; and Europe was to know that sceptre on which there is no dove.
>
> The instant evidence that Europe was in the grip of the savage was as simple as it was sinister. The invaders behaved with an innocent impiety and bestiality that had never been known in those lands since Clovis was signed with the cross. To the naked pride of the new men nations simply were not. The struggling populations of two vast provinces were simply carried away like slaves into captivity, as after the sacking of some prehistoric town. France was fined for having pretended to be a nation; and the fine was planned to ruin her forever. Under the pressure of such impossible injustice France cried out to

---

12. In "The Nightmare" he also discusses another kind of nightmare—that of the apocalyptic creatures full of eyes beneath the throne of God. These he sees as healthy because they are not operating as separate and idolatrous gods (27–28).

> the Christian nations, one after another, and by name. Her last cry ended in a stillness like that which had encircled Denmark.
>
> One man answered; one who had quarrelled with the French and their Emperor; but who knew it was not an emperor that had fallen. Garibaldi, not always wise but to his end a hero, took his station, sword in hand, under the darkening sky of Christendom, and shared the last fate of France. A curious record remains, in which a German commander testifies to the energy and effect of the last strokes of the wounded lion of Aspromonte. But England went away sorrowful, for she had great possessions. (*Crimes* 351)

At one level, we are to take it very seriously. Chesterton truly believed that the crowning of Wilhelm I represented the unfolding of the imperial belligerence of a united German Empire; he really held the Franco-Prussian War to be a violation of the tradition of French liberty. He admired Giuseppe Garibaldi's switch in allegiance to the French Third Republic, even when most of Italy had come to support Prussia. Still, how many competing measures of truth are in play in such a passage? On the one hand, Chesterton is addressing what he believes are explicit politico-religious and ideological (i.e. philosophical and theological) dangers; on the other hand, he insists that we should not shatter the mirror of fairyland, that we should not seek to explain the power and magic therein contained. He invokes the language of allegory here, but it is hardly univocal; rather, he crafts a broad tale that ends with one man of valor standing against the coming spiritual darkness. We are to enter into the romance imaginatively. Wilhelm welds a scepter without the sign of the Holy Spirit, such as the British crown had maintained, and, therefore, as an unholy antichrist spreads his new pagan reign of savagery and slavery across the land. France is personified as a besieged and tragically abandoned woman crying into the cowardly silence. Chesterton pictures Garibaldi, who was in reality opposed to the Christian Church, with sword in hand going to his death for Christendom.

There is a dramatic swagger in passages such as these, and, of course, no one is surprised. Chesterton's symbols and rhetoric contained these disturbing possibilities all along. He was always a writer of violence and heroism, as well as of optimism and buoyancy. Chesterton throughout his career saw as essential to adventurous manhood the heroic ethos of courage, hand-to-hand combat, defense of the weak, protection of women (who were not often weak in his eyes), and gallant sacrifice. He argued in *Orthodoxy* for an irrational optimism that may even wish to destroy something out of love for it: "I do not deny that reform may be excessive; I only say that it is the mystic patriot who reforms" ("Flag" 273). This same kind of fervent excess is everywhere in *Crimes*, for he held as valuable "the great truth that hatred is beautiful, when it is hatred of the ugliness of the soul" (*Crimes* 348) He can preach like a crusader that the Great War, if not an end to injustice, will be "the end of the world. But we have sworn to make an end of that ending: warring on until, if only by a purgatory of the nations and the mountainous annihilation of men, the story of the world ends well" (348). In his zeal, Chesterton makes a thanatopic romance of mounting carnage, a purification by fire.

This valorization of violence is the difficulty many have with Chesterton's propaganda. Fantastic story is well and good, unless one turns with it to actual violence. Canovan opines that Chesterton's "inability to fight may have contributed to the fanaticism of [his] propaganda pamphlets" (109), and Quentin Lauer calls Chesterton's hatred of Erich Maria Remarque ("that dirty, sniveling pacifist") "this strange exception" growing out of Chesterton's intense loathing of pacifism (59–60). I suspect that part of this is Chesterton's life-long conviction that fighting is, for a certain type of man, part of who he is, and Chesterton often fantasized that he could be such.[13] Courage arises, according to Chesterton, not because of some kind of national ideal, but because the *patria* is tied to the local divinity. Men fight in war for the shrine and reject anarchy because it endangers the *religio* ("Flag" 271). Still, this does not excuse the fast-and-loose way Chesterton played with the historical realities of war. Ralph C. Wood's recent critique rivals Evelyn Waugh's in its ferocity.[14] In Wood's eyes, Chesterton betrayed his Christian faith: not only did he overlook the nature of total war and the powerful interests of large nation-states; he also neglected to listen to wiser voices, including those who shared his faith. His picture of an evil Prussia and of the rise of populist English localities served to paint over the hundreds of thousands of causalities. And Chesterton would continue to pay no heed to either the post-war military accounts or the anguished accounts of war poets such as Siegfried Sassoon or Wilfred Owen (83–90).[15]

---

13. Chesterton recalls buying a pistol as a kind of fantasy of protecting his wife against pirates (*Autobiography* 44). His famous sword-cane also comes to mind.

14. As Waugh charged: "Could Chesterton have written like that today, if he had lived to see the Common Man in arms, drab, grey and brown, the Storm Troopers and the Partisans, standard-bearers of the great popular movements of the century; had he lived to read in the evidence of the War Trials the sickening accumulation of brutality inflicted and condoned by common men, and seen, impassive on the bench, the agents of other criminals, vile, but free and triumphant?" (Waugh 74).

15. Wood is especially troubled by a vague valorization of violence in poems like *The Ballad of St. Barbara* "that violates Chesterton's own loyalty to the specific

Why did Chesterton fail in these ways, if indeed, we may judge them as failure? Chesterton served a God of battle and conflict, but not of these alone. Only two years earlier, in *The Victorian Age in Literature*, Chesterton could condemn Rudyard Kipling's imperialism as a failure to understand the God of the cross: "The fallacy of this whole philosophy is that if God is indeed present at a modern battle, he may be present not as on Gilboa but Golgotha" (446). One is hard pressed to find anything like this in Chesterton during the war years. Rather than the orchestrator of tragic blood and thunder and duty, God may be present in the act of sacrificial love. In Chesterton's imagination (and theology) the crucifixion of Christ outstrips the typical human project of the good life: "The spectacle of a God dying [...] suggests that awful changes have really entered the alchemy of the universe" (*Blake* 179), and as Wood also shows, Chesterton had the imaginative resources to find in Christmas a symbol of peace (91–96). But despite this check in his thought, Chesterton always possessed both desire and regret regarding violence. The conclusion of *The Napoleon of Notting Hill* is a case in point. The sword-wielding Adam Wayne and the prankster-ruler Auberon Quin confront one another only to conclude that perhaps they are but two mad parts of the same brain, "two essentials" of a far-off "equal and eternal human being" with no internal antagonism remaining (378–79). Is it fair to suggest that this basic tension in Chesterton lost its balance in *Crimes*? Perhaps, though the eschatological longing remained.

Freud is valuable according to Ricoeur for helping us to see human "resistance to the truth," especially the painfulness of self-recognition, and the tragic nature of life's harshness, our seeming inability to change, and our being subject to our wandering, conflicted libidos (*Conflict* 150–56). This vision of internally conflicted human beings, driven by warring desires, is one worth testing against Chesterton's own work. All of Ricoeur's masters of suspicion share notions of genealogy that uncover false self-consciousness. Freud's concepts of the dream system, wish fulfillment, and a balance of satisfaction and dissatisfaction purport to offer the revelation of people to themselves. One need not agree with the specific mechanics of Freud to let his method raise certain questions. Ricoeur insists that sublimated desires are always a building block of poetics; all works of art are sublimated. As Ricoeur points out, one object can stand for another in a way that has a

---

and concrete" (87) and wonders how Chesterton could have failed to see the Germans as his fellow Christians in need of repentance.

truth-claim, yet also act as an expression of desire (*Freud* 456), and all symbols are, thus, enclosing and disclosing at the same time.[16]

One can turn to Chesterton's nervous breakdown in 1914-1915 or his frustration with the Marconi scandal as psychological sources for his abundance of rage in *Crimes* (Dale 176–83; Ker 307–21). Certainly, they offer us a man conflicted not only within his own body, but with the body politic of Britain. Within *Crimes* there are plenty of symbols, too, one can subject to suspicion. The pamphlet, lest we forget, is an act of aggression. "The deep collapse and yawning chasm of your ineptitude leaves me upon a perilous spiritual elevation" he tells Professor Whirlwind in the first chapter (299). Strangely, it is Chesterton's own complicity as an Englishman that empowers him to oppose the German Empire. The judging consciousness calls itself under judgment: "I am that Englishman who has tortured Ireland, who has been tortured by South Africa; who knows all his mistakes, who is heavy with all his sins. And he tells you, Faultless Being, with a truth as deep as his own guilt, and as deathless as his own remembrance, that you shall not pass this way" (*Letters* 290). This passage from *Letters to an Old Garibaldian*, the appendix to the 1915 propaganda piece, *The Appetite of Tyranny*, foreshadows the overall structure of *Crimes*. It also suggests Chesterton's own conflict. In the same appendix, Chesterton reflects on how the war has united opposed sides within England and the United Kingdom and how this unity of purpose acts as spiritual ablution: "To give up one's love for one's country is great. But to give up one's hate for one's country, this may also have in it something of pride and something of purification" (*Letters* 275). Is it too much a stretch to see Chesterton's polarizing history lesson in *Crimes* as a driving need to be thought a patriot and a warrior, and for a season to be united rather than divided from the English leadership?

At one level, Chesterton's attack on Prussia operates as what historian Reinhart Koselleck called an "asymmetrical counterconcept," that is a term that assigns meanings to others that they themselves would not accept (159). At another level, Chesterton is seeking to continue to confess the interior moral diseases of the English past, even while he judges the German juggernaut as that ideological infection

---

16. Chesterton himself admitted to the fascination of the crack in the door and the hole in the fence that gives one the best view of architecture, to the keyhole that opens out to the landscape, to the mountain just beyond the "rabbit warren" of London ("London" 636–37).

and defilement. To do this, he must describe and affirm certain national characteristics for divided Germany and divided England.[17] At a third level, Chesterton also has the unfulfilled dream of Latin and European Christendom in mind and England's own conflicted relationship to it. That all three of these entities—Teutonic nihilism, English character, and European Christendom—might be only semiotic projections raises the troubling question of false consciousness on Chesterton's part. With his gift for caricature, what was he seeking to create and to hold? His use of fairy-tale evil to demonize his enemies is powerful for symbolical reasons, but it is easily subject to the critique of the Other, as his gift for generalization easily overflows into heavy (and historically inaccurate) pronouncements. The Alliance between England and Prussia meant not only "the ruin of anything and everything Irish" but also "the ruin of anything and everything English" (*Crimes* 331). The German materialist philosophy is monstrous and animalistic, "a pack of wolves" and "blonde […] lions whose nature it is to eat such lambs as the French." The historical Zeitgeist arises out of the forests of "savage superstition" as "perhaps the only ghost that was ever entirely fabulous." And the German autocracy gives freedoms, but only those given to a slave, "the liberty to dream, the liberty to rage; the liberty to indulge in any intellectual hypotheses about the unalterable world and state" (*Crimes* 356–57). There is a hysteria about these passages; a fear of the unreal warring on the unreal.

Chesterton was partially correct about the content of Teutonic philosophy. He did not have far to search for examples of Shakespeare or Michelangelo or Jesus as German to assist in his *reductio ad absurdum*. Yet this did not mean that its worst excesses had had the debilitating impact in England that Chesterton described. Even in its heyday in the 1870s, English Teutonism was not a monolithic cultural force. The Everyman edition of Green's *Short History of the English People* would continue to sell well into the Edwardian period, but Green was hardly the racialist that Freeman was, and Celticism was an equally strong counter-force during the late Victorian period (Mandler 93–98; Kenyon 160–63).[18] The

---

17. The inner-German division (*Crimes* 364–66) parallel with the inner English division (367).
18. Most of the major figures in *Crimes* interact with various figures who were historical signifiers for Teutonism or its counterpart—Napoleon, Bismarck, Napoleon III. Michael Bentley has suggested that the rhetorical sonority of Bishop William Stubbs's work had much to do with the staying power of the position, even after scholars had taken it to task, but the Teutonic foundation of Stubbs's constitutional history was by far the least influential part of his history (24–31).

dark sublimity of Chesterton's Teutonism threatens to mesmerize, and with this comes an almost Nietzschean resentment. His portrait of scandal in *Crimes*—like the one that his brother broke over government insider trading in the Marconi Company—still burned hot three years afterward: The libel laws were used "to crush truths about public life" amidst "a maze of loopholes" and "the monstrous presence of certain secret monies" all presided over by "a Wonderland king and queen, who cut off our heads" (*Crimes* 366). Chesterton is hardly at peace with himself.

There are dangers, however, in reducing Chesterton's picture of Teutonism to a mere stand-in for anger at Cecil's lost court case. Ricoeur, following Freud, suggests that a demystification of accusation removes from us a figure of wrath and also removes from us a figure of consolation, and thus, Ricoeur charges that it becomes something of "a work of mourning." It cannot, however, remove from us the desire for a better country of which obligation is but a secondary characteristic (*Conflict* 338–39, 342–44). It is tempting to see in Chesterton's ideal of Christendom something of this longed-for land, even if there are reasons to be suspicious. At its best, Christendom for Chesterton was never completely conflated with Europe. In *Orthodoxy*, Christendom is in constant renewal, and Europe is the remnant of the goods in old paganism that survived in Christianity ("Authority" 354). Christendom is also a mother that renews Chesterton's faith in European culture ("Authority" 360–61). Even if she disappoints, he can proclaim that "Christendom has no more truly Christian quality, even its degradation, than the power of laughing at itself" ("Young Turks" 130). It is perhaps for this reason that Chesterton would insist that England has inherited Christendom, while the Saxons inherited barbarism ("Whitewashing" 213–15).[19] In *Crimes*, Austria "has a kind of shadow of responsibility for Christendom" (313). Such moments in Chesterton strike one as desperate justification. Austria corrects the limitations of the French revolution with its secularist vision of freedom. For all her faults, she continues as holdover of what was good in Christendom: "if they had given men stones for bread, the stones

---

19. After the war had ended, Chesterton would continue to reason from this ideal: "Christendom has a memory because it has a meaning; and it must know what its settlement really means" ("Barbarian" 380). Christendom is the common culture of European civilization, not reducible to it, though shared by all of it ("Negative" 19). Chesterton recognized the culture of Europe and Christendom were older than the modern nation-states, but he feared that without a continued basis in the Christian religion, their modern incarnations could not continue, having forgotten "the tradition of their own fathers and the teeming vitality of the dead" ("Austria" 300).

were carved with kindly faces and fascinating tales," and her tortures were those of Purgatory instead of "Parisian and Prussian diabolists" carried out in the open-streets (*Crimes* 315). One can hardly imagine Chesterton giving this kind of pass to Prussia.

A Hopeful Naïveté

At the heart of this reading via suspicion is the reminder that Chesterton's own imaginative investment is real and fraught with potential failure. At the same time, Chesterton's affirmation of fairyland as a necessity for ethical courage may be a truth worth holding, even in his most dangerous passages that idealize the Crusades. The sublime terrifies, yet also compels. Can the longed-for country still be found even in a propaganda pamphlet so fraught with misinformation and resentment? I think so, because Chesterton's symbols overdetermine their referents, projecting them into a vaster field of aspiration and desire. Following Ricoeur's thinking in *Freud*, all cultural poetics must have an *archê* and a *telos*, both a creation and an ending; they represent two horizons of meaning and are needed for symbols to disclose themselves (459–60). Chesterton insisted that "Human nature simply cannot subsist without a hope and aim of some kind" ("Concluding" 203), and for him, the image of the cross was of a force "breaking out" as if being centrifugal ("Maniac" 231).

Chesterton idealized those underdogs who stood up for the common people. Along with William Cobbett and Garibaldi, Nicholas I of Montenegro was a little king in a little mountain kingdom, "a king—a real king, who sat listening to his people in front of his own house" and who stood up to the large oppressor (*Crimes* 360). Chesterton pictures him as a knight still willing to fight for Christendom:

> It was under a sky so leaden and on a road so strewn with bones that the little mountain democracy with its patriarchal prince went out, first and before all its friends, on the last and seemingly the most hopeless of the rebellions against the Ottoman Empire. Only one of the omens seemed other than disastrous; and even that was doubtful. [...] For days that seemed like months the microscopic state seemed to be attempting alone what the Crusades had failed to accomplish. And for days Europe and the great powers were thunderstruck, again and yet again, by the news of Turkish forts falling, Turkish cohorts collapsing, the unconquerable Crescent going down in blood. The Serbians, the Bulgarians, the Greeks had gathered and risen from their lairs; and men knew that these peasants had done what all the politicians had long despaired of doing, and that the spirit of the first Christian Emperor was already standing over the city that is named after his name. (362)

This description is profoundly poetic and profoundly troubling, yet it cannot be reduced to a simple justification for Eastern European aggression. As Maurice Merleau-Ponty was wont to say, the perceived object "announces more than it contains" (3). The description is a celebration of blood, yet a celebration of hope past hopelessness. What Chesterton fails to offer as *realpolitik*, he does offer in the way of an image of renewal. Nicholas is responsible before others, and his responsibility has a necessarily eschatological direction, for the dream here means nothing—in light of what comes next—if not an evocation of future promise, of what could still be. Chesterton sees Prussia as the symbol of the polities and economies of scale that detest the small and local: "chivalry was not a thing she neglected; it was a thing that tormented her as any bully is tormented by an unanswered challenge." The Germans are "on the side of the dragon against the knight, of the giant against the hero" (*Crimes* 363). Yet Nicholas's campaign still stands as an image of hope, and for similar reasons, Chesterton invests the beginnings of the Great War with imagery of promise: "Simple men with simple motives, the chief one a hate of injustice which grows simpler the longer we stare at it […] the islanders went forth from their island, as simply as the mountaineers had gone forth from their mountain, with their faces to the dawn" (367). Poor history, but as a stirring toward the future, it still pulls at the reader.

Chesterton understood the dangers of utopian desire, of what Eric Voeglin called "a fallacious immanentization of the Christian eschaton" (121). Utopias are only obtained in the New Jerusalem ("Eternal" 327). They are too serious; they lack the pleasure of festival: "Riot means being a rotter; and religion means knowing you are a rotter" ("Survival" 24). Chesterton could warn: "When the heavenly kingdom becomes an earthly paradise, it sometimes tends to be a hell upon earth" or worse a very weak imitation of utopia that practices institutional perpetuation ("World Government" 542–43). The language of Utopia can be used by the powerful to abuse the poor, offering "the Summum Bonum, / The Evolving Eden and Elysium, / The Pattern of Fate with its thread and thrum" as code for hygienic oppression of the underclasses ("Nursery Rhymes No.3" 507).

At the same time, the language of the New Jerusalem, for Chesterton, imagined the extent of freedom promised by the Resurrection of Christ. In *The Everlasting Man*, Chesterton could describe the resurrection as being the end of "the history that was merely human" and "the first day of a new creation." The world, having itself experienced its death, was now opening into the dawning future (*Everlasting* 345). By this Chesterton did not mean a cyclical nature myth. Christ does not stand for the sun, nor does the hope of renewal stand in for the returning spring, rather, the exact opposite: "my pleasure is in some promise yet possible and in the resurrection of the dead" (*A Miscellany of Men* 75). And it is this hope, however sublimated, that one may argue continues to exist in even Chesterton's jingoism:

> It was a league of all knights for the remains of all knighthood, of all brotherhood in arms or in arts, against that which is and has been radically unknightly and radically unbrotherly from the beginning. Much was to happen after—murder and flaming folly and madness in earth and sea and sky; but all men knew in their hearts that the third Prussian thrust had failed, and Christendom was delivered once more. The empire of blood and iron rolled slowly back towards the darkness of the northern forests; and the great nations of the West went forward; where side by side as after a long lover's quarrel, went the ensigns of St. Denys and St. George. (*Crimes* 372–73)

In such a conclusion, *Crimes* conflates Chesterton's medievalism, his Christian hope, and his support for the War. He invests in it an image of two Christian peoples united as all shall be in the last days, yet this union must come at the price of enduring a terrible apocalypse. Ricoeur insisted that symbols cannot be taken literally, for their absolute meaning is still in the future, especially the language of evil implies a future resolution. Perhaps this is why Waugh could see "Chesterton's cheerfulness" as "abundantly redeemed, from vulgarity only by his innocence" (Waugh 74).

Should, then, fantasy always be fictional? Chesterton's commitment to "the fairyland of furniture," to defamiliarizing the mundane with new wonder, might challenge that. Yet *The Crimes of England* also makes us aware of the need for an independent secondary world where fairy tale and chivalry and apocalypse may be safely imagined. *Crimes* points to the need for a multi-narrative discourse in historiography; the problem of singular and totalizing violence is a real one in any vision like Chesterton's, but especially so when made the foundations of actual war. Chesterton's own life showed us a man capable of charity to his enemies. He called the portrait in English inns of Frederick II's declining years "a conclusion that would be peaceful, humane, harmonious, and forgiving," that of a sign without any power except to raise a toast to a vague dream of something that inspired men, however wrongly (*Crimes* 301). Perhaps we can desire such charity for Chesterton's propaganda, as well, and if this, then perhaps also a wariness of things which we need fear and a hunger for that of which we might yet hope.

WORKS CITED

Blackstock, Alan R. *The Rhetoric of Redemption: Chesterton, Ethical Criticism, and the Common Man*. New York: Peter Lang, 2012. Print.
Canovan, Margaret. *G. K. Chesterton: Radical Populist*. Boston: Houghton, Mifflin, Harcourt, 1978. Print.
Chesterton, G. K. 'The Abuses of the Past." *Collected Works*. Vol. 34. San Francisco: Ignatius, 1991. 379–83. Print.
—. "The Age of Reason." *Collected Works*. Vol. 34. San Francisco: Ignatius, 1991. 185–89. Print.
—. "Austria and the Nazis." *Collected Works*. Vol. 36. San Francisco: Ignatius, 2011. 300–03. Print.
—. "Authority and the Adventurer." *Collected Works*. Vol. 1. San Francisco: Ignatius, 1986. 346–66. Print.
—. *The Autobiography of G. K. Chesterton*. *Collected Works*. Vol. 16. San Francisco: Ignatius, 1988. Print.
—. "The Barbarian in History." *Collected Works*. Vol. 31. San Francisco: Ignatius, 1989. 378–81. Print.
—. "Books and Enlightenment." *Collected Works*. Vol. 30. San Francisco: Ignatius, 1988. 33–36. Print.
—. "Comparing Two Centuries." *Collected Works*. Vol. 34. San Francisco: Ignatius, 1991. 181–84. Print.
—. "Concluding Remarks on the Importance of Orthodoxy." *Collected Works*. Vol. 1. San Francisco: Ignatius, 1986. 196–207. Print.
—. *The Crimes of England*. *Collected Works*. Vol. 5. San Francisco: Ignatius, 1987. 291–398. Print.
—. "The Eternal Revolution." *Collected Works*. Vol. 1. San Francisco: Ignatius, 1986. 307–28. Print.
—. *The Everlasting Man*. *Collected Works,* Vol. 2. San Francisco: Ignatius, 1986. 135–407. Print.
—. "The Flag of the World." *Collected Works*. Vol. 1. San Francisco: Ignatius, 1986. 269–84. Print.
—. "Frederick and the German Evil." *Collected Works*. Vol. 36. San Francisco: Ignatius, 2011. 377–80. Print.
—. "Historical Scepticism." *Collected Works*. Vol. 28. San Francisco: Ignatius, 1987. 491–95. Print.
—. "Letters to an Old Garibaldian." *Collected Works*. Vol. 5. San Francisco: Ignatius, 1987. 274–90. Print.
—. "London." *Collected Works*. Vol. 20. San Francisco: Ignatius, 2001. 631–37. Print.
—. "The Maniac." *Collected Works*. Vol. 1. San Francisco: Ignatius, 1986. 216–32. Print.
—. *A Miscellany of Men*. Norfolk: IHS Press, 2003. Print.
—. "Mr. Bernard Shaw." *Collected Works*. Vol. 1. San Francisco: Ignatius, 1986. 63–70. Print.
—. *The Napoleon of Notting Hill*. *Collected Works*. Vol. 6. San Francisco: Ignatius, 1991. 215–380.
—. "The Need for Historical Humility." *Collected Works*. Vol. 33. San Francisco: Ignatius, 1990. 607–10. Print.
—. "Negative and Positive Morality." *Collected Works*. Vol. 32. San Francisco: Ignatius, 1989. 17–20. Print.
—. "The Nightmare." *Alarms and Discursions*. NY: Dodd and Mead, 1911. 23–29. Print.
—. "Nursery Rhymes No. 3." *Collected Works*. Vol. 10A. San Francisco: Ignatius, 1994. 506–07. Print.

—. "Paganism and Mr. Lowes Dickinson." *Collected Works.* Vol.1. San Francisco: Ignatius, 1986. 122–31. Print.
—. "The Romance and Realities of the Middle Ages." *Collected Works.* Vol. 30. San Francisco: Ignatius, 1988. 114–18. Print.
—. "Survival of Christmas." *Collected Works.* Vol. 28. San Francisco: Ignatius, 1987. 21–26. Print.
—. "The Teaching of History." *Collected Works.* Vol. 32. San Francisco: Ignatius, 1989. 316–19. Print.
—. "Thomas Carlyle." *Collected Works.* Vol. 18. San Francisco: Ignatius, 1991. 19–32. Print.
—. *The Victorian Age in Literature. Collected Works.* Vol. 15. San Francisco: Ignatius, 1989. 413–530. Print.
—. "The Whitewashing of the Barbarian." *Collected Works.* Vol. 31. San Francisco: Ignatius, 1989. 212–16. Print.
—. *William Blake.* London: Duckworth, 1910. Print.
—. "World Government, Again." *Collected Works.* Vol. 34. San Francisco: Ignatius, 1991. 540–44. Print.
—. "The Young Turks and their Western Models." *Collected Works.* Vol. 34. San Francisco: Ignatius, 1988. 130–34. Print.
Dale, Alzina Stone. *The Outline of Sanity: a Life of G. K. Chesterton.* Grand Rapids: Eerdmans, 1982. Print.
Hill, Roland. *Lord Acton.* New Haven: Yale UP, 2000. Print.
Kenyon, John. *The History Men: The Historical Profession in England since the Renaissance.* Pittsburgh: U of Pittsburgh P, 1983. Print.
Ker, Ian. *G. K. Chesterton: A Biography.* Oxford: Oxford UP, 2011. Print.
Koselleck, Reinhart. *Futures Past: On the Semantics of Historical Time.* Trans. Keith Tribe. New York: Columbia UP, 2004. Print.
Lauer, Quentin. *G. K. Chesterton: Philosopher without Portfolio.* New York: Fordham UP, 1988. Print.
Mandler, Peter. *The English National Character: The History of an Idea from Edmund Burke to Tony Blair.* New Haven: Yale UP, 2006. Print.
Merleau-Ponty, Maurice. *Phenomenology of Perception.* Trans. Colin Smith. London: Routledge, 1962. Print.
Pearce, Joseph. *Wisdom and Innocence: A Life of G. K. Chesterton.* San Francisco: Ignatius, 1996. Print.
Ricoeur, Paul. *The Conflict of Interpretations: Essays in Hermeneutics.* Ed. Don Ihde. Evanston: Northwestern UP, 1974. Print.
—. *Freud & Philosophy: An Essay on Interpretation.* Trans. Denis Savage. New Haven: Yale UP, 1970. Print.
—. *The Symbolism of Evil.* Trans. Emerson Buchanan. Boston: Beacon Press, 1967. Print.
Stapleton, Julia. *Christianity, Patriotism, and Nationhood: The England of G. K. Chesterton.* Lanham: Lexington Books, 2009. Print.
Voeglin, Eric. *The New Science of Politics: An Introduction.* Chicago: U of Chicago P, 1987. Print.
Ward, Maisie. *Gilbert Keith Chesterton.* Lanham: Rowman & Littlefield, 2006. Print.
Waugh, Evelyn. "The Man Who Was Thursday." *G. K .Chesterton: the Critical Judgments: Part 1: 1900–1937.* Ed. D. J. Conlon. Antwerp: Antwerp Studies in English Literature, 1976. 72–74. Print.
Wood, Ralph C. *Chesterton: The Nightmare Goodness of God.* Waco: Baylor UP, 2011. Print.

Lord Dunsany and the Great War:
Don Rodriguez and the Rebirth of Romance

DAVID J. CARLSON

IN HIS CLASSIC CULTURAL HISTORY of the First World War, *The Great War and Modern Memory*, Paul Fussell reminds his readers that "[i]rony is the attendant of hope, and the fuel of hope is innocence" (18). Fussell goes on to point out that the greatest casualty of four years of carnage at places like Ypres was precisely this spirit of innocence. The "Great War," as those who lived through the conflict came to call it, became "a hideous embarrassment to the prevailing Meliorist myth which had dominated public consciousness for a century. It reversed the Idea of Progress" (8). Of course, attempts were made at the time (as they still are) to perpetuate the kind of romantic views of warfare that held sway during the glory days of European imperialism. Such idealism proved difficult to sustain, though, especially when confronted with the recent memory of thousands of miles of muddy graves in France and Belgium. The result was that much of the greatest English writing of the time came to reflect a profound sense of loss and disillusionment. Wilfred Owen's "Dulce et Decorum Est" eulogized English patriotism with a quiet and dignified pathos. In *Goodbye to All That*, Robert Graves offered up a representative autobiography of declension and cynicism. Finally, just a few years after the war, T. S. Eliot's *The Waste Land* claimed its preeminence as the greatest poetic lament for the chaotic implosion which the modern age had just experienced. In Great Britain, certainly, spiritual malaise, cultural fragmentation, and a profound skepticism about the old "heroic" ideals seem to have been the defining characteristics of the literary age.

On the surface, this particular *zeitgeist* would seem to offer the most inauspicious of all backdrops for the development of modern fantasy literature, especially heroic fantasy. Yet as some critics have begun to point out, the Great War seems in fact to have spawned some of the most seminal works of the 20th century—texts that would go on to define the shape of the genre of fantasy for decades to come. The relationship between these works and the war varies, of course, but one common thread seems to be an attempt to resuscitate some form of faith in heroic idealism. E. R. Eddison's *The Worm Ouroboros* (1922), for example, speaks quite directly to the First World War's legacy of brutal futility. In Eddison's romance, the endless struggle between the opposing forces of Demonland and King Gorice is presented as noble, albeit tragic. This tale of a perpetual cycle of violence (the ouroboric circle suggested by the book's title) becomes, in the end, a story of heroic grandeur, suggesting that a sense of higher purpose in life might be found through martial valor. To take another example, the influence of World War I on the imagination and subsequent writings of J. R. R. Tolkien has been well-documented by a number of writers (including Humphrey Carpenter, Tom Shippey, Jane Chance, and Janet Croft). While Tolkien's *Lord of the Rings* offers a less laudatory vision of heroic death than Eddison's romance, it nevertheless does seem to stress the potential for meaningful sacrifice in the context of war. The moral clarity of Tolkien's Middle-earth provides the kind of structure, the ethos, that was missing in such struggles in 1917.

Writers such as Eddison and Tolkien engaged with the legacy of the Great War by writing their own novels of "global" war. Their fantasies take us, quite literally, into conflicts that engulf the entirety of their invented worlds. But what about the more isolated hero—the individual questing "knight" in search of fame and honor? How could this kind of "fantastic" character continue to resonate after the "war to end all wars"? To begin answering that question we must turn to the work of a different kind of fantasist, the Irish nobleman, sportsman, and author Lord Dunsany. In 1922, after having written a series of brilliant fantastic short stories in the first phase of his literary career, Dunsany published his first novel-length fantasy, *Don Rodriguez: Chronicles of Shadow Valley*.[1] As in the works of many of his contemporaries (both in fantasy and mainstream English literature), we can find in *Don Rodriguez* a pointed confrontation with the post-war *zeitgeist*. In the novel, Dunsany directly attempts to cultivate an audience culled from a war-weary and disillusioned readership. With its highly self-conscious narration and selective renovation of the romance-tradition, *Don Rodriguez* thus stands as a remarkable (and underappreciated) attempt to re-legitimize a specific form of fantasy in the most unpropitious of historical moments. In the end, I would argue that the book reflects Dunsany's conviction that fantastic literature in the romance tradition *could* resonate in the post-war world, provided that the writer remain in careful rhetorical control of his material. It the reading that follows, then, I would like to explore

---

1. The title of the British edition, published six months before the American, was *The Chronicles of Rodriguez*. For a survey of the shape of Dunsany's career, see Joshi (1995, 1996) and Schweitzer (1980, 1989). For a general biography of Dunsany, see Amory.

Dunsany's careful attempt to bring about a rebirth of romance and to offer his own commentary on the meaning of the Great War.

ಌ ಅ

A key element of any rhetorical performance, be it in speech or fiction, is an awareness of potential resistance by the audience to the message being conveyed. The likelihood of such resistance to heroic fantasy in nations which had just lost an entire generation of young men should be obvious, even to those of us born into a very different era. It is not surprising, then, given its context, that *Don Rodriguez* establishes itself within its first two pages as a carefully crafted rhetorical performance, constantly foregrounding the issue of its own reception. The first gesture in this vein addresses the question of genre.[2] At the outset, Dunsany's playful choice of subtitle for the work, *Chronicles of Shadow Valley*, reveals his gently ironic manipulation of audience expectations regarding the kind of book they will read. The term "chronicle," of course, recalls a specific body of historical writing produced during the Middle Ages and Renaissance, texts ranging from the 9th century *Anglo-Saxon Chronicle* to the early 17th century *A Mirror for Magistrates*. In thus labeling his work, Dunsany associates his fantasy novel with a form of episodic history, a claim he further develops in the one-page "Chronology" that functions as a kind of preface. "After long and patient research," he writes, "I am still unable to give to the reader of these Chronicles the exact date of the times that they tell of. Were it *merely* a matter of history there could be no doubts about the period; but where *magic* is concerned, to however slight an extent, there must always be some element of mystery" (my emphasis, xiv). Novelists' claims to be historical truth-tellers are hardly uncommon in the history of English literature; they often appear when the writer wishes to fend off criticism about the lack of moral value in the work. Dunsany's particular variation on the topos, defining his book as a *magical* history, serves a similar kind of rhetorical function. Clearly no reader would actually credit the assertion that *Don Rodriguez* is an "historical" work, so why even use the term? In my view, Dunsany's phrasing represents a canny appeal to ethos, one that begins to reveal his understanding of the challenges involved in writing fantasy for a modern audience. The Chronology authorizes a range of reader responses to the text that follows. First, with an ironic tone of worldliness, Dunsany foregrounds his text's fictiveness, anticipating post-war

---

2. Reader-response theory provides useful insights into the relationship between an awareness of genre and patterns of textual reception. On this issue, see Jauss.

cynicism and suggesting the possibility that the book might be read as a kind of fantastic satire (perhaps in the vein of his more cynical American contemporary James Branch Cabell): "This text really is a history (wink, wink)," the first sentence seems to say. At the same time, the introduction of "magic" licenses an alternative approach to reading the work. The second sentence suggests that we might indulge in the escapist pleasure of reading a dream-vision of a mythic past. This kind of attempt to balance conflicting responses to the very idea and appeal of fantasy seems to undergird *Don Rodriguez* from the start. Indeed, I would argue that the rhetorical approach of the novel as a whole is to subtly undermine modern cynicism and *gradually* restore a more idealistic faith in at least some of the values of the romance tradition.[3]

Moving beyond the Chronology's cagey treatment of generic reception, we can see Dunsany's choice of setting and tone to be another key element in his careful courtship of audience. Here, the appeal relies upon that audience's awareness of Western literary history and affection for one of its classics. Setting *Don Rodriguez* in "the later years of the Golden Age of Spain" (vii), Dunsany transports the reader back to the Spain of one of the greatest fantasists in the Western tradition, Don Quixote. Once there, though, *Don Rodriguez* stealthily begins to restore some of the luster to the romance tradition that Cervantes had so brilliantly satirized. Dunsany's novel *starts* with the assumption that readers will share Cervantes's skepticism of romance, but the book seeks to gradually overcome that skepticism, restoring that tradition in a way designed to be palatable to a world-weary post-war reader. In this sense, Dunsany cleverly reverses the historical shift from what Northrop Frye calls the "high mimetic" to the "low mimetic," the shift that led Western writers from the romance to the modern novel.[4] We can see the process gradually taking place from the very first pages of the opening chronicle, "How He Met and Said Farewell to Mine Host of the Dragon and Knight," which I would like to consider in some detail.

At first, it would seem that readers expecting a quixotic satire will not be disappointed in Dunsany's writing. Indeed, the text begins in a comic mode Cervantes would have appreciated, with Rodriguez's mar-

---

3. The juxtaposition of magical and familiar, the tonal blending of comic and serious passages is a hallmark of Dunsany's prose style. For a helpful general introduction to that style, see Anderson. For a discussion of the "decadent narcissism" of Dunsany's "language-conscious mode of writing" see Duperray.

4. On this distinction, see Frye's "Theory of Modes" in *Anatomy of Criticism* (33–67). See also Frye's *The Secular Scripture* (35–61).

ginally senile and dying father, the Lord of the Valleys of Arguento Harez, summoning his eldest son to discuss his inheritance. In the course of a conversation interrupted by confused and amusing digressions, the Lord of the Valley inverts both the traditional laws of primogeniture and the conventions of romance by giving his lands and title to his youngest son, whom he describes both as "dull" and as one "on whom those traits that women love have not been bestowed by God" (3) To his eldest son Rodriguez, the rightful heir, he offers instead two gifts (which later prove to be central symbols in the book)—an ancient Castilian blade and a mandolin. These represent skill in war and love, traits that are "most needful in a Christian man" (5). With these bequests, the Lord sends Rodriguez out into the world to conquer, both in the wars and on moonlit balconies, and then abruptly, almost absurdly, "[falls] back dead" (6). Our young hero has been sent on his way, but the tone of the opening (characterized by the rambling of an old man needing to be frequently "reminded of his discourse" [4]) is likely to leave the reader more bemused than enchanted by his quest. Four pages into the novel, then, Don Rodriguez's story shows a strong, tonal resemblance to Don Quixote's.

A few paragraphs into the opening chronicle, though, things begin to change. Whereas the death of Quixote in Volume 2 of Cervantes' novel signals the *end* of romantic *illusions* (and a literary tradition) here the death of the quixotic Lord of the Valley signals the *beginning* of romantic *adventure* (and the resurgence of the tradition). Dunsany's tale quickly begins to read as a kind of parody of the earlier parody. (It is here that we can most clearly see the author's self-conscious reversal of the "low mimetic" mode). Almost as soon as Rodriguez assumes the role of a romance-hero, he begins to infuse it with dignity, a dignity marked also by a tonal shift to Dunsany's more characteristic, lyrical prose style. When Rodriguez departs home in search of love and adventure, he strides forth into the Spain of springtime, a world whose distance from the modern reader's (both geographically and temporally) is clearly indicated, but which is nevertheless presented lovingly, poetically, and without a hint of derision or satire.

> Now the time of the year was Spring, not Spring as we know it in England, for it was but early March, but it was the time when Spring coming up out of Africa, or unknown lands to the south, first touches Spain, and multitudes of anemones come forth at her feet. [...]
>
>   And all the way as he went, the young man looked at the flame of those southern flowers, flashing on either side of him all the way, as though the rainbow had been broken in Heaven, and its fragments fallen on Spain. All the way as he went he gazed at those flowers, the first anemones of the year; and long after, whenever he sang to old airs of Spain, he thought of Spain as it appeared that day in all

the wonder of Spring; the memory lent a beauty to his voice and a wistfulness to his eyes that accorded not ill with the theme of the songs he sang, and were more than once to melt proud hearts deemed cold. (7)

There is nothing like this kind of ecstatic, lyrical description to be found in Cervantes, whose novel is dominated by its (low mimetic) comic situations and dialogues. In contrast, Dunsany gives us an imagined Spain that is both exotic and fecund, one designed to appeal to his reader's dreams and desires. His anemones mark the beginning of a rebirth of idealism and beauty. This early into the book, of course, it remains only a beginning. With strong memories of the trenches and of a generation of dead sons and husbands, the rebirth of romance will be hard won. It is to Dunsany's credit, though, that *Don Rodriguez* avoids becoming a naive retreat into an idealized past. Instead, the book builds on this opening to offer a kind of critical re-investigation of the romance tradition.

The narrator's talk of Rodriguez's wistful songs and descriptions of the quest's idyllic setting mark the initiation of a process that will span the novel's entire length, giving some shape to its otherwise episodic plot. The novel takes both reader and hero on a journey of self-discovery; having re-initiated us into the world of romance Dunsany then induces us (and the protagonist) to gradually interrogate *which* values of that literary world are truly essential and worthy of faith. This revision of the romance tradition begins as soon as Rodriguez steps out into his world of anemones and old airs. It is probably not a coincidence that at this stage of the novel Rodriguez's "memorable servant," Morāno, joins him, staying for the remainder of the book. Playing Sancho to Rodriguez's Quixote, Morāno is largely what readers familiar with Cervantes would expect him to be—a paradoxical mixture of earthy common sense, comic relief, and idealistic aspiration. Initially, his primary function in the novel seems to be satiric: he repeatedly reminds Rodriguez, for instance, to do something that few romance heroes ever seem to do—eat a simple meal. In this respect, Morāno's presence first seems another example of the rhetorical hedging in the novel. Through him, Dunsany offers cynical readers another bone to chew on, with the intrusive narrator periodically chiming in to reinforce the effect. When Morāno initially joins Rodriguez, for example, that narrator describes the servant's expressions of gratitude to his new master as being "in keeping with that flowery period in Spain, and might appear ridiculous were I to expose them to the eyes of such an age in which one in Morāno's place on such an occasion would have merely said 'Damned good of you old nut, not half,' and let the matter drop" (29–30). However, if the figure of Morāno *initially* reinforces a sense of distance between the modern world and the world of romance (and also ridicules certain aspects of the latter), he soon comes to represent a strangely "rational" faith in the dream-world of adventure. We have already seen that "flowery" is not a contemptible adjective in Dunsany's golden age. Not surprisingly, then, before long Morāno's belief in Rodriguez's quest seems stronger even than his master's. By the end of the Second Chronicle and his first few days with Rodriguez we find "gross Morāno" lying curled up on the ground on his humble bed of straw, dreaming peacefully of walking on "golden shoes" in Aragon, "proud among lesser princes" (47). Most significantly, our narrator sees no need to comment critically on those dreams.

The narrative strategies, the invocation of an extant literary tradition, and the tonal shifts between high and low mimetic styles that I have been discussing thus far provide the recurrent pattern for *Don Rodriguez* as a whole. As the pair of adventurers journeys on together, our narrator periodically hedges about whether readers should commit themselves wholly to his re-invented world, while the narrative itself encourages us to sift through elements of the received tradition, keeping some and discarding others. The final issue we need to consider then, is how specifically Dunsany wishes to re-work the romance-mode. With few exceptions, it seems to me, it is the naive idealization of heroic violence that comes under the strongest criticism, a point that makes sense when we recall the novel's post-war context. The place where we see this most clearly is in Chronicles III and IV, where Rodriguez and Morāno happen upon the "House of Wonder," the mysterious mountainside dwelling-place of a powerful enchanter. In Chronicle III, the aforementioned enchanter asks Rodriguez about the nature of his quest. Told that the young man seeks the wars, he offers to show him battles of past and future through a pair of magic windows. If there were any doubt that the shadow of World War I looms large over this novel, this point in the narrative dispels it. Turning his eyes to the past, Rodriguez comes face to face with the fraudulent idealization of combat in myth, legend, and history. "Retreats" turn out to have been "routs," and "heroes" win victories through merest accidents and "without knowing that they had won." The narrator sums up *our* hero's experience by noting that "never had man pried before so shamelessly upon History, or found her such a liar" (64). Yet this is not the end of Rodriguez's (and the reader's) re-education. Next he turns to look at the wars of the future, a sight that leaves Rodriguez stunned into silence. He sees man make a new "ally," one "who was only cruel and strong and had no purpose but killing" (69). The ally is, of course, the machine. With this revelation, and with Rodriguez standing silently and blocking faithful Morāno's view, our narrator intrudes with the bitterest lines of the entire book: "Blame not the age," he says, "it is now too late to stop [...] we cannot stop content with mustard-gas; it is the age of Progress, and our motto is Onwards" (71). With such a view of the past and future of war, readers are forced to question Rodriguez's present purpose. It is difficult to imagine a more striking, pointed assault of the heroic warrior-ideal that motivates at least half of his quest.[5]

Yet Rodriguez and Morāno are not finished in the House of Wonder. The next Chronicle relates how the enchanter sunders their spirit forms from their bodies through alchemy, sending them on a mystical journey to the mountains of the sun. Here their very dreams are called into question by the immensity and chaos of solar energies. What starts out as a potentially positive, mystical experience (human eyes are described as a "barrier between us and the immensities") quickly turns into something terrible. Up close, the sun suddenly appears as an enormous catastrophe, and Rodriguez and Morāno begin to believe that "the purpose of Creation is evil" (83). Significantly, the timeless, almost unreal horror of the experience is compared to that of World War I:

> There is nothing in the empty space between the Sun and Mercury with which time is at all concerned. Far less is there meaning in time wherever the spirits of men are under stress. A few minutes' bombardment in a trench, a few hours in a battle, a few weeks' traveling in a trackless country; these minutes, these hours, these weeks can never be few. (80)

The connection between the spiritual insight provided by the mysterious enchanter and the legacy of World War I is further reinforced by the ending of the journey to the sun. Rodriguez and Morāno fall into despair, feeling both a sense of utter insignificance before the energies of the cosmos and a fear that the tendency of the universe is to destruction. Aptly enough, upon their return to their Earthly bodies, both master and servant appear to suffer from a form of shell-shock. What allows their earthly journey to go on and redeems them, if only marginally, is the suggestion that the enchanter may either be a kind of diabolical agent or, at the very least, an unappealing representative of a world without faith. (As he prepares to send them off on another spirit-journey, Morāno drives him off with a makeshift cross, a moment that can

---

5. For a brief discussion of some of Dunsany's other fictional critiques of violence, see Pashka.

be read either literally, as an exorcism, or symbolically, as the conquest of faith over thoughts of a meaningless universe.) In the end, then, the reader is left to wonder how much of these lessons should be credited. If we are to question the ideals of heroic combat, are we also to abandon all dreams and aspiration before a Schopenhauerian universe bent only on our destruction? It seems to me that the balance of the novel argues against such a notion. Indeed, the very impulse to despair that Rodriguez and Morāno feel in the House of Wonder seems to necessitate the continuation and completion of their quest. And besides, as we should recall, Rodriguez was given another gift besides his Castilian blade—the mandolin.

The middle chronicles of the book re-introduce the theme of love and, in doing so, set up a climactic conflict between the central chivalric virtues—love, loyalty, and martial valor—that shapes the remainder of the narrative. Rodriguez and Morāno arrive at the village of Lowlight, where the young hero falls in love with the beautiful Serafina, whom he sees briefly on a balcony. Singing to her in the moonlight, he is challenged to a duel by a man who proves to be her brother. As the two fight, Morāno repeatedly interferes, clubbing Rodriguez's opponent into insensibility with his iron frying pan. Although it is obvious that Rodriguez was outclassed and likely to be killed in the combat, he berates his servant for violating the laws of chivalry and drives him away for a time. Clearly the overall effect of this comic interlude is to provide yet another critique of the martial side of the romance tradition. Two strangers fighting a moonlit duel for no real purpose (a duel ended only by a pan-wielding rustic) raises serious questions about the role of violence in the heroic tradition. In contrast, though, love and the mandolin seem to represent more timeless values. The balance of the novel, consequently, shifts our focus there, onto the significance of the virtues of love and loyalty, faith and friendship.

In later chronicles, Rodriguez rescues a mysterious stranger about to be hung by soldiers (not doing so through violence, but through cleverness). This stranger proves to be the King of Shadow Valley, a man who will eventually provide him with his castle—not for his martial prowess, but as a reward for his fidelity and compassion. Rodriguez's subsequent experiences in the wars provide his final lessons in the false promises of chivalric violence. As he passes into France, he encounters refugees and fearful civilians ravaged by the memories of war—hardly a scene from the romance tradition. Finally locating an army which he can join, Rodriguez chooses and defeats an opponent in single combat, sparing his life in exchange for his "castle in Spain." Journeying back across the mountains with Morāno and his prisoner, though, Rodriguez again experiences disappointment. As readers might have expected, the prisoner's castle turns out to be a humble cottage, and our hero leaves the wars with no tangible reward. Yet Rodriguez *does* leave with a renewed aura of virtuous nobility; he refuses to punish his prisoner for his obvious deception, choosing instead to accept his ridiculous explanation that a mysterious enchanter has stolen the castle that once stood where the cottage now rests. (We should note that Rodriguez is no Don Quixote here, for the narrator strongly implies his awareness of the lie.) But if Rodriguez walks away, finally, from the empty promises of warfare and "romantic" violence, he does not abandon all of the chivalric virtues. In the penultimate Chronicle ("How He Turned to Gardening and His Sword Rested"), Rodriguez returns to Serafina, who avows her love for him despite his failure to win a castle. Finally, in a blend of a fairy-tale happy ending and logical allegorical closure, Dunsany provides our hero with his just reward. The mysterious King of Shadow Valley builds Rodriguez a woodland palace, names him his heir, and serves as godparent to the children of Serafina's and Rodriguez's consummated (not courtly) love.

In the end, Rodriguez discovers that faith, friendship, and love represent ideals worthy of devotion. The joy he experiences in Serafina's garden and, subsequently, in his sylvan realm has a solidity to it, born of experience. If Rodriguez's giants proved to be windmills, his Dulcinea, in contrast, is real. For this reader, at least, that fact that such a conclusion feels both earned and satisfactory is a testimony to Dunsany's great rhetorical skill in crafting his fantastic tale in the shadow of world war. Contemporary reviews of the work were mixed, but in my view, Dunsany's awareness of literary tradition, historical context, and audience—issues I have tried to trace here—makes *Don Rodriguez* an important and successful early example of modern fantasy, as well as a commentary on the defining event of its age. Dunsany's belief that "timeless," archetypal narratives and high ideals have a role to play in even the darkest moments of human history strikes me as a powerful insight, one worth continued exploration. As the carefully orchestrated rebirth of romance in *Don Rodriguez* seems to suggest, well-crafted modern myths can demonstrate a vital kind of critical and moral intelligence. Thankfully, many other writers of modern fantasy seem to share this conviction.

ACKNOWLEDGMENT
I would like to thank the members of the Science Fiction and Fantasy Area of the SW/Texas Popular Culture Association for helpful comments on this essay.

This article was published originally in Mythlore *25.1/2 (#95/96) (2006): 93–104. It is reprinted here with permission.*

WORKS CITED
Anderson, Angelee Sailer. "Lord Dunsany: The Potency of Words and the Wonder of Things." *Mythlore* 15.1 (#55) (1988): 10–12. Print.
Amory, Mark. *Biography of Lord Dunsany*. London: Collins, 1972. Print.
Carpenter, Humphrey. *J. R. R. Tolkien: A Biography*. New York: Houghton Mifflin, 2000. Print.
Cervantes, Miguel. *Don Quixote*. 1605. New York: Modern Library, 1998. Print.
Chance, Jane. *Tolkien's Art: A Mythology for England*. Lexington: U of Kentucky P, 1979. Print.
Croft, Janet Brennan. *War and the Works of J. R. R. Tolkien*. Westport: Praeger, 2004. Print. Contributions to the Study of Science Fiction and Fantasy 106.
Dunsany, Lord. *Don Rodriguez: Chronicles of Shadow Valley*. 1922. New York: Ballantine, 1971. Print.
Duperray, Max. "Lord Dunsany Revisited." *Studies in Weird Fiction* 13 (Summer 1993): 10–15. Print.
Eddison, E. R. *The Worm Ouroboros*. 1922. New York: Ballantine, 1962. Print.
Eliot, T. S. *The Waste Land*. 1922. San Diego: Harcourt Brace, 1997. Print.
Frye, Northrop. *Anatomy of Criticism*. Princeton: Princeton UP, 1957. Print.
—. *The Secular Scripture: A Study of the Structure of Romance*. Cambridge: Harvard UP, 1976. Print.
Fussell, Paul. *The Great War and Modern Memory*. New York: Oxford UP, 1975. Print.
Graves, Robert. *Good-Bye To All That: an Autobiography*. 1929. Providence: Berghahn, 1995. Print.
Jauss, Hans Robert. *Toward and Aesthetic of Reception*. Minneapolis: U of Minnesota P, 1982. Print.
Joshi, S. J. "Lord Dunsany: The Career of a Fantaisiste." *Discovering Classic Fantasy Fiction*. Ed. Darrell Schweitzer. Gillette: Wildside, 1996. 7–48. Print.
—. *Lord Dunsany: Master of the Anglo-Irish Imagination*. Westport: Greenwood, 1995. Print.
Owen, Wilfred. *The Works of Wilfred Owen*. Herts: Wordsworth Poetic Library, 1994. Print.
Paska, Linda. " 'Hunting for Allegories' in the Prose Fantasy of Lord Dunsany." *Studies in Weird Fiction* 12 (Spring 1993): 19–24. Print.
Schweitzer, Darrell. "Lord Dunsany: Visions of Wonder." *Studies in Weird Fiction* 5 (Spring 1989): 20–26. Print.
—. "The Novels of Lord Dunsany." [Part 1]. *Mythlore* 7.4 (#26) (1980): 39–42. Print.
Shippey, Tom. *J. R. R. Tolkien: Author of the Century*. New York: Houghton Mifflin, 2001. Print.

From *Lolly Willowes* to *Kingdoms of Elfin*:
The Poetics of Socio-Political Commentary in Sylvia Townsend Warner's Fantasy Narratives

MEYRAV KOREN-KUIK

> This is the world exactly as Adam had it –
> Spring now, and willows flowering, and I alone
> In an ash-wood, with the birds around me
> Clamoring and flying, the small birds like leaves' shadows
> Threading through the hedge.
>   (Warner, *I'll Stand by You* 5)

> No hand, no footfall,
> Nothing to see at all –
> But a queen's presence when the night
> Stepped out of the wood.
>   (Warner, *New Collected Poems* 336)

LAURA WILLOWES, THE UNLIKELY HEROINE of Sylvia Townsend Warner's debut novel, *Lolly Willowes or The Loving Huntsman* (1926), is a casualty of the Great War; her old self, a mundane aging spinster, dies, and like a phoenix from the ashes of war she is resurrected as a witch. After spending her childhood and youth in the country, Laura (Lolly) Willowes takes up residence with her brother Henry and his wife Caroline in London. From that moment on, life becomes flat, restricted by conventions, and for the meek and submissive Lolly, space and time cease to exist. The end of the Great War finds her physically and emotionally numb, as well as mentally disconnected from her surroundings: "Four times a week she went to a depot and did up parcels. […] [N]o one thought of offering her a change of work. […] She continued to do up parcels until the eleventh day of November 1918. Then, when she heard the noise of cheering and the sounding of hooters, she left her work and went home. The house was empty" (*Lolly Willowes* [*LW*] 63–64). At home Laura faints and is confined to her chambers with a bad case of influenza. Her recovery, in the tomb-like, womb-like, darkened room, marks a rebirth; Laura's perception of the world around her is altered, as if a veil has been lifted and she can see clearly again: "Laura looked at her relations. She felt as though she had woken, unchanged, from a twenty-year slumber, to find them almost unrecognizable. […]

They were carpeted with experience. No new event could set jarring feet on them but they would absorb and muffle the impact" (84).

Laura's 'twenty-year slumber' refers to the time she spent in London with Henry, Caroline and their children after her forced departure from country life. The date that signifies the beginning of Laura's personal process of awakening, and the only explicit date in the novel, is November 11, 1918, the end of the First World War, and a date which signals the collective realization that reality has altered and will never revert back to its pre-war course. For Laura Willowes, time begins to flow again and accordingly, a change of space must follow. Unlike her relatives who are bound by tradition and a socio-cultural ideology that results in a static intransigent existence, Laura feels an irresistible compulsion to regain her 'country' self and let the witch, suppressed in the depths of her being, materialize. In *Lolly Willowes*, Sylvia Townsend Warner expresses both her critique of patriarchal social order and her call for women to take action and reclaim their birthright, by utilizing the dynamics of a split space/time construct; country and city are juxtaposed, and the flow of time is dependent upon the heroine's subjective view of consensus reality and the stagnation that plagues it.

Likewise, a split spatial and temporal narrative poetics is essential to Warner's last book, the short story collection *Kingdoms of Elfin* (1977), her only other book-length writing in the fantastic genre. As in *Lolly Willowes*, the mechanism of a split space/time is utilized, yet again, to evoke socio-political commentary. In the fictional world of *Kingdoms of Elfin*, elves and humans exist in segregated milieus, and their perception of time is accordingly different. In the story "Visitors to a Castle," for instance, a group of Elfin from the kingdom of Castle Ash Grove tries to make a mountain disappear by singing to it. Seeing as they have achieved a partial success in their endeavor they resolve to continue singing until the stubborn landmark permanently vanishes. They sing for centuries, which for them seem like minutes; time is of little consequence for the Elfin. "By now," writes Warner, "we are within sight of the twentieth century. It was a fine autumn evening in 1893" (*Kingdom of Elfin* [KE] 97).

The "twentieth century" brings change to the quiet Elfin kingdom. Humans are no longer staying away and Castle Ash Grove is frequented by visitors who hinder the preordained segregation between humans and Elfin. One of the visitors, an overbearing district nurse, disturbs the traditional order of the kingdom with the offensive odors of modern medicine to such an extent that Dame Bronwen, an Elfin matron, faints.

Upon regaining consciousness she explains: " 'When I fainted it was because of what was shown me. I saw trees blighted and grass burned brown and birds falling out of the sky. I saw the end of our world [...] the end of Elfin. [...]' [S]he spoke with such intensity it was impossible not to believe her" (102). Although, as Hannah Priest remarks about *Kingdoms of Elfin* "many of Warner's stories include historical specificities which allow us to place them on a human timeline" (7), only one explicit date is given in the entire collection of stories—1893, the year that saw "Gandhi's first act of civil disobedience" (History.com).[1] The year also foresaw the disintegration of Empire, the fading away of what Jennifer Paulos Nesbitt refers to in her article "Footsteps in Red Ink: Body and Landscape in *Lolly Willowes*" as "the geographies of imperial domination" (451). The mentioning of a date in the narrative momentarily bridges the temporal split between humans and Elfin and becomes a signifier of change in both the Elfin kingdoms and the human domain which they mirror, as well as suggesting the destabilizing effect of the spatial transformation of Empire on the British socio-political and socio-cultural collective perception of consensus reality.

These examples demonstrate Sylvia Townsend Warner's reliance on the dynamics of spatial/temporal split to construct socio-political commentary in both *Lolly Willowes* and *Kingdom of Elfin*. It will be further shown how this dynamics defines the poetics of socio-political commentary in both these books. Nevertheless, while criticism in *Lolly Willowes* is voiced in a mild tone tinged with irony, it takes on the form of sharp satire in *Kingdoms of Elfin*. Nesbitt observes: "Spaces and places become signifying systems that are the conditions of possibility for the subjects inhabiting them. These observations implicitly call for reconsideration of settings not as a background, symbolic or not, against which characters move and think, but as an ideological force in literary texts" (452); indeed it is the construction of separate and sometimes opposite milieus in the novel that underline the manner in which criticism is constructed.

Mikhail Bakhtin's concept of the chronotope provides a useful lens in the analysis of the temporal and spatial dimensions of narratives; he

---

1. Although this took place not in India, but on a train in South Africa, where Gandhi was working a lawyer until his return to India in 1914, this act of refusing "to comply with racial segregation rules on a South African train" marked the beginning of Gandhi's life-long dedication to political activism which will bring about change not only to colonial India but to the British Empire as a whole. The reference in Warner's story to "a mortal [...] a civil old man in a single garment" (*KE* 93) as the one who advocated to the Elfins that "Faith can remove mountains" strengthens the implied connection to Gandhi's actions.

defines chronotope as "the intrinsic connectedness of temporal and spatial relationships that are artistically expressed in literature" (15). By moving away from viewing a narrative as a primarily temporal construct, this definition of the chronotope takes the first step toward acknowledging the importance of space, as well as the impact of the narrative's spatial aspects upon its perception and interpretation. Nevertheless, Bakhtin's exploration of the chronotope still heavily relies on the traditional view which sees a narrative as a construct anchored in temporality. Critic Susan Stanford Friedman advocates "Spatialization" as "A Strategy for Reading Narrative"; she accordingly sees a narrative as "the play of desire in space as well as in time" (217). Friedman's suggestion augments the model presented by Bakhtin by stressing the importance of a story's spatial dimension. The chronotope split in Warner's fantasy narratives is both spatial and temporal.

The riven chronotope in *Lolly Willowes*, through which Warner expresses her socio-political commentary, relies on a temporal split between past and present and a spatial divide between country and city. Warner utilizes the role of the country and the city in the British national imagination to juxtapose a sense of nostalgic longing for country life with the forward gaze of industrial development associated with the city. In his seminal examination the role of the country and the city within the English socio-cultural dynamics Raymond Williams remarks:

> For it is a critical fact that [...] English attitudes to the country, and to ideas of rural life, persisted with extraordinary power, so even after the society was predominantly urban its literature, for a generation, was still predominantly rural; and even in the twentieth century, in an urban and industrial land, forms of the older ideas and experiences still remarkably persist. All this gives the English experience and interpretation of the country and the city a permanent [...] importance. (2)

Elsewhere in his treatise Williams makes a critical observation about the role of the city of London within the English socio-cultural fabric: "London [...] was plural and various [...] [a] dominant part of the life of the nation was reflected but also created within it. [...] [I]t was producing and reproducing, to a dominant degree, the social reality of the nation as a whole" (147–48). Furthermore, as Mary Jacobs observes, the sense of nostalgia about the rural was particularly strong "[d]uring the inter-war period," when "the countryside was the subject of huge ideological investment [...] part of a conservative nostalgic discourse which evokes an idealised pre-war English countryside" (62). It is between this persistent sense of nostalgia toward the idea of the rural and the overwhelming power of advancement and transformation represented by the city that Warner positions her subversive heroine, the timid Laura Willowes.

Clair Harman, Warner's biographer, describes the two books that sparked her idea to write *Lolly Willowes or The Loving Huntsman*, the story of "a contemporary witch": "She had read Margaret Murray's book *The Witch-Cult in Western Europe* when it was published in 1921 and, more recently, Pitcairn's *Criminal Trials of Scotland*" (59). Harman quotes Warner's reaction to Pitcairn's book: "The actual speech of the accused impressed on me that these witches were witches for love; that witchcraft was […] the romance of their hard lives, their release from dull futures" (59). Laura's childhood and early adulthood life in the country had suited her perfectly: she had been a free spirit, a witch in the making and mistress of her father's house hold.

> She had no wish for ways other than those she had grown up in […] enamored of the comfortable amble of day by day as she was. At certain seasons a fresh resinous smell would haunt the house like some rustic spirit. […] She roved the countryside for herbs and simples, and many were the washes and decoctions that she made from sweet-gale, water purslane, cowslips, and the roots of succory, while her salads gathered in the fields and hedges were eaten […] with flattering appetite. (*LW* 29–31)

After the death of her father, Laura is forced to leave her rural existence and move to London to live under the care of her brother Henry and his wife Caroline. This displacement, dictated by a patriarchal social structure, effectively destroys the budding natural country witch in Laura; her spirit is crushed in the hard and unnourishing urban environment. "She would become an inmate of the tall house in Apsley Terrace […] which had baffled her so one night when she lay awake trying to assemble the house inside the box of its outer walls" (7). The London residence is both a prison and a maze, an ominous spatial enigma undecipherable and unescapable. Accordingly, Laura defends herself by going into spiritual hibernation; on the outside she abides by the rules of a place which make no sense to her, while inwardly she withers away. Reflecting the industry of the city, Caroline's household works as a machine into which Laura is "introduced as a sort of extra wheel," she soon becomes "part of the mechanism […] interworking with the other wheels, went around as busily as they" (44).

Oddly enough, this patriarchal demand that she assume an urban existence is enforced by another female character in the novel—Laura's sister-in-law Caroline. Her perfect demeanor, which marks her as the epitome of the Victorian ideal of "the angel in the house" and the enforcer of Victorian social ideology, is scrutinized and criticized by both Warner's derisive tone and her silent acceptance yet perplexed perception of Laura's own actions. Laura's observations of Caroline's conduct and her relationship with Henry do not result in Laura's admiration and imitation, but in a conclusion that her sister-in-law is doing something innately wrong with a pointless, and to Laura's mind even counter-effective, result:

> After some years in his house she came to the conclusion that Caroline had been very bad for his character. Caroline was a good woman and a good wife. She was slightly self-righteous, and fairly rightly so, but she yielded to Henry's judgment in every dispute, she bowed her good sense to his will and blinkered her wider views in obedience to his prejudices. Henry had a high opinion of her merits, but thinking her to be so admirable and finding her to be so acquiescent had encouraged him to have an even higher opinion of his own. (50–51)

Caroline and Henry's relationship—a text book late-Victorian interaction—demonstrates not only the nullification of female power of thought and decision making ability, but points to Caroline herself as the instigator of this dynamics. This critique of Caroline's behavior is justified upon Laura's discovery of Henry's financial failure.

When Laura realizes her awakening, in a little London shop among fresh country flowers and homemade preserves, she resolves to leave the city and relocate back to a rural environment:

> As Laura stood waiting she felt a great longing. It weighed upon her like the load of ripened fruit upon a tree. She forgot the shop, the other customers […], she forgot the whole of her London life. She seemed to be standing alone in a darkening orchard, her feet in the grass, her arms stretched up […]. (79–80)

Laura intuitively understands that in order to be alive again, to regain her former self and reclaim the existence that is her birthright, she must forsake the city and relocate back to the country. She turns to her brother Henry, the warden of her inheritance, to ask for the money that is rightfully hers: the funds which will secure her a better and more suitable future in the little village of Great Mop. To her dismay Henry does not approve of her plan and demands that she "drop this idea. It is not sensible. Or suitable" (94). Nevertheless, Laura stands her ground, exclaiming "No, Henry. I don't feel inclined to; I'd much rather get it over now. Besides, if you are going to disapprove as violently as this, the sooner I pack up and start the better" (95). As the conversation progresses, Laura is shocked to find out that Henry's objections to her plan are insincere and designed to conceal the fact that he lost most of her money in speculative business ventures which did not pan out quite as he expected. Laura's fierce reaction positions her outside the role forced upon her by her relations and her social circumstances, and she finally gains independence from her family and freedom from the rigid social dogma by which they operate, as she aptly conveys to Henry:

> "Go on, Henry. I have understood quite well so far. You have administered all my money into something that doesn't pay. [...]"
> Laura stamped her foot with impatience. "Have done with trumpery red herrings!" she cried.
> She had never lost her temper like this before. It was a glorious sensation. [...]
> "You say you bought those shares at eight and something, and that they are now four. [...] Very well. You will sell them immediately [...] and reinvest the money in something quite unspeculative [...]. I shall still have enough to manage on. " [...]
> Ten days later Laura arrived at Great Mop. (96–99)

Laura's act of standing her ground and her fierce tone reverse the balance of power between her and Henry, tipping the scales in Laura's favor. This interaction further enhances the previously established critique of Caroline's submissiveness toward her spouse, by contrasting Laura's and Caroline's conduct. In light of this juxtaposition, Henry's financial failure becomes a metaphor for the disintegration of patriarchal structure and the failure of Victorian gender ideology to provide an adequate socio-cultural model for post-war reality.

As the story progresses, Warner uses contrast mirroring again to further critique Henry's patriarchal role and present it as unsuitable and unenlightened; this time she contrasts Henry with Mr. Saunters, Laura's country acquaintance and temporary employer. Seen from Laura's perspective, Mr. Saunters becomes a heroic figure:

> She leant on the gate and watched him. This young man who had been a bank-clerk and a soldier walked with the easy, slow strides of a born countryman; he seemed to possess the earth with each step. No doubt but he was like Adam. [...] [S]een from above, walking among his flocks and herds—for even hens seemed ennobled into something Biblical by their relation to him—was an impressive figure. (128–29)

Much like Laura, Mr. Saunters choses to abandoned his former urban existence as a "bank-clerk and a soldier" to become a chicken farmer in Great Mop, creating for himself a simple, rural post-war identity. Warner uses his choice to support her socio-political critique, contrasting his dynamic and productive country existence with Henry's stagnant lifestyle and outdated views.

Shortly after she settles in the little village, Laura makes Mr. Saunters's acquaintance and becomes aware of his temporary need for a farm hand. She volunteers to help him out. For a while Laura and Mr. Saunters work together in idyllic unison, in a little "utopian enclave" (Jameson 15)[2] reflecting the utopian properties of the village and countryside which surrounds it—until this country paradise is invaded by a representative of the city and the tranquility of Laura's new life is disturbed.

Laura's idle nephew Titus shows up in Great Mop for a visit and overstays his welcome. The chronotope split of country versus city is broken as Titus brings London with him back into Laura's life. Prior to his visit, Warner foreshadows this transgression of city space into rural territory and the emotional distress it causes Laura when she encounters a train on one of her nature strolls:

> The spent gusts left the beech-hangers throbbing like sea caverns through which the wave had passed; the fir plantation seemed to chant some never-ending rune.
> Listening to these voices, another voice came to her ear—the far-off pulsation of a goods train laboring up a steep cutting. It was scarcely audible, more perceptible as feeling than as sound, but by its regularity it dominated all the other voices. It seemed to come nearer and nearer, to inform her like the drumming of blood in her ears. She began to feel defenseless, exposed to the possibility of an overwhelming terror. Though the noise came from an ordinary goods train, no amount of reasoning could stave off this terror. (122–23)

The sound of the train, the ultimate harbinger of progress, a symbol for all that is mechanized, industrial, and urban, permeates the countryside and terrifies Laura. It engulfs her with the possibility of reverting back to her former existence by reminding her that the city and all it stands for is still out there beyond the fragile borders of her new-found Eden. When it seems to Laura that Titus intends to stay, she is overcome by these same fears again; she realizes she must collect herself and fight back. In order to do so, Laura completes her transition from a mere woman to witch, sealing her unspoken contract with Satan by accepting his gift of a minion of her own, a little cat she names Vinegar. Together, with a little touch of country magic, Laura and Vinegar bring about Titus's overdue departure from Great Mop. Laura becomes a fully-fledged witch, and is deemed ready by the coven to experience her first witches' Sabbath.

---

2. Fredric Jameson defines the "utopian enclave" as "an imaginary enclave within real social space" (15).

When Laura's landlady Mrs. Leak silently leads her to the Sabbath, Laura quickly grasps what is happening: " 'Where are you taking me?' she said. Mrs. Leak made no answer, but in the darkness she took hold of Laura's hand. There was no need for further explanation. They were going to the Witches' Sabbath" (170). To Laura's disappointment the event turns out to be no more than an awkward open-air dance party. When Satan finally appears to welcome Laura into the coven, she suspects that he is a mere mortal in disguise; dismayed, she leaves the Sabbath:

> Without glancing left or right she walked out of the field, and the dancers made way for her in silence. She was furious at the affront, raging at Satan, at Mrs. Leak, at Miss Larpent, with the unreasoning anger of a woman who had allowed herself to be put in a false position. This was what came of attending Sabbaths, or rather, this was what came of submitting her good sense to politeness. (182)

Laura's irritated reaction to the event stems from the realization that belonging to the Great Mop community of witches requires much the same sacrifice that she made when she was part of her brother's household in London. Here again Laura finds herself in a situation where she is expected to become a part of a community which will box her within a set of rules that are as false and as artificial as the ones that bound her before she came to the country; this time she turns her back to the offer of membership, and walks away with her freedom intact. After a night sleeping under the stars, Laura meets Satan in the woods, disguised as an old gamekeeper. Satan converses with Laura and reassures her that she may rely on his help whenever she needs it: "Satan had come to renew his promise and to reassure her. He had put on this shape that she might not fear him" (188).

But Satan, as Laura stated earlier in her musings, is "a huntsman. His interest in mankind is that of a [...] naturalist [...] [H]unt he must; it is his destiny" (162). Laura no longer wants to be hunted, to become someone else's charge and possession, no matter what advantages such position holds. If Laura is a witch and a charge of Satan she will be so in her own way, without pretenses and without compromising her integrity. Laura's last encounter with Satan, in the novel's closing scene, establishes the status-quo which Laura longs for; she walks back to Great Mop a content and free witch: "The pursuit was over, as far as she was concerned. She could sleep where she pleased, a hind couched in the Devil's coverts, a witch made free of her Master's immunity; while he, wakeful and stealthy, was already out after new game. So he would not disturb her" (222). As Gillian Beer remarks: "Warner imagines a different way for female self-discovery. Warner nonchalantly topples the whole Faustian edifice of the devil's bargain: masculine knowledge may be achieved only at the cost of death but female knowledge, it seems, can triumph as independent life" (18).

The thematic similarities between Warner's *Lolly Willowes* and Virginia Woolf's pivotal manifesto-style essay "A Room of One's Own" have been previously noted by critics.[3] Woolf's essay was published in 1929, three years after the publication of *Lolly Willowes*; both texts envision women's rights to personal freedom and a space to accommodate this right and enable its practice. In 1959, three decades after Woolf's essay was published, Warner gave an address titled "Women and Writing" which advocated and reiterated much of what Woolf wrote. It is interesting to note that the poetics of chronotope split was used by Warner in this address as well, as she ironically describes the perceived notion of a woman's ability to multitask:

> It is well known that a woman can be in two places at once; at her desk and at her washing-machine. She can practice a mental bi-location also, pinning down some slippery adverb while saying aloud, 'No, not Hobbs, Nokes. And the address is 17 Dalmeny Crescent'. Her mind is so extensive that it can simultaneously follow a train of thought, remember what it was she had to tell the electrician, answer the telephone, keep an eye on time, and not forget about the potatoes. Obstinacy and slyness still have their uses. (*With The Hunted* 234)

More than three decades after writing *Lolly Willowes*, Warner returned to her metaphor of a woman as a witch; for to be a woman is to seemingly possess extraordinary abilities.

In the only other fantasy text in Warner's oeuvre, the story collection *Kingdoms of Elfin*, the same narrative poetics of chronotope split exist, though a broader range of socio-political critique is offered.

In the endeavor which concluded her literary career, Warner revisited the genre of fantasy writing a string of loosely-linked stories which first appear in the *New Yorker* and were collected later on in a volume titled *Kingdoms of Elfin,* which was published in 1977. The Elfin stories, with their often dry matter-of-factly account of events, have the feel of a historical document about them; the events described, and the issues they raise, reflect a reality different than our own and yet feel uncannily familiar, as if projected back to us like an eerie distorted reflection in a surrealistic funfair mirror. This mirroring effect is a common trait of fairy tales, as Jack Zipes tells us: "the tales are reflections of the social order in a given historical epoch […] either affirming the dominant social values and norms or revealing the necessity to change them. […]

---

3. See Shin, Beer, Swaab, Knoll, and Lurie in the bibliography.

Each historical epoch and each community altered the original folk tales according to its needs" (7–8); and as J. R. R. Tolkien surmises in relation to the creation of fantasy narratives in general, "Probably every writer making a secondary world, a fantasy, every sub-creator, wishes in some measure to be a real maker, or hopes that he is drawing on reality: hopes that the peculiar quality of this secondary world (if not all the details) are derived from reality, or are flowing into it" (77). Indeed, as Hannah Priest remarks about the Elfin stories, "these creations are not ahistorical. They are rooted in in a set of social and cultural concerns that are visible elsewhere in Warner's writing" (3). Yet the reflection of reality in Warner's *Kingdoms of Elfin* is not a straightforward allegorical one, where each story element has a clear counterpart in the real world; though the Elfin clearly represent a faction of society which is in essence aristocratic or high born, their interactions at times mirror governmental policies and political decision making processes. The Elfin stories thus escape the narrow definition of allegory and instead represent a satirical deliberation on human follies.

In his introduction to *With the Hunted*, a collection of Warner essays, Peter Tolhurst observes: "The Elfin Stories [...] contained some of her finest writing according to William Maxwell, her editor at The *New Yorker*, and 'an eerie authenticity that suggests first-hand knowledge'. These satires on the human condition brought to a close Warner's literary career" (i). In the Elfin stories, Warner imagines a fictional world in which fairies or elves exist; the stories give an account of their social hierarchy, traditions, beliefs, and mannerisms, as well as detailing their manner of interaction with the 'other' social body existing alongside theirs—that of humans. The Elfin do not exist in another realm; they share space with humans, but the two societies are effectively segregated due to an Elfin attitude of general disinterest in humans as beings. On the whole, if humans have any value to the Elfin it is as commodities: pets, serfs, and playthings. As Tolkien writes in his essay "On Fairy-Stories," "if elves are true, and really exist independently of our tales about them, then this also is certainly true: elves are not primarily concerned with us, nor we with them. Our fates are sundered, and our paths seldom meet" (32). Accordingly, the structure of the fictional world in *Kingdoms of Elfin* is modeled on a split chronotope of two segregated societies that are both spatially and temporally removed from each other: the Elfin courts, castles, and mounds are usually inaccessible to humans, and sometimes even invisible. Additionally, the longevity of the Elfin folk results in a perspective on time which is unique to them. This chronotope split defines Warner's fictional world and becomes the basic structure out of which other partitions (class, race, belief systems) are formed. As with her practice in *Lolly Willowes*, the generation of socio-political commentary relies on this dynamic of segregated chronotopes. Nevertheless, the role fantasy takes in the production of socio-political critic is different in the two narratives. In *Lolly Willowes* the fantastic emerges as an organic result of the story against an otherwise realistic backdrop, thereby critiquing elements of socio-political reality as it is presented in the novel, by counter-effecting the real with a fantastic element (woman turned witch). Conversely, the Elfin stories present a fictional world which is in essence imaginary and designed to mirror aspects of consensus reality, not by its aesthetics but by the absurdity of the actions characters take and the interactions between them. What is reflected back to readers by this mirroring-effect is a distortion of the practices which are perceived as normal within consensus reality; these practices thus become a source of satire and their depiction is continuously laced with a sense of the ridiculous. Warner uses these dynamics to examine and critique notions relating to tradition, religion, class, race and government.

Members of the Elfin aristocracy do not use their wings in order to take flight and move about; flying is considered a breach of etiquette and is reserved to the servants among the Elfin. Flight, an ability which sets humans and elves apart, becomes within Elfin society a primary marker of class separation. The foolishness of flight-related politeness is remarked upon derisively: "The fault lay in the unnaturalness of a society where the privileged classes debar themselves from their birthright of flying in order to assert a hereditary claim to go on foot, as though they were mortals. Mortals, meanwhile, long, like pigs in a proverb, for wings" (*KE* 110). Consequently, the perversion of flying is depicted as an act of defying tradition, and its circumstances and consequences critique the kind of tradition that is essentially senseless. It is interesting to note that instances in which flight is exercised by highborn Elfin women are depicted as an acts of defiance which assert individuals' right to freedom from an absurd and decadent tradition, a connecting thematic line to *Lolly Willowes*.

In the first story in the collection, "The One and the Other," the child Titania takes flight to the dismay of Tiffany, her human companion and the former lover of the present Elfin Queen. Titania, who takes flight in order to spite her nurse, flies out of pure and natural childish pleasure. It is Tiffany's concern about this act of defiance that highlights how hollow and unreasonable the non-flying stipulation really is:

> Titania was overhead. Five times she flew down the whole length of the gallery and back again. She folded her wings and alighted beside him, as dexterously as though she had spent her whole life flying on errands. "Titania!" he exclaimed. "What ever will you do next? You know you mustn't fly." [...] Titania was wilful as a kitten, tart as a green fruit. She established a bond of mutual guilt between them: her reckless indecorum of flying, his disloyalty of consenting to it. [...] If it were known that Titania flew, her reputation would be lost. (8–9)

The distinction between those who are allowed to fly and those who must remain earthbound as a matter of etiquette is that of class. Warner uses this unnatural segregation to make a satirical allusion to all manners of tradition that suppress natural tendencies, at the expense of one's basic rights, for mere decorum. The story implies that restrictions generated for the sake of politeness are meaningless, and therefore have no logical purpose; as such they are a folly to maintain. This point of view is echoed in Tiffany's concern over Titania's possible punishment, which he voices out of his feverish mind as he lies dying and abandoned after being cast out of Elfhame: "Titania! Titania! What have they done to your wings? [...] Oh, they've caught her! They've tied her! [...] My bird is in a cage, and the cage has a black cloth over it" (13). Though Titania was really in no danger of such cruel fate, Tiffany's lament on Titania's loss of freedom serves to further highlight Warner's critique.

In another story, "The Search for an Ancestress," Warner's critique of the practice of holding on to meaningless traditions again manifests itself through the mechanism of flight. The highborn Joost, from the Elfin Court of Zuy,[4] is travelling to Persia in search of the Peri, an old race of beings from which, according to a common belief among the Elfin, "All Elfindom was descended" (139). On the basis of this assumption about Elfin genealogy, many ridiculous customs are practiced. In the Court of Brocéliande, for example, which "claimed that it had preserved the pure tradition of ancient Persia, where the elfin race originated" (57) many unreasonable practices are exercised in the name of the long lost Persian ancestry: "Its queens wore a pink turban instead of the usual crown; the royal wand was of cedarwood [...] so massively encrusted with jewels that it took a team of courtiers to wave it [...] it kept a particular breed of long-furred cats and an astrologer" (57). When Joost, after a long perilous voyage, reaches Persia and locates the legendary Peri, he finds to his surprise that none of the Kingdoms' traditions are observed by the Peri: no pink turban, no

---

4. Zuy paralleled the Dutch colonial empire, being experts in overseas commerce and located in the "Low Countries" (*KE* 138).

bejeweled staff, and no cats. Flight, however, is regularly exercised by Peri of all ranks, and queen Pehlevi frequently flies back and forth from the mainland to the fantastic rotating island from which she rules her domain. As the fascinated Joost observes: "A Queen so careless of her dignity that she flew like any working fairy […]. This Peri Kingdom was indeed a far cry from Zuy" (143).

Here again the sense of satire, as well as the critique attached to it, emerges out of the dynamic of a split chronotope. Joost essentially travels back in time and into another territory in order to track down the mythical Peri. The realization that Elfin customs and traditions are alien to the Peri turns these traditions from plainly ridiculous to categorically meaningless; a reflection that denotes the pointlessness of empty archaic traditions and beliefs. Eventually, the practice of flight saves Joost's life, as he must flee the Kingdom of the Peri before he is killed upon the instructions of queen Pehlevi, who has lost interest in his company. It seems that the one tradition that the Peri and the Elfin do have in common is the view that all outsiders who are not of their race are mere playthings to be brutalized at will.

Indeed, much socio-political commentary relating to race, class, and general mistreatment of the 'other' is generated by the divide between humans and Elfin. Elfin queens, for instance, regularly take humans as lovers. These men live among the Elfin even after they are discarded in favor of a new bedroom-playmate. Nevertheless, as soon as they begin to display signs of aging, they are unceremoniously cast out of the Elfin courts with nothing but the clothes on their backs, and are forced to spend their dying days isolated and disoriented back in the world of humans, a space to which they no longer belong. The Elfin often kidnap babies to serve as animated toys to the court members' pleasure. These changelings are often regarded and treated as pets. Queen Tiphane of Elfhame kept, as pets for her amusement, a monkey and a pair of human children, twins by the names of Morel and Amanita. Laying on her deathbed and no longer caring about neither monkey nor children, her 'pets' suffer a gruesome fate:

> Morel and Amanita seized the monkey. At first they caressed it; then they began to dispute as to which of them loved it best, whose monkey it should be. Their quarrel flared into fury and they tore it in half.
>
> The smell of blood and entrails still hung about the room when the sub-Archivist took up his evening watch. […] Tiphane had been given a composing draught and was asleep. That deplorable business with the monkey had made no impression on her, so the Court Physician assured him. She might even be the better for it. Morel and Amanita had been strangled and their bodies thrown on the moor as a charity to crows. (21–22)

The dispassionate tone of this account makes the events described all the more disturbing. Regarding other races as inferior, and the practice of disregarding the 'other,' sanction in the world of the Elfin deeds which project a sense of amorality. This same careless attitude is evident in other interaction with humans in the Elfin stories. In "Winged Creatures" the Elfin queen Alionde of Bourrasque is fascinated by the devastating effect pestilence has on the local peasantry: "she insisted on having the latest news of it: which villages it had reached, how many had died, how long it took them. She kept a tally of deaths, comparing it with the figures of other pestilences, calculating if this one would beat them" (124). The suffering of the human peasants becomes a game, a source of amusement to the Elfin queen and her subjects. No consideration is given to the suffering of their neighbors, and the thought of helping the humans never crosses the queen's mind. Yet the peasants were serfs of the Elfin court; it was their produce which kept the court well stocked and well fed. Once the plague rendered the humans unable to work the fields, the Elfin began to feel the burden of the pandemic in their bellies, and once the plague subsides the humans exert their revenge: "The survivors outside the walls railed against the palace people, who had done nothing for them, feasted while they starved, danced while they were dying, deserted them" (128). In a description reminiscent of the storming of the Winter Palace in Russia during the October Revolution, Warner, ever the communist, demonstrates the peasants' discontent with their Elfin lords. The tale projects a distorted image of the feudal system of lords and serfdom; the relationship within the story is not one of mutual support—peasants provide food, lords protection. It is a one-sided, unbalanced system, one in which the humans are not just mistreated but are viewed as objects, pawns in a game designed for Elfin amusement. Through this dynamic, Warner offers a reflection on our own consensus reality.

Partitions based on prejudice are not limited to the Elfin associations, or rather disassociations, with humans. They exist even within the fairies' own social structure. In the story "Elphenor and Weasel" two elves fall in love, but cannot live as a couple in any Elfin court due to the fact that they have a different skin color: Elphenor's skin is fair, while Weasel's is green. When Elphenor says he would like to visit the fairy hill in which Weasel was born, she exclaims: "No! You can't come. It's impossible. They'd set on you, you'd be driven out. *You're not green.*" Elphenor sadly retorts "It's the same where I come from. [...] [T]hey might be rather politer, but they'd never forgive you for being green" (emphasis in original; 29). Unequipped with the knowledge and skills to enable them to survive in the domain of humans, they eventually suffer a horrible death.

The touching affair of Elphenor and Weasel highlights another reason the schism between humans and Elfin is so profound. Their inherent lack of interest in mingling produces misinterpretations and misreading of the other race's way of life and manner of thinking; in other words, the fairies and the humans occupy two particular chronotopes. Different life spans and different spaces of living produce two distinct world views which are more often than not incompatible. Frequently these misunderstandings of the other race's traditions and customs produce comical instances which serve as reflections on the meanings of these customs. One such instance involves an Elfin lady by the name of Ellin, who witnesses a country religious ceremony and recounts the event to her companions, a group of dissident fairies playing at politics: "No one was slaughtered. At intervals, everyone sang. Finally they paid to go away. When Ellin recounted what she had seen there was a volley of explanations. […] It was a mass migration, it was a fertility rite […], it was an endurance test, it was a way of keeping warm" (196). The Elfin are baffled by proceedings which seem utterly strange and pointless from their perspective. What is reflected back to the readers as a result of this comical encounter is the realization that religion reduced to ceremonies is devoid of meaning.

Warner continues to explore the socio-political effects a belief system has in two other stories in the collection: "The Late Sir Glamie" and "The Climate of Exile." Sir Glamie is a ghost who joyfully haunts the corridors and the residents of the Elfin Court of Rings. The members of the court wish to vanquish Sir Glamie not because they fear his presence but because it serves as a constant reminder that Elfin might in some way be connected to humans:

> his reappearance proved that he had not been so well-bred. […] Elfins have no souls: when they die, they are dead: it is as simple as that. Therefore, at some point or other of Sir Glamie's pedigree an Elfin lady must have yielded to a mortal lover, and immortality, like the pox, has run in the family ever since. […] Most painful of all was the threat to the calm negation on which all Elfindom reposes. Once this was undermined by Sir Glamie's reappearances, libertine speculations and surmises would widen the breach, superstition, proselytizing, fear of an awaiting life after death, would rush in, and Elfins sink to the level of mortals. (169–70)

The Elfin are not immortal; they live for centuries but eventually die. In a tongue-in-cheek reversal of perceptions, they regard mortals as possessing the ability to live beyond death because of the professed immortality of the human soul. In "The Climate of Exile" the Elfin Sir Bodach is viewed as a heretic because he chooses to believe he possesses a soul, and for trying to convince others to 'convert'—he becomes a preacher of a new belief system and for that he is exiled from the kingdom of his birth and eventually sentenced to death. Sir Bodach explains to Snipe, his companion in exile: "Heresy […] is to believe in what other people don't believe in. […] Elfindom rejects any idea of the immortal soul. It is considered anti-social and subversive […] I am here on the strict understanding that I don't proselytize" (158, 160). But the need to preach is strong, and Sir Bodach is seen trying to baptize some unsuspecting Elfin folks, and for this transgression he is sentenced for execution. Nevertheless, in contrast to the eventual ending of the story of Christ, to which the tale of Sir Bodach alludes, the crafty old Elfin exercises another type of social heresy: he takes wing and flies away to freedom. Warner brings her criticism full circle as the freedom to choose one's beliefs is secured by the ability to fly, the very act that signifies freedom in her *Kingdoms of Elfin*.

In *Kingdoms of Elfin*, as in *Lolly Willowes* before it, Warner's poetics of socio-political commentary relies on the mechanism of the split chronotope. Warner aptly chose the fantastic medium to express the type of critique each of the two narratives exposes. In *Lolly Willows*, a post-WWI text, the commentary centers on the social condition of women and the blindness and shortcomings of the traditional patriarchal system in failing to recognize and address women's plight. For the purpose of critiquing women's condition Warner creates a witch—a fantastical entity who can transcend the boundaries set by a given socio-cultural ideology. The commentary in *Kingdoms of Elfin* encompasses an entire continent still ailed by prejudice and narrow-mindedness even after two supposedly-formative Great Wars. The scope of the socio-political critique in the Elfin stories demands a whole nation of fantastic creatures; Warner's fickle fairies place before us the proverbial mirror which reflects back a satirical image of our own reality.

WORKS CITED

Bakhtin, M. M. "Forms of Time and of the Chronotope in the Novel: Notes Toward a Historical Poetics." *Narrative Dynamics*. Ed. Brian Richardson. Columbus: Ohio State UP, 2002. 15–24. Print.

Beer, Gillian. "Sylvia Townsend Warner: 'The Centrifugal Kick'." *Journal of the Sylvia Townsend Warner Society* (2004): 18–31. Print.

Friedman, Susan Stanford. "Spatialization: A Strategy for Reading Narrative." *Narrative Dynamics*. Ed. Brian Richardson. Columbus: Ohio State UP, 2002. 217–28. Print.

Harman, Claire. *Sylvia Townsend Warner: A Biography*. London: Minerva, 1991. Print.

Jacobs, Mary. "Sylvia Townsend Warner and the Politics of the English Pastoral, 1925–1934." *Critical Essays on Sylvia Townsend Warner, English Novelist 1893–1978*. Ed. Gill Davies, et al. Lewiston: Edwin Mellen Press, 2006. 61–82. Print.

Jameson, Fredric. *Archaeologies of the Future: The Desire called Utopia and Other Science Fictions*. London: Verso, 2005. Print.

Knoll, Bruce. " 'An Existence Doled Out': Passive Resistance as Dead End in Sylvia Townsend Warner's *Lolly Willowes*." *Twentieth Century Literature: A Scholarly and Critical Journal* 39:3 (Autumn 1993): 344–63. Print.

Lurie, Alison. "Introduction." *Lolly Willowes: or the Loving Huntsman*. New York: New York Review Books, 1999. vii–xiii. Print.

Nesbitt, Jennifer Paulos. "Footsteps in Red Ink: Body and Landscape in *Lolly Willowes*." *Twentieth Century Literature*. 49:4 (Winter 2003): 449–71. Print.

Priest, Hannah. "The Unnaturalness of Society: Class Division and Conflict in Sylvia Townsend Warner's *Kingdoms of Elfin*." *Journal of the Sylvia Townsend Warner Society* (2010): 1–16. Print.

Shin, Jacqueline. "Lolly Willowes and the Arts of Dispossession." *Modernism/modernity* 16:4 (November 2009): 709–25. Print.

Swaab, Peter. "The Unnaturalness of Society: Class Division and Conflict in Sylvia Townsend Warner's *Kingdoms of Elfin*." *Journal of the Sylvia Townsend Warner Society* (2010): 29–52. Print.

This Day in History, June 7, 1893. "Gandhi First Act of Civil Disobedience." *History*. Web. 29 Apr. 2014.

Tolkien, J. R. R. "On Fairy-stories". *Tolkien on Fairy-Stories*. Ed. Verlyn Flieger and Douglas A. Anderson. London: HarperCollins, 2008. 27–84. Print.

Warner, Sylvia Townsend. *Kingdoms of Elfin*. London: Chatto & Windus, 1977. Print.

—. *Lolly Willowes: or the Loving Huntsman*. New York: New York Review Books, 1999. Print.

—. *New Collected Poems*. Ed. Clair Harman. Manchester: Fyfield*Books* Carcanet, 2008. Print.

—. *With the Hunted: Selected Writings Sylvia Townsend Warner*. Ed. Peter Tolhurst. Norwich: Black Dog Books, 2012. Print.

— and Valentine Ackland. *I'll Stand by You: Selected Letters of Sylvia Townsend Warner and Valentine Ackland*. Ed. Susanna Pinney. London: Pimlico, 1998. Print.

Williams, Raymond. *The Country and the City*. Oxford: Oxford UP, 1975. Print.

Zipes, Jack. *Breaking the Magic Spell: Radical Theories of Folk and Fairy Tales*. Lexington: UP of Kentucky, 2002. Print.

The Conqueror *Worm*:
Eddison, Modernism, and the War To End All Wars

Jon Garrad

In the first place, I must begin this essay with an apology, or perhaps a disclaimer. Since proposing an essay on *The Worm Ouroboros* and modernism, I have been informed of a trend in literary studies by which a given work, or author, or genre, is claimed as part of the ever-expanding territory of modernism—identified as a prerequisite, or response, or even closet contributor to the modernist project. Such is absolutely not my intention here. Not for a second am I about to claim that we have misunderstood E. R. Eddison all along, and that he belongs not in the genre of fantasy as a semi-obscure acquaintance of the Inklings but as a modernist and a contemporary of the Bloomsbury Group. Perish the thought!

What I am about to claim, however, is that Eddison's *The Worm Ouroboros* bears certain similarities to the modernist movement's canonical texts, in both its technical execution and its inspiration—the construction and character of the mirror which Eddison holds up to life. In technique, I will assess the willful difficulty of his prose, and the attitudes toward conflict exhibited by the novel's events and characters. In inspiration, I will consider the First World War, of course, and a broader reactionary process by which Eddison turns away from the twentieth century and into archaism, in order to find, and/or express, an alternative philosophical position. The essence of my argument is that Eddison is responding to the same social and emotional forces as the modernists, in a way which has some technical similarities, but with an extraordinary difference in outcome.

The comparison between Eddison and the modernists began, for me, with three observations. Eddison is every bit as difficult a read as, say, T. S. Eliot; Eddison and the modernists are contemporaries, writing in the immediate aftermath of the First World War; Eddison and the modernists are proposing alternative modes and philosophies as a means of surviving that aftermath. My guideline in this comparison is Joseph Young's assertion that Eddison's novels are "anything but gratuitous, being composed in strict accordance with an extensive, dearly held, deceptively humane reworking of moral philosophy" ("On This I Stake My Salvation" 73).

First Observation: Eddison Is Difficult

The first task ahead of me, in justifying this observation, is to define and describe a theory of difficulty. Leonard Diepeveen frames "difficulty" as a major cultural concept and battleground of the early twentieth century. With an assertion often made that good literature was difficult, and difficult literature good, the concept became a device by which to define literature and set the boundaries of the literary canon—an approach by which the writers of thorny texts framed themselves as the intellectual elite. The difficulty of the modernist work derives, according to Diepeveen, from several of its aspects, and is deliberately striven for.

Firstly, it can be described as "erudite," "obscure," or "complex," or "nonsense," depending on the aim of the describer in defining it as difficult. It may rely on the use of unusual but "real" words; "made-up" words which hint at meaning despite being outside the usual, comprehensible lexicon; metaphorical statements which rely on a system of reference so private that it defies an outsider's understanding; or a bewildering breadth of allusions to other texts.

Secondly, it is out of kilter with the norm. It is not commonplace or concerned with the everyday. It disorients the "ordinary" reader; it is not what the reader expects; it is, perhaps, "not for them" by design, a caution to be uttered as though patting the layman on the head like a baffled infant.

Thirdly, it is fashionable. It is aligned with some sort of movement; some collective of persons engaged in the production, discussion, and apparent understanding of similar works; a group of intellectuals for whom it *is* "for," thus suggesting that people who are in some ways special can overcome the difficulty and derive value from the work.

Finally, it is only of value *once it has been understood*—once the ways in which it thwarts one's usual tools of reading, comprehending and establishing meaning have been overcome, and some conclusion drawn about what it means.

So: if this is difficulty, is *Ouroboros* difficult?

Young observes that, while praised by such luminaries of fantasy as Lewis and Tolkien, Eddison has remained relatively unnoticed by academia, and by the wider readership of the genre, since his works "are too firmly grounded in Eddison's intricate philosophical conceits and demanding compositional style to be accessible to casual readers, or to be in any immediate danger of being adapted for the screen" ("Foundations" 183). This is essentially accurate; Eddison's prose style, which specializes in rich descriptions, anachronistic spellings and elaborate turns of phrase, is rather heavy going, and yet is arguably the source of the novels' appeal. Le Guin claims that Eddison "really did write Elizabethan prose in the nineteen-thirties. [...] Many, with reason, find him somewhat crabbed and most damnably long," but "if you love language for its own sake he is irresistible" (150).

It seems customary, in an essay on Eddison, to quote one's favorite of his lush descriptive passages, which in many cases border on the absurdly overdone, and yet do serve to create a totality of aesthetic impression, with a wealth of details which, if parsed successfully, *do* evoke an immersive reality. Far be it from me to break with tradition, or fail to provide an example in support of my claims; the length of the quotation will, I hope, be forgiven, as the length of Eddison's descriptions contributes both to their effectiveness and their difficulty:

> Like a black eagle surveying earth from some high mountain the King passed by in his majesty. His byrny was of black chain mail, its collar, sleeves and skirt edged with plates of dull gold set with hyacinths and black opals. His hose were black, cross-gartered with bands of seal-skin trimmed with diamonds. On his left thumb was his great signet ring fashioned in gold in the semblance of the worm Ouroboros that eateth his own tail: the bezel of the ring the head of the worm, made of a peach-coloured ruby of the bigness of a sparrow's egg. His cloak was woven of the skins of black cobras stitched together with gold wire, its lining of black silk sprinkled with dust of gold. The iron crown of Witchland weighed on his brow, the claws of the crab erect like horns; and the sheen of its jewels was many-coloured like the rays of Sirius on a clear night of frost and wind at Yule-tide. (103)

It may be useful to apply Diepeveen's criteria to this passage and establish the purely practical difficulty of Eddison's prose. On the one hand, the first simile deployed is simple and direct. The repetition and reiteration of "black" and "gold," appearing five and four times, respectively, connote King Gorice's malice and wealth at a glance. The regular identification of the dead animals whose skins comprise Gorice's cloak suggests both finery and mortality. On the other hand, "byrny" and "hose" and "bezel" are highly specific and archaic terms; the phrase "bigness of a sparrow's egg" is unwieldy to modern ears and perhaps less useful as a simile; the closing simile is so particular in its detailing as to, perhaps, be useless as a comparison. Yet, at the last, one does not need to have *seen* Sirius at Yuletide to receive the impression of chill radiance: the overall effect gives an impression of sensation and semiotic implication without the need to assimilate every word. There is a partial correspondence with Diepeveen's terms: the unusual but "real" vocabulary, the obscure and perhaps personal metaphor, and the distance from the everyday. There is a kinship, but not an identicality, with modernism.

In a broader sense, Eddison relies heavily on a grab-bag of invented place-names. Some, like Witchland, Demonland, Impland, et al, are comparatively commonplace, relying on connotations of the English words. Some, like the implausible mountains of Koshtra Belorn and Koshtra Pivrarcha, seem to contain hints of consistent linguistics ("Koshtra" suggesting the English "Mount"). Sometimes, though, Owlswicks and Crossby Outsikes and Breakingdales and Upper and Lower Tivarandardales and Onwardlithes crowd one another out in a cacophony of syllables, which seem to be thrown together largely because Eddison liked the sound of them.

As for the allusions: my edition of *Ouroboros* contains a bibliography of thirty-three poetic utterances, of which all but three are derived from other authors, ranging from the Classical period to the sixteen-sixties. Is it necessary to know that they are allusions in order to understand the novel? Arguably not; Eddison is selective in his deployment of borrowed verses, assigning them to moments where the surrounding events contextualize and frame them. It is, perhaps, more odd that characters from another world quote so extensively from the poetry of this one, and that—given Eddison's facility for invention, as demonstrated by the three poems not attributed to other sources—it was necessary for Eddison to do so at all.

It is possible that the simple answer is the true one: that the poems are there because Eddison liked them. They certainly do no harm, though they vex mildly if one attempts to consider Eddison's Mercury as self-contained invented world, as does the use of Mercury itself. Given our awareness of that planet as a sun-baked, toxic, uninhabitable hellhole, it is perhaps hard to accept this fantasy novel allegedly set there; Helmut Pesch identifies it as "less the astronomers' than the astrologers' Mercury, 'the mutable unpredictable planet where anything can happen'." This is all well and good if one knows anything about astrology, but may well have our hypothetical "layman" reader scratching his head.

As with the poems, this is an allusion that, once noticed, nags the reader out of full immersion in Eddison's creation. Perhaps this is deliberate after all—by reminding us, now and then, that his Mercury is an invention, is Eddison is challenging us to ask why it is invented? Why Mercury? Why this poem now? If Eddison is, as Young suggests, putting forth a philosophical position in his novels, he needs us to be alert and ready to detect it, not lulled by the fictional events in which the novel is framed.

A comparison might be drawn between Eddison's epic fantasy and the 'epic theatre' of Bertold Brecht, which "does not reproduce conditions but, rather, reveals them," through the interruption of the fictional illusion (Benjamin 4). Brecht, it should be noted, is another contemporary of the modernists, another didactic writer with a perspective to outline, and another notoriously "difficult" practitioner in his medium. Perhaps the Brechtian theatre might be a better venue for an adaptation of *Ouroboros* than the cinema—but I digress.

Assuming that one understands and is charmed by Eddison's style, his content proves to be a further challenge. Young noted in an earlier essay that "his books demand a great deal from the reader, offering few concessions to readability and only making complete sense as a dense, complicated, 1,500-page unit" ("Aphrodite on the Home Front" 71). This may be true of the *Zimiamvia* trilogy, the three later novels of Eddison's career, although I would argue that *Ouroboros*, appropriately, stands alone and self-contained as a reflection on war, an expression of what is worth fighting for.

Even with this charitable concession made, however, the content is not to the liking of every reader, even the fellow-travelers among whom Eddison finds his admirers. Tolkien, besides disliking the majority of *Ouroboros*'s characters and Eddison's haphazardness of nomenclature, held forth that "Eddison thought what I admire 'soft' (his word: one of complete condemnation, I gathered); I thought that, corrupted by an evil and indeed silly 'philosophy', he was coming to admire, more and more, arrogance and cruelty" (*Letters* 258). De Camp describes the arrogance and indifference of Eddison's kings and lords to their social inferiors (132), while Attebury confirms the moral code espoused in Eddison's work as "Nietzschean" (531).

All of this is in essence true, and the said arrogance, cruelty, and ignorance are displayed by both protagonist and antagonist alike, so the excuse that such tendencies are in some way framed as 'bad' or 'naughty' within the novel does not stand. Eddison presents a world which is obsessed with the personal actions of great heroes, who are willing to squander lives by the thousand and risk the fates of nations on settling personal vendettas.

Consider by way of example the magical sending of the reincarnated King Gorice against our nominal protagonists, the Lords of Demonland. If Gorice attempts such a sending twice in one lifetime, then he will be afforded no further reincarnations; he will die, and his kingdom Witchland will fall with him. Gorice's first act upon his return from the grave is to unleash this terrible power against Goldry Bluzsco, the Lord of Demonland who killed his previous incarnation in a duel, gambling his immortality and his kingdom on vengeance and—of course—ironically spurring the Demons on to their later conflicts. In these conflicts the Lords of Demonland spend months attempting to retrieve Goldry, in one perilous or foolish expedition after another, knowingly and willfully spiting their tactical sense, as Lord Brandoch Daha observes: "Let my opinion sway thee once. Why, a schoolboy should tell thee, clear thy flank and rear ere thou go forward" (*Ouroboros* 401).

Wherever these kings and lords go, pursuing their grudges and their glory, the deaths of peasant Witches, Demons, Goblins, et al., in their thousands are mentioned offhand, largely as a way of keeping score. Eddison's descriptive focus remains firmly on the duels between heroes and the material aspects of nobility—the beauty of Demonland's great halls, despoiled by the occupying Witches, and the somber majesty of besieged Carcë when the Worm turns and Witchland is assailed. This tendency both confirms the accusations of arrogance, cruelty, and indifference to the sufferings of lesser men, and vindicates Eddison of these vices, for his concern is not to champion the little people but to demonstrate the virtue and vitality of the big ones. Heroism, Eddison seems to say, is what makes all this slaughter worthwhile.

Toward the end of *Ouroboros*, the Witches are defeated, Goldry is restored, Demonland is liberated, and the immortal Queen Sophonisba, fosterling of the gods, is free to walk among mortals again. A happy ending, bought at the cost of many lives. However, the reaction of the Demons to their victory is unusual to say the least. After the moment of triumph, they look upon their swords with such sentiments as these:

> We may well cast down our swords as a last offering on Witchland's grave. For now must they rust: seamanship and all high arts of war must wither: and, now that our great enemies are dead and gone, we that were lords of all the world must turn shepherds and hunters, lest we become mere mountebanks and fops [...]. Thinking that we, that fought but for fighting's sake, have in the end fought so well we may never fight more; unless it should be in fratricidal rage each against each. And ere that should betide, may earth close over us and our memory perish. (*Ouroboros* 502–03)

Like Alexander, the Demons weep because there is no more world to conquer—or, in their case, to save. Their world has been plunged into war and carnage, and they have saved it, and now they have the nerve to regret doing so. It is a difficult perspective to understand—Sophonisba, for her part, is baffled. To understand it, it is perhaps necessary to turn to history.

SECOND OBSERVATION: EDDISON AND THE MODERNISTS ARE CONTEMPORARIES

This observation is more than simply a moment of critical serendipity. *Ouroboros* saw publication in 1922; the same year as *Ulysses*, *The Waste Land* and *À la recherche du temps perdu*. However, as Young notes, Eddison began the writing of *Ouroboros* in 1917, and evidence exists that elements of Eddison's invented world had existed for a great deal longer ("Foundations" 197). That *Ouroboros* was published at all indicates that there must have been some market for it, despite what Matthews observes about the readership of the time:

> At that time literary modernism was in vogue among the most thoughtful readers—those who had the kind of literary minds [...] complex fiction demands. Instead of reading fantasy, many of them were attracted by the new experimental realism of D. H. Lawrence, Gertrude Stein, Ernest Hemingway, James Joyce, Virginia Woolf, and T. S. Eliot. (23)

At first glance, Eddison's elaborate fantasy is a million miles away from "experimental realism"—indeed, it might as well be on Mercury, and the readership of the 1920s on Earth. However, an inspection of the modernist canon reveals some areas of correspondence: authorship as reaction to the First World War, and depictions of male friendship.

The idea of modernism as reaction to the First World War is old hat—so much so that, when Sherry interrogates the assumption, there are some points of critical awkwardness. As Sherry observes, it is "the rule of well-established associations" that designates the effect of the First World War—"a centering event, if a destructive legacy" on literature (6–8). However, the majority of the leading figures in modernism were rooted in a civilian culture which responded to the war at a distance, and its response was not to recount first-hand experience (though, as with Eliot's *Gerontion*, such experience was sometimes imitated or adopted as a theme).

Trudi Tate states a very similar case. From her position, the First World War was "a time of darkness and silence in which no one, including the combatants, knew what was going on nor why they were involved. Whole nations found themselves bearing witness to events they did not understand and, by and large, could not see." The direct outcome of this state of affairs was a literature primarily concerned with position of the self in relation to the past, recent and distant: "a history one has lived through and not seen, or seen only partially" (1). Tate also notes the scholarly lacuna surrounding modernism and war narratives, to whit that they are seldom read alongside one another for critical purposes, despite the authors involved reading and reviewing one another's work, and despite this shared social and emotional background.

From her perspective, modernism is a highly specific kind of war writing. It is very similar to the position taken by Sherry, who claims that, rather than narrating the experience of war in a traditional style, the civilian response to war was to narrate the absence of that experience, with a radical alteration in how writing was done (14)—a turn toward the difficulty described by Diepeveen and discussed previously.

Their world was Eddison's. Their response, correspondingly, was Eddison's: a drift away from the rational and mundane, toward a difficult style expressing a difficult position. Eddison, however, *focuses* on near-apocalyptic conflict rather than eliding it, describing the deaths of thousands on the field of battle in the "wrestling for Demonland" (*Ouroboros* 24), and he does so unrepentantly, being preoccupied with individual feats of valor on the part of the great leaders.

Yet in this preoccupation he continues to share ground with his contemporaries. Sarah Cole traces the development of male friendship from the Victorians through modernism, within Eddison's lifetime, and draws conclusions which are illuminating to a reader of *Ouroboros*. Cole claims that:

> in the early twentieth century, both the power and the potential for bereavement associated with male friendship were typically intertwined with such major cultural narratives as imperialism and war, and the sense of heightened importance that friendship often projected derived from those weighty connections. (3)

Central to Cole's analysis is the idea of the pseudocouple; the two men depicted as sharing extraordinary emotional intimacy, of a depth and intensity paralleling romance. Formed through hardship and personal strife, the pseudocouple (or pseudotriple) is central to the Victorian adventure narratives and the survival narratives of the First World War which Cole claims are evoked by the modernist and para-modernist literature of the 1920s (3).

In *Ouroboros*, this pairing appears again and again, each time expressing a different kind of friendship. Among the Demons, there is the friendship of Lord Juss and Lord Goldry Bluzsco, of whom Juss says "truly I care not greatly for my life that Goldry is gone from me" (84); that Goldry "for want of whom my whole soul languisheth in sorrow this year gone by" (228).

Scarce less close is the bond between Lord Juss and Lord Brandoch Daha, who journey across the world to rescue Goldry: their relationship is characterized by a graceful one-upmanship, born of mutual respect. In the Bed of the Mantichores there occurs the following exchange, which characterizes that association perfectly:

> "It is to be said of thee, O Brandoch Daha, that thou to-day hast done both the worst and the best. The worst, when thou wast so stubborn set to fare upon this climb which hath come within a little of spilling both thee and me. The best, whenas thou didst smite off his tail. Was that by policy or by chance?"
> "Why", said he, "I was never so poor a man of my hands that I need turn braggart. 'Twas handiest to my sword, and it disliked me to see it wagging. Did aught lie on it?"
> "The sting of his tail," answered Juss, "were competent for thine or my destruction, and it grazed but our little finger."
> "Thou speakest like a book," said Brandoch Daha. "Else might I scarce know thee for my noble friend, being berayed with blood as a buffalo with mire. Be not angry with me, if I am most at east to windward of thee." (208–09)

Such banter on the verge of death indicates a more earthy kind of friendship than the spiritual, life-defining association of Juss and Goldry, but it is an indestructible bond all the same, reiterated through the call-and-response wordplay of these two throughout their adventures.

Even the Witches, rotters to a man, have one such pseudocouple in King Gorice and Lord Gro, both of whom recognize in the other a merit and a depth lacking in the boozing, scheming court of braggarts and thugs who surround them. Gro deduces Gorice's immortality, and is intimately familiar with the prophecies concerning Gorice's and Witchland's future (*Ouroboros* 61–62); Gorice recognizes Gro's statesmanship and insight, unique among the Witches: "Art thou not a very jewel of wisdom and discretion? Let me embrace thee and love thee for ever" (*Ouroboros* 63). Gro is the only member of Gorice's court trusted to aid Gorice in the dangerous "sending against Demonland," and it is only with Gro's aid that the sending is completed at all; it is Gro who is chosen to crown Gorice as twelfth king of Witchland; and as Gorice remarks to his court, "Whoso among you shall so serve me and so water the growth of this Witchland as hath Gro in this night gone by, unto him will I do like honour" (*Ouroboros* 75).

These pseudocouples are created and maintained through hardship, and it is the *type* of hardship that is of greatest interest here. Gertrude Stein described the literary depiction of war encountered by a voracious reader like herself as not realistic, but romantic: "not to believe in, but to dream" (qtd. in Tate 4). Here, perhaps, is the source of Eddison's fantasy, and a vindication of sorts for his preoccupation with the posturings of individuals. Eddison depicts the war to end all wars, and is every bit as interested in its outcome for the Lords of Demonland as Virginia Woolf is in her tragic Septimus Warren Smith, but he does not pursue the course of realism that drives Septimus to suicide. The Lords of Demonland have another way out. Instead of lying down to die, their ideologies shattered and their purpose lost by victory, they ask Sophonisba to intercede with the gods on their behalf and grant them a final blessing:

> Would they might give us our good gift, that should be youth for ever, and war; and unwaning strength and skill in arms. Would they might but give us our great enemies alive and whole again. For better it were we should run hazard again of utter destruction, than thus live out our lives like cattle fattening for the slaughter, or like silly garden plants. (*Ouroboros* 504)

Having won the war to end all wars, they ask to do it all again, rather than face the loss of self and purpose that comes with peace, and it can be inferred that if they win again, they will make the same demand "for ever." Why would Eddison, who prepared the book in the latter years and during the aftermath of the First World War, react in *this* way? The final observation, which contrasts Eddison with the high modernists, looks in search of answers to the philosophy which he espoused.

THIRD OBSERVATION: EDDISON AND THE MODERNISTS PROPOSE ALTERNATIVES

Sherry describes the underlying project of high modernism as an effort to "reenact the disestablishment of a rationalistic attitude and practice in language, in the verbal culture of a war for which Liberal apologies and rationales provided the daily material of London journalism" (14): the exact outcome of this project are texts characterized such themes as "alienation, disconsolation and a desperately troubled relationship with the past" (Cole 20). This is potentially true of Eddison's *Ouroboros*, to an extent, but not to a complete or a convincing one: the comfort with which Eddison deploys his resources and comes to represent his world does not strike me as "troubled" in the slightest. That said, some of Eddison's devices do express an alienation with the contemporary world and a disconsolation at having to live within it, most obviously the means by which his invented world is accessed.

Ouroboros begins thus: "There was a man named Lessingham dwelt in an old low house in Wastdale, set in a gray old garden where yew-trees flourished that had seen Vikings in Copeland in their seedling time" (1). This Lessingham, like his creator, is a Northerner, and very much aware of his history: the Eddison who would go on to translate *Egil's Saga* creates a man who reads *Njal* over his after-dinner cigars. Supremely comfortable with the past, Lessingham is somewhat outlandish in the present. He keeps a "Lotus Room" which seems to have supernal properties, in which "it is a long way and several years too, sometimes [...] even though it is all over next morning" (3); he ascribes unexplained significance to the name of a piano piece by Couperin; he has taught his companion Mary her language. There is an unidentified and unspoken strangeness about this pair; reference to a peculiar past, shaded with mystery, which Eddison would only explore in the later novels comprising the *Zimiamvia* trilogy.

Within the Lotus Room, Lessingham is translated to Mercury and introduced to the Lords of Demonland. It is through his eyes that their finery and valor is first encountered, as a bridging device which gradually closes the gap between reader and imagined world. Eddison abandons Lessingham by the opening of the fourth chapter, and so completely are we immersed in Mercury that the single mention of Lessingham's name thereafter comes as a mild shock to the senses. It is as though this disconnected, rather eldritch contemporary man upon whom "Mercury had a finger" (3) simply and alchemically dissolves into Mercury upon arriving there.

Tempting though it would be to equate Eddison directly with Lessingham, and from my armchair pronounce the analysis that Eddison sought to lose himself in escapist fantasy, I cannot pretend that such an approach would hold up for long. It is too scant; Lessingham seems far too comfortable in his surroundings on Earth to be a disconsolate and alienated modernist. He is strange, and somewhat fantastic in his own right, but he does not strike me as a means of escape; only of exploration. Going further, the approach would do disservice not merely to Eddison, but to epic fantasy as a genre. Just because one leaves reality behind does not mean one is fleeing from it or troubled by one's own reality—it can mean that one sees something else in fantasy that is worth travelling toward.

Sarah Shoker explores the charge often levelled at epic fantasy— that it is an escapist genre underwritten by a "high toryism" ideology, characterized by an acceptance of class differences and social inequity leavened with a sense of *noblesse oblige* on the part of the upper crust— and claims the accusation of escapism to have been issued by the protomodernists of the nineteenth century. This emergent ideology, prioritizing style over story and with its growing conviction that what was not difficult to read was not worth reading, was fundamentally at odds with epic fantasy's reliance on an accessible style and a continuous narrative which smooth over the reader's integration into the invented world.

It has already been seen that *Ouroboros* is far from accessible or commonplace in its style—that it is at least partially difficult for the same value of difficulty as the texts of high modernism, though the manner of its difficulty varies considerably. In style, meanwhile, *Ouroboros* begins with a discontinuous approach which both is and is not concerned with readerly immersion. On the one hand, Lessingham is an undeniable bridging device; a contemporary observer of a fantasy world, a familiar lens through which to view the unfamiliar. On the other, Lessingham is downright peculiar, and his commentary on the appearance of the Lords of Demonland and the novel's first shift in time and place—"How could I have fallen asleep? [...] Where is the castle of the Demons, and how did we leave the great presence chamber where they saw the Ambassador?" (*Ouroboros* 24)—downright intrusive, a reminder that our perspective is shifting in time and place, that we are reading a constructed narrative.

Only when Lessingham is abandoned does *Ouroboros* settle down into the immersive and straightforward relation of story, and while there are shifts in place and time—the most jarring of which is the movement away from the Lords of Demonland for a lengthy passage in which the internal politics of Witchland are explored in admittedly charming detail—these are hardly the alienating jolts and switchbacks of the modernist text. Once again, *Ouroboros* would seem to squint toward modernism and hold out a hand to refuse it, at one and the same time; there would seem to be a similar elitism and distance from the commonplace, but a distinct interest in immersion and continuity.

Shoker also observes that, despite the association of post-Tolkienian fantasy with a rural high Toryism, there is nothing inherently binding the epic fantasy to a conservative ideology, citing the cases of China Miéville and Ursula K. Le Guin as evidence. Here, Eddison is on trickier ground: the ideology which he espouses is not precisely high Tory, but the crown fits better than the bowler hat or flat cap (Shoker). However, the devil is in the details, and Eddison's particular brand of conservatism has its own definition of *noblesse oblige* which is almost as subversive as Shoker suggests fantasy can, should, or is obliged to be.

Eddison stakes his salvation on a philosophical perspective which is expressed more clearly in the *Zimiamvia* novels and, in particular, a lengthy letter which was published as an appendix to the Dell collected edition of those novels. This philosophy is characterized by an inverted idealism; where the conventional idealist might strive toward a rationalized perfection, Eddison is only interested in perfection as it is made manifest in empirically observable, beautiful things or deeds. Such things have an inherent and transcendent value outside systems of value which, since they place the idea first and the manifestation second (unlike Eddison), are unable to fit the facts of the world as is: here it should be apparent that Attebury's description of Eddison's philosophy as Nietzschean is not without substance, since Eddison's drive toward an ultimate negation of systems and valuing of things as things in themselves. The only criterion by which the thing-in-itself is valued is beauty—feminized Beauty which rules over masculine Love, which protects, adores, and is enslaved by the feminine ideal.

This is hardly the troubled, alienated, disconsolate perspective of the modernists; Eddison's philosophy is confidently, though obtusely, evident throughout his body of works. Though it is arguable that *Ouroboros* does not articulate—or perhaps render observable—Eddison's philosophy to the extent that his later books manage, the germs of it can be seen in *Ouroboros*. They are most evident in the delicate, powerful, radiantly beautiful yet ultimately confined Queen Sophonisba who is central to the quest to retrieve Goldry Bluzsco; to a lesser extent, they are apparent in Queen Prezmyra and the Lady Mevrian, whose charm appears the deciding factor in the habitual treacheries of Lord Gro.

As it happens, Lord Gro—the only one of Eddison's characters whom Tolkien did not despise, and perhaps the only one who could be described as having the complex 'inner life' that welcomes cinematic adaptation—is the character who comes closest to directly articulating the attitudes of his creator. As I reach the end of these observations, I will indulge once more in quoting a favored passage: a speech of Gro's that indicates Eddison's value-system almost directly, suggesting exactly what it is that Eddison prizes as more ultimately valuable than human life, for which it is worth fighting, dying, betraying and, at the last, rewinding time to do it all again:

> But because day at her dawning hours hath so bewitched me, must I yet love her when glutted with triumph she settles to garish noon? Rather turn now as I turn to Demonland, in the sad sunset of her pride. And who dares call me turncoat, who do but follow now as I have followed this rare wisdom all my days: to love the sunrise and the sundown and the morning and the evening star? since only there abideth the soul of nobility, true love, and wonder, and the glory of hope and fear. (366)

Expulsion

All basking in Eddison's prose aside, some effort at closure must be made; we cannot simply vanish like Lessingham into the imaginary world. Three observations were made by which Eddison can be compared to and contrasted with his contemporaries, the high modernists, and areas of common or distinct ground between them located.

Firstly, that Eddison is difficult. To be difficult in the same way as the modernists, he must be erudite, obscure, or complex; out of kilter with the times; fashionable; and of value only when understood, when some new frame of meaning defined by rather than defining his work has been constructed. His allusions are erudite, though not always obscure, and his themes are deceptively complex, though at their simplest in *Ouroboros*. His prose is out of kilter with the times, and it is arguable that his pursuit of the fantasy epic during the nineteen-twenties is likewise. He is of value only when his prose is savored, and his philosophy detected and decoded through the actions of his characters. He is, however, far from fashionable. Critically, he is a byword in the notes of Northrop Frye (299); influentially, he is a writer's writer, an influence on Lewis, Tolkien, and the fantasy role-playing movement, a citation only, seldom engaged in his own right. This said, three out of four is by no means a bad match.

Secondly, that Eddison is a contemporary of the modernists, and moved by the same social forces. As part of a body of civilian literature, detached from first-hand accounts of the Great War, both Eddison and the high modernists drift away from conventional prose and into difficulty. Eddison, however, turns toward rather than away from the grand scale of conflict, and he cleaves to the Victorian adventure yarn and the War survivor's narrative, particularly in his construction and deployment of male friendship as a warrior bond, forged in strife.

Thirdly, that Eddison, like the modernists, is striving toward an alternative philosophy, some means of responding to and parsing the influence of the First World War. Faced with the inadequacy of Victorian rationalism, Eddison pursues a stark, Nietzschean vision of empirical beauty as ultimate value—beauty which, in *Ouroboros*, is expressed both through the physical, feminized goddess and through the more abstract beauty of glorious, heroic conflict against overwhelming odds. This is an ideological vision quite distinct from the modernist insistence on jarringly-expressed, rather ugly realism, as different as is the generic choice of epic fantasy or the prose style of gorgeously overwrought archaism, and is—I hope—the final firm insistence that my goal here is not, absolutely not, to identify Eddison as a closet modernist; merely to highlight the similarities between a writer and a movement active at a particular point in socio-cultural time.

In conclusion, I turn again to Cole and her claim that:

> other works from the [post-First-World-War] period, which may operate without the authorizing sign of high modernism, take up the promise and the burden of narrating male friendship: acting almost as modernist shadows, these texts construct the kind of resonant, self-legitimizing voices we often associate with modernism [...]. [M]odernism shares its topics, preoccupations and outcomes with the broader culture that surrounded and helped to produce it. (20)

Eddison operates without Cole's "authorizing sign," but he is no shadow. A more fitting metaphor might be this: the First World War looms over English literary culture, and in the cold light of dawn on Armistice Day, long shadows are cast in different directions. High modernism is one: epic fantasy is another. They are not the same, but they are cast from the same source, and there are darker patches where the shadows cross and merge, in similarity.

WORKS CITED

Attebury, Brian. "E. R. Eddison." *Supernatural Fiction Writers: Fantasy and Horror.* Vol. 2. Ed. E. F. Bleiler. New York: Scribner, 1985. 529–34. Print.

Benjamin, Walter. *Understanding Brecht.* Trans. Anna Bostock. 1966. London: Verso, 1992. Print.

Cole, Sarah. *Modernism, Male Friendship and the First World War* Cambridge: Cambridge UP, 2003. Print.

de Camp, L. Sprague. "Superman in a Bowler: E. R. Eddison." *Literary Swordsmen and Sorcerers: The Creators of Modern Fantasy.* Sauk City: Arkham House, 1976. 114–34. Print.

Diepeveen, Leonard. *The Difficulties of Modernism.* New York: Routledge, 2003. Print.

Eddison, E. R. *The Worm Ouroboros.* 1926. New York: Ballantine Books, 1971. Print.

—. *Zimiamvia: A Trilogy.* New York: Dell, 1992. Print.

Frye, Northrop. *Northrop Frye's Notebooks on Romance.* Toronto: U of Toronto P, 2004. Print.

Le Guin, Ursula K. "From Elfland to Poughkeepsie." 1973. *Fantastic Literature: A Critical Reader.* Ed. David Sandner. Greenwood: Greenwood, 2004. 144–55. Print.

Matthews, Richard. *Fantasy: the Liberation of Imagination.* New York: Twayne, 1997. Print.

Pesch, Helmut W. *The Sign of the Worm: Images of Death and Immortality in the Fiction of E. R. Eddison.* 1985. Web. 13 June 2014.

Sherry, Vincent. *The Great War and the Language of Modernism.* Oxford: Oxford UP, 2003. Print.

Shoker, Sarah. "Jailers Hate Escapism: Epic Fantasy as Subversive Literature." 2013. *The Hooded Utilitarian.* Web. 13 June 2014.

Tate, Trudi. *Modernism, History and the First World War.* Manchester: Manchester UP, 1998. Print.

Tolkien, J. R. R. *The Letters of J. R. R. Tolkien.* Ed. Humphrey Carpenter. Boston: Houghton Mifflin, 2000. Print.

Young, Joseph. "Aphrodite on the Home Front." *Mythlore* 30.3/4 (#117/118) (2012): 71–88. Print.
—. "The Foundations of E. R. Eddison's *The Worm Ouroboros*." *Extrapolation* 54.2 (2013): 183–203. Print.
—. " 'On This I Stake My Salvation': E. R. Eddison's Easter Manifesto." *Extrapolation* 54:1 (2013): 73–93. Print.

E. R. Eddison and the Age of Catastrophe

Joe Young

Historian Eric Hobsbawm observes that readers could be forgiven for overlooking the fact that Jane Austen's novels were written, published and set during the Napoleonic Wars. He makes the point to illustrate the difference between the wars of Austen's day and those of the twentieth century. Modern warfare engages entire societies. Troops are deployed in far greater numbers, and proportionately fewer of them come home. Entire economies must be reorganized to provide the torrent of equipment necessary for victory. With industrial workforces involved in the war effort, the general populace must often accept its position as a military target. Little of this was true in Austen's time. With the social impact of war relatively modest in her day, it could be deemphasized, or even ignored altogether, in literary depictions of her society. "It is inconceivable," says Hobsbawm, "that any novelist could write about Britain in the twentieth-century wars in this manner" (44).

The work of E. R. Eddison provides a particularly interesting test case for this idea. Eddison's first novel *The Worm Ouroboros* (1922) has been criticized as a celebration of amoral slaughter, unaffected by the social crisis of World War I. Closer examination of the behavior of heroes of *The Worm Ouroboros* suggests that this criticism is unfair. As Eddison's career continued, furthermore, the war and its after-effects became an integral part of his plots and, indeed, his authorial motivations. In Eddison's later novels, fantasy worlds overlap with real ones in complicated ways, and large sections of his penultimate book *A Fish Dinner in Memison* (1941) are set on Earth in the years 1908–1933. These episodes bear out Hobsbawm's comments about literary presentations of twentieth-century Britain by depicting the trials of that time and place. By incorporating fantasy elements into those depictions, Eddison was able to articulate daring criticisms of those trials.

Eddison's literary career in fact coincides almost exactly with what Hobsbawm has dubbed "the Age of Catastrophe." Hobsbawm argues that the social, political and emotional vicissitudes of World War I were not, by any means, forestalled by the armistice of 1918. Rather, he suggests, the war marked the beginning of a new and frightening period in history, in which "the end of a considerable proportion of the human race" (22) seemed a distinct possibility. As society digested the events of World War I, Hobsbawm argues, they began to see those events as dire precedents. Governments struggled to prevent war on behalf of populations increasingly skeptical of the possibility of any future peace. Once that assumption became entrenched, Hobsbawm suggests, society became too disheartened to prevent a slide back to war in the 1930s. Those who sought to prevent that slide were unable to compete with the pro-war fascist parties, themselves downstream effects of World War I, that came to power in many nations. This was the background against which Eddison wrote, and he had much to say it.

Eddison's first novel was *The Worm Ouroboros*, which in synopsis seems to have escaped influence by World War I. Depicting the struggle between the Demons and Witches of Mercury, it is a meandering catalogue of military adventures, with "high arts of war" (502) celebrated throughout. Given that Eddison, aged 32 in 1914, lacked direct military experience, it may be tempting to dismiss this as the naïve work of a reactionary writer shutting his eyes to recent history. This argument has certainly been made:

> To Eddison, apparently, war was a romantic adventure. This view was widespread in Western culture in Eddison's generation. People born before 1900 still visualised war as fought with bands and banners, and cavalry charging with sword and lance. Not until realistic accounts of the grim butchery of the Kaiserian War became current in the 1920s was there a reaction against this attitude. (de Camp 116–17)

Even if we share de Camp's assumption that texts are unedited, uncritical facsimiles of their author's perceptions of reality, there is a serious flaw in this assessment—Eddison appears not to have started writing *The Worm Ouroboros* until the war was well underway. Eddison claimed to spend around five years on each of his books (Bodleian Library [BL] MS Eng. misc. e. 456 249), which would mean he started this one in around 1917. The earliest dated progress on the manuscript—not all of which is dated—was recorded on 6th April 1918 (Leeds Central Library SRQ 823.91 ED23). The novel had its genesis in boyhood games, but by the time Eddison began seriously writing it down, Britain was dealing with the continuation of a long-standing conflict, not the launch of a long-expected one.

This seriously handicaps any suggestion that the novel reflects romantic adventurism. By 1917 Britain was, as Hobsbawm notes, a nation, not an army, at war. Expectations of quick victory had long since evaporated, and the public mood was one of grim determination rather than optimistic naiveté. Britain instituted compulsory military service in May 1916, prompted by manpower shortages and dwindling volunteer numbers (Joll 200). In the following months the Battle of the Somme caused 600,000 Allied casualties. (207) In April 1917 elements of the French army mutinied, and the British picked up the strain, at great human cost. (212) Until some breakthrough could be made, men and material had to be supplied to a modern, industrialized battlefront, beggaring nations and eroding optimism. By the time Eddison began his novel, put simply, nobody expected anybody home by Christmas. Hundreds of thousands had in fact already been advised not to expect their son home at all, ever. What Eddison thought when the war began is unrecorded, but by the time he began writing he lived in a society coping with its effects on an unprecedented scale. Furthermore, he wrote in the time he could spare from a civil service career that required him to take an interest in British foreign policy. To suggest he continued in such a position while retaining the idea that war was "a romantic adventure" would be to voice a low opinion of him indeed.

Such opinions are difficult to justify. *The Worm Ouroboros* is hardly a pacifistic story, but de Camp's suggestion, accompanying that made above, that the heroes show no concern for human life (116) contradicts their actual behavior. Consider, for example, the actions of Lady Mevrian, a young Demon forced to oversee the defense of her family castle when the Witches invade Demonland. Assailed by the overwhelming army of the Witch general Corinius, she carries wine to one of her officers and outlines her plan to "yield up the keep unto Corinius under promise of a safe conduct for Astar and Ravnor and all her men" (347). She reached this decision after contemplating a portrait of the castle's rightful castellan, missing in action in Impland:

> She fell to gazing on her brother's picture, the Lord Brandoch Daha, standing in his jewelled hauberk laced about with gold, his hand on his sword. And that lazy laughter-loving yet imperious look of the eyes which in life he had was there, wondrous lively caught by the painter's art, and the lovely lines of his brow and lip and jaw, where power and masterful determination slumbered, as brazen Ares might slumber in the arms of the Queen of Love.
>
> A long while Mevrian looked on that picture, musing. Then, burying her face in the cushions of the long low seat she sat on, she burst into a great passion of tears. (341)

Here, in the middle of a novel criticized for reactionary amorality, is a display of human emotion strikingly topical for the period in which it was written. By 1917, hundreds of thousands of British homes contained a picture of a brave-looking young soldier in his splendid uniform, and in all too many of those homes, a distraught sister had broken down in front of that image. Eddison's immediate family were spared this, but he probably had friends who were bereaved. Even if he did not, he will have known it was happening; the scale of the war made its depredations impossible to overlook. That being the case, it is hard to avoid the suspicion that this episode is informed by that situation.

The safety of Mevrian's men is foremost among her conditions in her parley (348). In taking this course Mevrian actually compromises her own safety as Corinius, vilely ungracious in victory, accosts her in the very hall in which she wept for her brother (352). Enduring such degradation to spare the lives of a crowd of mostly anonymous spear-carriers is hardly the act of a character, or the imagining of a writer, laboring under misconceptions about war as a consequence-free adventure. If the episode must be compared to contemporary events, it surely makes more sense to interpret it as a moment of wish-fulfilment during a war in which enlisted men were dying in droves. At the very least, the episode depicts a Demon displaying obvious concern for the lives of those involved in the conflict.

Nor is this the only instance of such concern. Later, when the tables are turned and a Demon army stands at the gates of the Witch-king's castle, their leader Juss makes King Gorice a magnanimous offer:

> "that we will depart out of thy country and do no more unpeaceful deeds against thee (till thou provoke us again); and thou, of thy part, of all the land of Demonland shalt give up thy quarrel, and of Pixyland and Impland beside, and thou shalt yield me up Corsus and Corinius thy servants that I may punish them for the beastly deeds they did in our land whenas we were not there to guard it." (458)

The Demons came to Witchland seeking justice rather than bloodshed. Corsus, for the record, was operating under Gorice's specific instructions to "spoyl ravysche and depopulate" (266) Demonland while Demon civilians have composed songs comparing Corinius to a millstone grinding them under his cruel lordship (383). The Demons seem justified in wanting these two to answer for their actions. As to what sort of punishment the Witches might expect, Corsus has been at the mercy of the Demons once before. They captured him when he raided their allies the Goblins. An eyewitness recalls how Brandoch Daha "stripped him stark naked, shaved him all of one side smooth as a tennis ball and painted him yellow and sent him home with mickle shame to Witchland" (283). Mickle shame, perhaps, but an intact skin.

It would be possible, given more space, to cite more evidence in this vein, but the point has perhaps been made. *The Worm Ouroboros* is, to be sure, no anti-war polemic, but de Camp's claim that it celebrates amoral bloodlust or naive adventurism is hardly fair. The Demons make few apologies for the violence they undoubtedly commit, and at times even gloat over putting their foes to bloody rout (392–95). Nevertheless they repeatedly display what the Witches dismiss as "silly phantasies of honour and courtesy" (477), offering terms, grieving casualties, proscribing shameful tactics and sharing risks in ways that Eddison's villains do not. The Demons appreciate that, in Hobsbawm's words, "[v]iolence has its rules" (50)—rules that were frequently overlooked amid the dispassionate, mechanical attrition of World War I. It is unlikely that the conduct of the Demons is a deliberate, calculated critique of that carnage, but de Camp's theory that their adventures stem from naiveté on Eddison's part seems even less plausible. Eddison lived and wrote through a modern, industrialized war, and as Hobsbawm avers, the scale and consequences of such wars are impossible to overlook. With that point in mind, it is possible to detect—in events such as the capitulation of Mevrian—faint but likely resonances of wartime stress in Eddison's presentation of principled, chivalrous warfare. At any rate, it is important to note that *The Worm Ouroboros* is not the catalogue of unrestrained, amoral bloodshed that de Camp complains about.

In the wake of World War I, social opinion turned away from militarism. This shift was slower and more complicated than may be appreciated by modern observers (Adams 124–26). Nevertheless governments have their own reasons—financial and diplomatic as well as humanitarian—for avoiding war, and British diplomats took an early and leading role in trying to forestall future conflicts. Britain was a founding member of the League of Nations, set up by the Treaty of Versailles in 1919. The 1925 Locarno Pact, an attempt to cool the simmering tensions Versailles had created, was signed in London. Public opinion gradually fell into line with such initiatives (Fink 550). There is little to suggest that, at the time, Eddison bucked this trend. Some tacit approval for it might be read into his literary activity in the 1920s. Eddison's work in the decade after *The Worm Ouroboros* features far more scattered and remote depictions of warfare. *Styrbiorn the Strong* (published in 1926, set in medieval Scandinavia) and his 1930 translation of *Egil's Saga* both feature wars, but of strictly historical nature. His next fantasy, *Mistress of Mistresses* (1935) features only brief fictional battles scattered through a long, luxuriant catalogue of courtly and romantic intrigues. It may well be that these works reflect the shift in public mood and taste away from militarism.

However morally laudable that shift might have been, it was, according to Hobsbawm, symptomatic of a dangerous trend in societal self-perception. He argues that, as hindsight accumulated, World War I came to be seen as a grim precedent. Recalling his own upbringing, Hobsbawm suggests this perception gave rise to further assumptions:

> [A] new world war was not only predictable, but routinely predicted. Those who became adults in the 1930s expected it. The image of fleets of fleets of airplanes dropping bombs on cities and of nightmare figures in gasmasks tapping their way like blind people through the fog of poison gas, haunted my generation: prophetically in one case, mistakenly in the other. (35)

The retreat from militarism in the 1920s was an attempt to prevent such occurrences. It coincided, however, with attempts to enforce the penal settlements of World War I, which had created intractable geopolitical tensions (34–37). Such objectives were largely incompatible, at least after the Great Depression stoked the fires of resentment in the defeated nations. Desperate to prevent wars within their own borders, governments became accustomed to letting them happen elsewhere, tolerating inhumanities in which they themselves eventually became embroiled (26–27). In their fear of war, diplomats of the post-1918 era failed to meaningfully oppose it.

World War I also produced, Hobsbawm argues, a "brutalising" effect on society. Warfare had also become impersonal—"opposite the permanently fixed guns of the western front were not people but statistics" (50). This trend was expected to continue, as indeed it did in World War II. World War I gave rise not only to the means to butcher millions, but also the acceptance of the use of such means, to their full extent, as a matter of course. Hobsbawm attributes many of the horrors of twentieth-century history to this "steep decline in the values of civilisation" (28). While the deaths of forty people in a pogrom in the Russian city of Kishinev in 1903 "outraged the world," Lithuanians responded to the 1941 German invasion of the USSR by killing 3,800 Jewish residents of Vilnius "before the systematic exterminations got underway" (120–21).

As society struggled to cope with these shifts, it encountered another phenomenon Hobsbawm blames on World War I—fascism. Noting how many fascists, both leaders and followers, were veterans, Hobsbawm blames these movements on men who had drawn sufficient self-esteem from the war to have overlooked its human consequences. Such men sought to address the perceived and real social problems of the day by exercising the same uncompromising aggression they had used on the battlefield. If the result of such brutality was another war, so much the better; they could once again exercise the strength they believed they had found in trenches (26). The result of the collision of these two consequences of World War I—demoralized, diffident pacifism in one camp and amoral, provocative militarism in the other—was the doomed Appeasement policy, in which Britain took a lead role (Fink 551–52). This, then, was the true legacy of World War I—a society that had lost its stomach for war but could not work productively toward an alternative, lost its moral center in its fatalistic acceptance of a future of unrestrained bloodshed, and consequently lacked the emotional or political equipment to resist a minority of vicious, militaristic bullies.

This trend was reaching its bitter fruition as Eddison worked on his last completed book, *A Fish Dinner in Memison*. The Austrian Anschluss, the 1939 Munich Conference and the early stages of World War II itself were underway as he wrote this book, which contains explicit commentary on the historical events that brought Europe to this crisis. The novel weaves together two narratives. One takes place in the paradisiacal fantasy realm of Zimiamvia, in which the members of an idealized, superhuman aristocracy pursue an endless succession of courtly and romantic intrigues. The other is set on Earth. Certain of the perfect beings of Zimiamvia have entered Earth, hoping to experience a different world from within (535–36; *The Mezentian Gate* 783). They live mortal lives here as Edward Lessingham and Mary Scarnside, provincial British gentlefolk who marry in 1908 and enjoy fifteen years of life together. The episodes Eddison provides from that life prove Hobsbawm's point about depictions of the era by openly acknowledging the events of the Age of Catastrophe. Eddison's narrative does so in a fascinatingly original way, however. Offering only vague, circumstantial hints that they are aware of their Zimiamvian existences (329; 498–99; 504), Edward and Mary nevertheless retain the superhuman perspectives of their fictional homeland. They therefore comment on the disasters and difficulties of their earthly epoch from the standpoint of idealized literary characters. By placing discussion of the real world in the mouths of fantasy characters with fantasy viewpoints, Eddison voices a penetrating critique of reality. He repeatedly raises issues arising from World War I as discussion points in this critique. This commentary on the war is, furthermore, very similar to that subsequently offered by Hobsbawm.

Some of Eddison's depictions are conventional, but very cleverly staged. For example, Edward and Mary go on an idyllic holiday in Wolkenstein in the Alps in 1914, chatting at length about the relief of being at their ease (420–22). At first glance this seems like an authorial indulgence, an excuse for Eddison to put his characters in a setting conducive of the lush descriptive passages that are a feature of his work. Details of timing, however, reveal a clear purpose to the episode. The Lessinghams leave Wolkenstein separately; Mary arrives home early on the morning of June 27th, "swinging her hat in her hand for the pleasure of the air" (434; cf. Thomas 968). The following day, Archduke Ferdinand will be shot in Sarajevo. It is hard to believe that Eddison, having lived through the July crisis of 1914 and its results, conceived this timetable by accident. Discussing public attitudes in the 1930s, Hobsbawm recalls that " 'Peace' meant 'before 1914'; after that came something that no longer deserved the name" (22). Writing in the same era, Eddison signals this transition precisely, thrusting World War I into the foreground of his narrative. The holiday constitutes the last few moments of ironic, self-assured happiness before the world is pitched into an unprecedented crisis.

Other examples of Eddison's commentary on this crisis are less subtle. Out riding in coastal Norfolk in 1923, for example, Mary encounters old practice trenches, which she wishes the authorities would fill in; her companion Anne Bremmerdale notes they would be "useful for the next war" (492). Anne communicates the sense of fatalism that Hobsbawm recalls from his own adolescence (35). Her melancholy remark sets Mary to thinking about absent friends:

> Jack Bailey, killed. Major Rustham, Hesper Dagworth, Captain Feveringhay, killed, killed, killed. Norman Rustham, that delightful little boy, gone down with the *Hawke*. Nigel Howard, killed: poor Lucy. And her brother married to that—well, we won't use Edward's word for her. And Tom Chedisford, of all people, drinking himself to death, it seems: incredible, appalling. (493)

Mary grew up with these people; they were all present, poignantly, at a cheerful cricket match in a section of the novel set in 1908 (339–63). Combined with that pre-war idyll of upper-middle-class British life, the passage is an unambiguous acknowledgement of the toll that World War I extracted, and the effect that loss had on those left to cope with it. Mary, who lost two brothers in the war (494), struggles to believe what has happened—her word for it, incredible, of course means "not credible."

She manages to believe it, however, delving into fine historical detail in the process. One of her friends went "down with the *Hawke*." The Royal Navy cruiser *HMS Hawke* was sunk by a German U-boat on 15th October 1914, with the loss of 544 lives (Paine 532). This reference demonstrates that Eddison was no unworldly daydreamer. Mary may not be parroting his precise opinions on the loss of the *Hawke*, but for her to have known about it at all, he must also have done so. As the context of Mary's recollection makes clear, he was all too aware of the toll World War I had extracted. Furthermore, the reference shows that he was not content with vague, general allusions to the war and its aftermath. He made a conscious effort to incorporate specific, unpleasant details of very real history into his work, imbuing that work with deliberate and timely purpose. *A Fish Dinner in Memison* is an ingenious philosophical novel. Mary, it must be remembered, is an expatriate Zimiamvian (566; Harris-Fain 78), a purpose-written ideal of distaff aristocracy predisposed to operate in a perfect world and think in utopian terms. In this capacity she is visiting Earth to observe its imperfections. The loss of the *Hawke* is one of the more incredible and appalling of those imperfections. Eddison has raised very precise details of the history attending World War I in his inquiry into the gap between utopia and reality.

The bulk of that inquiry is conducted by Edward Lessingham, who is no happier about the consequences of the war than his wife. He expresses his impressions differently, however. In 1919, he announces his contempt for the treaty being negotiated in Versailles:

> "As it is, I fancy we're going to be rather less than generous. And a load of mischief to come of it. Even if it doesn't cost us the fruits of these past four years, and leave us the job to do all over again." (484)

Society had been shoring up holes in the Versailles settlement for years by the time Eddison wrote this (Fink 548–53), so he should not be credited with any particular foresight here. Rather, he attributes such foresight to Edward by having him dismiss the treaty before it is even signed. Edward is not, furthermore, suggesting that the previous four years bore many fruits:

> "We have defeated 'Prussianism.' Have we so? I thought the object in war was to defeat your enemy, not defeat some absurd abstraction. We gave him an armistice when, at the last gasp, he asked for it. Now we're going to dictate terms of peace, in Paris apparently, I'd rather have carried the war to destruction clean through Germany, defeated him bloodily beyond cavil or equivocation, let him taste it at his own fireside, and dictated peace in Berlin. If we'd lost a hundred thousand lives by doing it (and we shouldn't have: nothing like it) it would have been worth the price."
> "And you one of them, perhaps?" said Charles.
> "Certainly: gladly: and I one of them." (484)

This outburst should not be mistaken for uncritical militarism, on Edward's part or Eddison's. Rather, it is an expression of frustration by a person used operating on an entirely different frame of reference from that in which he has found himself. Edward, like Mary, is not of this world. He is an expatriate Zimiamvian (566; Harris-Fain 78), an idealized warrior-aristocrat "larger than life and about half as natural" (557), characterized with explicit reference to Homeric poetry (482) and Icelandic saga (486). Zimiamvia is a land of ruthless schemers, brilliant generals, impassioned artists, and godlike kings, a stage for displays of superhuman emotion and swashbuckling heroism akin to those of Achilles or Egil Skallagrimsson. Zimiamvians can behave this way because their world is, like Troy or nameless north of the sagas, a literary artefact specifically designed to facilitate and celebrate such activity. The wars of Zimiamvia, like those of Homer's *Iliad*, are motivated by love and lordship. They are also individual affairs; fictional characters, after all, compete against other characters, not abstract historical and ideological forces. That is the frame of reference to which Edward Lessingham is accustomed.

In *A Fish Dinner in Memison*, however, Edward has been plucked from his natural habitat and transported to Earth, and at a time when, according to Hobsbawm, the world wars defined society. As Mary's reverie demonstrates, Eddison does not shrink from this, but he acknowledges the point in an idiosyncratic way. Asked for his thoughts on this milieu, Edward expresses frustration with complications that the likes of Achilles and Hector never had to contend with. Ours is not a world in which wars are fought for the sort of clearly-defined, concrete, finite ends that Homer sang about. It is a world in which people not only fight wars over "absurd abstractions" such as Prussian militarism—the extinguishment of which was seen by British strategists as a central war aim in 1914 (Calder 12–13)—but also believe that war can put an end to such idiocies. This makes no sense to a grand literary hero like Edward. Agamemnon, after all, fought to retrieve his abducted sister-in-law, not to discourage some quirk of Trojan thinking. By showing what an Agamemnon or a Sigurd would make of twentieth-century Earth, Eddison casts the difficulties of the age into high relief, the better to assess their true nature. Rather than betraying Eddison as the naïve, pro-war reactionary that de Camp suggests he is, Edward's statements here precisely demonstrate that his creator *did* understand the difference between fiction and reality, and expressed that appreciation in his work. He has simply done so in a roundabout way, having a character unused to such differences encounter them for the first time. From that position, Edward scrutinizes Earth and diagnoses its ills in a way that no earthly character could.

Edward's complaints frequently anticipate Hobsbawm's analysis of the post-war world. As Hobsbawm stated, "bloodbaths like 1914–18 would no longer be tolerated by the voters" (26). Democratic opinion is something else that Edward, like Agamemnon, is unused to. The idea of a nation involving itself in a war but not wanting to bring that conflict to a final, decisive conclusion is therefore alien to him. Thus he sees it as unusual that, to be quit of the war, the allies gave the nearly-defeated Germany an armistice. This is, to Edward's mind, a dreadful cop-out. How can the allies, having demonstrated such lack of resolve, now expect a firmly penal peace to hold? Of course, they could not; as Hobsbawm notes (26–27), interwar timidity on the part of the Allies hastened World War II and made it worse when it came. Edward's unique position, in the world but not of it, grants him the foresight to damn such prevarication as a false humanitarian economy in 1919, and indeed to wash his hands of it. Despite urging from his earthly family, he refuses to become involved with British politics (420; 480). By 1919, when he mentions that refusal a second time, Edward's experiences and observations in and around the war have led him to a conclusion that anticipates Hobsbawm's assessment of interwar politics—in its fear of war, society made future conflict virtually inevitable.

As the loss of Mary's friend aboard the *Hawke* demonstrates, Eddison was given to placing characters in very particular historical situations, sometimes going so far as to explain seating arrangements in specific, real buildings (*Mistress of Mistresses* 11–12; Thomas 867). Some of those deployments are open to interpretation. For example, Edward embarks on the 1914 holiday after seeing to a matter of personal finance, which he describes as "much more amusing than Berlin in nineteen-twelve" (415). He has always hated "money-grubbing" (416; cf. 326), so whatever happened in Berlin must have been dismal indeed, but he is interrupted before he can explain himself. The reference therefore takes some thought on the reader's part—doubtless Eddison's intention. Thomas (924) suggests that Edward was in Berlin trying to prevent the Balkan Wars of 1912–1913. Given Edward's work with the British Foreign Office (490), this suggestion makes sense, but there are further, intriguing dimensions to the issue. Anglo-German cooperation on the Balkan crisis of 1912 was less about preventing a war than preventing any of the Great Powers from making geopolitical capital from them, it preserving the delicate balance of European power (Neilson and Steiner 118). One of the central British victories of this cooperation was, in fact, to keep the Germans talking during a tense time in Anglo-German relations (113). One of the major tensions in Europe at the time was the rivalry between Germany and Britain for naval superiority, and therefore control of much of the shipping into Europe. This issue simmered for years before World War I, ultimately contributing to its outbreak, and took a grave turn in 1912. That February, a British delegation visited Berlin, led by Lord Chancellor Haldane, attempting to bring

Kaiser Wilhelm II to an agreement on this issue. This mission was unproductive, and subsequent talks "languished" (103). Haldane's communiques eventually convinced Wilhelm of British antagonism toward his empire. That December, therefore, the Kaiser ordered a series of military bills, investigations and reforms, most of them subsequently enacted, designed to prepare for a major, multi-party war in one to two years (Rohl 164–87). He was, obviously, not disappointed. Eddison, writing twenty-five years later, will have known of this, at least in broad terms. He completed *A Fish Dinner in Memison* after retiring as Deputy Overseas Comptroller for the Board of Trade (Harris-Fain 74), a body that administered British shipping throughout his career. This position will have required an understanding of the naval situation in Europe. In Eddison's mind, therefore, Anglo-German naval tension probably loomed large among the causes of World War I. Edward's cryptic comment appears to be a reference to the issue, and perhaps specifically to Haldane's February conference.

What makes this diplomatic disaster such a likely subject for Edward's allusion is that Edward is here to assess differences between Earth and Zimiamvia, and events in Berlin in 1912 demonstrate one such difference that particularly irritates him. During his earthly life he develops a deep suspicion of modern military technology, which as he sees it allows people to win wars whether they deserve to or not. He dislikes "[g]unpowder, the first mighty leveller" (*Fish Dinner* 544), a weapon that allows its owner to kill a foe without actually proving themselves to be the better fighter. Consequently, he says later, a great man defeated by "the dead weight of the machine" (*Mezentian Gate* 590) has little to be ashamed of. And yet such men are still defeated. Such a situation would be impossible in Zimiamvia, where battles turn on skill, courage, panache and passion. In *Mistress of Mistresses* Lessingham, campaigning in Rerek against two numerically superior armies, brilliantly outmaneuvers one, taking a route through mountains nobody else is so "fantastical" as to attempt. Shattering that foe, he then lays a brilliant trap for the other, shrewdly ignoring advice to spring that trap until the time is ripe. Having won the battle, and bleeding from an injury, he interrogates the opposing general, discovers common cause with him and shows mercy to the vanquished (263–70). He does not just win the campaign—he proves that he deserves to win it. Such is the nature of fiction.

History is less romantic, as Haldane's Berlin conference demonstrates. His published reports of that meeting contain no mention of human skill or gallantry. Rather, he and the Kaiser dwelt "at great length" (Gooch and Temperley 6.680) on the mathematical issue of who could build the most battleships. Battleships are fundamentally different from the longships of the Icelandic heroes to which Edward is compared, which serve to facilitate heroism by ferrying doughty warriors to their battlefields. Battleships render doughtiness and heroism irrelevant, allowing their owners to pull levers and achieve victories whether they deserve them or not. Wilhelm sought to win the coming war not by human means, but by amassing the largest possible collection of these contraptions and unleashing them on his enemy. Events in Berlin in 1912 thus serve as perfect illustrations of something that Edward comes to despise. It seems likely that by 1914, when he recalls his Berlin experience, Edward is recalling the discovery that earthly wars are not only fought for preposterous reasons, they are fought by preposterous means—in this world a general may purchase victory rather than earn it. Warfare therefore becomes the dispassionate, inhuman mathematical exercise Hobsbawm identified (50). Edward, a literary hero brought to Earth to examine the difference between literature and history, looks upon this trend from without, and dislikes what he sees. It is, he says, "a game not for men but for termites" (*Fish Dinner* 545).

In teaching Edward this lesson, furthermore, Eddison is not critiquing industrialization itself. He was of the opinion that "machinery […] is neither good nor bad, progressive nor reactionary, but as its user makes it" (BL, MS Eng. lett. e. 231, 112).[1] Machines could be put to ill use, however. Edward cites World War I (541) as an example of a trend in which people, professing to use progress to extend control of their circumstances, in fact do precisely the opposite. He argues that one of the major flaws of this world is "the cold lechery of *more and more*" (545)—the idea that because progress allows conflict and government on ever-increasing scales, it is inescapably necessary to conduct such endeavors on those scales. Individual human contributions, celebrated in Zimiamvia, are therefore diluted unto irrelevance. Without such contributions, the noblest abstract ideas end in tears (542). World War I, as analyzed by Hobsbawm, is an excellent example of what he is discussing. The uncompromising pursuit of war aims emerging from the abstract mathematical demands of expanding imperial government (Hobsbawm 29–30) caused men to die in unprecedented numbers. Such deaths did not facilitate the nobility of the commanders, a compensation accorded to literary spear-carriers in Zimiamvia or Troy. Little

---

1. Archival material quoted in this essay is © Anne Al-Shahi and used with her kind permission.

such nobility was in evidence. After all, the man who ordered the construction of the U-boat that killed Mary's "delightful" friend (493) was not displaying any of the qualities with which Lessingham earns his victories in Zimiamvia. Rather, he was an early adopter of a policy identified by Hobsbawm as an intractable consequence of the war—the unquestioning conduct of war as dispassionate, mechanical slaughter (50). Again, therefore, Eddison's unconventional method of critiquing events surrounding World War I produces conclusions that dovetail neatly with subsequent historical opinion; expanding power blunted our humanity.

Edward has also acquired first-hand knowledge of what earthly frames of reference will produce. During the Wolkenstein trip he recalls

> the slack weight in your arms beside the Struma: poor old Fred: like you born for a fighter, berserk taint, brothers in blood: 'Strike thunder and strike loud when I farewell:' thud of shells bursting, whining of them in the air: but the thinness, the shrivelled lack of actuality—was it all for this?—of the actual fact: of the end: trying to say something: bubbling of red froth between his front teeth: rattle of machine-guns: peas in a pig's bladder. (429)

The Struma is a river that flows through Bulgaria and Greece; Fred died in 1912 (415). These hints are rather clearer than Edward's comments about Berlin: he fought in the Balkan Wars (Thomas 924). These wars broke out in October 1912 (six months after naval talks in Berlin reached an impasse; Edward was not in two places at once). Wasserstein styles World War I as "the Third Balkan War" (37) since the first two enflamed the nationalist tensions that led to the murder of Archduke Ferdinand. Note the prominence of artillery and machine-guns in Edward's memory; these wars provided a "gruesome foretaste" (Hupchick 314) of the trench warfare that became such a defining feature of World War I. This, then, is Edward's first-hand experience of trench warfare, and it has confirmed his worst suspicions; great warriors like Fred will die in a mechanical dispute over who can afford the most artillery shells. To Edward, the experience was hollow and "shrivelled." Heroism may exist in such conflicts, but will not contribute to their outcomes.

When World War I itself breaks out, therefore, Edward participates "mainly" (*Mistress of Mistresses* 14) in Britain's attack on German East Africa. This is not cowardice—remember, he claims he would "gladly" (484) have died in France if it would have achieved anything—but a desire to use his superhuman skill where it will count for something, which in France it will not. None of his exploits in Africa are discussed, but his superiors laud him as his century's "finest tactician in irregular warfare" (558). Nevertheless the East African campaign was so marginal to the war that returning veterans encountered civilians unaware that it had even happened. (Parotti 159) Today, of course, the campaign is quite overlooked alongside the far-reaching cultural trauma of the trenches; "military action outside Europe," Hobsbawm claims, "was not very significant" (23). The very obscurity of this action, however, further underlines Eddison's point. Edward Lessingham is a great warrior, but this is not a world fitted for great warriors. Here, skill, courage and passion are forgotten, understandably and justifiably, alongside the human consequences of an amoral, macroeconomic spending spree in which great men can make no impact.

Edward's 1919 claim that he would have "gladly" died in World War I if doing so would have served a purpose is no ignorant vainglorious boast. It is a comment on what he would have done if the world was operating on what he sees as sound principles. It is a purely hypothetical statement, a frustrated wish that he lived in a world in which anything he understands as heroism, even heroic deaths, could actually solve anything. This wish is made in well-informed recognition of the fact that Earth does not work that way, at the instigation of an author committed to an unflinchingly realistic depiction of the difficulties of his time. References to such relative obscurities as the East African Campaign, the Balkan Wars and the sinking of the *Hawke* show Eddison paying close, specific attention to events attending World War I and acknowledging them as disasters. Fantasy allowed Eddison to critique these disasters from without. As Hobsbawm avers, society had lost sight of its capacity for goodness in the wake of World War I, allowing itself to be swept along on a tide of abstract ideas and meaningless violence, and those living in such times must be portrayed in that light. Anne Bremmerdale, Mary's fatalistic riding companion, is an example of such a portrayal. Edward Lessingham, however, comes from a place—fiction—that exists for the specific purpose of portraying the kernels of humanity, where ideas are never abstract and where warfare and violence, when they happen, serve considered authorial purposes. Coming from that frame of reference, he is ill-equipped to alter the course of earthly history, but he is uniquely qualified to point that course out to those caught up in it. Fantasy literature had, in fact, allowed Eddison a way to critique his times as a whole. Through a process of trial and error that nobody native to this world would think to undertake, Edward explores the Age of Catastrophe, ascertains its essential features, and reports findings very similar to those Hobsbawm offered fifty years later.

Not everybody living in the Age of Catastrophe possessed such detachment. The fascists, as analyzed by Hobsbawm, were so caught up in the brutality of World War I as to lose humanitarian perspective (26–27). They therefore felt that great men could solve problems via the application of further brutal force, and used appeals to an imagined past of militarized glory to justify horrifying atrocities (118). Edward Lessingham certainly exemplifies an imagined past. And yet in 1923, when a friend asks his opinion on the then-ascendant Mussolini:

> Lessingham answered with a shrug. "There is the better always, and there is the worse. But the mischief is more in the game than in the player. In mankind, not in particular men. The field, and the apparatus, are too much overgrown and sprawling." (543)

Eddison thus brings fascism into Edward's aforementioned critique of Earthly statecraft (541–45) in order to have his hero dismiss it as more of the same. The decision to explicitly name Mussolini here invites the reader to consider regimes such as his in light of that discussion. Doing so is an intriguing exercise. Fascists preached human courage and valor but practiced impersonal, industrialized pragmatism, coveting size, quantity and extent. Their armament campaigns—so much in the news as Eddison wrote—illustrate well "the cold lechery of *more and more*," inimical, in Edward's estimation, to the very sort of courage and honor they were supposed to empower. Edward's shrug is therefore predictable. He critiques the game ahead of the player, but he has little time for those who persist in playing a game that will reduce men to termites, particularly, it seems, if they are going to strut on balconies claiming it will do the opposite. Hobsbawm agrees, lambasting the fascist pursuit of chimerical traditions via "technological modernity," a contradiction appealing to "the resentments of little men" (118–19). Edward is a chimera himself, but Eddison has him spurn a perfect opportunity to praise fascism, instead having him critique the phenomenon in ways that anticipate subsequent historians. Eddison is therefore hardly the nascent fascist that de Camp (133) suggests he is. This is not the story of a little man contributing to the horrors of the Age of Catastrophe. It is a creative, searching portrayal of a great man grasping the constraints on his potential and doing his best in an imperfect world.

Edward remains great, however. As he grasps his position as an inapplicable ideal, he nevertheless remains a towering and unshakeable idealist. What makes him so is Mary. The Lessingham marriage is an idealized literary love writ large on Earth, a perfect combination of physical and spiritual pleasures. Zimiamvia is a utopia because, in that happy land, love conquers all; it is the only relevant motivation and those acting in its service are unquestionably assumed to be acting heroically. Edward brings that mentality to Earth by acting in the service of this redheaded, Grecian-profiled, cheerfully self-possessed "treasure of all hearts" (429), hence his fabulous career. In her name he scales mountains, creates statues, paints beautiful portraits, builds a gorgeous house, rediscovers lost Viking treasures and seeks out places of outstanding natural beauty, jobs that take unquestioned precedence over the empty termite-work of government (420). He ventures into the public sphere where he can be of use—he is revealed to have been covertly instrumental in the downfall of Bela Kun, a communist despot who briefly controlled post-imperial Hungary in 1919 (558; cf. Joll 248–49)—but love, not war, guides his actions. He asserts in 1919 that

> A man can build his freedom in any age, any land. I can live as well today as I could have in Egil Skallagrimson's time, or Walter Ralegh's [sic] [...] If I couldn't, I'd be a failure then too. (482)

He can live well because a properly-motivated man is always great, and can always rise above his troubles and do great things. The absurdities of Earth may well mean that Edward's flesh is inapplicably weak, but his motivation—his spirit—remains untarnished, because that motivation is eternal. The only circumstance that love is subject to, after all, is the presence of the beloved. This point is brought home to Edward in 1923, when Mary is killed in a train wreck. Only a 1933 visitation from Aphrodite, the goddess of love (560–63), stills thoughts of suicide (552; 562), and even then he subsequently confines his activities to fields and places "outside the ordinary texture of modern life" (*Mistress of Mistresses* 16). Mary's importance is clarified by her absence; all that is of value is accomplished out of love. This is essentially what this Zimiamvian hero has been sent on his fish-out-of-water expedition to appreciate.

Eddison firmly believed that it was by keeping mindful of this point that his contemporaries could end the Age of Catastrophe. When wartime paper shortages prevented the publication of a British edition of *A Fish Dinner in Memison* in 1941, he argued passionately with his publishers for the topical value of his book. This correspondence is peppered with such statements as this:

> I have a strong impression that there is a growing public (more than ever, perhaps, in wartime) for books that offer a taste of new air, not so much irrelevant to our troubles as above them. Such air is champagne; not dope, but a tonic, & a foundation-rock for action and endurance. (BL, MS Eng. lett. c. 232, 173)

World War II was a terrible burden, and would cost Britain dearly. Eddison understood this all too well; by the time he wrote the letter quoted above, his son-in-law had been killed flying with the RAF (that the novel is dedicated to his memory is further proof, if such is needed, of Eddison's lack of fascist sympathies). Nevertheless he remained steadfastly convinced this new war would be won by the right party, and the British would once again have the freedom to attend to the loves and passions that made life worth living. What concerned Eddison was that people might become so caught up in the all-encompassing utilitarian mechanisms of modern warfare as to forget those human passions, as the fascists had. Something had to be done to restore British society's self-belief and faith in their future. He argued that *A Fish Dinner in Memison*, a portrayal of a man grasping the imperfections of the world and yet remaining mindful of an eternal ideal, would reaffirm that faith. It would encourage readers, steadying their nerves and stiffening their resolve in the fight against fascism. So emboldened, he was sure, Britain could not be defeated.[2] Exactly how successful this exercise would have been is impossible know; the publishers were not swayed.[3] Nevertheless Eddison's claims for the novel rest on an assessment of evolving public mood over his literary career that, once again, anticipates subsequent historical analysis of the matter. Hobsbawm suggests, for example, that the capitulation of France to the Nazi invasion of 1940 was caused more by the demoralization of a nation traumatized by the previous war than by German military superiority (30). Eddison feared Britain might go the same way. He employed fantasy, with its unique ability to portray and affirm human ideals, in his attempt to forestall that possibility. It had helped him remain grounded in a bewildering time in history, and he wished to share that affirmation with others. In time, of course, his confidence was vindicated.

Fantasy literature allows authors to create fictional spaces that throw the conundrums of reality into new lights. E. R. Eddison gradually grew into that power over the course of his career, and World War I proved to be a significant spur to that maturation. His first novel, written during and after the war, does not explicitly depict it. This should not be taken as a sign of ignorance on his part; the impact of the war was inescapable, and faint resonances of it can be detected in Eddison's

---

2. Eddison's argument on this matter is discussed in detail in my article "Aphrodite on the Home Front: E. R. Eddison and World War II"; the article also examines his rejection of fascism in further detail.

3. At least in Britain; the book's 1941 publication date refers to a separate American edition that appeared in that year.

fictional conflict. As the long-term consequences of the war became apparent, furthermore, Eddison addressed them explicitly and innovatively. In *A Fish Dinner in Memison* he uses fantasy not to deny the troubles engendered by World War I, but to offer new, strikingly well-informed critiques of them—critiques that closely parallel those made by subsequent historians. In doing so he offered his contemporaries no easy answers, but encouraged them to know their enemies—both the bugbears of their own minds and the fools who had lost themselves in this dark new age—the better to defeat them. So Eddison must not be seen as a naïve reactionary. He was an overtly and consciously timely writer pushing the didactic and interrogative potential of his genre to address a particularly difficult time in history, and a thinker of eccentric but sincere and triumphant humanity.

WORKS CITED

Adams, Michael C. C. *The Great Adventure: Male Desire and the Coming of World War I.* Bloomington: Indiana UP, 1990. Print.

Calder, Kenneth J. *Britain and the Origins of the New Europe 1914–1918.* Cambridge: Cambridge UP, 1976. Print.

de Camp, L. Sprague. "Superman in a Bowler: E. R. Eddison." *Literary Swordsmen and Sorcerers: The Creators of Modern Fantasy.* Sauk City: Arkham House, 1976. 114–34. Print.

Eddison, E. R. Eddison papers. SRQ 823.91 ED23. Leeds Central Library, local history division. Note that this file contains several hundred pages of manuscripts, letters and miscellaneous papers, but has no internal inventory or pagination. It is therefore not possible to be more specific when referring to its contents.

—. Eddison papers. MS Eng. lett. e. 231. Bodleian Library, Oxford.

—. Eddison papers. MS Eng. lett., c. 232. Bodleian Library, Oxford.

—. Eddison papers. MS Eng. misc. e. 456. Bodleian Library, Oxford.

—. *A Fish Dinner in Memison.* 1941. *Zimiamvia: A Trilogy.* Ed. Paul Edmund Thomas. New York: Dell, 1992. 309–569. Print.

—. *The Mezentian Gate.* 1958. *Zimiamvia: A Trilogy.* Ed. Paul Edmund Thomas. New York: Dell, 1992. 581–856. Print.

—. *Mistress of Mistresses.* 1935. *Zimiamvia: A Trilogy.* Ed. Paul Edmund Thomas. New York: Dell, 1992. 1–307. Print.

—. *The Worm Ouroboros.* 1922. London: Ballantine, 1962. Print.

Fink, Carole. "The Peace Settlement 1919–1939." *A Companion to World War I.* Ed. John Horne. Oxford: Blackwell, 2012. 543–57. Print.

Gooch, G. P., and Harold Temperley, eds. *British Documents on the Origins of the War 1898–1914.* Vol. 6. London: His Majesty's Stationary Office, 1930. Print.

Harris-Fain, Darren. "E. R. Eddison." *Dictionary of Literary Biography.* Ed. Darren Harris-Fain. Vol. 255. Farmington Hills: Gale Group, 2002. 74–81. Print.

Hobsbawm, Eric J. *Age of Extremes: The Short Twentieth Century 1914–1991.* London: Abacus, 1995. Print.

Hupchick, Dennis P. *The Balkans from Constantinople to Communism.* New York: Palgrave, 2002. Print.

Joll, James. *Europe Since 1870: An International History.* 4th ed. London: Penguin 1990. Print.

Paine, Lincoln P. *Ships of the World: An Historical Encyclopedia.* New York: Houghton Mifflin, 1997. Print.
Parotti, Phillip. "War in the Tropics: East Africa and Burma." *The Great World War 1914–1945.* Vol. 1. Ed. John Bourne, Peter Liddle and Ian Whitehead. London: HarperCollins, 2000. 159–79. Print.
Röhl, John C. G. *The Kaiser and His Court: Wilhelm II and the Government of Germany.* Cambridge: Cambridge UP, 1994. Print.
Steiner, Zara S., and Keith Neilson. *Britain and the Origins of the First World War.* 2nd ed. New York: Palgrave MacMillan, 2003. Print.
Thomas, Paul Edmund. Introduction and notes. *Zimiamvia: A Trilogy.* Ed. Paul Edmund Thomas. New York: Dell, 1992. xix–xlvii and 857–965. Print.
Wasserstein, Bernard. *Barbarism and Civilization; A History of Europe in Our Time.* Oxford: Oxford UP, 2007. Print.
Young, Joseph. "Aphrodite on the Home Front: E. R. Eddison and World War II." *Mythlore* 30.3/4 (#117/118) (Spring/Summer 2012): 71–88. Print.

T. H. White and the Lasting Influence of World War I:
King Arthur at War

ASHLEY PFEIFFER

UNLIKE OTHER FANTASY NOVELISTS who came to prominence in the era after World War I, Terrance Hanbury White never served in the war. However, he grew up in a world greatly changed by it, and the question of the justness of war pervades his work, especially his best known work. White's *The Once and Future King* tells the story of King Arthur from his childhood as Wart to his end in battle against his son, Mordred. However, White concerns himself with more than just the history and romance of Arthur's story. He has set a question before his audience: Why do human beings war among each other? White explores this question throughout the five novels of his Arthurian series. The Romantic and chivalrous Arthurian figures are juxtaposed against modern British events and ideas in order to reveal disparities between traditional depictions of Victorian and Arthurian warfare and the new method of Total War born out of World Wars I and II.

T. H. White was born on May 29, 1906 (Warner 25). He was too young to have experienced any of the battles of World War I first hand, but came in to his prime during the Interwar period that lasted from 1918-1939. White was part of a unique, transitional generation of British cultural history, which lived through the massive emotional upheaval caused by World War I (Green 48). Notions of chivalrous, gentlemanly war could not survive the Great War. As Paul Fussell notes, for example, "Dawn has never recovered from what the Great War did to it" (*Great War and Modern Memory* 63). Dawn, especially in the Romantic painting and poetry that were the traditional staples of Arthuriana, symbolized "tokens of hope and peace, and rural charm" (52). However, following the Great War, dawn lost these positive associations, instead gaining "modern associations [...]: cold, the death of multitudes, insensate marching in files, battle, and corpses too shallowly interred" (63). Dawn becomes inextricably linked with battle, its beauty overshadowed by the battles that begin at sunrise and dangers that increase with the light. *The Once and Future King* highlights a similar rupture between the Romantic and the postwar by contrasting the story of the idealistic young Wart and the embittered, exhausted Arthur. The Interwar period during which White grew up and taught continued the process of denigrating Romantic ideals by drawing attention to the hypocrisy and callousness of the leaders of the Great War and their willingness to sacrifice the young (Green 52). Victorian ideals returned in satires and parodies, rather than as a true revival (28). World War II finally put an end to Victorian notion of war, and it was during this war that White completed *The Once and Future King* (Warner 186).

Although White lacked the combat experience that marked other significant fantasy writers influenced by World War I, he still grew up in a world changed and scarred by the war. His father, Garrick White, a member of the Indian Police, retired shortly after the end of the war, and he and his wife reunited with their son in England (Warner 32). "England was full of the retired, the disbanded, the disabled, the ex-servicemen who had given up jobs to fight and found no jobs after the war had ended, and who were scraping up livelihoods as chicken-farmers, salesmen, secretaries to golf-clubs" (32). The England White inhabited had been significantly changed by the war. The need for labor was not high enough to meet the demand for employment. Returning veterans and a diminished need for a large standing army affected White's original plan to join the service after his schooling (33). Instead, he was encouraged by his headmasters and tutors to continue his education and eventually attended Queens' College (34). While at Queens' College, White began the literary education that in conjunction with his personal and cultural education become the essential foundation for writing *The Once and Future King*.

White's Arthur represents a number of different time periods. While describing his novels to his good friend, Sydney Cockerell, White stated "I am trying to write of *an imaginary world which was imagined in the 15th century*" (Warner 133, emphasis in original). White had the benefit of using both Malory and the sources Malory used to write *Le Morte d'Arthur*. However, White did not just wish to tell the story of King Arthur; he wanted to provide a "good allusive criticism of chivalry" (*Letters* 94) and an antidote to war. "One of White's major aims in dealing with historical material in *The Once and Future King* was to draw parallels between past and present" (Brewer 206). These parallels are meant to guide the present generation in avoiding the mistakes of their predecessors. Arthur's triumphs and tribulations provide a guide for the boys of White's audience, many of whom were preparing for World War II when *The Sword in the Stone* was written. White hoped to use the Arthur's example, paired with modern allusions, to warn the present generation of the fruitlessness of war.

The groundwork for White's Arthurian saga began during his time at Queens' College, when he studied Thomas Malory and *Le Morte d'Arthur*. While seemingly unimpressed with the power of the language of the text, White was later drawn to the cultural implications of the value of *Morte d'Arthur* as a story. He describes this discovery and the publication of *The Sword in the Stone* in a letter to his longtime friend, mentor, and correspondent, L. J. Potts:

> I think it [*The Sword and the Stone*] is one of my better books, so probably no one else will. It is a preface to Malory. Do you remember I once wrote a thesis on the *Morte d'Arthur*? Naturally I did not read Malory when writing the thesis on him, but one time last autumn I got desperate among my books and picked him up in lack of anything else. Then I was thrilled and astonished to find that (a) The thing was a perfect tragedy, with a beginning, a middle and an end implicit in the beginning and (b) the characters were real people with recognisable reactions which could be forecast. Mordred was hateful, Kay a decent chap with an inferiority complex, Gawaine that rarest of literary productions, a swine with a solid streak of decency. He was a sterling fellow to his own clan. Arthur, Lancelot and even Galahad were really glorious people-- not pre-raphaelite prigs. (*Letters* 93)

White, aside from demonstrating the study habits recognizable to any who has written a thesis, makes an important distinction between his conception of Malory's work and the past's. T. H. White is not interested in reproducing the language of the *Morte d'Arthur* or the characterizations of works like *Idylls of the King*. Instead, he will produce a narrative of Arthur's journey from boy to man to king, and through this journey make a flat caricature into a rounded character.

The Once and Future King grows along with Arthur and matures as he does. The first two sections of the novel, *The Sword and the Stone* and *The Queen of Air and Darkness,* are concerned with disabusing Arthur of the notion that war is a game. Merlyn fears that Arthur will suffer from the same vices as his predecessors: "The trouble with Norman Aristocracy is that they are games-mad, that is what it is, games-mad" (55). Arthur, at the beginning of Merlyn's education, is unable to think beyond the glory of knighthood and what good fun fighting will be. After a minor battle in the second Gaelic War, Arthur muses that "Well it was a good battle […] It was a jolly battle, and I won it myself, and it was fun" (227). Until Merlyn reminds Arthur about the loss of "seven hundred" kerns and "one [knight] who [was injured] falling off [his] horse" (227), Arthur cannot think beyond the simple schoolboy terms of winning and losing. Merlyn laments that "the link between Norman warfare and Victorian foxhunting is perfect" (240). However, the link can be made between the general Victorian attitudes toward sports in general and warfare, not just foxhunting.

Victorian warfare differed greatly from the warfare that of World War I and later. Most wars that took place during the Victorian era were a result of skirmishes over expanding imperial borders. The image of the typical British soldier (reflected in Arthur's kern) improved slightly from that of an "idle, drunken, hard-swearing fighting man" (Newsome 106) to a necessary component of the British Empire. However, Victorians refused to compromise on their traditional image of an officer. David Newsome states that the "Duke of Cambridge was never shaken in his conviction that 'the British officer should be a gentleman first and an officer second' " (107). Chivalry was a trait the Victorians held dear, and a young man's participation in games was an excellent way to prove that he had the makings of a gentleman. Games and sportsmanship grew in importance as the Empire and its definitions of a gentleman and a Briton both expanded. "Decency, fortitude, grit, civilization, Christianity, commerce, all blend into one—the game!" (Eksteins 122). The "games-mad" (White 55) gentlemen that Merlyn warns Arthur against use their tournaments and quests to define themselves as English, as a part of Arthur's Round Table.

"Sports [...] were to serve both a moral and a physical purpose; they would encourage self-reliance and team spirit; they would build up the individual and integrate him into the group" (Eksteins 121). However, in *The Once and Future King*, these purposes failed; sports did not integrate the knights into a group. Tournaments and quests instead contributed to fracturing alliances and, eventually, the Round Table; sport in Gramarye pitted knights against one another, creating tension and bad blood:

> The people walking round the ground in their best frocks, from Grand Stand to Refreshment Tent, must have found the fighting very like the game [of cricket]. It took a frightfully long time—Sir Lancelot's innings frequently lasted all day, if he were battling against a good knight—and the movements had a feeling of slow-motion, because of the weight of the armor. When the sword-play had begun, the combatants stood opposite each other in the green acre like batsman and bowler—except that they stood closer together—and perhaps Sir Gawaine would start with an in-swinger, which Sir Lancelot would put away to leg with a beautiful leg-glide, and then Lancelot would reply with a yorker under Gawaine's guard—it was called "foining"—and all the people round the field would clap. (330)

White's use of cricket imagery to describe jousting conveys vital information about the attitude of Arthur's court toward games and class. Until the Interwar period, cricket was not only England's " 'best loved game', it was also 'more than a game'. It was held to embody a style of behavior and a system of values that were distinctively English" (Cronin and Holt 115). White could have used no better sport than cricket to compare to jousting, as no sport carries the same chivalric, upper class connotations. "Cricket involved self-control, instant acceptance of the umpire's decision, obedience to the captain and respect for the other team" (Cronin and Holt 115). Thus, by comparing Lancelot to the best modern cricket players in the world, "Bradman and Woolley," White transposed the traits of a world-class cricket player to Lancelot, proving to a modern "games-mad" audience that Lancelot was "the greatest knight King Arthur had" (330).

The real-world Victorian attitude toward warfare ends with the dawn of total war. Arthur's introduction to total warfare occurs in *The Queen of Air and Darkness* during the Battle of Bedegraine. After Merlyn enlightens Arthur as to the casualties among the kerns in a minor battle, Arthur decides the eleven kings must be taught that war is not a game (240). Lot is now "faced by an enemy who seemed to accept the death of gentlemen as a part of warfare" (311). Arthur's new brand of total war does not spare the rich, chivalrous, or powerful. The "Victorian" view of war as game has been dealt a swift blow by the Battle of Bedegraine. The Gaelic kings expect the war to continue until Arthur capitulates and pays a hefty ransom, but they foresee few casualties (306); however, Arthur refuses to continue the war according to the traditional rules of combat. Merlyn warns that if he fails to subdue the eleven kings, he will fight territorial skirmishes for his whole career (240). By choosing to annihilate the kings in one battle, collapsing the classes of knight and kern, Arthur breaks the battle traditions prized by the Gaelic kings and establishes his own. These new rules begin to slowly disrupt the games-mania associated with the idealized style of "Victorian" warfare.

Arthur commits two atrocities when he introduces total warfare to the Gaelic Kings. He interrupts the traditional scheduling practices for battle that Lot and the other Gaelic Kings follow when fighting, and he eschews the traditional fighting partners:

> The first one was that he did not wait the fashionable hour. He ought to have marshaled his Battle opposite Lot's, as soon as their breakfast was over, and then, at about midday when the lines were properly in order, he should have given the signal to begin. The signal having been given, he should have charged Lot's footmen with his knights, while Lot's knights charged his footmen, and there would have been a splendid slaughter. [...]
>
> The King's second atrocity was that he neglected the kerns themselves. That part of the battle, the racial struggle which had a

> certain reality even if it was a wicked one, he left to the races themselves. (308–09)

Arthur refuses to play by the rules of war established by the Gaelic Kings. The practice of warfare by the Kings resembles a game or a sport; there is a set time and method to practicing the game. The loss of human lives is diminished by naming the participants as their roles, rather than as autonomous actors. The old traditions described in the passage above could just as easily describe a chess match as a massive battle. Arthur interrupts the game of war with the reality of war.

As *The Once and Future King* closely mirrors the history of White's modern England, the Battle of Bedegraine parallels the beginning of World War I, England's introduction to total war. "[T]he Great War took place in what was, compared with ours, a static world, where the values appeared stable and where the meanings of abstractions seemed permanent and reliable" (Fussell, *Great War* 21). This "static world" and its adherence to old rules allow Arthur to win the Battle of Bedegraine. The other kings are unable to fathom changes to traditional ways of warfare. However, this "static world" also contributes to Arthur's downfall, as he will wrestle with the concepts of chivalry and might versus right for his entire reign. For Arthur and his generation, chivalry holds value and does not need to be redefined after the introduction of total war. However, Mordred and his generation have little to no respect for chivalry. "Mordred and Agravaine thought Arthur hypocritical—as all decent men must be, if you assume decency can't exist" (505). The word is intangible. Past standards for decency, Arthur's standards for decency, mean little to Mordred because of the disruption between the past and present generations; just as Lot's version of decency is dismissed and toppled by Arthur, so too is Arthur's version of decency dismissed by Mordred. However, Arthur exists in a key transitional generation where he can acknowledge the faults within his own generation, yet cannot acknowledge the slippage and disruption of words like *chivalrous* and *decent* when used by men like Mordred and Agravaine to undermine the words' very definition. A conversation between Arthur and Mordred about decency would be conducted in something akin to two different languages.

The Battle of Bedegraine signals the beginning of the death of innocence that characterizes the *Queen of Air and Darkness*. Fussell states that the beginning of the Great War "was more innocent" than previous wars (*Great War* 18). However, White concludes *The Queen of Air and Darkness* by acknowledging "in tragedy, that innocence is not enough" (323). At the Battle of Bedegraine, Arthur defeats Lot; as a result, Queen

Morgause, Lot's wife, decides to bring her children and retinue to pay tribute to Arthur. While at Arthur's court, Morgause seduces Arthur, a virgin (322) and the epitome of innocence; however, by entangling himself with Morgause and begetting Mordred, he loses this innocence. White commented that "the real reason why Arthur came to a bad end was because he had slept with his sister. It is a perfectly Aristotelian tragedy and it was the offspring of this union who finally killed him" (qtd. in Brewer 49). As a result of his loss of innocence, Arthur eventually loses his life and his kingdom.

Before Arthur's fractious relationship with his son becomes a factor in the later books of *The Once and Future King*, White introduces another critical issue for Arthur to overcome. The king needs to find a way to control his growing number of knights and to divert their attention in order to keep them from warring amongst themselves or falling victim to "Games-Mania" (455). Arthur decides the best course of action is to send his knights away from court on a quest for the Holy Grail. "If our [Arthur's] Might was given a channel so that it worked for God, instead of for the rights of man, surely that would stop the rot, and be worth doing?" (457). Arthur loses half of his knights in the quest, and the ones who return from the quest are the knights who were not holy enough to succeed; the quest left Arthur's kingdom worse off than when he began (459). Arthur's quest is less religiously motivated than politically motivated. He is engaging in social imperialism: "A combination of an imperialist foreign policy and programmes of social reform, frequently introduced in order to quell internal social upheaval" (*OED*). Arthur uses the Grail Quest to consolidate his power in England by removing the troubling influence of the knights and allowing his kingdom to function without the infighting between them. However, by sending the knights away and accepting the failed questers who return, Arthur severely weakens his kingdom. The best and brightest of Arthur's kingdom, Galahad and Percivale, are dead. Other knights have murdered their brothers. Some knights "came limping on crutches, or leading spent horses which could carry them no longer, or, as one did who had lost a hand in battle, carrying the one hand in the other. All these men looked worn and confused. Their face were fanatical, and they babbled of dreams" (459). The men returning from The Grail Quest mirror the wounded returning from the battlefields for World War I. Men returned wounded, crippled, or suffering from neurasthenia (Eksteins 173). Arthur's Grail Quest weakened his kingdom sufficiently for Mordred to begin his own machinations for the throne.

The relationship between Mordred and Arthur was suggestive of the relationship of upper class fathers and sons of England in the 1930s (Green 71):

> The golden lads had been sacrificed, it was felt, by "the old men," "the generals," and "the hard-faced men who did well out of the war." [...] For [the young] men the war meant not so much the great mistake as the great failure—it was the political diminishment of England and the moral enfeeblement of the new postwar Englishman. But both interpretations aroused the same feeling of the horror of the war, and of the official patriotism that had energized it. The men of letters remembered that, and since the nation as a whole was not going to change, they in some sense withdrew from the nation.
>
> There was also a feeling that England's old hierarchical order had been injured irreparably, in various ways. One was the breaking up of landed estates, a process that had, in fact, begun before but that felt like a post war phenomenon. Another, less tangible, was the decline in sports. (Green 52–54)

Looking at *The Once in Future King* in these terms, Arthur is part of the successful, older generation which condemns the younger generation to death for personal gain. In fact, upon finding out that Mordred's fate would be to overthrow him, Arthur "let them make a proclamation that all the children born at a certain time were to be put in a big ship and floated out to sea" (579). However, Mordred survives Arthur's attempt at infanticide and plots to overthrow his father as a result.

While Mordred survives the shipwreck, it leaves him with a "hunchback" (586). This hunchback means that "he has a weak body that he has failed in [Arthur's] sports" (580). As a failure at both tournaments and knighthood, Mordred has little value in Arthur's kingdom. Yet his lack of value is a direct result of Arthur's actions when Mordred was a child; Arthur has crippled his son, ruining the prospects of the new generation. Since Mordred cannot find a place in Arthur's court, he chooses to make his own, like the younger generation in Britain in the 1930s. These Bright Young Things attempted to break the prevailing social as an act of defiance against the generation they saw as having weakened their country and kin (Green 72). White delights in describing the reformed court, after the grail quest: "Marital fidelity has become 'news.' Clothes had become fantastic. [...] Mordred wore his ridiculous shoes contemptuously: they were a satire on himself. They court was modern" (504–05). The younger court is inscrutable to Arthur's generation; they were too sick-making.

However, Mordred also resembles another, darker rebellious figure of the 1930s, Adolf Hitler (Gallix 283). Mordred takes advantage of the social upheaval caused by the infighting between Lancelot and Gawaine and forms his "New Order" (624):

> Their aims were some kind of nationalism with Gaelic autonomy, and a massacre of the Jews as well, in revenge for a mythical saint called Hugh of Lincoln. There were already thousands, spread over the country, who carried his badge of a scarlet fist clenching a whip, and who called themselves Thrashers. (628)

While the mention of Hugh of Lincoln, a figure evoked in English literature as early as Chaucer's "The Prioress's Tale," connects Mordred to England's own complex history of anti-Semitism, the similarities to Hitler are pronounced and undeniable. White's modern audience would read the propaganda calling for the extermination of Jews as a reference to the Nazi party, which was formed during the 1930s under the pretense of reuniting and rebuilding Germany after World War I. The "scarlet badge" evokes the red badge with the black swastika favored by Hitler's Nazis. Just as Mordred's dandy costume represents his ties to Britain of the 1930s, his Thrasher costume ties him to Nazi Germany. "Both [Gawaine and Mordred] were in black. [...] Mordred had begun dressing with this dramatic simplicity since he had become a leader of the popular party" (628). "Mordred's uniform is a manifestation of his political aims, but at the same time his splendid outward appearance helps to conceal his madness" (Berger 138). Mordred's simple black uniform evokes images of the SS uniforms worn by the special police in the late 1930s and World War II as well as foreshadowing his key role in the outbreak of the upcoming war and Arthur's demise.

" 'Civilization seems to have become insane' [Guenever] said. 'Yes, and it seems we that we have made it so' " was Lancelot's response (625). This conversation, occurring during a lull in the fighting between Lancelot and Arthur, represents a common theme in the literature of both World Wars. "The absurdity of it all became an obsession" (Fussell, *Great War* 64). Lancelot and Guenever recognize that collapse of the Round Table is caused by internal issues, a lack of understanding between all parties involved. Inaction on Arthur's part and mistrust, betrayal, and miscommunication between key figures like Gawaine and Lancelot have allowed young insurgents like Mordred to gain control.

The final blow against Arthur's regime in *The Once and Future King* is not Arthur's death, which does not occur in the novel, but the siege of the Tower of London (658). The Queen has barred herself in the Tower, and Mordred is besieging the battlement with cannons. Arthur declares "Now that the guns have come, the Table is over" (658). This scene was written shortly after the London Blitzkrieg, which occurred in 1940. A characteristic of World War II was the belief that precision bombing could cripple a nation and effectively win the war (Fussell 16), a belief that carried over from the introduction of bombing in World War I. Mordred is the first character to use cannons in *The Once and Future King*, and as the Bishop of Rochester laments, the first "to use cannons against men!" (658). Mordred's use of the cannon brings the narrative's allusions into the era of World War II, but it places Mordred in a position of authority, rather than Arthur. During the Battle of Bedegraine, Arthur had the advantage over King Lot as he was utilizing the "atrocity" of total war, but now Mordred has the advantage of new technology, a technology that evokes the image of a recently destroyed London, which would have wrung an emotional response from White's original audience.

Although White did not fight in World War II, he considered his Arthurian saga a small wartime service. "Since there is no justification for war, a writer must not write propaganda about airplanes and air power; his duty is to write about mankind" (Lott 7). White undertook this duty in order to educate his readers about the causes of war and possible solutions. While White uses the life and times of King Arthur to tell a frame narrative about the ills of war, he also uses a variety of animal parables to teach young Wart, and by extension the audience, about the causes of war. The clearest and best understood of the examples are those of the geese and the ants.

While confined to his sick room after an adventure with Robin Wood, Wart is transformed into an ant by Merlyn and placed into the enclosure housing two different tribes (White 120). Wart finds the ants to be a war-like society that shares traits with fascists and communists. The ants have no individual property, not even their own bodies (127). The ants also make use of war propaganda:

> A. We are so numerous that we are starving.
> B. Therefore we must encourage still larger families so as to become more numerous and starving.
> C. When we are so numerous and starving as all that, obviously we shall have a right to take other people's stores of seed. Besides, we shall by then have a numerous and starving army. (127–28)

This propaganda closely mirrors the Nazi doctrine of *Lebensraum*, living space, which was the belief espoused by Adolf Hitler that the German people were so numerous that they needed to expand in order to continue to feed and house their expanding population (Gallix 289). Wart finds that the ants will fight and kill any ant from a different nest, so when ants from a new nest begin wandering over a rush bridge Wart and Merlyn created, war erupts (White 127). Merlyn removes Wart before he is forced to participate in the war.

After the ants, Merlyn again uses his magic to transform Wart into a goose and sends his charge on a journey with them. When asked about war, a goose responds "what creature could be so low as to go about in bands, to murder others of its own blood?" (171). The geese have no concept of war, unlike the ants, and White illustrates their main political difference as the belief in national boundaries. Ants believe firmly in boundaries, murdering ants from other nests, but "There are no boundaries among the geese" (172). Humankind's belief in national boundaries is a direct cause of their tendency to war among themselves: "It was geography which was the cause [of war]—political geography. It was nothing else. […] Countries would have to become counties— but counties which could keep their own culture and local laws. The imaginary lines on the earth's surface only needed to be unimagined" (676). The abolition of national boundaries appears to be White's ideal solution, as presented by Merlyn and again by an aged Arthur. However, White presents another solution to war simply by recounting the history of King Arthur.

The Once and Future King ends before the final battle between Arthur and Mordred. As Mordred represents Hitler and Arthur, England, *The Once and Future King* ends on the eve of an allegorical World War II. According to his diary, White believed "Pendragon [could] still be saved" (Warner 176). By ending the novel on the eve of battle, rather than with the death of Arthur, White places the characters in stasis. They are forever locked in a state of indecision, leaving the audience hoping that they will make decisions that will prove in opposition to hundreds of years of Arthurian literature. This stasis forces the audience to evaluate the costs and benefits of war. White ends the story with a small cameo by Tom of Newbold Revell, or Thomas Malory. Arthur passes his tale on to young Tom with instructions to make sure he is remembered (674). Elisabeth Brewer notes the optimism of this ending: "in keeping the candle burning, in keeping the story of Arthur alive, Tom can give him immortality and perhaps save future generations from the hell on earth of war. So there is both a grandeur and a hopeful finality in White's ending" (Brewer 125). By including this cameo by Thomas Malory, White serves two purposes. He gives his book a source to trace itself back to, and he emphasizes the importance of Arthur's antiwar sentiments on the eve of his final battle.

> In explicitly identifying the text with the interwar period and subsequent outbreak of the Second World War, White's alignment to Malory has the effect of dissociating *The Sword in the Stone* [and *The Once and Future King*] from the last major retelling of the story, namely

Alfred Lord Tennyson's *Idylls of the King* (1859–85) and the pseudo-medievalism of High Victorian Arthuriana. (Jackson 46)

Arthur's final act as king in *The Once and Future King* is to renounce the Victorian interpretation of his story, which no longer applies to post-WWI England, and to champion a renewal of Malory's version of the tale, which closely mirrors the troubled and uncertain British Empire of White's era.

Although White completed the final book in his Arthurian saga in 1941, *The Once and Future King* was not published until 1958 (Brewer 227). The topic of war could not have been far from White's mind during the writing of the books comprising *The Once and Future King* during early days of World War II. In writing about England's hero, King Arthur, in a dark time in England's history, White chose to examine changes in his country's attitudes toward war from the Victorians to his own generation through the historical ideal of King Arthur. *The Once and Future King* is more than just a children's story or an Arthurian Romance; it is a plea for an end to senseless war, a lament for humankind's past mistakes, and a proposal for a better future.

Works Consulted

Berger, Christiane. "More than Fashion: T. H. White's Use of Dress as a Means of Characterization." *Connotations* 7.1 (1997/98): 135–40. Print.

Brewer, Elisabeth. *T. H. White's The Once and Future King*. Cambridge: D. S. Brewer, 1993. Print.

Cronin, Mike and Richard Holt. "The Imperial Game in Crisis: English Cricket and Decolonisation." *British Culture and the End of Empire*. Ed. Stuart Ward. New York: Manchester UP, 2001. 111–27. Print.

Eksteins, Modris. *Rites of Spring*. New York: Mariner Books, 2000. Print.

Fussell, Paul. *The Great War and Modern Memory*. 25th anniv. ed. New York: Oxford UP, 2000. Print.

—. *Wartime*. New York: Oxford UP, 1989. Print.

Gallix, François, ed. "T. H. White and the Legend of King Arthur: From Animal Fantasy to Political Morality." *King Arthur: A Casebook*. New York: Garland, 1996. 281–97. Print.

Green, Martin. *Children of the Sun*. Mount Jackson: Axios Press, 2008. Print.

Jackson, Aaron Isaac. "Writing Arthur, Writing England: Myth and Modernity in T. H. White's the Sword in the Stone." *Lion and the Unicorn* 33.1 (2009): 44–59. Print.

Lott, Hershel Woodley. *The Social and Political Ideals in the Major Writings of T. H. White*. Diss. U of Southern Mississippi, 1970. Ann Arbor: UMI, 1990. Print.

Newsome, David. *The Victorian World Picture*. New Brunswick: Rutgers UP, 1997. Print.

Warner, Sylvia Townsend. *T. H. White*. London: Jonathan Cape, 1967. Print.

White, T. H. *Letters to a Friend: The Correspondence Between T. H. White and L. J. Potts*. Ed. François Gallix. New York: Viking, 1968. Print.

—. *The Once and Future King*. New York: Penguin, 1996. Print.

Contributors

NORA ALFAIZ holds an M.A. in Literature from American University, and is currently a Ph.D. student in British and Postcolonial Studies at George Washington University. She attended summer courses at Oxford University over a few years and completed a seminar on J. R. R. Tolkien and his work. She is a regular contributor at *Oasis Magazine*, where she has written articles ranging from book to art reviews.

DAVID J. CARLSON is Professor of English at California State University, where he specializes in American Indian Literatures and early American Literature. Professor Carlson is the author of *Sovereign Selves: American Indian Autobiography and the Law* (University of Illinois Press, 2006) and of several articles and book chapters focused on American Indian literature and other American writers. He is currently completing a new book entitled *Reading Sovereignty: The Discourse of Self-Determination in American Indian Law and Literature*. Professor Carlson is also founding co-editor of the on-line journal *Transmotion*, which focuses on avant-garde, transnational, and post-modern indigenous literatures.

S. BRETT CARTER studied English and Art History at the University of Alabama before receiving an M.A. in English from The Citadel. In addition to the works of Tolkien, his areas of interest include cultural studies, counterculture literature, and composition pedagogy. His most recent research has explored the benefits of using popular culture to teach first-year composition. He has also written papers examining the adaptation and simulation of drug use in film and the relationship between comic book superhero mythology and the counterculture movement of the 1960s. He currently teaches at Birmingham-Southern College in Birmingham, Alabama.

E. J. CHRISTIE is an Associate Professor of English at Georgia State University, where he teaches medieval English language and literature. His previously published articles—for example, in *Modern Philology*, *postmedieval*, and *A Handbook of Anglo-Saxon Studies* (Wiley-Blackwell, 2012)—mainly focus on writing and the metaphorics of inscription in Anglo-Saxon England. He is currently at work on a book about knowledge and secrecy in Old English literature.

JANET BRENNAN CROFT is Head of Access and Delivery Services and Assistant Professor at Rutgers University Libraries. She is the author of *War in the Works of J. R. R. Tolkien* (2005 winner, Mythopoeic Society

Award for Inklings Studies). She is the editor of the refereed scholarly journal *Mythlore* and has edited or co-edited four other collections of literary essays: *Tolkien on Film: Essays on Peter Jackson's* The Lord of the Rings; *Tolkien and Shakespeare: Essays on Shared Themes and Language; Tolkien in the New Century: Essays in Honor of Tom Shippey*; and *Perilous and Fair: Women in J. R. R. Tolkien's Work and Life*. She has also written on Lois McMaster Bujold, Terry Pratchett, J. K. Rowling, and other authors.

JON GARRAD is an independent researcher and occasional lecturer, currently based in London. He has presented on the history of necromancy, fantasy gaming and economic recession, and identities in online gaming. Jon is also active in the Green Party of England and Wales, and has been blogging for five years at kaptainvon.wordpress.com.

PETER GRYBAUSKAS teaches English at the University of Maryland. Previously, he taught in Italy and collaborated with the Roman Association of Tolkien Studies. His work has appeared in *Tolkien Studies, Mythlore*, and the Italian collection, *C'era una volta ... Lo Hobbit — Alle origini del Signore degli Anelli*.

MEYRAV KOREN-KUIK is a doctoral student at Tel Aviv University. Her research interests include narrative theory, Victorian literature and culture, science fiction, fantasy, and the intersection of visual arts, literature and space. She published (among others) essays in the collections *Film and Modernism, and Fan CULTure: An Examination of Participatory Fandom in the 21st Century*, and an article in the scholarly journal *Symbolism: An International Annual of Critical Aesthetics*. Meyrav has presented papers at several conferences; including the annual conferences of the International Society for the Study of Narrative, the International Gothic Association, and London Film and Media.

ANDREW KROKSTROM currently serves as an Officer in the United States Army and is a graduate of the University of Missouri. He is a loving dog owner and possesses the best jump shot in St. Louis County.

PHILIPPE LAFERRIÈRE is a Visual Artist based in Thessaloniki, Greece, who was born in Toulouse, France. After a few years at the École des Beaux Arts in Toulouse, he studied History of Art and graduated with a Master's degree in Classical Archaeology at the University of Aix-en-Provence. A survey about the painting of Macedonian Tombs brought him to Greece in 2000 where he worked as an art conservator. Since 2010, he has devoted his time to painting, taking part in many group exhibitions and regularly showing his work through solo exhibitions and performances (action painting) in Greece.

MICHAEL LIVINGSTON, an award-winning writer and professor, holds degrees in History, Medieval Studies, and English, and he currently serves as an Associate Professor of English at The Citadel. He specializes in the Middle Ages and in medievalism. He is the co-editor of *The Battle of Crécy: A Casebook* (Liverpool, 2015) and the author of the historical fantasy novel *The Shards of Heaven* (Tor, 2015).

TIFFANY BROOKE MARTIN has a Ph.D. in English from Idaho State University; while writing her dissertation " 'For the Future': Consciousness, Fantasy, and Imagination in Owen Barfield's Fiction," she had the privilege to access Barfield and Inklings special collections at the Bodleian Library. She has transcribed and edited poems, stories, and letters for the Owen Barfield Literary Estate and continues to work with Barfield's grandson and literary trustee, Owen A. Barfield, in making more Barfield material available to the public.

BRIAN MELTON is an Associate Professor of History and Instructional Mentor at Liberty University, an instructor for Regent University, and is on the faculty of the Liberty University On-line Academy. Befitting his status as an academic mercenary, he has been published in several historical fields, most notably the history of the American Civil War (*Sherman's Forgotten General: Henry W. Slocum* and *Robert E. Lee: A Life*), in addition to Lewis studies. He lives with his family in the Blue Ridge Mountains in Central Virginia.

NICK MILNE'S research focuses on Modern British Literature, with a particular emphasis on British literary propaganda and print culture during World War I. His doctoral thesis, in the University of Ottawa's Department of English, examines the intersections of literary scholarship, historiography, and commercial culture in WWI studies throughout the twentieth century. He is a regular contributor to the University of Oxford's WWI centenary blog, *WW1C*, and his work has appeared in *Slate* and on BBC Radio 3 and 4.

PHILIP IRVING MITCHELL is an Associate Professor of English at Dallas Baptist University, where he teaches early modern and modern humanities and directs the University Honors Program. A contributor to *Christianity and Literature*, *Logos*, *Mythlore*, *Seven*, and *Tolkien Studies*, as well as other published collections and journals, he is at work on monographs concerning G. K. Chesterton's practice of history and biography and concerning Austin Farrer and C. S. Lewis's intellectual and theological relationship.

ASHLEY PFEIFFER is from the Philadelphia area. While attending La Salle University, she took a class on King Arthur that piqued her interest in T. H. White. During her time in Lehigh University's Master's program, she expanded her interest in World War I and Interwar writers and finished this essay. Currently, she is pursuing a career in nonprofit development.

MARGARET SINEX is Professor of English at Western Illinois University where she teaches medieval British literature, Arthurian romance, Northern European mythology, Tolkien, and introductory Latin. She has published several articles in *Tolkien Studies* and an essay in *Tolkien the Medievalist*.

SHANDI STEVENSON is a teacher and freelance writer who lives in Travelers Rest, South Carolina. Shandi holds a B.A. in Literature in English from Excelsior College and a Master of Humanities with a concentration in history from California State University. Her previous publications on J. R. R. Tolkien and C. S. Lewis have appeared in *Doors in the Air: C. S. Lewis and the Imaginative World,* edited by Anna Slack, and *The Mirror Crack'd: Fear and Horror in J. R. R. Tolkien's Major Works* edited by Lynn Forest-Hill.

JOE YOUNG lives and works in Dunedin, New Zealand, where he pursues research interests including modern fantasy, intellectual history, the Gothic tradition and expressions of idealism in post-Enlightenment literature. He recently began work on a book examining E. R. Eddison's maturation as a philosophical novelist.

Index

Achilles 25, 288
advertising 168, 173, 202
Ælfric of Eynsham. *Glossary* 73; "Homily for the Common of a Confessor" 76
Afghanistan War 140
Agamemnon 288
air warfare 64, 108, 284, 308
Aldington, Richard. *Death of a Hero* 191n10
Alexander the Great 189, 268
Alfred, King. Translation of Boethius 73
alienation 65, 172–73, 176, 195, 272, 274–75
allegory 9, 60, 72, 76, 93, 217, 220, 222–23, 243, 255
alternate history genre 187–206
ambush tactics 28–29
American Civil War 189, 193
American Expeditionary Force 148
anarchy and anarchism 110, 220, 224
Andersen, Hans Christian 178, 217. "The Tin Soldier" 217
Anderson, Sherwood 18n14
Anglo-Saxon Chronicle 236
Anthroposophy 167; Anthroposophical Society 167n2
apocalyptic themes and imagery 168–69, 210–11, 215, 220, 222n12, 231, 270
archaism 72, 263, 265, 276
Arras (France), Battle of 131, 135, 137, 148
Arthur, King and Arthurian legends 217, 299–300, 309–10; *see also* Malory, Tennyson, and White for fictional treatment
astrology and horoscopes 177–78, 257, 266
atomic bomb 9
Austen, Jane 279
Austria 219, 228; Austrian Anschluss 285
Austria-Hungary 145; Austro-Hungarian Ultimatum 192
authoritarianism 181
Ayers, Harry 136, 148

Bakhtin, Mikhail 247–48
Balkan Wars (1912–1913) 289, 292–93
Ballot Act 61
barbed wire 146, 209
Barfield, Owen 165–83. Military service 2, 165, 167, 177–78; brother Harry Barfield 165; conscientious objection 173–74; at Oxford 169; theories on human consciousness and meaning 166–69, 178, 221 *Works:* "Day" 167; "The Devastated Area" 165–66, 168, 172, 174, 174n9, 176–77; "Dope" 166, 169–70, 172–77; *Eager Spring* 177; *Night Operation* 177, 180n15; *Poetic Diction* 171n6; review of Wilfrid Owen's poetry 165, 176; *The Rose on the Ash-Heap* 178, 180n15; *The Silver Trumpet* 166, 178–81; "The Superman" 166, 169–72, 176; *This Ever Diverse Pair* 177
batmen 20, 23
battleships 291
Belgium 146, 178, 195, 198, 234; Mons 178
Belloc, Hilaire 191
Beorhtnoth 35
Beowulf (character) 35, 124; *Beowulf* (poem) 74, 77, 98, 98n13
Berlin 196, 217, 289–92
Bhabha, Homi. "DessemiNation" 81, 88
Bible, Old English translations 73
Birmingham (England) 60, 82
Bismarck, Otto von 217, 227n18
Blackadder Goes Forth 203
blitzkrieg tactics 193n12, 307
Bloomsbury Group 263
Blücher, Gebhard von 217
bodies, dead 12, 21, 137, 139, 147, 152–53, 218, 299
bodies, male 38–39, 46–59, 306
Boer War 46
Boethius. *Consolation of Philosophy* 73–74; *see also* Alfred, King
Bok, Sisella 62
Bolsheviks 63
Brecht, Bertolt 267
Bright Young Things 306
British Army 11, 27, 134; Staff College 202
British Empire and imperialism 175, 177, 195, 198, 225, 247, 247n1, 302, 310
British Foreign Office 289
Brittain, Vera. *Testament of Youth* 123–24, 191n10
Buchan, John 202, 202n16. *Greenmantle* 196
Bulgaria 229, 292
Byron, Lord 191

Cabell, James Branch 237
Cambrai, Battle of 193
Cambridge Modern History 213n4
camouflage 27–29
Canada 198
Carlyle, Thomas. *On Heroes, Hero-Worship and the Heroic in History* 117, 200, 213n7, 217; *see also* great man theory of history
Carpenter, Humphrey 235
castles *see* fortifications
catharsis 43
Catholicism, Catholic Church, and Catholic beliefs 125–26, 213n7, 214
cavalry and cavalry tactics 201, 280
Cecil Rhodes Trust 198
Celticism 227
censorship 61
Cervantes. *Don Quixote* 237–39, 243
Chance, Jane 235
charity 61
Charity Organization Society 61
Chaucer. "The Prioress's Tale" 307
chemical weapons 24; *see also* gas
Chesney, George Tomkyns. *The Battle of Dorking* 188n1, 194
Chesterton, G. K. (Gilbert Keith) 191, 209–31. Lack of military service 224; religious upbringing 212; education 212; idealism 210–11; nervous breakdown 226; violence in his works 223–25
  Works: *Autobiography* 224n13; *The Crimes of England* 209–33; *The Everlasting Man* 230; *Illustrated London News* columns 209; *The Napleon of Notting Hill* 225; *Orthodoxy* 215, 223, 228; "Three Ways of Writing History" 212; *The Victorian Age in Literature* 225
Childers, Erskine. *The Riddle of the Sands* 188n3, 194, 196
children's literature 154, 178–81, 218, 221–22
chivalry and chivalric imagery 113, 210–12, 230–31, 242–43, 283, 299–300, 302–04
Christ 73, 75, 122, 125, 215, 225, 227, 230–31, 261
Christ II 75
Christianity and Christian beliefs 2, 63, 73, 112–13, 119–20, 124, 126, 150, 212, 221, 223, 225n15, 227–28, 228n19, 231, 302
Christmas 178n11, 225
chronicle (literary form) 89, 236

chronotope and chronotope split 247–61; *see also* Bakhtin, city vs. country, spatio/temporal split
Churchill, Winston S. 191, 197, 204–05; memoirs 204
cinema and film 35n2, 163n3, 203, 206, 267
city vs. country 246, 248–52
civil service 61, 281
civilian war efforts 29
civilians 18n16, 39, 45–46, 48, 50, 57, 63, 150, 161, 269–70, 276, 293
Clarke, Susanna. *Jonathan Strange and Mr. Norrell* 189n4
class and social status 61, 90, 214n9, 286, 302–03, 306; class discrimination 61, 230; class divide 30, 256–58, 273
classical literature 113, 151, 266
Clovis, King of France 222
Cobbett, William 209n1, 216n10, 229
Coghill, Nevill 2, 173–74
Coleridge, Samuel Taylor 180
Collingwood, R. C. 213
combat stress 14n11; *see also* shell-shock, post-traumatic stress disorder
Commission for Relief in Belgium 198
communism 110, 259, 308
Conrad, Joseph 58
Conroy, Robert. *1920: America's Great War* 206
conscientious objection 174
conscription and draft 83, 133–34, 161, 280–81
consensus reality 172, 247, 256, 259
Constantinople 229
counsel and counsellors 47, 53, 55, 75
Couperin, François 273
courage 36, 51, 113–15, 125, 141, 148, 151, 223–24, 229, 293–94
courtesy 115, 283
cowardice 51–52, 55, 292
cricket (game) 302–03
Croft, Janet Brennan. *War and the Works of J. R. R. Tolkien* 10n6, 160, 162, 235
Crusades 159, 215, 229
cynicism 237

Daedalus 64
Daily Mail 195
Dardanelles 205
Darwinism 117

316 | *Baptism of Fire:*

Index

de Camp, L. Sprague 267, 280–83, 288, 294. *Lest Darkness Fall* 189n4
death 63–64, 68–69, 76, 87, 112, 116, 124, 135, 139, 148, 152, 168, 254, 260–61, 293
Deathwatch (movie) 206
demonization of the enemy 162–63, 227
Denmark 217, 223
Denys, Saint 231
Derrida, Jacques 62, 76. *The Gift of Death* 63
despair 119, 124–28, 182
Dick, Philip K. *The Man in the High Castle* 189n4
Diepeveen, Leonard. Theory of difficulty 264–65, 270
disabilities 38–39, 45–51, 54, 57, 141, 300
disillusionment 18n14–15, 25, 111, 118
Disraeli, Benjamin. *The Wondrous Tale of Alroy* 189
Dorsett, Lyle 178
Doyle, Arthur Conan. Lack of military service 203. Works: "Danger!" 188n1; "The Death Voyage" 189, 197, 200–01
dragons 38, 124, 151, 230
dreams 168, 210–11, 218, 225
Dundas-Grant, Jim 2
Dunsany, Lord. Violence in his works 241, 241n5, 242
  Works: *The Book of Wonder* 174; "The City on Mallingham Moor" 174; *Don Rodriguez: Chronicles of Shadow Valley* 235–43; *Tales of Wonder* 174; "The Wonderful Window" 174
duty 34–36, 63–64, 114, 121–22, 126–27, 225
Dyson, Hugo 2

Eddison, E. R. Lack of military experience 280; civil service career 281, 289–90; attitudes on conflict 263; death of son-in-law 296; philosophy 263–64, 267, 274–76, 287, 295, of Beauty and Love 275–76, 295, 297; perception of amorality of his work 279, 281–83; place names in his work 266; violence in his works 283
  Works: *Egil's Saga* (translation) 283; *Styrbiorn the Strong* 283; *The Worm Ouroboros* 234–35, 263–83; *Zimiamvia* trilogy 267, 273–74 (*Mistress of Mistresses* 283, 289–90, 295; *A Fish Dinner in Memison* 279, 285–88, 290, 295–97; *The Mezentian Gate* 290)
  Characters: Anne Bremmerdale 286, 293; Aphrodite 295; Corinus 281–82; Corsus 282; Edward Lessingham 272–74, 276, 285, 287–95; King Gorice 235, 265, 267, 271, 282; Lady Mevrian 275, 281–83; Lord Brandoch Daha 268, 270–71, 281–82; Lord Goldry Bluzsco 267–68, 270–71, 275; Lord Gro 271, 275; Lord Juss 270–71, 282; Mary (Scarnside) Lessingham 273, 285–89, 292–95; Queen Prezmyra 275; Queen Sophonisba 268, 271, 275
  Settings: Earth 279, 285, 288, 290–91, 293, 295; Zimiamvia 285, 287, 290–92, 294–95; Mercury 266, 269, 273, 280
Eden 126, 230
education 115
Edward IV, King of England 11n7
Edwardian culture and literature 118, 141, 210, 212, 216, 227
Egil's Saga 273; Egil Skallagrimsson 288, 295
Eliot, T. S. 111, 166, 263. *The Criterion* (ed.) 174–75n9; *Four Quartets* 187, 206; *Gerontion* 269; *The Hollow Men* 142–43; *The Waste Land* 17, 172, 234, 269
elves 255; *see also* Tolkien, Warner
England and English culture 9, 45–47, 50, 53, 57–58, 60, 63, 65, 192, 195, 211, 217–31, 248, 300–01; English law 60–61
Enlightenment thought and philosophy 110–11, 113–15, 117, 124
enlisted men 20, 23, 30–32, 282, 302
epic literature 35
escapism 110, 123, 189, 273
espionage 60, 68
evil 18, 69, 77, 92, 115–16, 121, 151, 162–63, 211, 221, 227, 231, 241
Exeter Book riddles 74–75, 77
exile 126

fairy stories and tales 111, 210, 217, 220–23, 227, 229, 231, 243, 254
fall of man 126
fantasy role-playing games 276
fascists and fascism 172, 180, 280, 284, 294, 296, 308
fatalism 286
fate and doom 68–69, 127, 220
Faulks, Sebastian. *Birdsong* 203
Faustus 253

Index

Ferdinand, Archduke Franz, assassination of 145, 191n9, 192–93, 286, 292
festival 230
feudal system 259
Fitzgerald, F. Scott 18n14, 111
flashbacks (shell-shock symptom) 15
folklore and folk literature 215
Forster, E. M. 58. "Our Graves in Gallipoli" 205n20
fortifications 158–60, 162
foxhunting 301–02
France 9, 9n3, 13n10, 146–48, 152, 158–59, 161–63, 192, 195, 202, 222–23, 227, 234, 242, 292, 296
Franco-Prussian War (1870–1871) 194, 223
Frayn, Michael. *Balmoral* 206
Frederick II of Prussia (Frederick the Great) 211, 218–19, 231
free will 122, 162
freedom 62, 65, 69, 90, 254, 256
French Revolution 115, 117, 211, 216–17, 228
French, Sir John 205n19
Freud, Sigmund, and Freudian psychology 152, 212, 225, 228–29
Friedman, Susan Stanford. Concept of spatialization 248
friendship 62–64, 242–43, 269–71, 276–77; pseudocouples 270–71
Frye, Northrop 276. Theory of modes 1, 237–40; *see also* irony
Fussell, Paul. *The Great War and Modern Memory* 1, 18n16, 29, 31, 35, 83, 113, 116–18, 128, 166, 176, 193n10, 234, 299, 304, 307–08

Galileo 214
Gallipoli, Battle of 192, 205
Gandhi 247
Gardner, John. *Grendel* 94
Garibaldi, Giuseppe 223, 226, 229
Garth, John 2, 26–26, 29, 35, 81. *Tolkien and the Great War* 10n5, 11n8, 13, 26, 30, 32, 35, 60, 82n3, 92, 111
gas (in war) 24, 209, 241, 284
gaze 67, 73
Geats 74
gender criticism and ideology 58, 179, 251
genealogy 225
genre 102n16, 111, 151, 189, 190, 194, 215, 236–37, 263–64, 273, 297

Geoffroy-Chateau, Napoléon. *Napoléon et la conquête du monde* 189
George V, King 35, 197–98
George, Saint 231
Germanic languages 71
Germany and Germans, German society 9, 9n3, 11, 60, 63, 140–41, 160, 162–63, 200, 204, 215, 226–27, 287–89, 307–08; anti-German sentiment in England 189, 195, 197, 209; Anglo-German relations 195, 227, 289–90; German stereotypes 198; German philosophy 198, 227; German actions in WWI 135, 146–48, 158–60, 192–99, 211; German Revolution 196
Gilson, Rob 11, 24–25, 29, 32
God 74, 77, 182, 225
Golding, William 81
Gollancz, Victor 202
Gospels 73–74
Grahame, Kenneth 6
Graves, Robert. *Goodbye to All That* 98n11, 188, 191n10, 234
Great Depression 284
great man theory of history 117, 200–01; *see also* Carlyle, Thomas
The Great Martian War 206
Greece 229, 292; Greek history and warfare 24
Green, John Richard. *A Short History of the English People* 227
Greeves, Arthur 136–38, 147
Grendel 74
Gresham, Douglas 150, 153
Gresham, Joy (née Davidman, later Lewis) 142
Griffiths, Dom Bede 139
Grimm brothers 217
Guite, Malcolm 181
guns and machine-guns 11, 24–25, 146, 284, 209, 290, 292, 307

Haig, Douglas 146, 158, 205n19
hair color change (shell-shock symptom) 44, 58
Halbwachs, Maurice 80, 84–86
Haldane, Lord Chancellor 289–91
hallucinations (shell-shock symptom) 45
Hardy, Thomas 118
Hector 25, 288
Helen of Troy 288

318 | *Baptism of Fire:*

Hemingway, Ernest 18n14, 111, 113, 269; *A Farewell to Arms* 108, 191n10; *The Sun Also Rises* 140
Hengist and Horsa 217
heroes and heroism 23–36, 64, 76, 93–95, 115, 127, 151, 154, 211–12, 216–17, 220, 223, 230, 234–42, 267–70, 276, 279, 288, 291–95
Hipper, Admiral Franz von 196–97, 200
history and historiography 68, 70, 80–91, 93, 97–102, 107–08, 111–13, 117–18, 152, 167, 187–206, 210–22, 236–37, 240, 243, 269, 273, 279–80, 287, 290, 294–99
Hitler, Adolf 187, 200, 306–09
HMS Hawke, sinking of 286, 289, 293
Hobsbawm, Eric 279, 283–84, 286, 288–89, 291–94, 296. Concept of "Age of Catastrophe" 279–80, 285, 293–95
Hohenzollern dynasty 197–98, 219
Holland *see* Netherlands
Holy Roman Empire 215
Holy Spirit 223
Homer 34, 158, 287. *Iliad* 23, 25, 151, 288; *Odyssey* 35n2
honor 25, 27, 31, 35–36, 55, 113, 115, 154, 209, 283, 294
Hooper, Walter 147, 178
hope 1, 18, 111–12, 124–28, 229–31, 234, 299
horses 64, 153, 166, 178
Housman, A. E. 118
Hoyle, Fred. *October the First is Too Late* 189n4
Hugh of Lincoln 307
humility 26, 33, 36, 115, 213, 215
Hungary 295

Icarus 64
Icelandic sagas 287, 291
idealism 210–11, 234, 239, 243, 275, 294, 299
identity 47, 53, 67, 90
imagination 31, 35, 93, 126, 147, 151, 165, 167–68, 174, 181–82, 214, 221, 225
immortality 67, 86, 121, 260–61, 268, 271
imperialism 65, 234, 270, 291, 302
Imphal-Kohima, Battle of 19
India 195, 247n1
Indo-European language 72
industrialization 9, 248, 252, 279, 291, 294
influenza outbreak 245
injuries and dismemberment 38–40, 46, 50–52, 55–56, 131, 141, 156, 171, 300, 305

Inklings 2, 64, 82, 160, 165, 171, 178n11, 183, 263
Inquisition 220
insomnia (shell-shock symptom) 175
interrogation 73, 77; *see also* torture
intimacy 62, 64, 69
invasion literature 188, 194
invisibility 67, 70
Iraq War 140
Ireland 211, 220, 226–27
irony (literary mode) 1, 95, 113, 234, 236, 247, 286
isolation 24, 65–66, 69, 168–69, 171, 173, 176
Italy and the Italians 193n12, 223

Jackson, Peter 105
Jacobinism 110, 213n7
James, Edward. *Science Fiction and Fantasy Writers in the Great War* (website) 6
James, Henry 110
Jameson, Fredric. Concept of utopian enclave 252
Jews and anti-Semitism 284, 307
Joan of Arc 217
Jones, David 6
journalism 272
jousting 302–03
Joyce, James 111, 118, 166. *Ulysses* 168, 269
Juarès, Jean, assassination of 192
Judeo-Christian thought and philosophy 110, 117, 211
Jung, Carl 65, 77. *Modern Man in Search of a Soul* 62; *The Undiscovered Self* 62
just war 299

Kafka, Franz 111, 118
Kant 148
Katte, Hans Hermann von 218
Kiel 196, 201
kingship 198, 219
Kipling, Rudyard 6, 225
Kirkpatrick, William 132, 146
Kitchener, Lord 205n19
Kluck, Alexander von 192
knights and knighthood 27, 151, 229–31, 235, 301–06

Lancashire Fusiliers 13n9
language 165, 167–69, 173, 180–81, 217, 265, 272

Latin language 72–74
Lawrence, D. H. 111, 113, 166, 269
Le Guin, Ursula K. 265, 274
Le Queux, William. *The Great War in England in 1897* 188n1, 195; *The Invasion of 1910* 188n1, 195–96
Leacock, Stephen. Lack of military service 203. "The Devil and the Deep Sea" 198; "Germany From Within Out" 198; "The Hohenzollerns in America" 189, 197–200; *Sunshine Sketches of a Little Town* 198
leadership 30–31, 39, 47
League of Nations 283
Lebensraum 308
Lebow, Richard Ned. *Archduke Franz Ferdinand Lives! A World Without World War I* 206
Lenin, Vladimir 193
Lettow-Vorbeck, General Paul von 204, 204n18
Levinas, Emmanuel 62
Lewis, C. S. 2, 9n2, 64, 81, 92n1, 111–65, 178–79, 183, 264, 276. Military service 2, 83, 111–12, 131–37, 144–58, 160, 162–63; injury in battle 134n4, 136–38, 143, 147–48, 156–57; attitudes on dead bodies 152–53. At Malvern 132–33, 138–39, 149, Robert Capron 149; at Oxford (Maudlin) 133n1, 146–48. Death of mother 132, 138–39, 149, 152–53; relationship with father 132–34, 136–37, 139–40; friends and associates 133–34, 142. Christianity and conversion 112, 138; as apologist 132. Lacunae in autobiography and letters 136–38, 144; habit of compartmentalization 142, 149–50, 160
  Works: All My Road Before Me 112, 173–74, 178; *The Great Divorce* 117; *The Horse and His Boy* 120, 153–56, 159, 162; *The Last Battle* 145, 158, 162; "Learning in Wartime" 150–51; *Letters* 125–26, 133–34, 136–40, 143, 147; *The Lion, the Witch and the Wardrobe* 128, 145, 153–55, 158–59, 161; "On Three Ways of Writing for Children" 150–51, 153, 155–56; *Perelandra* 122, 127; *Prince Caspian* 120, 145, 153–54, 156, 159, 161–62; *The Screwtape Letters* 117, 127; *The Silver Chair* 115–16, 148; Space trilogy 120; *Spirits in Bondage* 147; *Surprised by Joy* 125–26, 131, 137–39, 142, 146–48; *That Hideous Strength* 116; *Till We Have Faces* 122–23; *Voyage of the "Dawn Treader"* 145; "Why I am Not a Pacifist" 150
  Characters: Aravis 154–55, 157; Aslan 115–16, 120, 128, 148, 152, 154–56, 159, 162–63; Bacchus 153; Calormenes 145, 161–62; Caspian 145, 154–55, 159, 161; Corin 153–54; Corradin 155, 162; Dr. Cornelius 159; Edmund Pevensie 154–57, 159; Eldils 120; Emeth 162; Fenris 145, 158, 161; Glozelle 162; Green Witch 148, 149n2, 163; Hermit of the Southern Waste 155; horses 155; Jill Pole 116; Lucy Pevensie 120, 128, 155–56, Lucy's cordial 153, 156–57; Lune 155; Maledil 122; Mark Studdock 116; Miraz 145, 154, 159; monsters 163; Mr. Beaver 154; Mrs. Beaver 156; N.I.C.E. 116; Narnians 148, 159–60, 163; Orual 122–23; Peter Pevensie 145, 153–55, 158–59; Psyche 122–23; Puddleglum 148; Rabadash 155, 159, 162; Ransom 122, 127–28; Reepicheep 156–57; Screwtape 117, 127; Shasta 120, 154, 157–58, as Cor 157; Shift 162; Spoesian 162; Susan Pevensie 128, 154; Telmarines 155, 159, 161–62; Tinidril 122; Tirian 145; Weston as "Un-Man" 127; White Witch (Jadis) 128, 153–56, 159, 161, 163
  Settings: Anvard 153–54, 157–59; Aslan's How 154, 159, 162; Cair Paravel 158–59, 161; Earth 122, 162; Jadis's Castle 158–59; Narnia 116, 120, 128, 132, 144–45, 149n2, 150–57, 159–61; Perelandra 122, 127; Stone Table 152
Lewis, Warren 2, 9n3, 149
libel laws 228
Liddell Hart, Basil 202
Lincoln, Abraham 191
literary canon 263–64
Lithuania—Vilnius massacre 284
Livy. *Ab Urbe Condita* 189
Lloyd George, David 11, 197. Memoirs 204
Locarno Pact 283
London 174, 226n16, 245–46, 248–50, 283
London blitzkrieg 307–08

Index

Lord of the Rings (films) 24n1, 105
loss 111, 119–22, 124, 126, 129
Lost Generation 18, 18n14, 20
Louis IX, King of France 222
love 49, 181–82, 238, 242–43, 275, 288, 294–95
love triangles 51, 55–56
loyalty 113–15, 122, 242
Ludwig, Emil 191
Lukács, Georg 61
Lusitania, sinking of 200

MacLeod, Ian R. *The Summer Isles* 206
magic 121, 128, 180, 223, 236–37, 252
Maginot Line 13n10
Maldon, Battle of 105; *Battle of Maldon* (poem) 126
Malory, Thomas. *Le Morte d'Arthur* 300–01, 309–10
Manhattan Project 9
Manning, Frederic. *The Middle Parts of Fortune* 191n10
maps 86–87
Marconi scandal 226, 228
Maria Theresa of Austria 219
Marne, Battle of the (First) 211
Marx, Karl, and Marxism 115, 117, 212
Mary, Mother of Jesus 73–74, 220
materialism and anti-materialism 165, 168
Maurois, André 191
Maxims I 75–77
mechanization 172–73; *see also* industrialization, technological advances
medieval period in northern Europe 64, 92n3, 125–26, 159, 166; medieval literature 215, 236; medieval warfare 161
medievalism 231, 310
memory, memory loss, and forgetfulness 40, 42, 80–93, 108, 176–77, 203, 210, 216–17
Mercury (planet) 241, 266, 269
metaphor 81, 117, 264–65
Michelangelo 227
Miéville, China 274
militarism 283–88
Milne, A. A. 6
Mirror for Magistrates, A 236
modern warfare 31, 36, 64, 161, 279, 297
modernism, modernity, and modernists 6, 93n5, 110, 114, 119–20, 123, 128, 166–75, 178, 181, 263–67, 269–70, 272–73, 277, 294; proto-modernism 273

Monocled Mutineer, The 203
monsters, monstrosity, and the monstrous 69, 98n12, 124, 163
Montenegro 229
Moore, Maureen 142, 147
Moore, Paddy 147
moral choice and responsibility 60, 62–63, 68, 116, 235; moral values and education 61, 111, 113–16, 213, 215, 259
Morocco 60
Morselli, Guido. *Contropassato prossimo: un'ipotesi retrospettiva* 206
Motts, F. W. *War Neuroses and Shell Shock* 40, 41n6, 43n9
Munich Conference 285
music therapy 43
Mussolini 294
Myers, C. S. 14
myth 1, 35, 81, 93, 110, 151, 167, 182, 210, 212, 214, 218, 221, 240
Mythlore: A Journal of J. R. R. Tolkien, C. S. Lewis, Charles Williams, and Mythopoeic Literature 1, 10n6

names and naming 70–71, 77, 170, 179
Napoleon I 187, 189–92, 196, 200, 204, 211, 216, 227n18; Napoleonic Wars 193, 279
Napoleon III 211, 227n18
nations and nationalism 80–82, 84–85, 87–91
nature and the natural world 173, 178, 180, 221; nature myths 230–31
Nazis and Nazism 197, 296, 307–08
Netherlands 197, 201
New Yorker (magazine) 254
Newman, Bernard. Military service 203; *The Cavalry Went Through!* 189, 193n12, 201–05
Newman, John Henry 213n7
Nicholas I of Montenegro 229–30
Nietzsche, Friedrich, and Nietzscheism 170, 212, 267, 275–76
nightmares (shell-shock symptom and in general) 15, 19, 81, 139–40, 150, 210–11, 222, 222n12
nihilism 128, 227
Njal's Saga 273
No-Man's Land 11–13, 21, 146, 152–53, 206
non-resistant anergic stupor (shell-shock symptom) 39, 41–45, 57
Nora, Pierre 80, 86, 89

Index

Northcliffe, Lord 193, 195
nostalgia 110, 113, 117, 121, 125, 248
novel (genre), modern 237
Novik, Naomi 189n4

officers 29–30, 302; Officer Training Corps 29; Officer Training Course 134
Official Secrets Act 60–61
Oh! What a Lovely War 203
Old English language and literature 60, 70–78, 125–26
optimism 128
oral story-telling and history 85, 89, 95
Orwell, George 81
Other, the 227, 258–59
Ottoman Empire 229
Owen, Wilfrid 165, 176, 224. "Dulce et Decorum Est" 234
Oxford University 60, 133n1, 134, 147–48, 169

pacifism 15–17, 150, 224, 284
paganism 228
paralysis *see* non-resistant anergic stupor
paranoia 64
Paris 18n14, 192
parody 238, 300
Patočka, Jan 63, 76
patriarchal social order 246, 249–51, 261
patriotism 65, 234
Pax Brittania 25
peace 26, 32, 36, 110, 125, 174, 200, 205, 225, 271, 280, 286, 289, 299
Peake, Mervyn 6
Petty, Anne C. *Tolkien and the Land of Heroes* 10n6
Pharisees 73
Pitt, William 211, 220
pity 32, 56, 113
Plato 62–63
Poland 219
postmodernism 94, 172
post-traumatic stress disorder 10, 14–19, 58, 131, 137, 140–41, 149–50; social stigma associated with 137, 140–43; *see also* combat stress, shell-shock
Potsdam 196
Pound, Ezra 113, 166
poverty 110, 115, 117
power 60, 64, 94n8
prisoners of war 52–53

privacy 61, 77
progress 110–11, 124, 234, 241, 252, 291
propaganda 63–65, 168, 175, 209, 211, 215, 224, 229, 231, 308; *see also* War Propaganda Bureau
Proust, Marcel. *À la recherché du temps perdu* 269
Prussia 215, 217–18, 222, 224, 226, 229–31; Prussianism 287–88
psychology 62, 114, 117, 179, 221

race, racism, and racial segregation 247n1, 256, 258–60, 303–04
Raleigh, Sir Walter 295
range weaponry tactics 27
Raws, John 12
reader-response theory 236n2
realism 81–82, 154–56, 216, 269, 276
realpolitik 210, 230
redemption 162–63
religion (in general) 256, 260–61
Remarque, Erich Maria. *All Quiet on the Western Front* 35, 131, 135, 191n10, 224; film adaptation 35n2
Ricoeur, Paul. Theories of suspicion, naiveté, and belief 210–31
ritual 62, 70, 166, 218
Roberts, Field Marshal Lord 195
robots 180n15
romance (literary genre) 237–40, 242
Romanticism 165, 167, 169, 299–300; neo-romanticism 168–70, 173
Rowling, J. K. 83
Royal Air Force 34
Russia and Russians 63, 146, 148, 190, 195, 259, 284; October Revolution 193, 259

sacred, the 61, 72, 74, 76
sacrifice 62, 113–15, 120–22, 126–28, 223, 225, 300
Saki. *When William Came* 188n1
Sarajevo 192, 286
Sassoon, Siegfried 19–20, 83n5, 93n5, 187–88, 224. *Memoirs of an Infantry Officer* 191n10, George Sherston (character) 187
satire 237–38, 247, 255–58, 261, 300
Saturday Evening Post 201
Scandinavia 283
secrecy 49, 54, 60–78
secret societies 66

Index

secularization 117
Serbia and Serbians 145, 192, 229
sex and sexuality 38, 47
Shakespeare, William 227
shell-shock 10, 14, 16, 17, 38, 40–43, 58, 175, 241, 305; *see also* combat stress; post-traumatic stress disorder; flashbacks; hair color change; hallucinations; insomnia; nightmares; non-resistant anergic stupor; somnambulism; Motts, F. W.; Smith, G. Elliot; Southard, E. E.
Sherriff, R. C. *Journey's End* 191n10
Shippey, Tom 81–83, 92, 235. Concept of traumatized authors 81, 118, 132
Sigurd 288
Simmel, Georg 63–65, 67, 77. "Sociology of Secrecy" 61
Singapore 11n7
Slocum, Henry W. 144
Smith, G. Elliot. *Shell Shock and its Lessons* 40
Smith, Geoffrey Bache 12, 18
Smuts, Jan Christiaan 204
Somme, Battle of the 9–14, 17, 18–21, 31, 36, 82, 92, 193, 281
somnambulism (shell-shock symptom) 42
song and national memory 84–86
South Africa 226, 247n1
Southard, E. E. *Shell-shock and Other Neuropsychiatric Problems* 40, 41n7
Spain 237–239, 242
spatial/temporal split 246–48
sports and games 301–05
Squire, J. C. *If It Had Happened Otherwise* 189–92
Stableford, Brian. *The Carnival of Destruction* 206
Stalin, Josef 9n3
stars 128–29, 166, 171
state security 61
stealth tactics 27–29, 54
Stein, Gertrude 18n14, 269, 271
Steiner, Rudolf 167n2
Stephen, Saint 177
Stephens, James 6
Stirling, S. M. 189n4
stories and story-telling 93–94, 97, 101, 119, 182, 216
Strand, The (magazine) 201
stream of consciousness storytelling 111, 168, 175

Stubbs, Bishop William 227n18
subjects (language) and subjectivity 62, 67, 69–70, 73, 94n8
submarines 63
suicide 175
suicide missions 31, 34
Superman *see* Übermensch
supernatural 167, 171, 182, 206, 211, 220–21
surreal and surrealism 170
surveillance 61, 64
survivor guilt 43, 63, 77
Swinburne, Algernon Charles 118
Switzerland 146
swords 15–17, 27, 32, 34, 48, 97, 105, 209, 224n13, 225, 238, 242–43
symbolism 81, 210–29, 238, 241, 247

T.C.B.S. *see* Tolkien, J. R. R.: Friends and associates
technological advances 146, 160, 173
Telegraph (newspaper) 195
Tennyson, Alfred. "Charge of the Light Brigade" 35; *Idylls of the King* 301, 310
terrorism 222
time 111–28, 168, 172, 176
Tolkien, Christopher 34, 38, 39n1, 40n3, 53, 64–65, 82, 94n7, 103–04, 108, 126
Tolkien, J. R. R. 1–128, 152, 160–61, 165, 178–79, 183, 264, 267, 274–76. Military service 2, 11–12, 17, 23, 35, 38, 80, 82–83, 90, 92–93, 111, 234; views on war 26, 34, 82n2; influence of World War II 10n4, 12–13, 90, 92–93. Academic achievements 31; King Edward's School 60, 82; Exeter College 35. Children 178–79; friends and acquaintances 10, 19, 24, 32, 35–36, 60, 64, 82–83, 93, 121–22; marriage 64. Languages 38, 57, 60, 65–66, 69, 72, 77, 108; as philologist 69–72, 80. Race in his works 6. As modernist 5, 77. Mythology and legendarium 21, 63, 69, 80, 91–92, 111, 120, 124; Music of the Ainur 69. Concept of eucatastrophe 125
Works: "Adventures of Tom Bombadil" 89; "Beowulf: The Monsters and the Critics" 124; *The Children of Húrin* 38–59, textual history 38–44, 48–49, 51–52, 55–56; *The Fall of Arthur* 103n17; *The Fall of Gil-galad* 95, 99, 101–03; "The Fall of Gondolin" 13n9; *The Hobbit* 20–21, 66–67, 69–70, 80–81,

Index

84, 88–90, 92, 97, "Far Over the Misty Mountains Cold" 84–86; *The Homecoming of Beorhtnoth Beorhthelm's Son* 98, 105–06; *Letters* 64–65, 80, 82, 90, 94n7, 111–12, 121, 125–26; *Letters from Father Christmas* 178n11; *The Lord of the Rings* 9–21, 23–36, 39n1, 60, 63, 66–68, 70–74, 77, 80, 82–83, 87–108, 114, 119, 121, 123–24, 127–28, 160–61, 234, "The Council of Elrond" 67, 87, 97, 102–03, 106; "On Fairy-stories" 1, 92n3, 103, 105, 255; *Roverandom* 178n11, 179n12; "A Secret Vice" 66; *The Silmarillion* 39n1, 68, 103–04, 120–24, 128; *Unfinished Tales* 104–05; "Valedictory Address to the University of Oxford" 65

Battles and Wars: Bragollach 50; Bywater 17; Dagorlad 99, 101, 103–04; Five Armies 105; Helm's Deep 107; Last Alliance 93–108; Nírnaith Arnoediad 39n1, 44, 51–56, 58; Pelennor Fields 31, 34, 125; War of the Ring 9n2, 26, 89, 95, 105; War of Wrath 101n15

Characters: Anárion 104; Aragorn 26–27, 30, 32, 35–36, 67, 95, 100–03, 105–08, 114, 124, as Strider 67; Ar-Pharazôn 68; Arwen 103; Balrog 98n13; Beleg 39–41, 43, 44n10, 51, 53; Beregond 30; Beren 53, 97n10, 121; Bilbo Baggins 19–21, 70, 73, 84–85, 87, 89–90, 98–99, 102, 104–05; Boromir 23n1, 27–28, 32–33, 35–36, 87, 99; Brandir 39, 44–51, 56–57; Celeborn 124; Déagol 60, 71–72, 74, 77; Denethor 29, 35, 88, 115, 119, 123, 127; Dorlas 49; Dwarves 66–67, 81, 84–87, 114; Eärendil 121; Edain 54; Elendil 97, 100–04, 106–07; Elrohir 106; Elrond 19, 28, 67, 95, 97, 99–104, 106–07; Elves 28–29, 44, 48–49, 54–55, 57, 66–69, 87, 96, 103, 114, 120–22; Ents 29; Éomer 23, 32, 35, 114, 127; Éowyn 24n1; Failivrin 55–56; Faramir 23–36, 99, 114–15; Fellowship 15, 26–28, 122; Finduilas 47, 55–56; Fingon 52; Flinding *see* Gwindor; Frodo Baggins 10, 13–20, 26, 32–33, 67–68, 70, 73, 77, 87, 89–90, 94–97, 100–01, 119, 121, 124–25, 127–28; Galadriel 19, 124, 127; Gandalf 16, 19–21, 67, 70–71, 84, 86–89, 95, 97–102, 108, 114, 119, 124; Gelmir 52–53, 55; Gil-galad 97, 100–04; Gimli 26, 98n13, 107, 114, 122; Glaurung 48, 53; Glorund *see* Glaurung; goblins 13; Gollum *see* Sméagol; Gwindor 38–39, 41–43, 45–48, 50–58; Handir 48; Hobbits 67, 72, 80–81, 89–90, 95–96; House of Hador 50; House of Haleth 49; Húrin 39, 44–45, 48, 50–51, 58, epithet Thalion "Steadfast" 44; Ilúvatar 67–69, 120, 128; Isildur 32, 87, 95–96, 99–101, 104–07; Istari (Wizards) 86; Labadal 45–47, 50–51, 57–58; Legolas 26, 107, 114, 122; Lotho Sackville-Baggins 17; Lúthien Tinúviel 101, 103, 121; Maedhros 53; Malbeth the Seer 106; Mandos 54; Manwë 54; Melkor/Melko *see* Morgoth; Men 68–69, 86–87, 96, 103, 114, 120, 128; Merry Brandybuck 16–17; Morgoth 44–45, 47, 51–56, 68, 121; Morwen 50, 57, epithet Eledhwen 57; Nazgûl 13, 16, 67–68, 101, 104; Niënor 45, 47–49, 56; Níniel *see* Niënor; Ohtar 106; orcs 26, 32, 52, 56, 96, 106–07, 160, 162; Orodreth 41, 48, 54–55; Peregrin Took 16–17, 30, 105; Rangers (Faramir's troops) 26–29; Ringwraiths *see* Nazgûl; Rodothlim 52, 56; Rohirrim 125, 127; Sador *see* Labadal; Sam Gamgee 13, 16, 19–20, 23, 26, 28, 32–33, 89–90, 94–99, 101–02, 106, 119, 127–28; Saruman 9, 13, 15n13, 16–17, 29, 88–89, 105, 119; Sauron 9n3, 13, 29, 31, 66–70, 73, 77, 81, 87, 95–107, 121, 127, 160, as the Black Hand 96–97; Shelob 15, 17, 19, 97n10; Smaug 84, 86, 97; Sméagol 60, 65–66, 68–75, 77, 93–98, 104–05, 108, 125; Southrons 28; Strider *see* Aragorn; Tamar *see* Brandir; Théoden 106–07, 127; Thorin Oakenshield 84–87; Thrór 86–87; Tída 98; Tom Bombadil 89; Totta 98, 106; Túrin Turambar 38–46, 48–58, 97n10, 103; Ulmo 43; Valar 68, 120–21, 123, 125, 128; women 13, 54, 58; Wormtongue 17

Objects: Aiglos (Spear of Gil-galad) 101–02; Arwen's gem 17; Elendilmir 105; Hammer of Wrath 13n9; Narsil/Anduril 97, 101–03, 106–07; One Ring and other rings of power 10, 15–17, 20, 32–33, 60, 66–71, 75, 77, 87–89,

95–97, 99–100, 103–04, 121–22, 125; palantíri 96, 107; The Red Book of Westmarch 80–81, 87, 89–91, 94; Secret Fire 67; Silver Crown 33, 96; Thrór's Map 66; White Tree 33, 96
Settings: Amon Obel 48; Anduin (Great River) 95; Angband 53, 55, 56n21; Bag End 17, 85–86, 98, 102; Barad Eithel 51; Barad-dûr 29, 104, 107, 114; Black Gate 96, 101, 105; Bree 106; Brethil 46–47, 49, 57; Cirith Ungol 15; Cracks of Doom 95, 97; Dead Marshes 9, 12–13, 96, 105; Doriath 57; Dorlómin 46, 50, 57; Edoras 107; Eithel Ivrin 42–43; Ephel Brandir 48; Erech 106; Fangorn 9; Ford of Bruinen 16; Gladden Fields 71, 96, 104–06; Gondolin 57; Gondor 9, 13n10, 81, 87–89, 95, 99, 102–03, 105, 125, 127, stewardship and kingship of 33, 36, 87–88; Great Mound 51; Green Dragon Inn 16; Grey Havens 19; Ithilien 15–16, 26, 30, 36; Lonely Mountain 66, 84, 87; Lothlórien 27, 121–22, 124, 127; Menegroth 39n1; Middle-earth 10, 15, 21, 66, 69, 72, 80–81, 86–87, 90, 99, 101, 121, 124–25, 128, 160–61; Minas Morgul 96, as Minas Ithil 96; Minas Tirith 30, 33, 88, 127; Misty Mountains 71, 104; Morannon 9, 12–13; Mordor 9, 13, 15, 20, 26, 30, 94, 95, 101, 128; Moria 15, 66; Mount Doom (Orodruin) 10, 15, 87, 97, 101, 104, 127; Nargothrond 46–49, 51, 53–55, 57–58; Númenor 68, 106, 123, 128; Orthanc 105, 107; Osgiliath 30–31, 34; Paths of the Dead 98n13, 106; Rammas Echor 13n10; Rivendell 28, 67, 95, 100–03, 121; Rohan 9n3, 72, 103; Shire 9, 13, 15n13, 16, 17, 19, 121; Silver Bowl 44; Stairs of Cirith Ungol 94; Thangorodrim 44n13, 45; Undying Lands 20; Weathertop 15, 16, 19, 102–03
Tolkien, Michael 83
Tolstoy 151
torture 95–96, 219–20; *see also* interrogation
Toryism (conservatism) 273–74
total war 299, 303–04
totalitarianism 172
Towton, Battle of 11n7

translation 73–74, 102, 214n9
Treaty of Versailles 197, 283, 287
trench fever 12, 147
trenches and trench warfare 11–12, 21, 24–26, 31, 45, 83, 128, 131, 135, 144, 150–51, 157–59, 162–63, 166, 175, 204, 209, 239, 241, 284, 286, 292–93
Trevelyan, G. M. "If Napoleon had Won the Battle of Waterloo" 190n8
Troy and the Trojan War 288, 291
Tuchman, Barbara. *The Guns of August* 123
Turkey and Turks 205, 229
Turtledove, Harry 189n4
twentieth-century culture 9, 24, 31, 35–36, 61, 64, 77, 111, 117, 125, 161, 172, 180, 194, 246, 248, 263–64, 279, 284, 288

Übermensch (Superman) 170
u-boats, German 286, 292
undead 210, 215, 219
uniforms 27, 30, 307
United States 11, 63, 195, 198
Unknown Warrior, The (play) 51
unreliable narrator 111
utopias 125, 230, 252, 287, 294

Vanity Fair (magazine) 198
Verdun 12
Versailles 222
veterans 13–14, 19, 34, 39, 44–47, 50–51, 53, 57–58, 131–32, 140–42, 144, 150, 152, 173–74, 176–77, 284, 300
Victoria, Queen 123
Victorian culture 18n14, 114, 118, 212, 227, 250–51, 270, 276, 300, 310; Victorian adventure stories 276; attitudes toward sports 301–02; Victorian warfare 299, 302–03, 310
Vietnam War 11, 149
Vimy Ridge, Battle of 192–93
violence 17, 64, 67, 70, 80–81, 83–84, 86, 117, 135, 138, 144, 223, 231, 240–42, 283, 293
Virgil 99. *Aeneid* 98
Voltaire 219n11

war poets 58–59, 176
War Propaganda Bureau 209–10, 226
war stories 93–94, 98–99, 269–70, 276
war, causes of 299, 308–09; rules of 303–04

warfare, ancient 23–25

Warner, Sylvia Townsend 245–61. *Kingdoms of Elfin* 246–47, 254–61; *Lolly Willows or The Loving Huntsman* 245–54, 256, 261, Satan (character) 252–53; *With the Hunted* 255; "Women and Writing" 254

warriors 33–34, 150, 241

Waterloo, Battle of 187, 191–92, 216, 222

Waugh, Evelyn 224, 231

Wells, H. G. *The War of the Worlds* 206

White, T. H. 81, 299–310. Lack of military service 299, 308; family 300; education 300–01; friends 300–01; use of animal parables 308–09. *The Once and Future King* 299–310 (*The Queen of Air and Darkness* 301, 303–04; *The Sword in the Stone* 300–01, 309). Battle of Bedegraine 303–04, 308; Siege of the Tower of London 307–08; Round Table 302, 307; Holy Grail and Grail Quest 305

Characters: Agravaine 304; Galahad 305; Gawaine 302, 307; Guenever 30; Kay 301; King Arthur 299, 303–10, as Wart 299, 308–09; King Lot 303–05, 308; Lancelot 302–03, 307; Merlyn 301–03, 308–09; Mordred 299, 304–09; Percivale 305; Queen Morgause 304–05

Wilhelm I, Kaiser 222–23

Wilhelm II, Kaiser 195–201, 289–91. *Memoirs* 197

Wilhelmina, Queen 197

Williams, Charles, 183. Lack of military service 2

Williams, Raymond 248

Wilson, Woodrow 128

wisdom and learning 31–32, 73–74, 76–77

witches 245–46, 249, 252–54, 256, 261

women in society 246, 249–50, 261; women in war 13; women's rights 254

Woolf, Virginia 111, 118, 166, 269, 271. *Mrs. Dalloway* 168, 175, 175n10, 271, Septimus Smith (character) 175, 271; "A Room of One's Own" 254

Wordsworth, William. "Resolution and Independence" 171

World War I and post-World War I mainstream literature and art 13, 18, 108, 110–14, 117, 124, 126–27, 160, 166, 189, 203, 206, 235, 248, 269, 277, 307; post-war and inter-war society 39, 46–47, 50, 57, 116, 119, 123, 128, 140, 176, 240, 248, 251, 261, 263, 271, 279, 284, 288–89, 299, 302, 306, 309; pre-war society 60, 111, 113, 117, 119, 124

World War I. In contrast to other wars 14, 18, 24–29, 34, 279–81, 302; causes 290; Allies 146, 158, 160, 281, 289, leadership 203, 300; Central Powers 140, 193n12; Western Front 9n1, 110, 117, 146, 161, 196, 201, 205, 284; East African campaign 204, 292–93; mutiny of French army 281; armistice 165, 196, 203, 245–46, 277, 279, 287, 289

World War II 10n4, 19–21, 34, 82, 92, 112, 127, 131, 139, 141, 145, 193, 280, 284–85, 289, 296, 299–300, 307–10; appeasement policy 285; War Trials 224n14; WWII literature 307

writing as therapy 177

Yeats, W. B. 166

Young, Joe 263, 266–67

Ypres, Battle of 234

326 | *Baptism of Fire:*

www.ingramcontent.com/pod-product-compliance
Lightning Source LLC
Chambersburg PA
CBHW031603110426
42742CB00037B/823